T0197975

Get the eBooks FREE!

(PDF, ePub, Kindle, and liveBook all included)

We believe that once you buy a book from us, you should be able to read it in any format we have available. To get electronic versions of this book at no additional cost to you, purchase and then register this book at the Manning website.

Go to https://www.manning.com/freebook and follow the instructions to complete your pBook registration.

That's it!
Thanks from Manning!

Get Programming with Node.js

Get Programming with
Node.js

Jonathan Wexler

Foreword by Kyle Simpson

MANNING
Shelter Island

For online information and ordering of this and other Manning books, please visit
www.manning.com. The publisher offers discounts on this book when ordered in quantity. For
more information, please contact

Special Sales Department
Manning Publications Co.
20 Baldwin Road
PO Box 761
Shelter Island, NY 11964
Email: orders@manning.com

Development editor: Toni Arritola
Technical development editor: John Guthrie
Review editor: Aleksandar Dragosavljević
Production editor: David Novak
Copyeditor: Kathy Simpson
Proofreader: Melody Dolab
Senior technical proofreader: Srihari Sriharan
Technical proofreader: German Frigerio
Typesetter: Dottie Marsico
Cover designer: Monica Kamsvaag

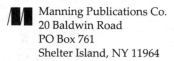

Manning Publications Co.
20 Baldwin Road
PO Box 761
Shelter Island, NY 11964

ISBN 9781617294747
Printed in the United States of America
1 2 3 4 5 6 7 8 9 10 – SP – 24 23 22 21 20 19

To the ones who got me programming and to my parents
(the two people I always know aren't reading my book),
with love.

Contents

Unit 0

GETTING SET UP   1

Unit 3

CONNECTING TO A DATABASE   133

Unit 4

BUILDING A USER MODEL   175

Unit 7

ADDING CHAT FUNCTIONALITY   349

Unit 8

DEPLOYING AND MANAGING CODE IN PRODUCTION 389

Foreword

I was fortunate enough to be among a crowd of about 250 folks who gathered at the first JSConf.EU conference in Berlin in late 2009, when a relatively unknown-at-the-time speaker stood up and introduced himself as Ryan Dahl. Over the next hour, he proceeded to deliver a simple, no-frills talk with dry humor and little affect—not exactly the kind of talk you'd expect to receive a rousing audience response.

But we all jumped to our feet and gave him a standing ovation, for multiple minutes. Why? Dahl had just changed the game for all JavaScript developers, and we knew it. He officially launched Node.js to the world. Nothing in JS would ever be the same again.

In the eight or so years since, Node.js has skyrocketed to practical ubiquity, not only within the JavaScript world, but also far beyond. Node.js represents a powerful, respected, first-class, enterprise server-side platform for global-scale web applications. It sparked an explosion of interest in embedding JS in practically any computing or electronic device you can imagine, from robots to television sets to light bulbs.

The Node.js ecosystem is built around hundreds of thousands of published module packages in npm—the largest code repository ever for any programming language by more than 6 times. That statistic doesn't include the countless privately installed packages comprising billions of lines of JavaScript.

With the enormous momentum around and attention to Node.js, it can be painfully daunting for someone who wants to learn this ecosystem to figure out where to start.

I think that's why I appreciate this book so much. From the first page, it lays out a refreshingly down-to-earth, pragmatic, clear path that shows you how to navigate your way into Node.js. You won't find unnecessary historical or philosophical fluff here; the book jumps right into showing you how to install and configure Node.js so that you can get to the code as quickly as possible.

The book is divided into short, digestible lessons. Each section is clearly organized, ensuring that you won't get lost in the weeds and lose sight of the bigger picture.

Reading this book is like having Jonathan sit next to you patiently while you dig into Node.js, prompting you with enough challenges to get you to the next section review.

When you're about 50 pages into the book, you'll look up and realize that you've already written a web server that responds to web requests. The feeling of having total control of your application, with no off-limits black boxes, is so empowering that you may want to give yourself a standing ovation, too!

As you progress through the book's lessons (almost 40 in total), you methodically expand the scope of your Node.js programming capabilities into API handling, databases, authentication, and more. This book lays out a solid checklist of what you need to learn and master to solidify Node.js as a vital tool in your programming toolbox.

That's what Node.js always has been to me, from the moment I first heard Ryan talk about it to the present. Node.js is a powerful tool that gives me, a JavaScript developer, the capability to own my entire application. I think that you'll find this book to be the guide you've been looking for as you cross over from knowing about Node.js to knowing how to wield it effectively as your favorite web application tool.

Jonathan's ready for you to begin this journey with him in Lesson 0, so what are you waiting for? Get programming with Node.js!

KYLE SIMPSON, GETIFY
OPEN WEB EVANGELIST

Preface

Nearly a quarter century after the internet became a public-facing tool for the world to use, the tech job market has never been larger. From new startups to large corporations, nearly all entities are looking for an online presence or, even better, sophisticated tools to push their brand and products. Luckily, you don't need a computer-science degree or a master's degree in data science to meet the needs of the market these days. Moreover, most of the skills you need to build these tools, you can acquire at little to no cost through open-sourced technologies.

During my time at The New York Code + Design Academy, instructing intensive courses on web development and building new curriculums, I recognized the strength of a full stack education. I've taught students with a variety of backgrounds, most of them without development experience, to realize their programming visions in as little as three months. So why not you?

I wrote this book to manifest the stages of learning web development in Node.js. Each unit guides you through a core concept in web development, with instructions on how to apply code and build your own application. I present the building blocks of a web server and show you how to piece together the components that your favorite web applications use. Using the same boot-camp learning strategy, I walk you through the development of a web application with dynamic web pages, user accounts, a database, and a live chat feature. By the end of the book, you'll have a fully functioning application published on the internet. The work you produce from this book could spark ideas for a new application, become the start of a product for your business, or showcase your development skills as a personal portfolio piece. However you choose to use this book, you can find everything here that you need to get programming with Node.js.

My goal is to make the learning process less intimidating and more exciting. The frustration that many new engineers feel is twofold: resources are scattered, and they don't always deliver the complete picture. Node.js is a relatively new platform for development, and although the online community can answer common questions, new web developers may struggle to find full ingredient lists and recipes for building a complete application from scratch. This book covers the surface aspects and a little extra.

Be ambitious while tackling the exercises in this book, and be patient while understanding the core concepts. Ask questions where you get stuck, and communicate with other readers through the book's forum. (They'll be hitting the same walls as you.) With a little practice and determination, you'll soon be demonstrating your Node.js talent to the sea of developer-hungry organizations.

Acknowledgments

I'm grateful for all the support I received in making this book possible. First, I'd like to thank Manning Publications for choosing me to curate and write its *Get Programming* book on Node.js. In particular, I want to thank my development editors for guiding the book through its many daunting phases. Dan Maharry, you were a great resource in preparing me for the task. Toni Arritola, your push to fill the book's gaps and help me meet important deadlines was the driving force behind its completion. I thank Srihari Sriharan, the senior technical proofreader, and German Frigerio, the technical proofreader, for making sure all the code examples were properly formatted and ran as intended. Also, to those who volunteered to review my book and offer the feedback that ultimately improved my final product, I'm appreciative for your time and comments: Ahmed Chicktay, Aindriu Mac Giolla Eoin, Alberto Manuel Brandão Simões, Alper Silistre, Barnaby Norman, Bryce Darling, Dan Posey, Daniela Zapata, David Pardo, Dermot Doran, Edwin Boatswain, Filipe Freire, Foster Haines, Jeremy Lange, Joseph White, Madhanmohan Savadamuthu, Michael Giambalvo, Michal Paszkiewicz, Patrick Regan, Rafael Aiquel, Roger Sperberg, Ron Lease, Ronald Muwonge, Vincent Zhu, Vinicius Miana Bezerra, and Vipul Gupta.

Thank you to everyone who helped propel my development and teaching career. Each of you instilled the confidence I needed to focus on the vision of this book and deliver a product that reflects the work ethic, teaching strategies, and development techniques we've evolved together over the years.

Thank you to The New York Code + Design Academy (NYCDA) and my former students for promoting this book and supporting me throughout its development. To all my students: I'm proud of what you've accomplished, and only through your success have I been convinced that this book can help others change careers and reach new development milestones.

Thank you, Zach Feldman, for initially hiring me, introducing me to the coding bootcamp world, and also for continuing to be a great friend, resource, and collaborator.

Thank you to everyone on the NYCDA development team for trusting my leadership and providing a fun, reliable work environment for me. Thank you, Sharon Kass, for your unconditional friendship and inclusiveness starting from my first day at Bloomberg LP.

I want to thank my family for their support of my career choices and for inspiring ambition over challenges big and small. Thank you, Dad and Eema, for supporting creative expression and encouraging me to do what makes me happy. Thank you, Kimmy and Matt, for helping me understand the legal side of this business, and Noa and Emmanuelle, for being my youngest reviewers and future students. Thank you, Jessie, for not losing my ski poles.

Thank you to my fellow developers and to the Philadelphia and New York tech communities. Thank you, Kevin Skogland, whose teaching style through his tutorial series influenced the way that I answer technical questions; thank you also for your friendship and engagement in my former classes. Thank you, Kyle Simpson, for your unique perspective on teaching and understanding JavaScript and for your support and willingness to review my book's draft. Thank you to those who reviewed earlier drafts of this publication and to my friends Michael "Sybles" Sklaroff, for checking in on me through development; Gurbakshish Singh, for your code suggestions; and Violeta Soued for persuading me to pursue a computer science degree in the first place.

Last, thank you to everyone who purchases this book. I know that you can find a lot of resources online and in print to learn to program with Node.js, and I thank you for showing interest in learning through my teaching style. I hope that I get to hear from many of you, in compliments or critiques, as well as learn how this book helped you reach new programming revelations and career achievements. As you read, keep this sentiment in mind: we take on challenges not to tell others that we did, but to remind our future selves that we can.

About this book

Before you get started, I'll discuss Node.js and what you'll learn in this book.

What is Node.js?

According to the Node.js website (https://nodejs.org/en/about/), Node.js is "an asynchronous event driven JavaScript runtime." Let me break down that definition. Node.js reads, or interprets, your JavaScript code. You write code in JavaScript and then use your version of Node.js to run the code. How does that process work, exactly?

The Node.js runtime uses a *JavaScript engine*, a program that reads JavaScript code and executes its commands on the fly. Specifically, Node.js uses Google's Chrome V8 JavaScript engine, an open-source interpreter that converts JavaScript to machine code—code that your computer can readily execute. This feature is useful because Google often updates and monitors its JavaScript engine for use in its Chrome web browser, where JavaScript engines traditionally run. Node.js adapts this engine to provide an environment for you to run JavaScript code that doesn't require a web browser. Now, instead of reserving JavaScript for scripting on web pages, you can use it to build an entire application on the server (see unit 1).

Defining the terms *asynchronous* and *event driven* is important, as they're fundamental elements of how JavaScript is used nowadays. Understanding their impact on Node.js applications is more important, however.

When a JavaScript application is launched, all the code in that application is loaded into memory. Every variable, function, and block of code is made available to the application, whether or not the code is executed right away. Why might certain code not run right away? Although defining and assigning a global variable may give that variable a value as soon as the application is launched, not all functions run unless they have a reason to do so. Some of these functions come in the form of *event listeners*—function objects that run a corresponding callback function when an event with a matching name is emitted. These functions sit around in memory until *event emitters*—objects that fire event names—trigger the event listeners to run their callback functions.

In this way, Node.js can run applications in a particularly fast, efficient manner. Whereas other platforms may need to recompile or run all of their code every time a request to run a certain command is made, Node.js loads JavaScript code only once, and it runs the functions and corresponding callback functions only when triggered to do so by events. JavaScript as a language supports event-driven development but doesn't require it. Node.js takes advantage of this architecture by promoting the use of events as a way for the server to execute most of an application's tasks, using the Node.js event-loop (see unit 1).

Last, why does it matter that Node.js is asynchronous? Well, JavaScript, by nature, is asynchronous, which means that tasks don't necessarily run sequentially. If I want to call a function, log a comment, and change the background color of my web page, all these commands could potentially run instantaneously, but they won't necessarily run in order. In fact, it's likely that my comment will be logged before anything else happens.

The code in the listing that follows demonstrates this phenomenon. Although I call my callMe function first, change the background color of my web page to green next, and log a comment at the end, the order of events is reversed when I run this code in my web browser's console.

Listing Example of asynchronous flow

Call the callMe function.   Change the web page
                                             background style to green.

```
callMe();
document.body.style.background = "green";
console.log("my comment");

function callMe(){ (4)
  setTimeout(function(){
    console.log("function called");
  }, 1000);
}
```

Log a comment
to the console.

Define the callMe
function.

Having an asynchronous runtime environment is great for web applications. Think about every time you've visited a website and the average time it took to load the page you requested. Suppose that you placed an order on Amazon.com and that while the order was processing (verifying your name, credit card information, shipping address, and other security measures), no other visitors to Amazon.com could load their web pages. This system would imply that the website used a single application process or *thread* (an operating-system resource dedicated to running a series of commands, handling every single task, and blocking other tasks from completion). Other web applications handle this scenario by creating new processes or threads, building bigger and more powerful machines to handle an influx of task requests.

Node.js requires only one executing thread (used by the event-loop), which can use other threads only when necessary for larger tasks. As a result, a Node.js application needs less processing power for creating and running tasks to completion because computer resources aren't necessarily assigned and dedicated to each incoming task. In the Amazon example, Node.js might use its main thread to handle your request to process an order, send your information off to be verified, and continue to process other users' requests to load web pages. When your order is processed, an event is emitted, triggering the main thread to let you know that your order was placed successfully. In other words, Node.js uses asynchrony to run parts of tasks and continue to other tasks before the first task completes. Instead of waiting for an operation from start to finish, Node.js registers event listeners, which are called when the task that was sent off is complete.

Ultimately, Node.js offers you a way to write JavaScript code without a web browser, and you can use this environment to design all types of applications. Most Node.js applications are web applications that use its asynchronous, event-driven nature to offer fast-loading, responsive web content.

In this book, you explore the architecture of a Node.js web application by evolving a basic JavaScript web server, using only the built-in Node.js tools, into a fully dynamic web application built with external open-source code libraries called Node.js *packages* (see unit 1).

Goals of the book

Node.js is only one of many platforms on which you can build an application. Because of its design, Node.js is particularly useful for building *web applications*—applications that handle requests over the internet and provide processed data and views in return. For many of you, the concept of building an application purely in JavaScript is both new and your ultimate goal. For others, this book is your introduction to web development. You've never built or fully understood the inner workings of a web application, and you've come here to learn how everything fits together.

Because the focus of this book is teaching web development through Node.js, I'm going to put a lot of focus on how a web application is architected, including initial setup, the ways dynamic pages are created, how a database is connected, and ways of preserving a user's activity on your application. The goal is to clearly explain these concepts through examples and code that you can use and modify to create your own applications.

Who should read this book

This book is intended, first and foremost, for anyone who's interested in learning about Node.js and the tools required to build a web application. If you have some familiarity with JavaScript but little experience with web development, this book is for you.

Because this book is project-based, readers need to be proficient in navigating their computers, typing, and working with a web browser. No experience in web-connected applications is expected. Readers with a background in backend or service technologies are good candidates for this book. New developers should have some familiarity with the following technologies:

- JavaScript
- HTML
- CSS
- Terminal/command line

Knowledge of JavaScript ES6 is beneficial but not required for this book.

How this book is organized: a road map

This book is divided into nine units. Each unit teaches a group of related concepts and builds on the preceding unit toward a more-complete, robust application. Unit 0 guides you through the Node.js installation and setup process, as well as the installation steps needed for other software used in this book. You continue from there to learn about some fundamental tools used in the Node.js core installation, including tools that come prepackaged with your installation of Node.js. In lesson 1, you start writing your first lines of JavaScript, which are run in the Node.js read-eval-print-loop (REPL), a window within your terminal window in which you can run JavaScript code. You end the unit by completing a few more exercises in the REPL environment and learning about Node.js modules.

Unit 1 jumps into building your first web server. The web server is the backbone of your web application, as it handles incoming requests for data to be processed and outgoing responses. Here, you learn how to initialize your Node.js application properly and load your first web page. Lessons 5 and 6 demonstrate how to use your web server to load images and other file types from your server. These lessons cover some of the fundamental concepts of interaction on the web. The unit concludes with your first capstone exercise: an opportunity to tie together the concepts you've learned by building your first web application.

The capstone exercise in unit 1 carries over into unit 2, where you learn about Express.js, a web framework. In this unit, you learn how web frameworks help speed up the development process by implementing much of the code you wrote in unit 1. Lessons 9 and 10 cover how to use Express.js to architect a standard web application, and lesson 11 teaches you how to handle errors that occur on your server. Unit 2 concludes with your second capstone exercise, in which you re-create your web application by using the Express.js web framework.

Unit 3 shows you how to save application data through the minimum database theory needed to connect a database and start persisting your application's data. In this unit, you learn about MongoDB, a leading database used in Node.js applications. You start by getting familiar with the MongoDB environment, creating database collections and documents. Then you connect your database to your application with the help of a Node.js package called Mongoose. Lessons 14 and 15 teach you how to organize your data in Mongoose models as one part of the model-view-controller (MVC) architecture taught in this book. The unit ends with an opportunity to add a database and models to your capstone project.

Unit 4 builds on the concept of models by discussing the standard functionality expected of your models. In this unit, you learn about create, read, update, and delete (CRUD) functions and see why they're helpful to have for the major models in your application. At this point, you develop the ability to create and modify data in your application from the web browser. This unit also helps you complete some of the code needed in your application controllers and shows you how to link web forms to your application's server and models. The unit concludes with a capstone exercise in which you build the CRUD functions for your user model.

Unit 5 introduces user authentication and the code you need to allow unique users to sign up for and log in to your application. In lesson 22, you add sessions and cookies to your application to allow information to be shared between the application server and your users' computers. This technique helps preserve a user's state while they navigate your application. Next, you learn how to encrypt your user passwords. This lesson guides you through the standard security practices expected in protecting your application data. Last, you set up an authentication system to analyze and approve user data and then apply these techniques to your capstone project. By the end of this unit, you'll have an application in which you can selectively display content to logged-in users.

Unit 6 focuses on an often-under-taught element of application development: application programming interfaces (APIs). In lesson 26, you're introduced to some ways that you can extend your application to serve data in other ways beyond a web page. These alternative data avenues enable your application to connect with external services that might use your application's data. You might later build a mobile app or Amazon Alexa skill that needs to use your application's data but can't read a normal web page's contents, for example. A useful API can deliver that data in multiple data formats. In lessons 27 and 28, you build out your application's API and use it within the application by creating a pop-out window with a list of data accessed through an API endpoint. At the end of the unit, you secure your API by creating an API token system and applying the same techniques to your capstone project.

When the core of your application is complete, you move to unit 7, where you learn about building a live-chat feature in your application. In Node.js, you use Socket.io, a library that connects to your application's normal web server and enhances it to allow open streams of communication among users. The lessons in this unit break down the steps you need to take to set up Socket.io and (later) to associate messages with users and save those associations in your database. By the end of the unit, you have a fully functioning chat system running in your capstone project.

In unit 8, you configure your application to get deployed online. Up to this point, you've viewed your work on your own machine, with no opportunity for external users to sign up for and use your application. In lesson 34, you save your application code to Git and upload the first live version of your application to Heroku. In this lesson, you're provided a URL with which you can share your application with family members, friends, and co-workers. Lessons 35 and 36 introduce some ways to clean your application code and monitor your application as it begins its journey on the internet. In the final lesson, I introduced some ways in which you can test your code. Testing is an important element in the development process; it may ensure that your code continues to function as expected as you make changes and add features.

About the code

This book contains many examples of source code, both in numbered listings and inline with normal text. In both cases, source code is formatted in a fixed-width font like this to separate it from ordinary text. Sometimes, code is also in bold to highlight code that it has changed from previous steps in the chapter, such as when a new feature adds to an existing line of code.

In many cases, the original source code has been reformatted; I've added line breaks and reworked indentation to accommodate the available page space in the book. In rare cases, even reformatting wasn't enough, so some listings include line-continuation markers (➡). Additionally, comments in the source code have often been removed from the listings when the code is described in the text. Code annotations accompany many of the listings, highlighting important concepts.

All code examples in this book are available for download from the Manning website at https://www.manning.com/books/get-programming-with-node-js and from GitHub at https://github.com/JonathanWexler/get-programming-with-nodejs. The code examples are organized by lesson and unit. Within each lesson's folder, you'll find a start folder, containing the code you can use and build on from the beginning of that lesson, and a finish folder, which contains the final working code for that lesson. Any future updates to this book's code will be added to lesson-specific folders titled updated.

Software requirements

For this book, you need a computer with at least 500 MB of RAM and 500 MB persistent memory. Most modern computers come with plenty of space and the specifications needed to run a Node.js application.

Node.js supports 32-bit and 64-bit Windows and Linux installations and the standard 64-bit Mac OS installation, as specified at https://nodejs.org/en/download/.

You also need a text editor to write your code. I recommend installing the Atom text editor, available for free at https://atom.io.

You need a web browser to test your web application. I recommend installing the Google Chrome browser, which is available for free at https://www.google.com/chrome

You also need to install the Heroku command-line interface and Git on your machine (instructions listed in unit 0).

liveBook discussion forum

Purchase of *Get Programming with Node.js* includes free access to a private web forum run by Manning Publications, where you can make comments about the book, ask technical questions, and receive help from the author and from other users. To access the forum, go to https://livebook.manning.com/#!/book/get-programming-with-node-js/dis-cussion. You can also learn more about Manning's forums and the rules of conduct at https://livebook.manning.com/#!/discussion.

Manning's commitment to our readers is to provide a venue where a meaningful dia-logue between individual readers and between readers and the author can take place. It isn't a commitment to any specific amount of participation on the part of the author, whose contribution to the forum remains voluntary (and unpaid). We suggest that you try asking the author some challenging questions lest his interest stray! The forum and the archives of previous discussions will be accessible from the publisher's website as long as the book is in print.

About the author

 Jonathan Wexler is a Philadelphia-native software engineer with degrees in neuroscience and computer science from Brandeis University. With years of experience building applications and teaching about web development, Jonathan has helped hundreds of clients and students unlock their technical potentials. Jonathan has partnered with organizations in Philadelphia and New York City to use technology to bridge social and economic gaps with organizations around the world. From building computer games for schools in India to leading the development team at The New York Code + Design Academy and software engineering for Bloomberg LP, Jonathan hopes to continue to adapt the best practices in program design and share his impressions of the path to development success.

Getting set up

Before I introduce you to working with Node.js as a web-development platform, you need to prepare your environment (the computer on which you'll be developing). In this unit, you'll install all the tools you need to get started with Node.js. These tools help you write the code to get your applications working and eventually running on the internet. By the end of this unit, you'll have installed everything you need to get started coding and running a Node.js application. Toward this goal, unit 0 covers the following topics:

- Lesson 0 discusses what you're going to learn in this book and why it's important. I introduce you to Node.js, giving you a little background and discussing why it's a good platform for web development. This lesson also covers what you should expect to get out of this book. I talk about some of the prerequisites and things to keep in mind as you work toward a robust web application.
- Lesson 1 walks you through the installation process for each tool and library of code you'll be using to start the next unit. Although installing Node.js is the focus of this lesson, setting up your computer as a development environment takes a few more steps.

- Lesson 2 introduces your first Node.js application and a few tests to ensure that you have a compatible version of Node.js running on your computer.

I begin by talking about Node.js.

SETTING UP NODE.JS AND THE JAVASCRIPT ENGINE

In this lesson, you get an overview of what you'll be learning in this book and why it's important. Whether you're new to web development or a seasoned developer looking to build better applications, this lesson acts as a starting guide for entering the world of Node.js.

This lesson covers

- Reviewing what you're going to learn
- Understanding Node.js
- Learning why we develop in Node.js
- Preparing yourself for this book

 ## 0.1   What you're going to learn

The goal of this book is to teach you how to build web applications on a platform called Node.js, using the JavaScript language. Starting with this lesson, each unit aims to build on the concepts and development skills of the last.

As you work through each lesson, you pick up new web development concepts, terminology, and coding skills that will help you build a web application. Although the book revolves around using Node.js, many of the concepts taught in the following units apply to other leading platforms and programming languages.

> **NOTE** Web development skills are different from typical software engineering or computer theory knowledge. In addition to teaching coding concepts, this book helps explain how the internet works beyond your project. I'll explain as much as I can to make things easier.

Following is an overview of what you'll learn in each unit:

- Unit 0 gives you the background knowledge you need to get started and walks you through the installation of Node.js and development tools.
- Unit 1 covers some basic web development concepts and provides guiding steps toward building your first web application in Node.js from scratch.
- Unit 2 introduces you to Express.js, a web framework that most Node.js developers use to build applications. You learn what Express.js offers, how it works, and what you can do to customize it. In this unit, you also learn about the model-view-controller (MVC) application architecture pattern.
- Unit 3 guides you through connecting your application to a database. This unit also helps you install a few new tools and structure your database with MongoDB.
- Unit 4 teaches you about building data models in your application, where CRUD operations are performed to create, read, update, and delete data from the database.
- Unit 5 helps you build code to represent user accounts in an object-oriented structure. In this unit, you learn about securing your data and building a login form for new users.
- Unit 6 introduces building an application programming interface (API). You learn what constitutes an API, how to secure it, and how to design it by using the REST architecture.
- Unit 7 invites you to build a live chat system into your application. This unit introduces polling, web sockets, and broadcasting data with Socket.io, a library that mainstream applications use to get data to their users faster and more efficiently.
- Unit 8 guides you through the deployment process. This unit helps you set up the necessary tools and accounts.

To start, let's talk a bit about exactly what Node.js is.

0.2 Understanding Node.js

Node.js is a platform for interpreting JavaScript code and running applications. JavaScript has been around for a couple of decades; with every improvement, it has shifted further from being a client-side scripting language to a full-fledged server-side programming language for managing data.

Because Node.js is built with Google Chrome's JavaScript engine (a tool used to interpret the JavaScript language into meaningful computer commands), it's considered to be powerful and able to support JavaScript as a server-side language. JavaScript can be used to both assist in web-page (client-side) interactions and handle incoming application data and database communications. (The latter jobs have often been reserved for languages such as C, Java, Python, and Ruby, among others). Developers can now commit to mastering JavaScript to build a complete web application instead of having to master multiple languages to accomplish the same task.

Client-side versus server-side

As a general overview, web development can largely be broken into two categories:

- *Client-side*—(front-end) refers to the code you write that results in something the user sees in his web browser. Client-side code typically includes JavaScript used to animate the user experience when a web page is loaded.
- *Server-side*—(back-end) refers to code used for application logic (how data is organized and saved to the database). Server-side code is responsible for authenticating users on a login page, running scheduled tasks, and even ensuring that the client-side code reaches the client.

In the following figure, the client represents the browser on which a user may view your application. The server is where your application runs and handles any data submitted by the user. Also, the server often renders the user interface in many cases in which the client expects one.

> **NOTE** *Application*, as used throughout this book, refers to a computer program written in a programming language and run on a computer. This book focuses on web applications written in JavaScript and run with Node.js.

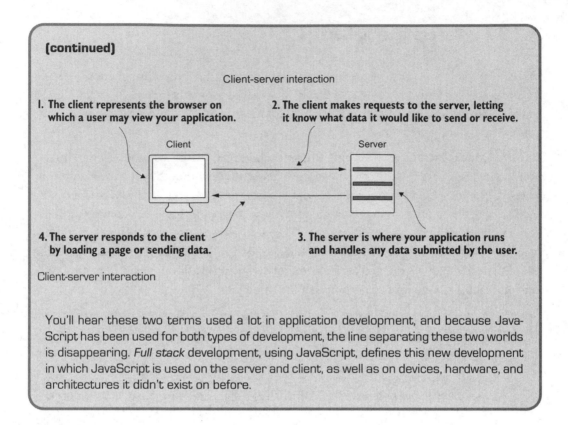

(continued)

Client-server interaction

1. The client represents the browser on which a user may view your application.

2. The client makes requests to the server, letting it know what data it would like to send or receive.

Client

Server

4. The server responds to the client by loading a page or sending data.

3. The server is where your application runs and handles any data submitted by the user.

Client-server interaction

You'll hear these two terms used a lot in application development, and because JavaScript has been used for both types of development, the line separating these two worlds is disappearing. *Full stack* development, using JavaScript, defines this new development in which JavaScript is used on the server and client, as well as on devices, hardware, and architectures it didn't exist on before.

Node.js operates on an event loop using a single thread. A *thread* is the bundle of computing power and resources needed for the execution of a programmed task. Generally, a thread is responsible for starting and completing a task; the more tasks needed to run simultaneously, the more threads are needed. In most other software, multiple tasks are matched and handled by a pool of threads that the computer can offer at the same time (concurrently). Node.js, however, handles only one task at a time and uses more threads only for tasks that can't be handled by the main thread.

This process may sound counterintuitive, but in most applications that don't require computationally intensive tasks (tasks requiring a lot of processing power from your computer), this single thread can quickly manage and execute all the tasks. See a simplified diagram of the event loop in figure 0.1. As tasks are prepared to run, they enter a queue to be processed by specific phases of the event loop.

As its name implies, the Node.js event loop cycles forever in a loop, listening for JavaScript events triggered by the server to notify of some new task or another task's

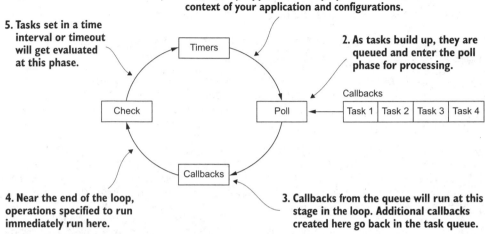

Node.js Event-loop

I. Your Node.js application will prepare the context of your application and configurations.

5. Tasks set in a time interval or timeout will get evaluated at this phase.

Timers

2. As tasks build up, they are queued and enter the poll phase for processing.

Callbacks

Check   Poll ← | Task 1 | Task 2 | Task 3 | Task 4 |

Callbacks

4. Near the end of the loop, operations specified to run immediately run here.

3. Callbacks from the queue will run at this stage in the loop. Additional callbacks created here go back in the task queue.

Figure 0.1   Simplified model of the Node.js event loop

completion. As the number of tasks increases, tasks line up in a queue to be incremen-tally processed by the event loop. You don't code with this fact in mind, though. You write your code by using asynchronous conventions, and the Node.js architecture schedules task handling for you behind the scenes. As a result, Node.js has become pop-ular for creating real-time applications that persistently listen for data being sent back and forth.

You can think of the event loop as being like an office manager. The office manager's role is to handle incoming messages, job assignments, and office-related tasks. The office manager could have a long list of tasks to complete, from delegating the creation of complete financial reports to answering the phone and putting up the office-party decorations. Because some tasks take more time than others, the office manager isn't obligated to complete any individual task before handling a new one. If she's setting up for a party and the phone rings, for example, she can stop setting up to answer the call. Better yet, she can answer the call and transfer the caller to another employee so that she can go back to decorating.

Similarly, the event loop handles a series of tasks, always working on one task at a time and using the computer's processing power to offload some larger tasks while the event loop shortens the list of tasks. On most other platforms, incoming tasks are assigned to new processes, creating a new event loop for each task. Increasing the number of tasks, however, is like increasing the number of employees in a finite space. You start to run into new issues such as cost, computing power, and shared resources. (What would you do if two employees need to use the phone at the same time, for example?)

Processes and threads

It's important to note that the Node.js event loop relies on a single thread to manage all its tasks, but it doesn't necessarily use that thread only to run each task to completion. In fact, Node.js is designed to pass larger tasks to the host computer, and the computer may create new threads and processes to operate those tasks.

A *thread* is an allocated bundle of computer resources used to run a series of instructions in a task. Usually, the tasks handled by threads are simple and fast. For this reason, the Node.js event loop needs only one thread to act as the manager of all other tasks. Threads are made available through computer processes, and some more-intensive tasks require their own process to run.

A *process* is also a bundle of computing power and resources used for a task's execution, though usually for larger tasks than those handled by threads. A process must exist to create a thread, which implies that each Node.js application runs on its own process.

Even though Node.js may be single-threaded, you can have multiple instances of processes running in parallel and processing incoming requests and tasks. For this reason, Node.js scales well; it schedules tasks asynchronously, using additional threads and processes only when necessary instead of generating new processes for every task. As more processes are needed to handle your task list, demand on your computer increases. Node.js works best to minimize the number of concurrent processes.

You may hear the terms *thread* and *process* in conjunction. For this book, you only need to know that Node.js depends on a single task handler at any given time. For more information on threads and processes in Node.js, read the article on Node.js scalability at https://medium.freecodecamp.org/node-js-child-processes-everything-you-need-to-know-e69498fe970a.

In this book, I further explore some Node.js strengths in building a web application. Before I dive deeper, however, let's talk about why Node.js is beneficial.

Quick check 0.1 True or false: The Node.js event loop runs each task to completion before handling the next task.

 0.3 Why learn to develop in Node.js?

It's likely that you've picked up this book to become a better programmer and to build a web application, which is also the main reason you'd use Node.js and get better at coding in JavaScript.

Plenty of other options, such as Ruby on Rails and PHP, could help you build an application that's indistinguishable to a user from a Node.js application. Consider the following reasons to learn Node.js instead:

- You can focus on JavaScript as the core language in development instead of balancing multiple languages to keep your application afloat.
- If you want to stream data continuously or have some chat functionality, Node.js has gained prominence over other platforms.
- Node.js is backed by Google's V8 JavaScript interpreter, meaning that it's widely supported and expected to grow in performance and features, and won't go away soon. Visit http://node.green/ to see what features are supported by each version of Node.js.
- Node.js has gained a lot of popularity in the web development community. You're likely to meet and get support from other developers who may have been developing with Node.js for up to five years. Additionally, more supportive, open-source tools are now being built for Node.js than for other, older platforms.
- More jobs are available for developers who have concrete JavaScript skills. You can apply for front-end or back-end development positions when you know Node.js.

If you're trying to enter the web development world as a new programmer, or if you've developed software before and are looking for the new thing that everyone's talking about, Node.js is your platform of choice, and this book is your book.

QC 0.1 answer   False. The Node.js event loop removes tasks from a queue sequentially, but it may offload the task to be handled by the machine on which the application is running or wait for certain tasks to complete while handling new tasks.

0.4   Preparing yourself for this book

From the first unit in this book, you're introduced to web development through the process of building a basic web server in Node.js. As the book progresses, you'll append code to your application to complete a robust web application.

To prime yourself to learn these new topics, make sure that you go through each lesson carefully and write all the code examples yourself. If you get into the habit of copying and pasting code instead, you'll likely run into some errors; more important, you won't learn the concepts.

Because JavaScript is an important prerequisite for this book, research best practices and other common solutions to your problems online if you struggle through a task. Throughout this book, you'll find exercises and "Quick check" questions to test your knowledge. (You completed your first "Quick check" in section 2.) At the end of each lesson starting with lesson 3, expect a section called "Try this," where you can practice some of the coding concepts presented earlier in the lesson.

The exercises and capstone projects at the end of each unit mark milestones on your way to creating a web application with all the bells and whistles.

Treat each unit like a course topic and each lesson as a lecture. You may find that some lessons take longer to comprehend or apply in code than others. Take your time, but also continually build your development skills through repetition and practice.

The goal of the book is to make you comfortable building a web application like the one built throughout the capstone lessons. In these capstones, you build a web application for a company called Confetti Cuisine, which offers cooking classes and allows users to sign up, connect, and chat with one another about recipes. Try to follow the guidelines of the capstone and redo part, or all, of the project after your first pass.

> **TIP** Consider working through an exercise three times. The first time, follow the guide; the second time, work with some reference from the guide; and the third time, work on your own without any help. By the third time, you'll have a concrete understanding of the concept involved.

Most of the exercises in this book ask you to use your computer's terminal (command line). Node.js is a cross-platform tool—meaning that it can run on Windows, Mac, and Linux machines—but I teach it from a UNIX perspective in this book. Windows users can use their built-in command line to run Node.js but may find some of the terminal commands to be different. As a result, I recommend that Windows users install Git Bash, a terminal window where you can use UNIX commands and follow all the examples in this book. You can accomplish a lot, however, with the Node.js command-line environment that comes with your Node.js installation. For information on installing Git Bash, visit https://git-scm.com/downloads.

After completing each unit, look back at the progress you've made since the last capstone exercise. By the end of unit 7, you'll have built a complete web application with Node.js.

I'll remind you about the following items along the way, but you should keep them in mind as you progress through this book:

- Source files are written in JavaScript and have a .js file extension.
- The main application file used in every example in the book is called main.js unless otherwise specified.
- I recommend using an up-to-date Google Chrome browser for running book exercises that require a web browser. You can download that browser from https://www.google.com/chrome/browser/.

In the lessons I do my best to explain new terms and concepts tangential to the Node.js learning experience. If you need more information on any topic mentioned in the book, however, you can reference any of the following resources:

- *HTML5 in Action* by Rob Crowther, Joe Lennon, Ash Blue, and Greg Wanish (Manning, 2014)
- *CSS in Depth* by Keith J. Grant (Manning, 2018)
- *You Don't Know JS: Up & Going* (https://github.com/getify/You-Dont-Know-JS), by Kyle Simpson (O'Reilly Media, 2015)
- *ES6 in Motion* (https://www.manning.com/livevideo/es6-in-motion), by Wes Higbee

 **Summary**

In this lesson, my objective was to teach you about the book's structure, what Node.js is, and why it's important. I also talked about how you should approach this book. If you treat this book as a course with subtopics and lectures, you'll build your knowledge and skills incrementally until you become a competent web developer. In the next lesson, you install the tools that you need to get coding.

LESSON 1

CONFIGURING YOUR ENVIRONMENT

In this lesson, you install all the tools you need to start building applications with
Node.js. You install a version of Node.js that's compatible with the latest JavaScript ES6
updates. Next, you install a text editor—software through which you'll write your
application's code. Last, you give Node.js a test drive from your computer's command-
line terminal by using a Node.js sandbox environment known as REPL.

This lesson covers

- Installing Node.js
- Installing a text editor
- Setting up SCM and deployment tools
- Working with the Node.js REPL in terminal

 1.1   Installing Node.js

Node.js is growing in popularity and support. For this reason, new versions to download are being deployed quite frequently, and it's important to stay up to date with the
latest versions to see how they may benefit or otherwise affect the applications you're
building. At this writing, the version of Node.js to download is 11.0.0 or later.

> **NOTE**   The release of Node.js 8.8.1 comes with support for ES6 syntax. ES6 (ECMAScript 2015) is a recent update to JavaScript, with syntax improvements for defining variables, functions, and OOP code. To keep up with updates to JavaScript, download the latest stable version of Node.js as your development progresses.

You have a couple of ways to download and install Node.js, all of which are listed on the Node.js main site, https://nodejs.org.

Because Node.js is platform-independent, you can download and install it on your Mac, Windows, or Linux computer and expect full functionality.

The simplest way to install Node.js is to go to the download link at https://nodejs.org/en/download/ and follow the instructions and prompts to download the installer for the latest version of Node.js (figure 1.1).

Downloads

Latest LTS Version: **8.11.3** (includes npm 5.6.0)

Download the Node.js source code or a pre-built installer for your platform, and start developing today.

LTS Recommended For Most Users		Current Latest Features
Windows Installer	macOS Installer	Source Code
node-v8.11.3-x86.msi	node-v8.11.3.pkg	node-v8.11.3.tar.gz

Figure 1.1   Node.js installer page

Node Version Manager

Alternatively, you may want to use the Node.js Version Manager (NVM) to handle your Node.js installation and manage one version or multiple versions of Node.js on your computer. The benefit of using a version manager is that you can test newer versions of Node.js as they're released while still having older, more stable, versions installed in case of compatibility issues. You can follow the installation instructions at https://github .com/creationix/nvm or follow these steps on a UNIX machine:

1 Run `curl -o https://raw.githubusercontent.com/creationix/nvm/v0.33.8/install .sh | bash` in a new terminal window. You may need to quit and relaunch terminal after this installation completes.

2 Run `nvm list` in a terminal window to see whether any versions of Node.js are already installed on your computer.

(continued)
3 Run nvm ls-remote in terminal to check what versions of Node.js are available to install.
4 Run nvm install 9.3.0 in terminal to install the current Node.js version.
5 Run node -v in terminal to verify that you have version 9.3.0 installed.

If you're comfortable with installing Node.js through NVM and without a graphical interface to walk you through the process, this setup is right for you. When installation is complete, don't install Node.js again by using the other set of instructions in this lesson.

> **NOTE**   NVM doesn't support Windows. You may work with one of two alternative version managers: nvm-windows and nodist, which you can install by following the instructions at https://github.com/coreybutler/nvm-windows and https://github.com/marcelklehr/nodist, respectively.

When you install Node.js, you also get npm, the Node.js ecosystem of external libraries (multiple files of code other people wrote) that can be imported into your future projects. npm is similar to pip in Python and gem in Ruby. You learn more about npm in unit 1.

When the installer file is downloaded, double-click the file in your browser's download panel or your computer's download folder. The installer opens a new window that looks like figure 1.2 and writes all necessary files and core Node.js libraries to your system. You may be asked to accept licensing agreements or give the installer permission to install Node.js on your computer. Follow the prompts to click through the installation.

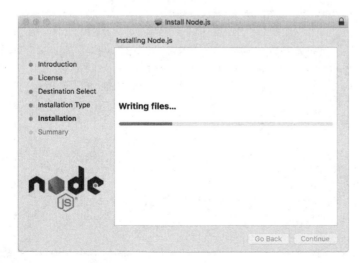

Figure 1.2   Node.js writing to your machine

Terminal and your PATH

You'll be working mostly in your computer's terminal, which is built-in software used to navigate and run commands on your computer without a graphical interface. This book teaches using UNIX terminal (Bash) commands. Those of you who are Windows users can follow along by using Window's CMD terminal window (but may need to look up command equivalents throughout the book). You can reference the table at https://access.redhat.com/documentation/en-US/Red_Hat_Enterprise_Linux/4/html/Step_by_Step_Guide/ap-doslinux.html, which compares Windows and UNIX commands. To make things easier in Windows, you can download and install an additional Bash terminal called Git Bash from http://git-scm.com/downloads.

Make a note of where your version of Node.js and npm are installed on your machine. That information appears in the final window of the installer. The installer attempts to add these directory locations to your system's PATH variable.

PATH is an *environmental variable*—a variable that can be set to influence the behavior of operations on your machine. Your computer's PATH variable specifies where to find directories and executable files needed to perform operations on your system.

This variable's value is the first place terminal will look for resources used in development. Think of the PATH variable as being like your computer's index for quickly finding the tools you need. When you add these tools' original file paths or directory locations to the PATH variable, terminal won't have any problems finding them.

The following figure shows how terminal refers to the PATH variable to identify directories of certain programs and executable files, as these directories may be in different locations on different computers. If you experience any problems starting Node.js in your terminal, follow the installation steps at https://www.tutorialspoint.com/nodejs/nodejs_environment_setup.htm.

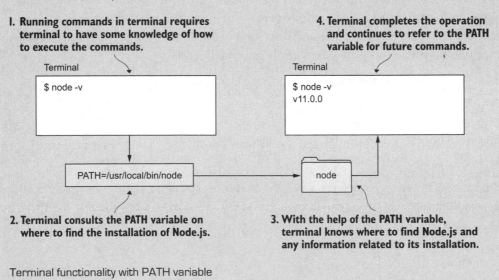

I. **Running commands in terminal requires terminal to have some knowledge of how to execute the commands.**

4. **Terminal completes the operation and continues to refer to the PATH variable for future commands.**

Terminal
```
$ node -v
```

Terminal
```
$ node -v
v11.0.0
```

PATH=/usr/local/bin/node → node

2. **Terminal consults the PATH variable on where to find the installation of Node.js.**

3. **With the help of the PATH variable, terminal knows where to find Node.js and any information related to its installation.**

Terminal functionality with PATH variable

Now that you have Node.js installed, use terminal to make sure that everything is installed correctly. Open terminal (or Git Bash), and type the following command at the prompt: node -v.

The output of this command should show you the version of Node.js you installed. Similarly, you can check the version of npm that you installed by running the command npm -v at the command prompt.

> **NOTE**   If your terminal responds with an error or with nothing, it's possible that your installation of Node.js was unsuccessful. In the case of an error, try copying and pasting that error into a search engine to look for common solutions. Otherwise, repeat the steps in this section.

Now that you have Node.js installed and your terminal running, you need somewhere to write your code.

> **TIP**   If you ever forget where you installed Node.js or npm, you can open a command window and type which node or which npm at the prompt to see the corresponding location. From a Windows command-line prompt, use where in place of which.

1.2   Installing a text editor

A *text editor* is a software application you use to write your code while developing an application. Although text editors come in many forms and can be used to make non-code files as well, the text editors designed for developers often come prepackaged with helpful tools and plugins.

For this book, I recommend downloading and installing the Atom text editor, a free open-source software application for developing in many programming languages. Atom was developed by GitHub and offers many additional plugins written in Node.js. Atom will help you write a Node.js application with ease.

Install Atom by following these steps:

1 In your browser, go to https://atom.io.
2 Click the Download link.
3 Follow the prompts to install the software on a Mac, Windows, or Linux computer.

When the installation completes, open the folder on your computer where applications are located. From there, you can launch the Atom editor by double-clicking the program file.

> **TIP** You may be interested in writing your code in an *integrated development environment* (IDE). IDEs such as Visual Studio Code (https://code.visualstudio.com/) offer helpful tools like a terminal window within the editor, code autocomplete, and debuggers for your project.

With your text editor in place, test some Node.js terminal commands.

 ## 1.3   Setting up SCM and deployment tools

In this section, you set up Git and the Heroku command-line interface (CLI), which you'll use at the end of the book to deploy your applications online. *Deployment* is a term used to describe the migration of your application from your computer to a place where it can be accessed and used publicly online. *Software configuration management* (SCM) is the process of managing your application in its different environments as new features and changes are applied to the code. You can use Git and the Heroku CLI together to deploy your code from development to production and manage your application.

Git is a version-control tool used to separate layers of your application's code evolution. It allows you to save, or take a snapshot, of your code at different stages of development, making it easy to return to a working state quickly if you find that your latest changes break your application's functionality. More important for this book, you need Git to send a version of your code to Heroku so that people can start using your application on the internet.

If you have a Mac, Git should already be installed. If you've installed Git Bash on your Windows machine, Git came packaged and installed too. If you aren't sure whether you have Git, you can enter `git --version` in a terminal window. Unless your window responds with a Git version number, you should download it directly from https://git-scm.com/downloads. Select your operating system, as shown in figure 1.3. The downloaded file opens a graphical interface through which you can install Git on your machine.

When Git is installed, you use it by initializing your project with `git init` in terminal. Then you can add individual project files to your new version by running `git add` followed by the relative path to the file. You can also add all the files in your project by running `git add.` (including the period in the command). To confirm these files, run `git commit -m "some message"`, where the message in quotations describes the changes you made. If you're familiar with Git, I recommend using it as you run the code in this book. Otherwise, you won't need it until unit 8. You learn more about using Git through videos and documentation at https://git-scm.com/doc.

Downloads

 Mac OS X   Windows

 Linux   Solaris

Older releases are available and the Git source repository is on GitHub.

Figure 1.3   Installing Git from the downloads page

TIP For a useful cheat sheet of Git commands, visit https://services.github.com/on-demand/downloads/github-git-cheat-sheet.pdf.

Heroku is a service you'll use to host your application online. To use Heroku, you need to create a new account at https://signup.heroku.com. Enter your name and other information in the required fields, and verify your email address. When your account is created, Heroku lets you upload three applications for free. The best part is that you can do all the work directly from terminal.

Next, you need to install the Heroku CLI. On a Mac you can install it with Homebrew. To install Homebrew, run the command shown in listing 1.1 in a terminal window. This installation process is described at https://brew.sh/.

Listing 1.1   Installing Homebrew on Unix computers in terminal

```
/usr/bin/ruby -e "$(curl -fsSL
  https://raw.githubusercontent.com/Homebrew/install/master/
  install)"          Run install command
                     in terminal window
```

Run brew install heroku/brew/heroku or download the installer at https://devcenter .heroku.com/articles/heroku-cli#macos. For Windows, you can find an installer at https:// devcenter.heroku.com/articles/heroku-cli#windows. Linux users can install the Heroku CLI by running sudo wget -q0- https://toolbelt.heroku.com/install-ubuntu.sh | sh in terminal. If you use the graphical installer, you can step through the default settings and prompts.

When the Heroku CLI is set up, you can use the heroku keyword in terminal. The last part of this setup process is logging in to your Heroku account from terminal. Enter heroku login and then enter the email address and password you used to set up your Heroku account. You're prepared to deploy to Heroku.

 ## 1.4   Working with the Node.js REPL in terminal

In this section, you begin using Node.js from terminal through the Node.js REPL environment. The interactive Node.js shell is the Node.js version of Read-Evaluate-Print Loop (REPL). This shell is a space in which you can write pure JavaScript and evaluate your code in the terminal window in real time. Within the window, your written code is read and evaluated by Node.js, with results printed back to your console. In this section, I look at a few things you can do in REPL.

You've already used terminal to check whether Node.js was installed correctly. Another way to see whether the installation was successful is to type node and press the Enter key. This action places you in the interactive Node.js shell. You'll know that this command is successful when you see the terminal prompt change to >. To exit this prompt, type .exit or press Ctrl-C twice.

Several keywords specific to Node.js allow your terminal and REPL environment to understand when you're running a Node.js command. In appendix A, I discuss keywords in Node.js and how they pertain to application development.

> **NOTE**   If you need more practice with terminal commands, look at Part 2 of *Learn Linux in a Month of Lunches* by Steven Ovadia (Manning, 2016).

You can get to REPL by entering the node keyword in your terminal window without any text to follow. When you're prompted by >, you can enter a command in JavaScript. Although this environment is reserved for testing and sandbox code, the node shell can offer a lot of benefits in development. You can enter and evaluate simple mathematical expressions, for example, or you can execute full JavaScript statements. You can also store values in variables and instantiate objects from your own custom class here. See listing 1.2 for some example REPL interactions.

In these code examples, I demonstrate some of the JavaScript ES6 syntax that appears throughout the book. In addition to the basic arithmetic I run in the REPL shell, I set up a variable with the let keyword. This keyword allows me to define a variable that's scoped to a code block. The blocks include function blocks, to which var-defined variables are scoped, as well as conditional blocks and loops.

I also use the new class syntax to define an object. The syntax here resembles that of object-oriented programming languages but mainly acts as a wrapper over the existing JavaScript prototype structure.

Listing 1.2 REPL command examples

```
$ node          ◄──── Enter REPL.
>
> 3 + 3         ◄────
6                       Perform basic commands
> 3 / 0                 and expressions.
Infinity
> console.log("Hello, Universe!");    ◄────
Hello, Universe!                              Log messages to
> let name = "Jon Wexler";                    the console.
> console.log(name);
Jon Wexler                    Create ES6 classes and
> class Goat {         ◄────  instantiate objects.
  eat(foodType) {
    console.log(`I love eating ${foodType}`);
  }
}

> let billy = new Goat();
> billy.eat("tin cans");
I love eating tin cans
```

In the REPL environment, you have access to all the core modules that come with Node.js. *Core modules* are JavaScript files that come with your Node.js installation. I talk more about modules in unit 1. You'll soon see in your own custom applications that you need to import some modules to use them in REPL. For a short list of commands to use in REPL, see table 1.1.

Table 1.1 REPL commands to remember

REPL command	Description
.break (or .clear)	Exits a block within the REPL session, which is useful if you get stuck in a block of code
.editor	Opens an internal editor for you to write multiple lines of code. ctrl-d saves and quits the editor
.exit	Quits the REPL session

Table 1.1 REPL commands to remember (continued)

REPL command	Description
.help	Lists other commands and useful tips to help you feel comfortable with this interactive shell environment
.load	Followed by a local filename; gives REPL access to that file's code
.save	Followed by a new filename of your choice; saves your REPL session's code to a file

Explore REPL by running some JavaScript commands you know. In the next lesson, you learn how to import previously written code into REPL.

 # Summary

In this lesson, you installed the Atom text editor and Node.js. You also verified that your Node.js environment is ready to evaluate JavaScript code by running some commands in REPL. In the next lesson, you learn how to use Node.js and terminal to build and launch an application.

RUNNING A NODE.JS APPLICATION

In this lesson, you write and run your first JavaScript file with Node.js. At the end, I show you how to import JavaScript files into REPL so you can work with prewritten code.

This lesson covers

- Creating and saving a JavaScript file
- Running your JavaScript file with Node.js
- Loading files into REPL

Consider this   You're testing some code that you've written in JavaScript. Suppose that this code is the function shown in the following snippet, which accepts an array of numbers and prints them to the screen.

> **NOTE**   In this code example, I use ES6 syntax to assign the variable `printNumbers` to a function defined with a single `arr` parameter and an arrow symbol in place of the traditional `function` keyword. I use another arrow function as the callback function within my `forEach` call.

```
let printNumbers = arr => {
  arr.forEach(num => console.log(num));    ← Print array
};                                             elements.
```

To test whether this code works, you could save it in a .js file, link it to an .html web page, and run that file in a browser, viewing the results in your browser's inspector window. With Node.js, you get immediate satisfaction by running JavaScript files directly in terminal.

 ## 2.1   Creating a JavaScript file

To get started with your first Node.js application, create a JavaScript file to print a message to the terminal console. To do that, follow these steps:

1 Open your text editor to a new window.
2 Type the following code in that empty file: `console.log("Hello, Universe!");`
3 Save this file as hello.js on your desktop.

That's all you need to do. You've created a JavaScript file that Node.js can execute. In the next section, you run that file.

Strict mode

In JavaScript, you can opt to write code in *strict mode*—a mode in which casual JavaScript mistakes are caught, even when the Node.js engine or web browsers you use let those mistakes pass.

To use strict mode, add "use strict"; to the top of every JavaScript file you write (before any other statements). For strict mode to work, all files in a related project must be tagged as using strict mode.

See strict mode's documentation at https://developer.mozilla.org/en-US/docs/Web/JavaScript/Reference/Strict_mode.

> **NOTE** Strict mode changes some previously-accepted mistakes into errors, so they're discovered and promptly fixed.

Some mistakes discovered by strict mode include

- *Accidentally creating global variables*—You won't be able to create a variable without the var, let, or const keywords.

(continued)

- *Assigning variables that can't be assigned*—You can't use undefined as a variable name, for example.
- *Using non-unique function parameter names or property names in an object literal*—You need to choose names that don't repeat within the same scope when assigning values.

  NOTE JavaScript has retained "use strict"; as a string for backward compatibility. Older JavaScript engines see it as a string and ignore it.

JavaScript can be forgiving, but for learning purposes and in anticipation of the casual mistakes that most developers make, I use strict mode in my code and recommend that you do the same. Although I may not show "use strict"; in the book's code examples, this line is present at the top of every JavaScript file I write and run.

 ## 2.2   Running your JavaScript file with Node.js

The Node.js JavaScript engine can interpret your JavaScript code from the terminal when you navigate to the location of a JavaScript file and preface the filename with the node keyword.

Complete the following steps to run your JavaScript file:

1 Open a new terminal window.
2 Navigate to your desktop by entering cd ~/Desktop.
3 Run your JavaScript file by entering the node keyword followed by the file's name. You can also run the same command without the file's extension. Type node hello at the prompt, for example, for a file named hello.js (figure 2.1).

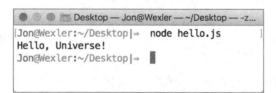

Figure 2.1 Running a JavaScript file with Node.js

If your file was created and run correctly, you should see Hello, Universe! printed on the screen. If you don't see a response, make sure that hello.js has content in it and that your latest changes are saved. Also, make sure that you run the command from that file's directory.

Exactly what is happening here? The Node.js `console.log` function allows you to output the result of any JavaScript command to the console window (or your terminal's standard output window). If you've debugged JavaScript in your browser before, you'll notice the parallel between using `console.log` in a Node.js console window and outputting to your debugging tool's console window.

> **TIP** For more information about console.log and other logging types, please reference appendix B.

Quick check 2.1 If you have a file called hello.js, what will happen if you run node `hello` in terminal?

2.3 Running individual JavaScript commands

Imagine that you're working on an application to send positive messages to your users. Before you fully incorporate your file of positive messages into the application, you want to test it in your Node.js REPL. You create a .js file with your messages as an array by creating a JavaScript file called messages.js with the code from the following listing.

Listing 2.1 Declaring a JavaScript variable in messages.js

```
let messages = [
  "A change of environment can be a good thing!",
  "You will make it!",
  "Just run with the code!"
];
```

List an array of messages.

Instead of executing this file with Node.js (which currently wouldn't offer anything), you initiate the REPL environment with the `node` keyword and import this file by using `.load messages.js`, as shown in listing 2.2. By importing the file, you give REPL access to the contents of that file. After the file is imported, the window responds with the file's contents. You also have access to the `messages` variable in your REPL environment.

QC 2.1 answer Because Node.js is primed for executing JavaScript code, it doesn't require adding the .js file extension when running files. You could run a file as node `hello.js` or node `hello`; either will work.

NOTE   Make sure that you start your REPL session from the same directory in which you saved the messages.js file; otherwise, you'll need to import the absolute path of the file instead of its relative path. The *absolute* path to a file is its location on your computer, starting from your root directory. On my computer, for example, /usr/local/bin/node is the absolute path to my installation of Node.js. The relative path from the local directory would be /bin/node.

Listing 2.2   Loading a JavaScript file into REPL

```
> .load messages.js
"use strict";
let messages = [
  "A change of environment can be a good thing!",
  "You will make it!",
  "Just run with the code!"
];
```
Loading an array
with three strings

You plan to list each of the messages to your users through your Node.js application. To test this list, loop through the array and broadcast each message by entering the code from the next listing directly in the REPL window.

Listing 2.3   Use a file's contents in REPL

```
> messages.forEach(message => console.log(message));
```
Log each message
by using a single-line
arrow function.

The messages print in their array order in the terminal window, as shown in the following listing.

Listing 2.4   Results from the console.log loop

```
A change of environment can be a good thing!
You will make it!
Just run with the code!
undefined
```
Printing messages and
showing undefined as
the return value

If you're happy with the code you wrote in the REPL window, you can save the code to a file called positiveMessages.js by typing `.save positiveMessages.js` in REPL. Doing so saves you the trouble of retyping any work that you produce in the REPL environment.

> **Quick check 2.2**
> 1 What are three ways in which you could exit the REPL environment?
> 2 How do you load a file that isn't in your project folder into REPL?
> 3 What happens if you run `.save` with a filename that already exists?

Ease in navigating the Node.js REPL environment comes with practice. Remember to access node in terminal for quick checking and testing of code that might take longer to modify in a big application. Next, you're off to start building web applications and setting them up the right way from scratch.

 # Summary

In this lesson, you learned that JavaScript files can be run with Node.js in your terminal. In your first outing with Node.js, you created and ran your first application. Then you explored the REPL environment by loading your JavaScript file and saving your REPL sandbox code. In the next lesson, you create a Node.js module and install tools with npm.

Try this

`console.log` will soon become one of your best friends in web development, as log notes will help you find bugs. Get to know your new friend with a little practice and variation. As mentioned earlier in this lesson, `console` is a global object in Node.js, from the Console class. `log` is only one of many instance methods you can run on this object.

QC 2.2 answer
 1 To exit your Node.js REPL environment, you can type `.exit`, press Ctrl-C twice, or press Ctrl-D twice.
 2 For files that aren't located within the directory you navigated to in terminal, you may need to use that file's absolute path.
 3 Running `.save` saves your REPL session to a file and overwrites any files that have the same name.

> **NOTE**   *String interpolation* means inserting a piece of text, represented by a variable, into another piece of text.

Try printing the following to console:

- A message with an interpolated string variable with `console.log("Hello %s", "Universe");`
- A message with an interpolated integer variable with `console.log("Score: %d", 100);`

Try building a file called `printer.js` with the code in the next listing inside.

Listing 2.5 String interpolation example

```
let x = "Universe";
console.log(`Hello, ${x}`);          Log an
                                      interpolated string.
```

What do you expect to happen when you run `node printer.js` in terminal?

Getting started with Node.js

Now that you've gone through unit 0 and have Node.js installed and running, it's time to see it working. Unit 1 is about building from the get-go. You begin by building a small web application in Node.js and gradually piece together the components that work behind the scenes. In this unit, you learn all you need to get a web server running on Node.js that serves some simple static content: HTML pages, pictures, and a stylesheet. Toward this goal, you look at the following topics:

- Lesson 3 introduces npm and discusses how to configure a new Node.js application. In this lesson, you build a Node.js module, and learn how packages and modules offer tools and support to your application.
- Lesson 4 introduces the idea of a web server running on Node.js as a way to launch a simple website. You learn how to set up the server and write code to get your website content viewable.
- Lesson 5 builds on lesson 2 by giving the app enough information to load web content based on different requests. In this lesson, you build your first application route—a system for connecting content to URLs in your application.

- Lesson 6 teaches you how to serve different HTML files from your web server rather than simple responses. This lesson adds support for application assets: CSS, JavaScript that runs on the user's device, and image loading. Together, these concepts enable you to organize and structure your application to handle more requests to your website with less code clutter.
- Finally, lesson 7 shows you how to put everything together by building a complete multipage application. You start a new application from scratch; then you add three views, routes for the views and assets, and a public client folder.

When you're solid on how to build a static site from scratch, unit 2 takes you to the next step: using a framework to build your application faster.

CREATING A NODE.JS MODULE

In this lesson, you kick off Node.js application development by creating a Node.js module (JavaScript file). Then you introduce npm to the development workflow and learn about some common npm commands and tools for setting up a new application.

This lesson covers

- Creating a Node.js module
- Constructing a Node.js application with npm
- Installing a Node.js package with npm

Consider this   You want to build an application to help people share food recipes and learn from one another. Through this application, users can subscribe, join online courses to practice cooking with the application's recipes, and connect with other users.

You plan to use Node.js to build this web application, and you want to start by verifying users' ZIP codes to determine the locations and demographics of your audience. Will you need to build a tool for checking ZIP codes in addition to the application?

Luckily, you can use npm to install Node.js *packages*—libraries of code others have written that add specific features to your application. In fact, a package for verifying locations based on ZIP codes is available. You take a look at that package and how to install it in this lesson.

A Node.js application is made up of many JavaScript files. For your application to stay organized and efficient, these files need to have access to one another's contents when necessary. Each JavaScript file or folder containing a code library is called a *module*.

Suppose that you're working on a recipe application using the positive messages from unit 0. You can create a file called messages.js with the following code: `let messages = ["You are great!", "You can accomplish anything!", "Success is in your future!"];`.

Keeping these messages separate from the code you'll write to display them makes your code more organized. To manage these messages in another file, you need to change the `let` variable definition to use the exports object, like so: `exports.messages = ["You are great!", "You can accomplish anything!", "Success is in your future!"];`. As with other JavaScript objects, you're adding a `messages` property to the Node.js exports object, and this property can be shared among modules.

> **NOTE** The `exports` object is a property of the `module` object. `module` is both the name of the code files in Node.js and one of its global objects. `exports` is shorthand for `module.exports`.

The module is ready to be required (imported) by another JavaScript file. You can test this module by creating another file called printMessages.js, the purpose of which is to loop through the messages and log them to your console with the code shown in the next listing. First, require the local module by using the `require` object and the module's filename (with or without the .js extension). Then refer to the module's array by the variable set up in printMessages.js, as shown in the next listing.

Listing 3.1   Log messages to console in printMessages.js

```
const messageModule = require("./messages");
messageModule.messages.forEach(m => console.log(m));
```

Require the local
messages.js module.

Refer to the module's
array through
messageModule.messages.

`require` is another Node.js global object used to locally introduce methods and objects from other modules. Node.js interprets `require("./messages")` to look for a module called `messages.js` within your project directory and allows code within `printMessages.js` to use any properties on the exports object in `messages.js`.

Using require

To load libraries of code and modules in Node.js, use `require()`. This `require` function, like `exports`, comes from `module.require`, which means that the function lives on the global `module` object.

Node.js uses CommonJS, a tool that helps JavaScript run outside a browser by helping define how modules are used. For module loading, CommonJS specifies the `require` function. For exporting modules, CommonJS provides the `exports` object for each module. Much of the syntax and structure you use in this book results from CommonJS module designs.

`require` is responsible for loading code into your module, and it does this by attaching the loaded module to your module's `exports` object. As a result, if the code you're importing needs to be reused in any way, it doesn't need to be reloaded each time.

The Module class also performs some extra steps to cache and properly manage required libraries, but the important thing to remember here is that once a module is required, the same instance of that module is used throughout your application.

In the next section, you use npm, another tool for adding modules to your project.

Quick check 3.1   What object is used to make functions or variables within one module available to others?

 ## 3.1   Running npm commands

With your installation of Node.js, you also got npm, a package manager for Node.js. npm is responsible for managing the external packages (modules that others built and made available online) in your application.

Throughout application development, you use npm to install, remove, and modify these packages. Entering `npm -l` in your terminal brings up a list of npm commands with brief explanations.

You'll want to know about the few npm commands listed in table 3.1.

QC 3.1 answer   `exports` is used to share module properties and functionality within an application. `module.exports` can also be used in its place.

Table 3.1   npm commands to know

npm command	Description
npm init	Initializes a Node.js application and creates a package.json file
npm install <package>	Installs a Node.js package
npm publish	Saves and uploads a package you build to the npm package community
npm start	Runs your Node.js application (provided that the package.json file is set up to use this command)
npm stop	Quits the running application
npm docs <package>	Opens the likely documentation page (web page) for your specified package

When you use npm install <package>, appending --save to your command installs the package as a dependency for your application. Appending --global installs the package globally on your computer, to be used anywhere within terminal. These command extensions, called *flags*, have the shorthand forms -S and -g, respectively. npm uninstall <package> reverses the install action. In unit 2, you'll use npm install express -S to install the Express.js framework for your project and npm install express-generator -g to install the Express.js generator for use as a command-line tool.

> **NOTE**   By default, your package installations appear in your dependencies as production-ready packages, which means that these packages will be used when your application goes live online. To explicitly install packages for production, use the --save-prod flag. If the package is used only for development purposes, use the --save-dev flag.

Later, when you prepare your application for production, making it available for the world to use, you may distinguish packages by using the --production flag.

Modules, packages, and dependencies

Throughout your development with Node.js, you'll hear the terms *modules*, *packages*, and *dependencies* thrown around a lot. Here's what you need to know:

- *Modules* are individual JavaScript files containing code that pertains to a single concept, functionality, or library.
- *Packages* may contain multiple modules or a single module. They're used to group files offering relevant tools.
- *Dependencies* are Node.js modules used by an application or another module. If a package is considered to be an application dependency, it must be installed (at the version specified by the application) before the application is expected to run successfully.

If you'd like to incorporate some functionality in your application, you can likely find a package that performs this task at https://www.npmjs.com. To your recipe application, add the ability to find where your users are located based on their ZIP codes. If you have this information, you can determine whether users live close enough together to cook with one another.

To add this feature, you need to install the cities package (https://www.npmjs.com/package/cities), which converts text addresses to location coordinates. But you still need one more thing for this project before you can install the package successfully. In the next section, you properly initialize a Node.js project and create a package.json file that npm will use to install cities.

> **Quick check 3.2**   What flag do you use if you want to install a package globally on your computer?

 ## 3.2   Initializing a Node.js application

Every Node.js application or module contains a package.json file to define the properties of that project. This file lives at the root level of your project. Typically, this file is where you specify the version of your current release, the name of your application, and the main application file. This file is important for npm to save any packages to the node community online.

To get started, create a folder called recipe_connection, navigate to your project directory in terminal, and use the npm init command to initialize your application. You'll be prompted to fill out the name of your project, the application's version, a short description, the name of the file from which you'll start the app (entry point), test files, Git repositories, your name (author), and a license code.

For now, be sure to enter your name, use main.js as the entry point, and press Enter to accept all the default options. When you confirm all these changes, you should see a new package.json file in your project directory. This file should resemble the contents of the next listing.

> **QC 3.2 answer**   The --global or -g flag installs a package for use as a command-line tool globally on your computer. The package can be accessible to other projects, not exclusively to the one you're working on.

Listing 3.2   Result of package.json file in recipe_connection project in terminal

```
{
  "name": "recipe_connection",
  "version": "1.0.0",
  "description": "An app to share cooking recipes",
  "main": "main.js",
  "scripts": {
    "test": "echo \"Error: no test specified\" && exit 1"
  },
  "author": "Jon Wexler",
  "license": "ISC"
}          Display contents of package.json, containing
           a name, version, description, starting file,
           custom scripts, author, and license.
```

Now your application has a starting point for saving and managing application configurations and packages. You should be able to install cities by navigating to your project folder in terminal and running the following command: npm install cities --save (figure 3.1).

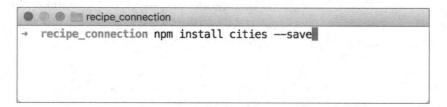

```
● ● ●   recipe_connection
→  recipe_connection npm install cities --save
```

Figure 3.1   Installing a package in terminal

After you run this command, your package.json gains a new dependencies section with a reference to your cities package installation and its version, as shown in the following listing.

Listing 3.3   Result of your package.json file after package installation in terminal

```
{
  "name": "recipe_connection",
  "version": "1.0.0",
  "description": "An app to share cooking recipes",
  "main": "main.js",
```

```
  "scripts": {
    "test": "echo \"Error: no test specified\" && exit 1"
  },
  "author": "Jon Wexler",
  "license": "ISC",
  "dependencies": {          ◄─────    Display dependencies
    "cities": "^2.0.0"                 section of
  }                                    package.json.
}
```

Also, with this installation, your project folder gains a new folder called node_modules.
Within this folder live the code contents of the cities package you installed (figure 3.2).

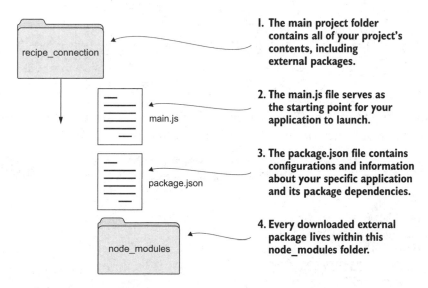

1. **The main project folder contains all of your project's contents, including external packages.**

2. **The main.js file serves as the starting point for your application to launch.**

3. **The package.json file contains configurations and information about your specific application and its package dependencies.**

4. **Every downloaded external package lives within this node_modules folder.**

Figure 3.2 Node.js application structure with node_modules

> **NOTE** You also see a package-lock.json file created at the root level of your project direc-
> tory. This file is automatically created and used by npm to keep track of your package instal-
> lations and to better manage the state and history of your project's dependencies. You
> shouldn't alter the contents of this file.

The --save flag saves the cities package as a dependency for this project. Check your
package.json file now to see how the package is listed under dependencies. Because your
node_modules folder will grow, I recommend that you don't include it when you share
the project code online. Anyone who downloads the project, however, can enter npm
install to automatically install all the project dependencies listed in this file.

Test this new package by adding the lines in listing 3.4 to main.js. Start by requiring the locally installed cities package, and make it available in this file. Then use the zip_lookup method from the cities package to find a city by that ZIP code. The result is stored in a variable called myCity.

> **NOTE** I'll continue to use the var keyword for variable definitions where appropriate. Because myCity is a variable that could change value, I use var here. The cities variable represents a module, so I use const. I use the let variable when the scope of my code could specifically benefit from its use.

Listing 3.4 Implementing the cities **package in main.js**

Require the cities
package.

```
const cities = require("cities");
var myCity = cities.zip_lookup("10016");
console.log(myCity);
```

Assign the resulting
city by using the
zip_lookup method.

Log the results
to your console.

The resulting data from that ZIP code is printed to console as shown in the following listing. The zip_lookup method returns a JavaScript object with coordinates.

Listing 3.5 Sample result from running main.js in terminal

```
{
  zipcode: "10016",
  state_abbr: "NY",
  latitude: "40.746180",
  longitude: "-73.97759",
  city: "New York",
  state: "New York"
}
```

Display the results from
the zip_lookup method.

> **Quick check 3.3** What terminal command initializes a Node.js application with a package.json file?

QC 3.3 answer npm init initializes a Node.js app and prompts you to create a package.json file.

 **Summary**

In this lesson, you learned about npm and how to use its array of tools to create a new Node.js application and install external packages. You built your own Node.js module and required it in your main application file. Last, you installed an external package and got it working in your sample app. The next step is integrating these tools into a web application. I discuss the first steps of building a web server in lesson 4.

Try this

Create a couple of new modules, and practice adding simple JavaScript objects and functions to the exports object.

You can add a function as shown in the following listing.

Listing 3.6 Exporting a function

```
exports.addNum = (x, y) => {
  return x + y;
};
```
Export a function.

See what happens when you require modules from within another directory in your project folder.

BUILDING A SIMPLE WEB SERVER IN NODE.JS

This lesson covers some basic functions of the `http` module, a Node.js library of code used for handling requests over the internet. The tech community raves about Node.js and its use of JavaScript as a server-side language. In this lesson, you build your first web server. In a few short steps, you convert a couple of lines of JavaScript to an application with which you can communicate on your web browser.

This lesson covers

- Generating a basic web server using Node.js and npm
- Writing code that processes requests from a browser and sends back a response
- Running a web server in your browser

Consider this You're on your way to building your first web application. Before you deliver a complete application, the cooking community would like to see a simple site with the flexibility to improve and add features in the future. How long do you think it will take you to build a prototype?

With Node.js, you can use the `http` module to get a web server with sufficient functionality built within hours.

4.1   Understanding web servers

Web servers are the foundation of most Node.js web applications. They allow you to
load images and HTML web pages to users of your app. Before you get started, I'll discuss some important web server concepts. After all, the final product will look and feel a
lot better if you have clear expectations of the result.

Web servers and HTTP

A *web server* is software designed to respond to requests over the internet by loading or
processing data. Think of a web server like a bank teller, whose job is to process your
request to deposit, withdraw, or view money in your account. Just as the bank teller follows a protocol to ensure that they process your request correctly, web servers follow
Hypertext Transfer Protocol (HTTP), a standardized system globally observed for the viewing of web pages and sending of data over the internet.

One way that a client (your computer) and server communicate is through HTTP verbs.
These verbs indicate what type of request is being made, such as whether the user is
trying to load a new web page or updating information in their profile page. The context
of a user's interaction with an application is an important part of the request-response
cycle.

Here are the two most widely used HTTP methods you'll encounter:

- GET—This method requests information from a server. Typically, a server
  responds with content that you can view back on your browser (such as by clicking a link to see the home page of a site).
- POST—This method sends information to the server. A server may respond with
  an HTML page or redirect you to another page in the application after processing your data (such as filling out and submitting a sign-up form).

I discuss a couple more methods in lesson 18.

Most web applications have made changes to adopt *HTTP Secure* (HTTPS), in which
transmission of data is encrypted. When your application is live on the internet, you'll
want to create a public key certificate signed by a trusted issuer of digital certificates.
This key resides on your server and allows for encrypted communication with your client.
Organizations such as https://letsencrypt.org offer free certificates that must be
renewed every 90 days. For more information about HTTPS, read the article at https:
//developers.google.com/web/fundamentals/security/encrypt-in-transit/why-https.

When you visit https://www.google.com, for example, behind the scenes you're making
a request to Google's servers, which in turn send a response back to you, rendering the

famous Google Search landing page. This request-response relationship allows for a channel of communication between the user and the application. In figure 4.1, a bundle of data is sent to the application's server in the form of a request, and when the server processes the request, it issues a bundle of data back in the form of a response. This process is how most of your interaction on the internet is facilitated.

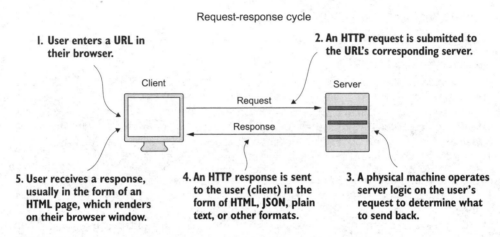

Figure 4.1 A web server sends your browser web pages, images, and other resources on request.

When you enter the URL you want to see in your browser, an HTTP request is sent to a physical computer elsewhere. This request contains some information indicating whether you want to load a web page or send information to that computer.

You may build a fancy application with many bells and whistles, but at the core lies a web server to handle its communication on the internet. (These concepts will make more sense to you as I discuss them throughout the book.) In the next section, you start building your web server.

Quick check 4.1 What does a web server receive from the client, and what does it send back?

QC 4.1 answer The web server receives requests from the client and sends back responses.

4.2   Initializing the application with npm

Before you get started with a Node.js web application, you need to initialize the project in your project folder in terminal. Open a terminal window, and create a new directory called simple_server with `mkdir`. You can initialize the project with `npm init`.

> **NOTE**   npm is Node.js' package manager. Your Node.js projects rely on this tool to install and build applications. You can learn more about npm and how it's used at https://docs .npmjs.com.

Running the `npm init` command initiates a prompt to create a package.json file. As the prompt explains, you'll walk through configuring the most basic settings of your Node.js application in this file. For now, you can add main.js as the entry point, along with a short description and your name as the author, and elect to use the default values offered by pressing the Enter key until you reach the end of the prompt

Then you're asked to confirm your settings with a preview of your package.json file. Press Enter to confirm and return to the regular terminal prompt.

 ## 4.3   Coding the application

When you installed Node.js, the core library was installed too. Within that library is a module called `http`. You'll use this module to build your web server. In this section, you also use a package called `http-status-codes` to provide constants for use where HTTP status codes are needed in your application's responses.

> **NOTE**   Modules in Node.js are libraries of code that come packaged to offer specific functionality to your application. Here, the `http` module helps you communicate across the web by using HTTP.

In your text editor, create a new file called main.js, and save it in the project folder called simple_server containing the package.json file you created earlier. This file will serve as the core application file, where your application will serve web pages to your users. Within this project's directory in terminal, run `npm i http-status-codes -S` to save the `http-status-codes` package as an application dependency.

Before I analyze every aspect of what you're about to build, take a look at all the code in listing 4.1. The first line of code assigns the port number you'll use for this application: 3000.

Then you use `require` to import a specific Node.js module called `http` and save it as a constant. This module is saved as a constant because you don't plan on reassigning the variable. You also require the `http-status-codes` package to provide constants representing HTTP status codes.

Next, you use the `http` variable as a reference to the HTTP module to create a server, using that module's `createServer` function, and store the resulting server in a variable called `app`.

The `createServer` function generates a new instance of `http.Server`, a built-in Node.js class with tools for evaluating HTTP communication. With this newly created server instance, your app is prepared to receive HTTP requests and send HTTP responses.

The argument in `createServer` is a callback function that's invoked whenever some event occurs within the server. When the server is running and your application's root URL (home page) is accessed, for example, an HTTP request event triggers this callback and allows you to run some custom code. In this case, the server returns a simple HTML response.

You log that a request was received from the client and use the `response` parameter in the callback function to send content back to the user, from whom you first received a request. The first line uses a `writeHead` method to define some basic properties of the response's HTTP header. *HTTP headers* contain fields of information that describe the content being transferred in a request or response. Header fields may contain dates, tokens, information about the origins of the request and response, and data describing the type of connection.

In this case, you're returning `httpStatus.OK`, which represents a `200` response code, and an HTML `content-type` to indicate that the server received a request successfully and will return content in the form of HTML. Following this block, you assign a local variable, `responseMessage`, with your response message in HTML.

Right below that line, you're writing a line of HTML in the response with write and clos-ing the response with end. You must end your response with end to tell the server that you're no longer writing content. Not doing so leaves the connection with the client open, preventing the client from receiving the response. You also log your response at this point so you can see that a response was sent from the server itself.

The last line of code takes the server instance, app, and runs the listen method to indi-cate that the server is ready for incoming requests at port 3000.

Listing 4.1 Simple web application code in main.js

Require the http and http-
status-codes modules.

Create the server with
request and response
parameters.

```
const port = 3000,
  http = require("http"),
  httpStatus = require("http-status-codes"),
  app = http.createServer((request, response) => {
    console.log("Received an incoming request!");
    response.writeHead(httpStatus.OK, {
      "Content-Type": "text/html"
    });

    let responseMessage = "<h1>Hello, Universe!</h1>";
    response.write(responseMessage);
    response.end();
    console.log(`Sent a response : ${responseMessage}`);
  });

app.listen(port);
console.log(`The server has started and is listening on port number:
  ${port}`);
```

Write the
response to
the client.

Tell the application server
to listen on port 3000.

> **NOTE** The response object is used by Node.js and carried throughout the application as a way to pass information about the current client transaction from function to function. Some methods on the response object allow you to add data to or remove data from the object; writeHead and write are two such functions.

There your application is, in all its glory! Not so terrible. In only a few lines of code, you'll also build a web server this way.

NOTE   If you don't specify a port number, your operating system will choose a port for you. This port number is what you'll soon use to confirm through your web browser that your web server is running.

Callbacks in Node.js

Part of what makes Node.js so fast and efficient is its use of callbacks. Callbacks aren't new to JavaScript, but they're overwhelmingly used throughout Node.js and worth mentioning here.

A *callback* is an anonymous function (a function without a name) that's set up to be invoked as soon as another function completes. The benefit of using callbacks is that you don't have to wait for the original function to complete processing before running other code.

Consider virtually depositing a check in your bank account by uploading a picture to your bank's mobile app. A callback is equivalent to receiving a notification a couple of days later that the check was verified and deposited. In the meantime, you were able to go about your normal routine.

In the `http` web server example, incoming requests from the client are received on a rolling basis and thereupon pass the request and response as JavaScript objects to a callback function, as shown in the following figure:

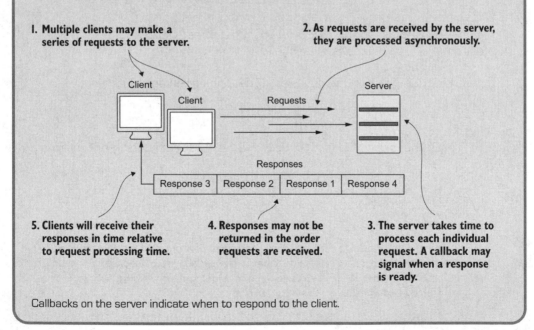

I. **Multiple clients may make a series of requests to the server.**

2. **As requests are received by the server, they are processed asynchronously.**

5. **Clients will receive their responses in time relative to request processing time.**

4. **Responses may not be returned in the order requests are received.**

3. **The server takes time to process each individual request. A callback may signal when a response is ready.**

Callbacks on the server indicate when to respond to the client.

With this code in place, you're ready to start your Node.js application from terminal.

Quick check 4.2   Why should you use `const` instead of `var` to store the HTTP server in your application?

4.4   Running the application

The last step is an easy one. Navigate to your project's directory with terminal, and run `node main` in your terminal window. Next, open any browser to the address `localhost:3000`. You see a message indicating that the server has started. Your terminal window should resemble figure 4.2.

```
simple_server — node main.js — node — node main.js — 68×5
→ simple_server node main.js
The server has started and is listening on port number: 3000
```

Figure 4.2   Running the a basic Node.js server

The browser window should greet you and the universe with salutations, as shown in figure 4.3. Congratulations! Your first Node.js web application is complete. It's big, and it's about to get bigger and better.

Figure 4.3   Display of your first web page

To stop the application, press Ctrl-C in your terminal window. You can also close the terminal window, but you may risk not shutting down the application properly, in which case the application could continue to run behind the scenes (requiring more command-line magic to kill the process).

> **Quick check 4.3** When you navigate to http://localhost:3000/ while your server is running, what type of HTTP request are you making?

 ## Summary

In this lesson, you learned that Node.js has built-in functionality for creating web servers via the http module. You configured a new Node.js application via the package.json file. Using the http module and createServer method, with minimal effort you created a web server, which is a stepping stone to building robust applications with Node.js. Through terminal, you were able to run a web-server application.

Complete the "Try this" exercise to check your understanding.

Try this

npm init interactively generates a package.json file, although you could create this file on your own.

Create a new package.json from scratch for the project in this lesson. Don't use npm init; see whether you can construct a similar JSON-structured file.

LESSON

HANDLING INCOMING DATA

In lesson 4, I introduced you to the web server and showed how you can create one with Node.js. Every time a user visits a URL that leads to your application, a request is made, and each request must be processed by the code you write. In this lesson, you learn how to gather and process some of the information in these requests. You also build application routes—code logic to match requests with appropriate responses.

This lesson covers

- Collecting and processing request data
- Submitting a POST request with the curl command
- Building a web application with basic routes

Consider this   As you plan web pages for your recipe application, you realize that the basic web server you've built knows how to respond only with single lines of HTML. What if you want to show a complete home page and different HTML content for a contact page?

Every web application uses routes alongside its web server to ensure that users get to see what they specifically requested. With Node.js, you can define these routes in as few steps as any conditional block.

5.1   Reworking your server code

To start this lesson, rearrange the code from lesson 4 to get a better idea of how the server is behaving. Create a new project called second_server within its own project directory, and inside, add a new main.js file.

> **NOTE**   In this lesson and following lessons, I expect you to initialize your Node.js application with npm init and to follow the guidance in lesson 4 to create a package.json file.

In your code, you have a server object that has a callback function, (req, res) ⇒ {}, which is run every time a request is made to the server. With your server running, if you visit localhost:3000 in your browser and refresh the page, that callback function is run twice—once on every refresh.

> **NOTE**   req and res represent the HTTP request and response. You can use any variable names here. Keep the order in mind; request always comes before response in this method.

In other words, upon receiving a request, the server passes a request and response object to a function where you can run your code. Another way to write the code for this server is shown in listing 5.1. The server fires the code in a callback function when a request event is triggered. When a user visits your application's web page, the code within the braces runs. Then the server prepares a response by assigning a response code of 200 and defines the type of content in the response as HTML. Last, the server sends the HTML content within the parentheses and simultaneously closes the connection with the client.

Listing 5.1 A simple server with a request event listener in main.js

```
const port = 3000,
  http = require("http"),
  httpStatus = require("http-status-codes"),
  app = http.createServer();                    Listen for
                                                requests.
app.on("request", (req, res) => {      ◄──────
  res.writeHead(httpStatus.OK, {
    "Content-Type": "text/html"
  });        ◄────────          Prepare a response.

  let responseMessage = "<h1>This will show on the screen.</h1>";
  res.end(responseMessage);
});                          ◄──────   Respond with
                                       HTML.
app.listen(port);
console.log(`The server has started and is listening on port number:
➥ ${port}`);
```

Run node main in terminal and visit http://localhost:3000/ in your web browser to view the response containing one line of HTML on the screen.

> **NOTE**:   You may need to reinstall the http-status-codes package again for this new project by runinng npm i http-status-codes –save-dev.

It's great to have some content on the screen, but you want to modify the content based on the type of request you get. If the user is visiting the contact page or submitting a form they filled out, for example, they'll want to see different content on the screen. The first step is determining which HTTP method and URL were in the headers of the request. In the next section, you look at these request attributes.

> **Quick check 5.1**   What is the name of the function your server calls every time a request is received?

 ## 5.2   Analyzing request data

Routing is a way for your application to determine how to respond to a requesting client. Some routes are designed by matching the URL in the request object. That method is how you're going to build your routes in this lesson.

Each request object has a url property. You can view which URL the client requested with req.url. Test this property and two other properties by logging them to your console. Add the code in the next listing to the app.on("request") code block.

Listing 5.2 Logging request data in main.js

```
console.log(req.method);        ←——— Log the HTTP method used.
console.log(req.url);           ←——— Log the request URL.
console.log(req.headers);       ←——— Log request headers.
```

Because some objects in the request can have within them other nested objects, convert the objects to more-readable strings by using JSON.stringify within your own custom wrapper function, getJSONString, as shown in listing 5.3. This function takes a JavaScript object as an argument and returns a string. Now you can change your log statements to

---

> **QC 5.1 answer**   The function that's called after each request is received is a callback function. Because the function doesn't have an identifying name, it's also considered to be an anonymous function.

use this function. You can print the request method, for example, by using `console.log` (`` `Method: ${getJSONString(req.method)}` ``);.

Listing 5.3   Logging request data in main.js

```
const getJSONString = obj => {
  return JSON.stringify(obj, null, 2);      Convert JavaScript
};                                          object to string.
```

When you restart your server, run main.js again, and access http://localhost:3000 in your web browser, you'll notice in your terminal window information indicating that a GET request was made to the / URL (the home page), followed by that request's header data. Try entering a different URL, such as http://localhost:3000/testing or http://localhost:3000/contact. Notice that you still get the same HTML text on the browser, but your console continues to log the URLs you type in the browser.

The types of requests you're largely dealing with are GET requests. If you were building an application with forms for users to fill out, though, your server should be able to process that form data and respond to the user to let them know that the data has been received.

The request object, like most objects in Node.js, can also listen for events, similarly to the server. If someone makes a POST request to the server (trying to send data to the server), the content of that POST lives in the request's body. Because a server never knows how much data is being sent, posted data comes into the http server via chunks.

> **NOTE**   Data chunks allow information to stream into and out of a server. Instead of waiting for a large set of information to arrive at the server, Node.js allows you to work with parts of that information as it arrives via the ReadableStream library.

To collect all the posted data with a server, you need to listen for each piece of data received and arrange the data yourself. Luckily, the request listens for a specific data event. `req.on("data")` is triggered when data is received for a specific request. You need to define a new array, body, outside this event handler and sequentially add the data chunks to it as they arrive at the server. Notice the exchange of posted data in figure 5.1. When all the data chunks are received, they can be collected as a single data item.

Within the `app.on("request")` code block, add the new request event handlers in listing 5.4 to read incoming data. In this code example, every time a request is made to the server, you execute the code in the callback function. An array is created and referred to as body, and every time data from the request is received, you process it in another callback function. The received data is added to the body array. When the transmission of data is

Posting data

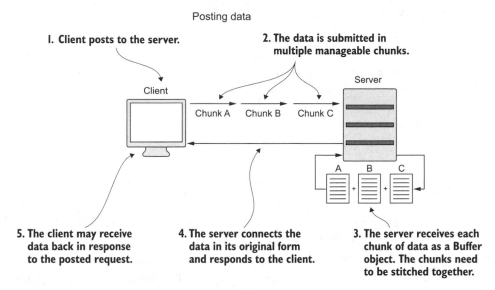

Figure 5.1   A web server collects posted data and arranges it.

complete, you execute code in a third callback function. The body array is turned into a String of text, and the request's contents are logged to your console.

Listing 5.4 Handling posted request data in main.js

Listen for requests.

Create an array to hold chunk contents.

Process it in another callback function.

Add received data to the body array.

Run code when data transmission ends.

Convert the body array to a String of text.

Log the request's contents to your console.

```
app.on("request", (req, res) => {
  var body = [];
  req.on("data", (bodyData) => {
    body.push(bodyData);
  });
  req.on("end", () => {
    body = Buffer.concat(body).toString();
    console.log(`Request Body Contents: ${body}`);
  });

  console.log(`Method: ${getJSONString(req.method)}`);
  console.log(`URL. ${getJSONString(req.url)}`);
  console.log(`Headers: ${getJSONString(req.headers)}`);
```

```
  res.writeHead(httpStatus.OK, {
    "Content-Type": "text/html"
  });

  let responseMessage = "<h1>This will show on the screen.</h1>";
  res.end(responseMessage);
});
app.listen(port);
console.log(`The server has started and is listening on port number:
➥ ${port}`);
```

With this added code, your application is prepared to receive posted data collected into an array and converted back to String format. When an event is triggered, indicating that some chunk of data reached the server, you handle that data by adding the chunk (represented as a Buffer object) to an array. When the event indicating the request's connected has ended, you follow up by taking all the array's contents and turn them into text you can read. To test this process, try sending a POST request to your server from terminal.

Because you haven't built a form yet, you can use a curl command. Follow these steps:

1 With your web server running in one terminal window, open a new terminal window.
2 In the new window. run the following command: curl --data "username=Jon&password=secret" http://localhost:3000

TIP curl is a simple way of mimicking a browser's request to a server. Using the curl keyword, you can use different flags, such as –data, to send information to a server via a POST request.

NOTE If you're a Windows user, before you install curl on your computer, install the software and package manager called Chocolatey (https://chocolatey.org/install). Then you can run choco install curl in your command line.

In the first terminal window, you should see the contents of the request's body logged to the screen, letting you know that a request was received and processed by your server (figure 5.2).

```
● ● ●    lesson_5 — node main.js — node — node main.js —...
⇒  node main.js
Request Body Contents: username=Jon&password=secret
```

Figure 5.2 Results of running a curl command

TIP   For a more user-friendly interface for submitting data to your application, install Insomnia [https://insomnia.rest/download/].

In lesson 8, you learn about simpler ways to handle request contents. For now, try to control what type of response you write back to the client based on the URL and method in the request.

> **Quick check 5.2**   True or false: Every submitted form sends its full contents in a single chunk of data.

 ## 5.3   Adding routes to a web application

A *route* is a way of determining how an application should respond to a request made to a specific URL. An application should route a request to the home page differently from a request to submit login information.

You've established that a user can make a request to your web server; from there, you can evaluate the type of request and prompt an appropriate response. Consider your simple HTTP web server code, which so far has one response to any request. This example accepts any request made to the server (localhost) at port 3000 and responds with a line of HTML on the screen.

Listing 5.5   Simple server example in main.js

```
const port = 3000,
  http = require("http"),
  httpStatus = require("http-status-codes"),
  app = http
    .createServer((req, res) => {
      res.writeHead(httpStatus.OK, {
        "Content-Type": "text/html"
      });
      let responseMessage = "<h1>Welcome!</h1>";
      res.end(responseMessage);        Respond with HTML
    })                                  to every request.
    .listen(port);
```

QC 5.2 answer   False. Data is streamed to the server in chunks, which allows the server to respond based on part of the received data or even the size of the collected data.

As a first web application, this application is a great accomplishment, but you need to start building an application with more functionality. If this project were a legitimate application live on the internet, for example, you might want to show content based on what the user is looking for. If the user wants to see an information page, you may want them to find that information at the /info URL (http://localhost:3000/info). Right now, if users visit those URLs, they'll be greeted by the same HTML welcome line.

The next step is checking the client's request and basing the response body on that request's contents. This structure is otherwise known as *application routing*. Routes identify specific URL paths, which can be targeted in the application logic and which allow you to specify the information to be sent to the client. Creating these routes is necessary for a fully integrated application experience.

Duplicate the simple_server project folder with a new name: simple_routes. Then add a few routes to the main.js file, as shown in listing 5.6.

You set up a mapping of routes to responses called routeResponseMap. When a request is made to http://localhost:3000/info, you check whether the request's URL has a match in routeResponseMap and respond with an info page heading. When a request is made to http://localhost:3000/contact, you respond with a contact page heading. To all other requests, you respond with a generic greeting.

Listing 5.6 Simple routing in a web server in main.js

```
const routeResponseMap = {
  "/info": "<h1>Info Page</h1>",              Define mapping of
  "/contact": "<h1>Contact Us</h1>",          routes with responses.
  "/about": "<h1>Learn More About Us.</h1>",
  "/hello": "<h1>Say hello by emailing us here</h1>",
  "/error": "<h1>Sorry the page you are looking for is not here.</h1>"
};

const port = 3000,
  http = require("http"),
  httpStatus = require("http-status-codes"),
  app = http.createServer((req, res) => {
    res.writeHead(200, {
      "Content-Type": "text/html"           Check whether a
    });                                      request route is
                                             defined in the map.
    if (routeResponseMap[req.url]) {
      res.end(routeResponseMap[req.url]);
    } else {
```

```
        res.end("<h1>Welcome!</h1>");
    }
});
```

Respond with
default HTML.

```
app.listen(port);
console.log(`The server has started and is listening on port number:
➥ ${port}`);
```

With the additions to your code, you can differentiate between a couple of URLs and offer different content accordingly. You're still not concerned with the HTTP method used in the request, but you can check whether the user was searching for the/info route or the /contact route. Users can more intuitively determine what URLs they need to type to get to that page's expected content.

Give the code a try. Save the code in listing 5.6 in a project file called main.js, and run that file in terminal. Then try accessing http://localhost:3000/info or http://localhost:3000/contact in your web browser. Any other URL should result in the original default welcome HTML line.

To mimic heavy processing or external calls made by your server, you can add the code in the following listing to a route to manually delay your response to the client.

Listing 5.7 Route with a timer in main.js

```
setTimeout(() => res.end(routeResponseMap[req.url]), 2000);
```

Wrap a response with
setTimeout to delay
the response manually.

If you run this file again, you'll notice that the page's load time is approximately two seconds longer. You have full control of what code is executed and what content is served to your user. Keep this fact in mind: as your application grows, your web pages' response times will naturally be longer.

Look at the browser screenshot for the /contact URL in figure 5.3.

Quick check 5.3 With what URL do you route requests to the home page?

QC 5.3 answer The / route represents the home page of the application.

Figure 5.3   Browser view
for the /contact URL

 **Summary**

In this lesson, you learned how to handle request content, respond with viewable HTML, and build a server route. By identifying a request's contents, you can process posted data from a request and separate response content based on targeted URLs. The creation of routes shapes your application logic. As a web application expands, its routes expand with it, and so do the types of content that it's able to deliver.

In the next lesson, I talk about serving individual HTML files, images, and web-page styles.

Try this

Your simple web application is handling two path requests with routes you created for /info and /contact. A normal application will likely have more pages to visit. Add three more routes to the application for the following paths:

- /about—When users access http://localhost:3000/about, respond with a line of HTML stating Learn More About Us.
- /hello—When users access http://localhost:3000/hello, respond with a line of HTML stating Say hello by emailing us here. Include an anchor tag linked to your email around the word here.
- /error—When users access http://localhost:3000/error, respond with a status code of 404 (indicating that no page was found) and a line of plain text stating Sorry, the page you are looking for is not here.

NOTE   Open multiple web browsers (such as Apple's Safari, Google Chrome, and Mozilla Firefox), and visit different URLs in those browsers. Notice how the request headers change. You should see the same host but a different user-agent.

WRITING BETTER ROUTES AND SERVING EXTERNAL FILES

In lesson 5, you directed URL traffic with a routing system that matched request URLs to custom responses. In this lesson, you learn how to serve whole HTML files and assets such as client-side JavaScript, CSS, and images. Say goodbye to plain-text responses. At the end of the lesson, you improve your route code and place your logic in its own module for cleaner organization.

This lesson covers

- Serving entire HTML files by using the fs module
- Serving static assets
- Creating a router module

Consider this   It's time to build a basic recipe website. The site should have three static pages with some images and styling. You quickly realize that all the applications you've built so far respond only with individual lines of HTML. How do you respond with rich content for each page without cluttering your main application file?

Using only the tools that came with your Node.js installation, you can serve HTML files from your project directory. You can create three individual pages with pure HTML and no longer need to place your HTML in main.js.

6.1   Serving static files with the fs module

With the goal of building a three-page static site, using these HTML snippets can get cumbersome and clutter your main.js file. Instead, build an HTML file that you'll use in future responses. This file lives within the same project directory as your server. See the project file structure in figure 6.1. In this application structure, all content you want to show the user goes in the views folder, and all the code determining which content you show goes in the main.js file.

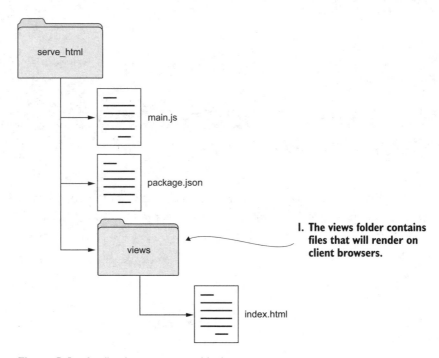

Figure 6.1   Application structure with views

The reason you're adding your HTML files to the views folder is twofold: All your HTML pages will be organized in one place. This convention is used by the web frameworks that you'll learn about in unit 2.

Follow these steps:

1   Create a new project folder called serve_html.
2   Within that folder, create a blank main.js file.

3 Create another folder called views within serve_html.

4 Within views, create an index.html file.

Add the HTML boilerplate code in the next listing to main.html.

Listing 6.1 Boilerplate HTML for the index.html page

```html
<!DOCTYPE html>
<html>
  <head>
    <meta charset="utf-8">
    <title>Home Page</title>
  </head>
  <body>
    <h1>Welcome!</h1>
  </body>
</html>
```

Add a basic HTML structure to your views.

> **NOTE** This book isn't about teaching HTML or CSS. For this example, I've provided some basic HTML to use, but for future examples, I won't provide the HTML so that I can get to the important stuff more quickly.

The client can see this page rendered in a browser only with the help of another Node.js core module: fs, which interacts with the filesystem on behalf of your application. Through the fs module, your server can access and read your index.html. You're going to call the fs.readFile method within an http server in your project's main.js file, as shown in listing 6.2.

First, require the fs module into a constant such as http. With the fs constant, you can specify a particular file in the relative directory (in this case, a file called index.html within the views folder). Then create a routeMap to pair routes with files on your server.

Next, locate and read the file contents of the file in your route mapping. fs.readFile returns any potential errors that may have occurred and the file's contents in two separate parameters: error and data. Last, use that data value as the response body being returned to the client.

Listing 6.2 Using the fs module in server responses in main.js

```js
const port = 3000,
  http = require("http"),
  httpStatus = require("http-status-codes"),
  fs = require("fs");
```

Require the fs module.

```
const routeMap = {
  "/": "views/index.html"
};
```
← Set up route mapping for HTML files.

```
http
  .createServer((req, res) => {
    res.writeHead(httpStatus.OK, {
      "Content-Type": "text/html"
    });
    if (routeMap[req.url]) {
      fs.readFile(routeMap[req.url], (error, data) => {
        res.write(data);
        res.end();
      });
    } else {
      res.end("<h1>Sorry, not found.</h1>");
    }
  })
  .listen(port);
console.log(`The server has started and is listening
⇨ on port number: ${port}`);
```
Read the contents of the mapped file.

Respond with file contents.

NOTE When files on your computer are being read, the files could be corrupt, unreadable, or missing. Your code doesn't necessarily know any of this before it executes, so if something goes wrong, you should expect an error as the first parameter in the callback function.

Run this file by entering this project's directory on your command line and entering node main.js. When you access http://localhost:3000, you should see your index.html page being rendered. Your simple route guides the response of any other URL extension requested to the Sorry, not found message.

TIP If you don't see the index.html file being rendered, make sure that all the files are in the correct folders. Also, don't forget to spell-check!

In the following example, you serve only the files specified in the URL of the request. If someone visits http://localhost:3000/sample.html, your code grabs the request's URL, /sample.html, and appends it to views to create one string: views/sample.html. Routes designed this way can look for files dynamically based on the user's request. Try rewriting your server to look like the code in listing 6.3. Create a new getViewUrl function to take the request's URL and interpolate it into a view's file path. If someone visits the /index path, for example, getViewUrl returns views/index.html. Next, replace the hard-coded filename in fs.readFile with the results from the call to getViewUrl. If the file doesn't exist in the views folder, this command will fail, responding with an error message and httpStatus.NOT_FOUND code. If there is no error, you pass the data from the read file to the client.

Listing 6.3 Using `fs` and routing to dynamically read and serve files in main.js

Create a function to
interpolate the URL
into the file path.

```
const getViewUrl = (url) => {
  return `views${url}.html`;
};

http.createServer((req, res) => {
  let viewUrl = getViewUrl(req.url);
  fs.readFile(viewUrl, (error, data) => {
    if (error) {
      res.writeHead(httpStatus.NOT_FOUND);
      res.write("<h1>FILE NOT FOUND</h1>");
    } else {
      res.writeHead(httpStatus.OK, {
      "Content-Type": "text/html"
      });
      res.write(data);
    }
    res.end();
  });
})
.listen(port);
console.log(`The server has started and is listening on port number:
  ${port}`);
```

Get the file-path
string.

Interpolate the
request URL into your
fs file search.

Handle errors
with a 404
response code.

Respond with file
contents.

> **NOTE** String interpolation in ES6 allows you to insert some text, number, or function results by using the ${} syntax. Through this new syntax, you can more easily concatenate strings and other data types.

Now you should be able to access http://localhost:3000/index, and your server will look for the URL at views/index.

> **WARNING** You'll need to handle any and all errors that may occur as requests come in, because there will likely be requests made for files that don't exist.

Add your new HTML files to your views folder, and try to access them by using their filenames as the URL. The problem now is that the index.html file isn't the only file you want to serve. Because the response body depends heavily on the request, you also need better routing. By the end of this lesson, you'll implement the design pattern laid out in figure 6.2.

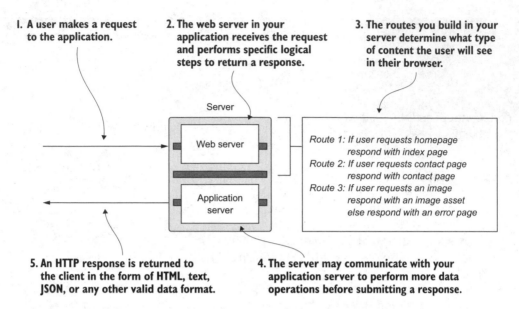

1. **A user makes a request to the application.**

2. **The web server in your application receives the request and performs specific logical steps to return a response.**

3. **The routes you build in your server determine what type of content the user will see in their browser.**

Server

Web server

Application server

Route 1: If user requests homepage respond with index page
Route 2: If user requests contact page respond with contact page
Route 3: If user requests an image respond with an image asset else respond with an error page

5. **An HTTP response is returned to the client in the form of HTML, text, JSON, or any other valid data format.**

4. **The server may communicate with your application server to perform more data operations before submitting a response.**

Figure 6.2   Server routing logic to render views

Quick check 6.1   What happens if you try to read a file that doesn't exist on your computer?

 ## 6.2   Serving assets

Your application's *assets* are the images, stylesheets, and JavaScript that work alongside your views on the client side. Like your HTML files, these file types, such as .jpg and .css, need their own routes to be served by your application.

To start this process, create a public folder at your project's root directory, and move all your assets there. Within the public folder, create a folder each for images, css, and js, and move each asset into its respective folder. By this point, your file structure should look like figure 6.3.

QC 6.1 answer   If you try to read a file that doesn't exist on your computer, the fs module passes an error in its callback. How you handle that error is up to you. You can have it crash your application or simply log it to your console.

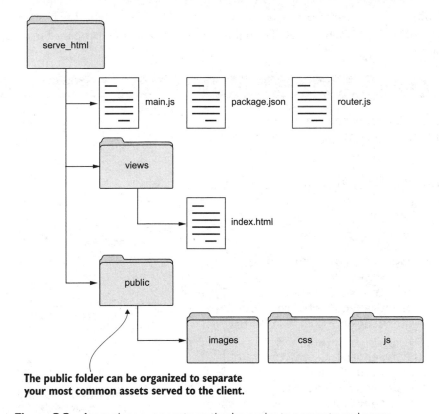

The public folder can be organized to separate your most common assets served to the client.

Figure 6.3 Arranging your assets so they're easier to separate and serve

Now that your application structure is organized, refine your routes to better match your goal in listing 6.4. This code may appear to be overwhelming, but all you're doing is moving the file-reading logic into its own function and adding if statements to handle specific file-type requests.

Upon receiving a request, save the request's URL in a variable url. With each condition, check url to see whether it contains a file's extension or mime type. Customize the response's content type to reflect the file being served. Call your own customReadFile function at the bottom of main.js to reduce repeated code. The last function uses fs.readFile to look for a file by the name requested, writes a response with that file's data, and logs any messages to your console.

Notice that in the first route, you're checking whether the URL contains .html; if it does, you try to read a file with the same name as the URL. You further abstract your routes by moving the code to read the file into its own readFile function. You need to check for specific file types, set the response headers, and pass the file path and response object to this method. With only a handful of dynamic routes, you're now prepared to respond to multiple file types.

Listing 6.4 A web server with specific routes for each file in your project

```
const sendErrorResponse = res => {
  res.writeHead(httpStatus.NOT_FOUND, {
    "Content-Type": "text/html"
  });
  res.write("<h1>File Not Found!</h1>");
  res.end();
};

http
  .createServer((req, res) => {
    let url = req.url;
    if (url.indexOf(".html") !== -1) {
      res.writeHead(httpStatus.OK, {
        "Content-Type": "text/html"
      });
      customReadFile(`./views${url}`, res);
    } else if (url.indexOf(".js") !== -1) {
      res.writeHead(httpStatus.OK, {
        "Content-Type": "text/javascript"
      });
      customReadFile(`./public/js${url}`, res);
    } else if (url.indexOf(".css") !== -1) {
      res.writeHead(httpStatus.OK, {
        "Content-Type": "text/css"
      });
      customReadFile(`./public/css${url}`, res);
    } else if (url.indexOf(".png") !== -1) {
      res.writeHead(httpStatus.OK, {
        "Content-Type": "image/png"
      });
      customReadFile(`./public/images${url}`, res);
    } else {
      sendErrorResponse(res);
    }
  })
  .listen(3000);
```

Create an error-handling function.

Store the request's URL in a variable url.

Check the URL to see whether it contains a file extension.

Call readFile to read file contents.

Customize the response's content type.

```
console.log(`The server is listening on port number: ${port}`);

const customReadFile = (file_path, res) => {                Look for a file
  if (fs.existsSync(file_path)) {                           by the name
    fs.readFile(file_path, (error, data) => {               requested.
      if (error) {
        console.log(error);
        sendErrorResponse(res);                             Check
        return;                                             whether the
      }                                                     file exists.
      res.write(data);
      res.end();
    });
  } else {
    sendErrorResponse(res);
  }
};
```

Now your application can properly handle requests for files that don't exist. You
can visit http://localhost:3000/test.js.html or even http://localhost:3000/test to see the
error message! To render the index page with these changes, append the file type to the
URL: http://localhost:3000/index.html.

The next section shows you how to further redefine your routing structure and give
your routes their own module.

Quick check 6.2 What should be your default response if a route isn't found?

 ## 6.3   Moving your routes to another file

The goal of this section is to make it easier to manage and edit your routes. If all your
routes are in an if-else block, when you decide to change or remove a route, that
change might affect the others in the block. Also, as your list of routes grows, you'll find
it easier to separate routes based on the HTTP method used. If the /contact path can
respond to POST and GET requests, for example, your code will route to the appropriate
function as soon as the request's method is identified.

QC 6.2 answer   If your application can't find a route for some request, you should send back a 404
HTTP status code with a message indicating the page that the client was looking for can't be found.

As the main.js file grows, your ability to filter through all the code you've written gets more complicated. You can easily find yourself with hundreds of lines of code representing routes alone!

To alleviate this problem, move your routes into a new file called router.js. Also restructure the way you store and handle your routes. Add the code in listing 6.5 to router.js. In the source code available at manning.com/books/get-programming-with-node-js, this code exists in a new project folder called better_routes.

In this file, you define a routes object to store routes mapped to POST and GET requests. As routes are created in your main.js, they'll be added to this routes object according to their method type (GET or POST). This object doesn't need to be accessed outside this file.

Next, create a function called handle to process the route's callback function. This function accesses the routes object by the request's HTTP method, using routes[req.method], and then finds the corresponding callback function through the request's target URL, using [req.url]. If you make a GET request for the /index.html URL path, for example, routes["GET"]["/index.html"] gives you the callback function predefined in your routes object. Last, whatever callback function is found in the routes object is called and passed the request and response so that you can properly respond to the client. If no route is found, respond with httpStatus.NOT_FOUND.

The handle function checks whether an incoming request matches a route in the routes object by its HTTP method and URL; otherwise, it logs an error. Use try-catch to attempt to route the incoming request and handle the error where the application would otherwise crash.

You also define get and post functions and add them to exports so that new routes can be registered from main.js. This way, in main.js you can add new callback associations, such as a /contact.html page, in the routes object by entering get("contact.html", <callback function>).

Listing 6.5   Adding functions to the module's exports **object in router.js**

```
const httpStatus = require("http-status-codes"),
  htmlContentType = {
    "Content-Type": "text/html"
  },                              Define a routes object to
  routes = {            ←        store routes mapped to
    "GET": {                      POST and GET requests.
      "/info": (req, res) => {
        res.writeHead(httpStatus.OK, {
```

```
          "Content-Type": "text/plain"
        })
        res.end("Welcome to the Info Page!")
      }
    },
    'POST': {}
  };
exports.handle = (req, res) => {
  try {
    if (routes[req.method][req.url]) {
      routes[req.method][req.url](req, res);
    } else {
      res.writeHead(httpStatus.NOT_FOUND, htmlContentType);
      res.end("<h1>No such file exists</h1>");
    }
  } catch (ex) {
    console.log("error: " + ex);
  }
};

exports.get = (url, action) => {
  routes["GET"][url] = action;
};

exports.post = (url, action) => {
  routes["POST"][url] = action;
};
```

Create a function called handle to process route callback functions.

Build get and post functions to register routes from main.js.

NOTE More HTTP methods could go here, but you don't need to worry about those methods until unit 4.

When you call get or post, you need to pass the URL of the route and the function you want to execute when that route is reached. These functions register your routes by adding them to the routes object, where they can be reached and used by the handle function.

Notice that in figure 6.4, the routes object is used internally by the handle, get, and post functions, which are made accessible to other project files through the module's exports object.

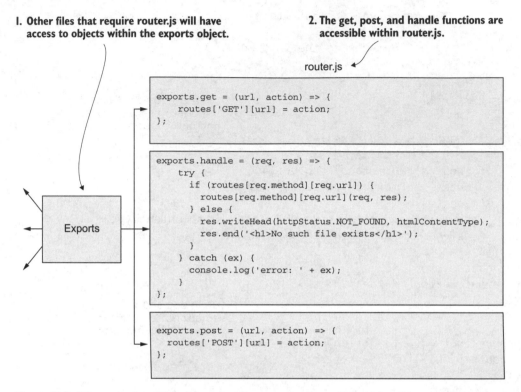

1. Other files that require router.js will have access to objects within the exports object.

2. The get, post, and handle functions are accessible within router.js.

router.js

```
exports.get = (url, action) => {
    routes['GET'][url] = action;
};
```

Exports

```
exports.handle = (req, res) => {
    try {
      if (routes[req.method][req.url]) {
        routes[req.method][req.url](req, res);
      } else {
        res.writeHead(httpStatus.NOT_FOUND, htmlContentType);
        res.end('<h1>No such file exists</h1>');
      }
    } catch (ex) {
      console.log('error: ' + ex);
    }
};
```

```
exports.post = (url, action) => {
  routes['POST'][url] = action;
};
```

Figure 6.4   The exports object gives other files access to specific functionality.

The last step involves importing router.js into main.js. You complete this the same way you import other modules, with require("./router").

You need to prepend router to every function call you make in main.js, as those functions now belong to the router. You can also import the fs module if you plan to serve assets and static HTML files as before. The code for your server should look like the code in listing 6.6.

With the creation of your server, every request is processed by the handle function in your router module, followed by a callback function. Now you can define your routes by using router.get or router.post to indicate the HTTP method you expect from requests to that route. The second argument is the callback you want to run when a request is received. Create a custom readFile function, called customReadFile, to make your code more reusable. In this function, you try to read the file passed in and respond with the file's contents.

Listing 6.6   Handling and managing your routes in main.js

```
const port = 3000,
  http = require("http"),
  httpStatusCodes = require("http-status-codes"),
  router = require("./router"),
  fs = require("fs"),
  plainTextContentType = {
    "Content-Type": "text/plain"
  },
  htmlContentType = {
    "Content-Type": "text/html"
  },
  customReadFile = (file, res) => {
    fs.readFile(`./${file}`, (errors, data) => {
      if (errors) {
        console.log("Error reading the file...");
      }
      res.end(data);
    });
  };

router.get("/", (req, res) => {
  res.writeHead(httpStatusCodes.OK, plainTextContentType);
  res.end("INDEX");
});

router.get("/index.html", (req, res) => {
  res.writeHead(httpStatusCodes.OK, htmlContentType);
  customReadFile("views/index.html", res);
});

router.post("/", (req, res) => {
  res.writeHead(httpStatusCodes.OK, plainTextContentType);
  res.end("POSTED");
});

http.createServer(router.handle).listen(3000);
console.log(`The server is listening on port number:
➥ ${port}`);
```

Create a custom readFile function to reduce code repetition.

Register routes with get and post.

Handle all requests through router.js.

After adding these changes, restart your Node.js application, and try to access your home page or /index.html route. This project structure follows some of the design patterns used by application frameworks. In unit 2, you learn more about frameworks and see why this type of organization makes your code more efficient and readable.

> **Quick check 6.3**   True or false: functions and objects that aren't added to their module's exports object are still accessible by other files.

 **Summary**

In this lesson, you learned how to serve individual files. First, you added the `fs` module to your application to look for HTML files in your `views` folder. Then you extended that functionality to application assets. You also learned how to apply your routing system to its own module and selectively register routes from your main application file. In unit 2, I talk about how you can use the application structure provided by Express.js, a Node.js web framework.

Try this

You currently have one route set up to read an HTML file from this lesson's examples. Try adding new routes in the style introduced in this lesson to load assets.

QC 6.3 answer   False. The `exports` object is intended to allow modules to share functions and objects. If an object isn't added to a module's `exports` object, it remains local to that module, as defined by CommonJS.

CAPSTONE: CREATING YOUR FIRST WEB APPLICATION

When I first got into web development, I really wanted to build a website where people could go to view interesting recipes. Luckily for me, a local cooking school, Confetti Cuisine, wants me to build them a site with a landing page to reflect their course offerings, a page of recipes, and a place where prospective students can sign up.

As a cooking enthusiast, I thought this project would be a good one that I could use daily. What's more, this site is going to be fun to build in Node.js. Piecing together all the preceding lessons into a complete multipage application, these steps should sufficiently prepare me to build a static site for Confetti Cuisine.

I'll start a new application from scratch and add three views, routes for the views and assets, and a public client folder. To start, I'll build out the application logic with the goal of clean, nonrepetitive code. Then I'll add some of the public-facing views and custom styling. At the end of this lesson, I'll have a web server to handle requests to specific files and assets in the project. The final product is one that I can gradually build on and connect to a database at my client's request.

To create this application, I use the following steps:

- Initialize the application package.json.
- Set up the project directory structure.

- Create application logic in main.js.
- Create three views, each of which should have a clickable image that can be served independently:
  - Index (home)
  - Courses
  - Contact
  - Thanks
  - Error
- Add custom assets.
- Build the application's router.
- Handle application errors.
- Run the application.

I'm ready to get cracking.

 ## 7.1   Initializing the application

To start, I use npm to create a package.json file with a summary of the application I'm developing. I navigate to a directory on my computer where I'd like to save this project and then create a new project folder, using the following commands in terminal: `mkdir confetti_cuisine && cd confetti_cuisine` and `npm init`.

I follow the command-line instructions and accept all default values except the following:

- Use main.js as the entry point.
- Change the description to "A site for booking classes for cooking."
- Add my name as the author.

Next, I install the `http-status-codes` package by running `npm install http-status-codes --save` in the project's terminal window. Within my confetti_cuisine folder, my package .json file should resemble the example in the next listing.

Listing 7.1   Project package.json file contents

```
{
  "name": "confetti_cuisine",
  "version": "1.0.0",
  "description": "A site for booking classes for cooking.",
  "main": "main.js",
  "scripts": {
    "test": "echo \"Error: no test specified\" && exit 1",
```

```
    },
    "author": "Jon Wexler",
    "license": "ISC",
      "dependencies": {
          "http-status-codes": "^1.3.0"
      }
}
```
Display my package.json
in terminal.

From this point forward, I'll be able to refer to this file as a summary of my application's configurations.

7.2   Understanding application directory structure

Before I continue with more code, I want to review the application's directory structure. In the project structure, I want my main.js, package.json, and router.js files to live at the root level of my directory. Any HTML content will be represented as individual .html files, which will live in a views folder within my project folder. My complete application project directory will look like the structure in the following listing.

Listing 7.2 Project directory structure for confetti_cuisine

```
.
|____main.js
|____router.js
|____public
| |____css
| | |____confetti_cuisine.css
| | |____bootstrap.css
| |____images
| | |____product.jpg
| | |____graph.png
| | |____cat.jpg
| | |____people.jpg
| |____js
| | |____confettiCuisine.js
|____package-lock.json
|____package.json
|____contentTypes.js
|____utils.js
|____views
```
Display of directory tree
from root folder

```
| |____index.html
| |____contact.html
| |____courses.html
| |____thanks.html
| |____error.html
```

My application server will respond with HTML files in my views folder. The assets on which those files rely will live in a folder called public.

> **NOTE**   HTML files will be viewed by the client, but they're not considered to be assets and don't go in the public folder.

The public folder contains an images, js, and css folder to hold the application's client-facing assets. These files define the styles and JavaScript interactions between my application and its user. To add some quick styling to my application, I download bootstrap .css from http://getbootstrap.com/docs/4.0/getting-started/download/ and add it to my css folder in public. I also create a confetti_cuisine.css file for any custom styling rules that I want to apply to this project.

Next, I set up the application logic.

 ## 7.3   Creating main.js and router.js

Now that I've set up my folder structure and initialized the project, I need to add the main application logic to the site to get it serving files on port 3000. I'm going to keep the routes in a separate file, so I'll need to require that file along with the fs module so that I can serve static files.

I create a new file called main.js. Within that file, I assign my application's port number, require the http and http-status-codes modules and the soon-to-be-built custom modules router, contentTypes, and utils, as shown in listing 7.3.

> **NOTE**   The contentTypes and utils modules simply help me organize my variables within main.js.

Listing 7.3   Contents of main.js with required modules

```
const port = 3000,          ←——— Import required modules.
  http = require("http"),
  httpStatus = require("http-status-codes"),
  router = require("./router"),
  contentTypes = require("./contentTypes"),
  utils = require("./utils");
```

The application won't start until I create my local modules, so I'll start by creating contentTypes.js, using the code in the following listing. In this file, I'm exporting an object that maps file types to their header values for use in my responses. Later, I'll access the HTML content type in main.js by using contentTypes.html.

Listing 7.4   Object mapping in contentTypes.js

```
module.exports = {                    ←——————  Export content type
  html: {                                       mapping object.
    "Content-Type": "text/html"
  },
  text: {
    "Content-Type": "text/plain"
  },
  js: {
    "Content-Type": "text/js"
  },
  jpg: {
    "Content-Type": "image/jpg"
  },
  png: {
    "Content-Type": "image/png"
  },
  css: {
    "Content-Type": "text/css"
  }
};
```

Next, I set up the function that I'll use to read file contents in a new `utils` module. Within utils.js, I add the code in the next listing. In this module, I export an object containing a `getFile` function. This function looks for a file at the provided path. If a file doesn't exist, I immediately return an error page.

Listing 7.5   Utility functions in utils.js

```
const fs = require("fs"),                              Import modules
  httpStatus = require("http-status-codes"),           for use in getFile.
  contentTypes = require("./contentTypes");    ←————

module.exports = {                      ←————————          Export a
  getFile: (file, res) => {                               function to read
    fs.readFile(`./${file}`, (error, data) => {          files and return
      if (error) {                                        a response.
```

```
        res.writeHead(httpStatus.INTERNAL_SERVER_ERROR,
          contentTypes.html);
        res.end("There was an error serving content!");
      }
      res.end(data);
    });
  }
};
```

Last, in a new file, I add the code in listing 7.6. This router.js file requires the http-status-codes and my two custom modules: contentTypes and utils.

The router module includes a routes object that holds key-value pairs mapped to GET requests through my get function and POST requests through my post function. The handle function is the one referred to as the callback function to createServer in main.js. The get and post functions take a URL and callback function and then map them to each other in the routes object. If no route is found, I use my custom getFile function in the utils module to respond with an error page.

Listing 7.6 Handling routes in router.js

```
const httpStatus = require("http-status-codes"),
  contentTypes = require("./contentTypes"),
  utils = require("./utils");

const routes = {                    Create a routes
  "GET": {},                        object to hold
  "POST": {}                        route functions.
};
                                    Create the handle function
exports.handle = (req, res) => {    to handle requests.
  try {
    routes[req.method][req.url](req, res);
  } catch (e) {
    res.writeHead(httpStatus.OK, contentTypes.html);
    utils.getFile("views/error.html", res);
  }
};

exports.get = (url, action) => {    Create the get and
  routes["GET"][url] = action;      post functions to
};                                  map route functions.

exports.post = (url, action) => {
```

```
    routes["POST"][url] = action;
};
```

To get my application server to run, I need to set up the application's routes and views.

 ## 7.4   Creating views

The views are client-facing and could make or break my user's experience with the application. I'll use a similar template for each page to reduce complexity in this application. The top of each HTML page should have some HTML layout, a head, a link to my soon-to-be-built custom stylesheet, and navigation. The home page for the Confetti Cuisine site will look like figure 7.1, with links to my three views in the top-left corner.

Figure 7.1   Example home page for Confetti Cuisine

For the home page, I'll create a new view called index.html in my views folder and add the content specific to the index page. Because I'm using bootstrap.css, I need to link to that file from my HTML pages by adding `<link rel="stylesheet" href="/bootstrap.css">` to my HTML `head` tag. I'll do the same for my custom stylesheet, `confetti_cuisine.css`.

Next, I create a courses.html file to show off a list of available cooking classes and a contact.html file with the following form. This form submits contact information via POST to the / route. The form's code should resemble the code in the next listing.

Listing 7.7 Example form that posts to the home-page route in contact.html

```html
<form class="contact-form" action="/" method="post">
  <input type="email" name="email" required>
  <input class="button" type="submit" value="submit">
</form>
```

Build a form
to submit a
name to the
the home
page.

My site's contact page will look like figure 7.2.

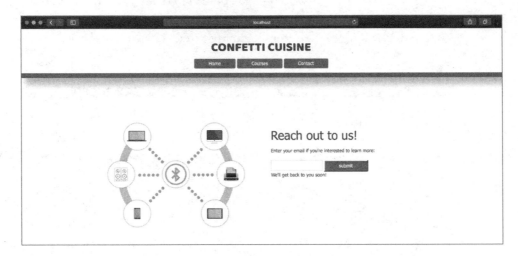

Figure 7.2   Example contact page for Confetti Cuisine

Each page links to the others through a navigation bar. I need to make sure that all the assets I'm using in these files are accounted for when I create my routes. If any assets are missing, my application could crash when it tries to look for their corresponding files.

I'll add these assets so that my pages will have resources for richer content.

 ## 7.5   Adding assets

For this application, I've created some custom styles to be used by each of the views. Any color, dimension, or placement changes I want to make in elements of my site will go in confetti_cuisine.css, which lives in public/css alongside bootstrap.css.

When this file is saved, my views will have colors and structure when loaded. If I decide to use any client-side JavaScript, I'll need to create a .js file, add it to my public/js folder, and link to it within each file by using <script> tags. Last, I'll add my images to public/ images. The names of these images should match the names I use within my HTML views.

The only step left is registering and handling my routes for each view and asset in my project.

 ## 7.6   Creating routes

The last piece of the puzzle is an important one: routes. The routes of my application will determine which URLs are accessible to the client and which files I'll serve.

I've specifically created a router.js file to handle my routes, but I still need to register them. Registering my routes essentially means passing a URL and callback function to my router.get or router.post function, depending on which HTTP method I'm handling. Those functions add my routes to router.routes, a JavaScript object that maps my URLs to the callback functions to be invoked when that URL is accessed.

To recap, to register a route, I need to state the following:

- Whether the request is a GET or a POST request
- The URL's path
- The name of the file to return
- An HTTP status code
- The type of the file being returned (as the content type)

In each callback function, I need to indicate the content type that will go in the response and use the fs module to read the contents of my views and assets into the response. I add the routes and code in the next listing below the require lines in main.js.

> **Listing 7.8 Registering individual routes with the** router **module in main.js**

```
router.get("/", (req, res) => {
  res.writeHead(httpStatus.OK, contentTypes.htm);
  utils.getFile("views/index.html", res);
});

router.get("/courses.html", (req, res) => {
  res.writeHead(httpStatus.OK, contentTypes.html);
  utils.getFile("views/courses.html", res);
```

Add a series of routes for web pages and assets.

```
});

router.get("/contact.html", (req, res) => {
  res.writeHead(httpStatus.OK, contentTypes.html);
  utils.getFile("views/contact.html", res);
});

router.post("/", (req, res) => {
  res.writeHead(httpStatus.OK, contentTypes.html);
  utils.getFile("views/thanks.html", res);
});

router.get("/graph.png", (req, res) => {
  res.writeHead(httpStatus.OK, contentTypes.png);
  utils.getFile("public/images/graph.png", res);
});
router.get("/people.jpg", (req, res) => {
  res.writeHead(httpStatus.OK, contentTypes.jpg);
  utils.getFile("public/images/people.jpg", res);
});
router.get("/product.jpg", (req, res) => {
  res.writeHead(httpStatus.OK, contentTypes.jpg);
  utils.getFile("public/images/product.jpg", res);
});
router.get("/confetti_cuisine.css", (req, res) => {
  res.writeHead(httpStatus.OK, contentTypes.css);
  utils.getFile("public/css/confetti_cuisine.css", res);
});
router.get("/bootstrap.css", (req, res) => {
  res.writeHead(httpStatus.OK, contentTypes.css);
  utils.getFile("public/css/bootstrap.css", res);
});
router.get("/confetti_cuisine.js", (req, res) => {
  res.writeHead(httpStatus.OK, contentTypes.js);
  utils.getFile("public/js/confetti_cuisine.js", res);
});

http.createServer(router.handle).listen(port);        ←
console.log(`The server is listening on
➡ port number: ${port}`);                      Start the server.
```

> **NOTE**   Notice the POST route, which will handle form submissions on the contact.html
> page. Instead of responding with another HTML page, this route responds with an HTML
> "thank you for supporting the product" page.

I should now be able to start my application with `node main` and navigate to http://localhost: 3000 to see my web application's home page.

> **NOTE**   I only create routes for the assets (images, js, and css) that I have represented as files within my project.

 # Summary

In this capstone exercise, I built a complete web application serving static web pages for Confetti Cuisine. To accomplish this task, I required my own router module into the main application file. Then I created a custom system for routing user requests to serve specific content. After building custom functions to register routes in an organized and systematic way, I created views and assets to be served from their respective directories.

A lot of code logic is going on here, and the code logic is on its way to a professional structure used by Node.js applications around the world.

In unit 3, I explore web frameworks and show you how they use this application structure and some scaffolding (prebuilt folders and structure) to accomplish the same application in fewer steps and with fewer headaches.

Easier web development with Express.js

Unit 1 taught you how web servers work with Node.js and how to build meaningful content with built-in modules. This unit is about taking your application to a more robust and professional level by using a web framework and dynamic content. A *web framework* is a predefined application structure and a library of development tools designed to make building a web application easier and more consistent.

In this unit, you learn how to set up an application with Express.js and organize your application file structure to optimize communication of data among your pages. You're also introduced to the model-view-controller (MVC) application architecture, which organizes your code into three distinct responsibilities:

- Giving structure to your data
- Displaying that data
- Handling requests to interact with that data

With the goals of building on the lessons you learned in unit 1 and modifying your code to take full advantage of Express.js, this unit covers the following topics:

- Lesson 8 introduces Express.js and shows how to configure a new Node.js application.

In this lesson, you get an overview of how a web framework helps you develop an application.

- Lesson 9 covers routing with Express.js. You've already learned about writing routes from scratch. This lesson introduces you to the style of routing you'll use throughout the rest of the book. You also learn about MVC and see how routes can behave like controllers in that structure.

- Lesson 10 introduces the concepts of layouts and dynamically rendered views. So far, you've worked only with static content, but in this lesson, you use Express.js to feed content to your views on every page reload. This lesson also discusses templating in Node.js. In Express.js, templating engines are at work to allow you to write placeholders for dynamic content into your HTML pages.

- Lesson 11 builds on the preceding lessons to show how to handle application errors and configure a start-up script with npm.

- Finally, lesson 12 shows how to rebuild your project from unit 1 by using Express.js. You re-create the three front-facing views for the cooking school's website and add functionality to dynamically fill content from your application server.

This unit is your first step into web applications that may feel more familiar. Getting comfortable with Express.js and external packages will make you a more skilled developer. When your Node.js application is running successfully on Express.js, unit 3 talks about how to connect your app to a database and save user information.

SETTING UP AN APP WITH EXPRESS.JS

Building a web application has become a simpler task with the addition of web frameworks. A web framework in Node.js is a module that offers structure to your application. Through this structure, you can easily build and customize the way your application feels without worrying about building certain features from scratch, such as serving individual files. By the end of this lesson, you'll know where to begin with web frameworks and how the one used in this book, Express.js, can reduce the time it takes you to get your application running.

This lesson covers

- Setting up a Node.js application with Express.js
- Navigating a web framework

Consider this   Your static web app from unit 1 is a success. The cooking community wants you to add more functionality and serve more web pages. You realize that your application isn't fully prepared to handle more routes, let alone handling errors or serving other types of assets. Could there be an easier way to start development with some structure already in place?

Luckily, you can install a web framework with your Node.js application. Express.js, the framework you use in this book, handles a lot of the tasks most applications need right out of the box, such as error handling and static-asset serving. The more familiar you get with this framework's methods and keywords, the faster you can build your applications.

8.1   Installing the Express.js package

Express.js increases development speed and provides a stable structure on which to build applications. Like Node.js, Express.js offers tools that are open-source and managed by a large online community.

First, I'll talk about why Express.js is the web framework you should learn. With each passing year, Node.js gains new frameworks, some of which provide convincing reasons to switch to its library. Express.js came out in 2010, and since then, other reliable frameworks have grown in popularity. Table 8.1 lays out some other frameworks you can look into.

Table 8.1   Node.js frameworks to know

Node.js frameworks	Description
Koa.js	Designed by developers who built Express.js with a focus on a library of methods not offered in Express.js (http://koajs.com/)
Hapi.js	Designed with a similar architecture to Express.js and a focus on writing less code (https://hapijs.com/)
Sails.js	Built on top of Express.js, offering more structure, as well as a larger library and less opportunity for customization (https://sailsjs.com/)
Total.js	Built on the core HTTP module and acclaimed for its high-performance request handling and responses (https://www.totaljs.com/)

> **NOTE**   For more information about Node.js web frameworks, you can view an updated list of GitHub repositories at http://nodeframework.com/.

Ultimately, a framework is intended to help you overcome some common development challenges in building a web application from scratch. Express.js is the most used framework in the Node.js community, ensuring that you find the support you need compared with the support offered by other, newer frameworks. Although I recommend using Total.js for its performance and scalability ratings, it's not necessarily the best framework to start with.

Because you're working with Node.js to build a web application for the first time, you need some tools to help you along the way. A web framework is designed to offer some of the common tools used in web development. Express.js provides methods and modules to assist with handling requests, serving static and dynamic content, connecting databases, and keeping track of user activity, for example. You find out more about how Express.js provides this support in later lessons.

Express.js is used by new and professional Node.js developers alike, so if you feel over-whelmed at any time, know that thousands of others can help you overcome your development obstacles.

Now you're ready to jump into initializing an application with Express.js. To begin, you need to initialize your application by creating a new project directory called first_ express_project, entering that directory within a new terminal window, and entering npm init. You can follow the prompt to save main.js as the entry point and to save all the other default values.

> **NOTE**   As discussed in lesson 1, initializing a new project creates a package.json file with which you can define some attributes of your application, including the packages you down-load and depend on.

Because Express.js is an external package, it doesn't come preinstalled with Node.js. You need to download and install it by running the following command within your project directory in terminal: npm install express --save.

> **NOTE**   At this writing, the latest version of Express.js is 4.16.3. To ensure that your ver-sion of Express.js is consistent with the one used in this book, install the package by running npm install express@4.16.3 --save.

> **WARNING**   If you try to install Express.js in a specific project before you create pack-age.json, you may see an error complaining that there's no directory or file with which the installation can complete.

Use the --save flag so that Express.js is listed as an application dependency. In other words, your application depends on Express.js to work, so you need to ensure that it's installed. Open package.json to see this Express.js package installation under the depen-dencies listing.

> **TIP**   If you want to access the Express.js package documentation from your terminal win-dow, type npm docs express. This command opens your default web browser to http:// expressjs.com.

In the next section, you create your first Express.js application.

> **Quick check 8.1**   What happens if you don't use the --save flag when installing Express.js for your application?

QC 8.1 answer   Without the --save flag, your Express.js installation won't be marked as an applica-tion dependency. Your application will still run locally, because Express.js will be downloaded to your proj-ect's node_modules folder, but if you upload your application code without that folder, there's no indication in your package.json file that the Express.js package is needed to run your application.

8.2   Building your first Express.js application

To start using Express.js, you need to create a main application file and require the express module. Save the code in listing 8.1 to a file called main.js within your project.

You require Express.js by referring to the module name express and storing it as a constant. express offers a library of methods and functionality, including a class with built-in web server functionality. The express webserver application is instantiated and stored in a constant to be referred to as app. Throughout the rest of the project, you'll use app to access most of Express.js' resources.

As in the first capstone project, Express.js offers a way to define a GET route and its callback function without building out an extra module. If a request is made to the home page, Express.js catches it and allows you to respond.

A response in plain text is sent to the browser. Notice the Express.js method send, which behaves similarly to write from the http module. Express.js also supports http module methods. Remember to use end to complete your response if you use write. Finally, you set up the application to listen for requests on port 3000 of your local host and ask for a helpful message to be logged to your console when the application is running successfully.

Listing 8.1   Simple Express.js web application in main.js

Add the express module to your application.

Assign the express application to the app constant.

Set up a GET route for the home page.

Issue a response from the server to the client with res.send.

```
const port = 3000,
  express = require("express"),
  app = express();

app.get("/", (req, res) => {
  res.send("Hello, Universe!");
})
.listen(port, () => {
  console.log(`The Express.js server has started and is listening
  on port number: ${port}`);
});
```

Set up the application to listen at port 3000.

Give it a shot. Make sure that you're in your project directory on your command line. Run node main, and go to http://localhost:3000. If you see Hello, Universe! on the screen, you've built your first successful Express.js application.

Installing and using nodemon

To see your application server code changes in effect, you need to restart the server in terminal. Close your existing server by pressing Command-D (Ctrl-C for Windows) and entering node `main.js` again.

The more changes you apply to your application, the more tedious this task becomes. That's why I recommend installing the nodemon package. You can use this package to start your application the first time and automatically restart it when application files change.

To install nodemon globally, enter npm i nodemon -g. You may need to prepend that command with sudo or run it in terminal as an administrator.

Alternatively, you can install nodemon as a development dependency (devDependency) or a resource that you use only during development of an application. Run npm i nodemon --save-dev or npm i nodemon -D. nodemon starts with your npm start script (discussed in lesson 11). The benefit of installing as a devDependency is that each project has its own nodemon modules, reflecting the most up-to-date version of the package at the time of development.

When nodemon is installed, it's simple to use: nodemon picks up on the main property in your package.json. Your package.json should also be modified to include the npm start script. Add "start": "nodemon main.js", to the scripts section in package.json so that you may run your application using nodemon with npm start. Go to your project directory in terminal, and enter nodemon. This command launches your application, and any future changes you make signal nodemon to restart without your needing to enter another command.

You can shut down the server by pressing the same key combination (Command-D or Ctrl-C for Windows) in the nodemon window in terminal.

NOTE The express constant is still used for some Express.js tools related to configuring your application. app is used mainly for anything created for the application's movement of data and user interaction.

In the next section, I talk about some of the ways that Express.js offers support as a web framework.

Quick check 8.2   What's the difference between the express and app constants?

QC 8.2 answer   app represents most of your application, the routes, and access to other modules. express represents a wider range of methods that aren't necessarily scoped to your application. express could offer a method to analyze or parse some text on which your application doesn't necessarily depend.

8.3   Working your way around a web framework

A web framework is designed to do a lot of the tedious tasks for you and leave you with an intuitive structure for customizing your app. Express.js provides a way to listen for requests to specific URLs and respond by using a callback function.

A web framework like Express.js operates through functions considered to be middleware because they sit between HTTP interaction on the web and the Node.js platform. *Middleware* is a general term applied to code that assists in listening for, analyzing, filtering, and handling HTTP communication before data interacts with application logic.

You can think of middleware as being like a post office. Before your package can go into the delivery network, a postal worker needs to inspect the size of your box and to ensure that it's properly paid for and adheres to delivery policies (nothing dangerous in your package). See the diagram on middleware in figure 8.1.

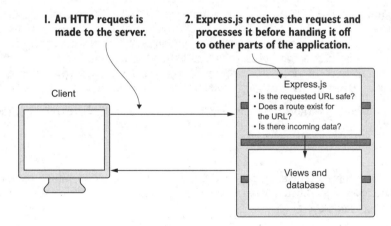

Figure 8.1   Express.js stands between the HTTP requests and your application code.

NOTE   Middleware can come in smaller packages than Express.js. Some play a security role in checking incoming requests before data passes through to the core application.

Because you're still dealing with HTTP methods, the overall interaction between your application and the browser doesn't change much from your application that uses the http module in unit 1. You get the same request and response objects, containing a lot of rich information about the sender and its contents. Express.js offers methods that make it easier for you to get that information.

In addition to the send method on the response object, Express.js provides simpler ways to pull and log data from the request body. Add the code in the next listing to your GET route handler in main.js.

Listing 8.2   Request object methods in Express.js in main.js

```
console.log(req.params);        ◄─┐
console.log(req.body);            │  Access request
console.log(req.url);             │  parameters.
console.log(req.query);
```

From the request, you can pull the values in table 8.2.

Table 8.2   Request object data items

Request data object	Description
params	Allows you to extract IDs and tokens from the URL. When you learn about RESTful routes in unit 4, this request attribute allows you to identify which items are being requested in an e-commerce site or what user profile you should navigate to.
body	Contains much of the contents of the request, which often includes data coming from a POST request, such as a submitted form. From the request body, you can collect information quickly and save it in a database.
url	Provides information about the URL being visited (similar to req.url in unit 1's basic web server).
query	Like body, lets you pull data being submitted to the application server. This data isn't necessarily from a POST request, however, and is often requested in the URL as a query string.

Upon restarting your application and visiting http://localhost:3000, you see these values logged to your server's terminal window. You explore how to make better use of the request body when you learn about Express.js routes in lesson 9.

> **TIP**   A query string is text represented as key/value pairs in the URL following a question mark (?) after the hostname. http://localhost:3000?name=jon, for example, is sending the name (key) paired with jon (value). This data can be extracted and used in the route handler.

Quick check 8.3   Why do most developers use web frameworks instead of building web applications from scratch?

 **Summary**

In this lesson, you learned how to initialize an Express.js project and started a simple application that said hello in your web browser. You also learned about Express.js as a web framework and saw how you'll benefit from its methods moving forward. In lesson 9, you apply some Express.js methods in building a routing system.

Try this

Change the get method in your index.js file to post. Restart your application, and see how your application behaves differently when you try to access the home page at http://localhost:3000. You should see a default error message from Express, telling you that there's no GET route for /.

The reason is that you changed the request method you're listening for. If you make a curl POST request to the home page, you see your original response content.

QC 8.3 answer   Web frameworks make development work a lot easier. Web development is fun, and the best parts aren't the tedious tasks that are most subject to errors. With web frameworks, developers and businesses alike can focus on the more interesting parts of applications.

ROUTING IN EXPRESS.JS

In lesson 8, I introduced Express.js as a framework for Node.js web applications. The rest of this unit is dedicated to exploring Express.js functionality and using its convenient methods. This lesson covers routing and how a few more Express.js methods allow you to send meaningful data to the user before building a view. You also walk through the process of collecting a request's query string. The lesson ends by touching on the MVC design pattern.

This lesson covers

- Setting up routes for your application
- Responding with data from another module
- Collecting request URL parameters
- Moving route callbacks to controllers

Consider this   You want to build a home-page view for your recipe application that people can visit to see an estimated date of completion for your application. With your new, clean Express.js setup, you'd like to keep the date variable in a separate file that you can easily change without modifying your main.js file.

After setting up your routes, you'll be able to store some data in a separate module and respond dynamically with that data. With the separate module, you'll be able to modify that file's contents without needing to edit your main application file. This structure helps prevent you from making mistakes in your code while constantly changing values.

9.1   Building routes with Express.js

In lesson 8, you constructed your first Express.js application, consisting of a route handling GET requests to your home-page URL. Another way to describe this route is as an application endpoint that takes an HTTP method and path (URL). Routes in Express.js should look familiar to you because you built the same routing structure at the end of unit 1. In Express.js, a route definition starts with your app object, followed by a lower-case HTTP method and its arguments: the route path and callback function.

A route handling POST requests to the /contact path should look like the following listing. This example uses the post method provided by Express.js.

Listing 9.1   Express.js POST route in main.js

```
app.post("/contact", (req, res) => {
  res.send("Contact information submitted successfully.");
});
```

Handle requests with the Express.js post method.

You can use these HTTP methods on the app object because app is an instance of the main Express.js framework class. By installing this package, you inherited routing methods without needing to write any other code.

Express.js lets you write routes with parameters in the path. These parameters are a way of sending data through the request. (Another way is with query strings, which I talk about at the end of this lesson.) Route parameters have a colon (:) before the parameter and can exist anywhere in the path. Listing 9.2 shows an example of a route with parameters. The route in this listing expects a request made to /items/ plus some vegetable name or number. A request to "/items/lettuce", for example, would trigger the route and its callback function. The response sends the item from the URL back to the user through the params property of the request object.

Listing 9.2   Using route parameters to indicate vegetable type in main.js

```
app.get("/items/:vegetable", (req, res) => {
  res.send(req.params.vegetable);
});
```

Respond with path parameters.

Initialize a new project called express_routes, install Express.js, and add the code to require and instantiate the Express.js module. Then create a route with parameters, and respond with that parameter as shown in listing 9.2. At this point, your main.js should look like the code in the next listing.

Listing 9.3 Complete Express.js example in main.js

```
const port = 3000,
  express = require("express"),
  app = express();

app.get("/items/:vegetable", (req, res) => {        ← Add a route to get
  let veg = req.params.vegetable;                       URL parameters.
  res.send(`This is the page for ${veg}`);
});

app.listen(port, () => {
  console.log(`Server running on port: ${port}`);
});
```

Route parameters are handy for specifying data objects in your application. When you start saving user accounts and course listings in a database, for example, you might access a user's profile or specific course with the /users/:id and/course/:type paths, respectively. This structure is necessary for developing a representational state transfer (REST) architecture, as you learn in unit 4.

One last note on Express.js routes: I talked about how Express.js is a type of middleware because it adds a layer between a request being received and that request being processed. This feature is great, but you may want to add your own custom middleware. You may want to log the path of every request made to your application for your own records, for example. You can accomplish this task by adding a log message to every route or by creating the middleware function in listing 9.4. This listing defines a middleware function with an additional next argument, logs the request's path to your terminal console, and then calls the next function to continue the chain in the request-response cycle.

next is provided as a way of calling the next function in your request-response execution flow. From the time a request enters the server, it accesses a series of middleware functions. Depending on where you add your own custom middleware function, you can use next to let Express.js know that your function is complete and that you want to continue to whatever function is next in the chain.

As with HTTP methods, you can create a route with app.use that runs on every request. The difference is that you're adding an additional argument in the callback: the next function. This middleware function allows you to run custom code on the request before its URL path matches with any other routes in your application. When your custom code completes, next points the request to the next route that matches its path.

Try adding this middleware function to your express_routes application. If a request is made to /items/lettuce, the request is processed first by your middleware function and then by the app.get("/items/:vegetable") route you created previously.

Listing 9.4 Express.js middleware function for logging request path in main.js

```
app.use((req, res, next) => {                          Define a middleware
  console.log(`request made to: ${req.url}`);          function.
  next();
});            Call the next                            Log the
              function.                                 request's path
                                                        to console.
```

> **WARNING** Calling next at the end of your function is necessary to alert Express.js that your code has completed. Not doing so leaves your request hanging. Middleware runs sequentially, so by not calling next, you're blocking your code from continuing until completion.

You can also specify a path for which you'd like your middleware function to run. app.use("/items", <callback>), for example, will run your custom callback function for every request made to a path starting with items. Figure 9.1 shows how middleware functions can interact with a request on the server.

In the next section, I talk about handling data in your routes and responding with that data.

Quick check 9.1   What does the Express.js use method do?

 ## 9.2   Analyzing request data

Preparing fancy and dynamic responses is important in your application, but eventually, you'll need to demonstrate the application's ability to capture data from the user's request.

QC 9.1 answer   The use method allows you to define the middleware functions you want to use with Express.js.

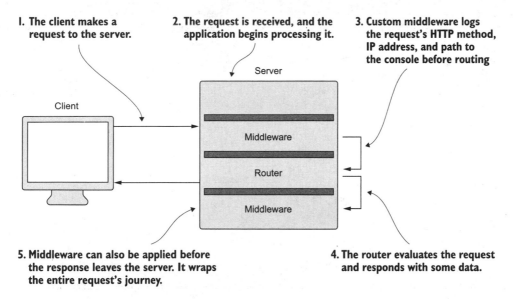

1. The client makes a request to the server.

2. The request is received, and the application begins processing it.

3. Custom middleware logs the request's HTTP method, IP address, and path to the console before routing

5. Middleware can also be applied before the response leaves the server. It wraps the entire request's journey.

4. The router evaluates the request and responds with some data.

Figure 9.1   The role of middleware functions

You have two main ways to get data from the user:

- Through the request body in a POST request
- Through the request's query string in the URL

In the first capstone project, you successfully built a form that submits data to a POST route (a route that listens for posted data to a specific URL). But http incoming data is represented as a Buffer stream, which is not human-readable and adds an extra step to making that data accessible for processing.

Express.js makes retrieving the request body easy with the body attribute. To assist in reading the body contents (as of Express.js version 4.16.0), you add express.json and express.urlencoded to your app instance to analyze incoming request bodies. Notice the use of req.body to log posted data to the console in listing 9.5. Add that code to your project's main.js. With Express.js' app.use, specify that you want to parse incoming requests that are URL-encoded (usually, form post and utf-8 content) and in JSON format. Then create a new route for posted data. This process is as simple as using the post method and specifying a URL. Finally, print the contents of a posted form with the request object and its body attribute.

Listing 9.5 Capturing posted data from the request body in main.js

```
app.use(
  express.urlencoded({
    extended: false
  })
);
app.use(express.json());

app.post("/", (req, res) => {
  console.log(req.body);
  console.log(req.query);
  res.send("POST Successful!");
});
```

Tell your Express.js application to parse URL-encoded data.

Create a new post route for the home page.

Log the request's body.

Test this code by submitting a POST request to http://localhost:3000, using the following curl command: curl --data "first_name=Jon&last_name=Wexler" http://localhost:3000.

You should see the body logged to your server's console window like so: { first_name: "Jon", last_name: "Wexler" }.

Now when you demo the backend code to your customers, you can show them, through a mocked form submission, how data will be collected on the server.

Another way to collect data is through the URL parameters. Without the need for an additional package, Express.js lets you collect values stored at the end of your URL's path, following a question mark (?). These values are called *query strings*, and they are often used for tracking user activity on a site and storing temporary information about a user's visited pages.

Examine the following sample URL: http://localhost:3000?cart=3&pagesVisited=4&utmcode=837623. This URL might be passing information about the number of items in a user's shopping cart, the number of pages they've visited, and a marketing code to let the site owners know how this user found your app in the first place.

To see these query strings on the server, add console.log(req.query); to your middleware function in main.js. Now try visiting the same URL. You should see { cart: "3", pagesVisited: "4", utmcode: "837623" } logged to your server's console window.

In the next section, I talk about MVC architecture and how Express.js routes fit into that structure.

9.3   Using MVC

This lesson is about processing request data within your routes. Express.js opens the door to custom modules and code to read, edit, and respond with data within the request-response cycle. To organize this growing code base, you're going to follow an application architecture known as MVC.

MVC architecture focuses on three main parts of your application's functionality: models, views, and controllers. You used views in past applications to display HTML in the response. See the breakdown and definitions in table 9.1.

Table 9.1   Model-view-controller parts

Views	Rendered displays of data from your application. In unit 3, you learn about models and even create your own.
Models	Classes that represent object-oriented data in your application and database. In your recipe application, you might create a model to represent a customer order. Within this model, you define what data an order should contain and the types of functions you can run on that data.
Controllers	The glue between views and models. Controllers perform most of the logic when a request is received to determine how request body data should be processed and how to involve the models and views. This process should sound familiar, because in an Express.js application, your route callback functions act as controllers.

To follow the MVC design pattern, move your callback functions to separate modules that reflect the purposes of those functions. Callback functions related to user account creation, deletion, or changes, for example, go in a file called usersController.js within the controllers folder. Functions for routes that render the home page or other informational pages can go in homeController.js by convention. Figure 9.2 shows the file structure that your application will follow.

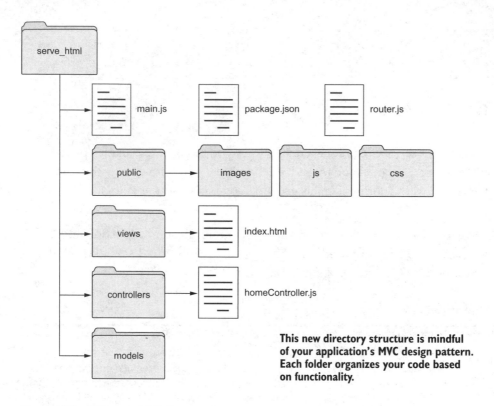

This new directory structure is mindful of your application's MVC design pattern. Each folder organizes your code based on functionality.

Figure 9.2   Express.js MVC file structure

Figure 9.3 shows Express.js as a layer over your application that handles requests but also feeds your application's controllers. The callbacks decide whether a view should be rendered or some data should be sent back to the client.

To restructure your express_routes application to adhere to this structure, follow these steps:

1   Create a controllers folder within your project folder.
2   Create a homeController.js file within controllers.
3   Require your home controller file into your application by adding the following to the top of main.js:

```
const homeController = require("./controllers/homeController");
```

4   Move your route callback functions to the home controller, and add them to that module's exports object.

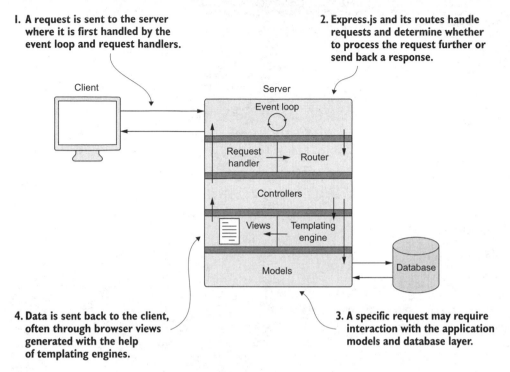

1. A request is sent to the server where it is first handled by the event loop and request handlers.

2. Express.js and its routes handle requests and determine whether to process the request further or send back a response.

4. Data is sent back to the client, often through browser views generated with the help of templating engines.

3. A specific request may require interaction with the application models and database layer.

Figure 9.3 Express.js can follow the MVC structure with routes feeding controllers

Your route to respond with a vegetable parameter, for example, can move to your home controller to look like listing 9.6.

In homeController.js, you assign exports.sendReqParam to the callback function. sendReqParam is a variable name, so you can choose your own name that describes the function.

Listing 9.6 Moving a callback to homeController.js

```
exports.sendReqParam = (req, res) => {
  let veg = req.params.vegetable;
  res.send(`This is the page for ${veg}`);
};
```

Create a function to handle route-specific requests.

5 Back in main.js, change the route to look like the next listing.

When a request is made to this path, the function assigned to sendReqParam in the home controller is run.

Listing 9.7   Replacing a callback with a controller function in main.js

```
app.get("/items/:vegetable", homeController.sendReqParam);
```

Handle GET requests
to "/items/:vegetable".

6 Apply this structure to the rest of your routes, and continue to use the controller
   modules to store the routes' callback function.
   You can move your request-logging middleware to a function in the home controller referenced as logRequestPaths, for example.

7 Restart your Node.js application, and see that the routes still work.
   With this setup, your Express.js application is taking on a new form with MVC in
   mind.

In the next lesson, I discuss how to serve views and assets with Express.js.

Installing and using express-generator

As you continue to evolve your Express.js application, you adhere to a specific file structure. You have many ways to construct your application, though, depending on its
intended use. To jump-start your application in the Express.js framework, you can use a
package called express-generator.

express-generator provides some boilerplate code for an application. This tool offers
scaffolding (prebuilt folders, modules, and configurations) that might have taken you a
few hours to build from scratch. To install this package, use the global flag with the npm
install command. Enter the following command in terminal: npm install express-
generator -g. For UNIX machines, you may need to prepend this command with sudo or
run it as an administrator.

When this package is installed, you can create a new project by entering express and
the project name in a new terminal window. If your project is called Generation Generator, for example, enter express generation_generator in terminal. The express keyword
in this context uses express-generator in terminal to construct the application with
some views and routes.

Although this tool is great for constructing applications quickly, I don't recommend using
it while running the exercises in this book. You should use a slightly different application
structure from the one provided by express-generator. For more information about this
package, visit https://expressjs.com/en/starter/generator.html.

Quick check 9.3 What is the role of controllers in MVC?

 **Summary**

In this lesson, you learned how to build routes and middleware functions with Express.js. Then you used middleware functions to work with Express.js in analyzing request body contents. At the end of the lesson, you learned about MVC and saw how routes can be rewritten to use controllers in your application. In lesson 10, you jump into views and a rich feature known as layouts. With these tools, you can build your views faster.

Try this

You have the directory structure set up for an MVC Express.js application. Try creating a POST route for the /sign_up path, using Express.js methods and controller functions for the route's callback.

The function's name in the controller can read something like userSignUpProcessor.

QC 9.3 answer   Controllers are responsible for processing data by communicating with models, performing code logic, and calling for a view to be rendered in a server's response.

CONNECTING VIEWS WITH TEMPLATES

In lesson 9, you constructed a routing system for your Express.js application. In this lesson, you learn about templating engines and see how to connect your routes to views. You learn how to work with Embedded JavaScript (EJS), a syntax for applying JavaScript functions and variables within your views, as well as how to pass data into those views from your controllers. You start by setting up EJS with your application and seeing how templating engines work. By the end of the lesson, you'll understand the syntax needed to master EJS in your Express.js applications. At the end of the lesson, you install the `express-ejs-layouts` package to use dynamic layouts in your application.

This lesson covers

- Connecting a templating engine to your application
- Passing data from your controllers to your views
- Setting up Express.js layouts

Consider this   You have some wireframes laying out how your application pages will look, and you notice that many of the pages share components. Your home page and contact page both use the same navigation bar. Instead of rewriting the HTML representing the navigation bar for each view, you want to write the code once and reuse it for each view.

With templating in a Node.js application, you can do just that. In fact, you'll be able to render a single layout for all your application pages or share view content in code snippets called *partials*.

10.1 Connecting a templating engine

In lesson 9, you reorganized your routes to serve responses with Express.js routing methods and an MVC application structure. The next step is using your routes to respond with more than single lines of text. As in unit 1, you'll render separate files, but these files aren't purely HTML, and you won't explicitly need the fs module to serve them.

Part of what makes Express.js so popular is its ability to work with other packages and tools. One such tool is the templating engine. *Templating* allows you to code your views with the ability to insert dynamic data. In this book, you'll be writing your views in HTML with EJS—data in the form of JavaScript objects embedded in the page with special syntax. These files have the .ejs extension. There are many templating languages like EJS, but this book assumes that you have moderate experience with HTML, and EJS proves to be the most effective and simplest templating language to learn with that background. If you want to explore other templating engines, consider some of the ones listed in table 10.1.

Table 10.1 Templating engines

Templating engine	Description
Mustache.js	Without the custom helpers offered by Handlebars.js, this templating engine is simple and lightweight, and it compiles for many languages other than JavaScript [https://mustache.github.io/].
Handlebars.js	Functionally similar to EJS, this templating engine focuses on the use of curly brackets, or *handlebars*, for inserting dynamic content into your views [http://handlebarsjs.com/].
Underscore.js	In addition to other JavaScript functions and libraries, this engine offers templating with customizable syntax and symbols [http://underscorejs .org/].
Pug.js	This engine offers syntax similar to Jade in Ruby, abbreviating HTML tag names for simplicity, and is indentation-sensitive [https://pugjs.org].

A *templating engine* is what Express.js uses to process your views and convert them to browser-readable HTML pages. Any non-HTML lines are converted to HTML, with values rendered where embedded variables once were. See figure 10.1 to understand the conversion process.

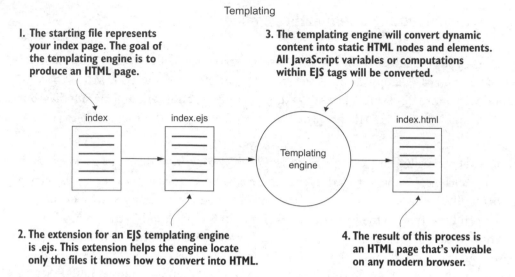

Figure 10.1   Converting EJS to HTML

In a new application project called express_templates, initialize your application, install express as a dependency, and create your controllers folder with a home controller. In your main.js file, require the normal Express.js module and *app* object, homeController.js, and set your server to listen on port 3000. Next, install the ejs package with the following terminal command: npm install ejs --save.

> **NOTE**   You can also install express and ejs in one line by running npm install express ejs --save.

The set method

set is often used to assign values to predefined configuration variables used by your application. Those variables, called *application settings properties*, are listed at https://expressjs.com/en/api.html#app.set. Some variables are used by *app* itself to allow your application to function on your computer. Assigning variables with set is another way to set the application's configurations.

You've been setting the port for your application to 3000. Although 3000 is a conventional port number used in web development, the port number won't stay the same when the application is deployed online.

app.set lets you assign a value to some key that you plan to reuse in your application. The following code will set port to the environment variable PORT value or 3000 if the former value is undefined. You could use app.set("port", process.env.PORT || 3000);, for example.

To use this set value, you need to replace your hardcoded 3000 at the end of the application main.js file with `app.get("port")`. Similarly, you could run `app.get("view engine")`. Now you can even replace your `console.log` with a more dynamic statement, such as `console .log(`Server running at http://localhost:${ app.get("port") }`);`

Restart this application with the added code to make sure that it still runs correctly.

Now that the `ejs` package is installed, you need to let your Express.js application know that you plan to use it for templating. To do so, add `app.set("view engine", "ejs")` below your require lines in main.js. This line tells your Express.js application to set its `view engine` as `ejs`. This line is how your application knows to expect EJS in your views folder in your main project directory.

Now that your application is ready to interpret EJS, create an index.ejs file in your views folder with the code in listing 10.1. In this code, you use the EJS syntax <% %> to define and assign a variable within your view. Everything within these characters runs as valid JavaScript. Each line of HTML contains an embedded variable. By using <%= %>, you're able to print that variable's value within the HTML tags.

Listing 10.1 Sample EJS content in your index.ejs view

```
<% let name = "Jon"; %>          Define and assign
<h1> Hello, <%= name %> </h1>    a variable in EJS.

          Embed a variable
          within HTML.
```

Last, create a route in main.js for the /name path. You can think of a name for the controller function that relates to what the function will do. The following example calls the function respondWithName: `app.get("/name", homeController.respondWithName)`. This route runs when a request is made to the /name path; then it calls the respondWithName function in the home controller.

In homeController.js, add the respondWithName function as shown in the next listing. You use the render method on the response object to respond with a view from your views folder.

Listing 10.2 Rendering a view from a controller action in homeController.js

```
exports.respondWithName = (req, res) => {
  res.render("index");          Respond with a
};                             custom EJS view.
```

> **NOTE**   Notice that you don't need the .ejs extension for the index.ejs view, and you don't need to specify the folder that this view lives in. Express.js takes care of all that for you. As long as you continue to add your views to the views folder and use EJS, your application will know what to do.

Restart your application, and visit http://localhost:3000/name in your browser. If you run into any issues, try reinstalling the ejs and express packages, and make sure that your files are in the correct folders.

In the next section, I talk about passing data from the controller to your EJS views.

Quick check 10.1   What is a templating engine?

 ## 10.2 Passing data from your controllers

Now that your templates are rendering, the best way to use them is to pass data from your controllers to your views instead of defining those variables directly in the view. To do so, remove the line in index.ejs that defines and assigns the name variable, but keep the H1 tag and its EJS contents.

Change your route to take a parameter in its path and then send that parameter to the view. Your route should look like the following code: `app.get("/name/:myName", homeController.respondWithName)`. Now the route takes a parameter at the end of the /name path.

To use this parameter, you need to access it from your request params in the `homeController.respondWithName` function. Then you can pass the name variable to your view in a JavaScript object. Your function should look like the code in the following listing. In this code block, you set the route parameter to a local variable; then you pass the name variable as a value for the `name` key (which should match the variable name in your view).

Listing 10.3 Passing a route parameter to your view in homeController.js

```
exports.respondWithName = (req, res) => {
  let paramsName = req.params.myName;
  res.render("index", { name: paramsName });
};
```

Assign a local variable to a request parameter.

Pass a local variable to a rendered view.

Restart your application, and visit http://localhost:3000/name/jon in your browser.

> **WARNING**   /name/jon is a different path from /name/. If you don't add a name as a route parameter, your application will complain that no route matches your request. You must add some text following the second forward slash in the URL.

In the next section, I talk about layouts and partials, and discuss how they allow you to write less code to get the same results in your views.

> **Quick check 10.2**   What is the format in which you send data from your controller to a view?

10.3 Setting up partials and layouts

In the preceding two sections, you introduced dynamic data to your views. In this section, you set up your views a little differently so that you can share view content across multiple pages.

To start, create an application layout. A *layout* is a shell in which your views are rendered. Think of layouts as being the content that doesn't change from page to page when you browse a website. The bottom (footer) of the page or navigation bar might stay the same, for example. Instead of re-creating the HTML for these components, add them to a layout.ejs file that other views can share.

To do so, install the express-ejs-layouts package, and require it in your main.js file by using const layouts = require("express-ejs-layouts"). Then let Express.js know to use this package as an additional middleware layer by adding app.use(layouts) to your main.js file.

QC 10.2 answer   To send data from your controller, you can pass a variable within a JavaScript object. The variable that's local to your controller's context follows the key, whose name should match the variable name in your view.

Next, create a layout.ejs file in your views folder. You can start with some simple HTML in the layout file, as shown in the next listing. The body keyword is used by Express.js and the layout express-ejs-layouts to fill your other views' contents in its place.

Listing 10.4 EJS layout file contents in layout.ejs

```
<body>
  <div id="nav">NAVIGATION</div>
    <%- body %>
  <div id="footer">FOOTER</div>        ← Wrap body with
</body>                                    boilerplate HTML.
```

When you visit a route that renders a view, you'll notice the navigation and footer text with your rendered view in between. This layout will continue to render along with your view on every page load. To see, restart your application, and visit the /name/:myName path in your browser.

Partials work similarly to layouts. *Partials* are snippets of view content that can be included in other views. In your recipe application, you may want to add a notification box on a few of the pages. To do so, create a partial called notification.ejs, and add it to select EJS views by using the include keyword. To create a partial for the navigation element, move your code for that div to a new file called navigation.ejs. Place that file in a new folder called partials within your views folder. Then include that file within your layout.ejs file by using the following code: <% include partials/navigation %>. With a little styling, your view should resemble figure 10.2.

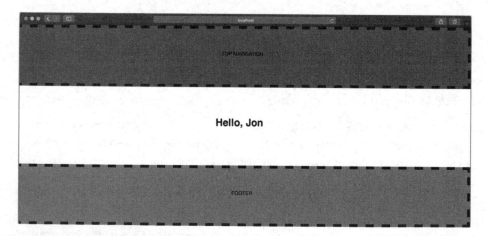

Figure 10.2   Example view of name page

Within the EJS carets, use the `include` keyword followed by a relative path to your partial. Because the layout is already in the views folder, it needs to look in the partials folder on the same directory level to find the navigation partial.

Restart your application, and visit the /name/:myName path again. If everything was set up correctly, nothing in that view should have changed since the addition of a layout file. To prove that the partial is working, try changing the text in the navigation partial or adding new tags to see how content changes in your browser.

NOTE When making changes in your views, you don't need to restart your application.

Now you have an application using an EJS templating engine, a layout, and partials that accept dynamic data. In lesson 11, you learn about handling errors and adding some configurations to your package.json file.

Quick check 10.3 What keyword do you use to share partials across multiple views?

Summary

In this lesson, you learned how to use templates in your application with EJS. You also learned how to pass data from your controllers to application views. At the end of the lesson, you learned how to create a layout with the `express-ejs-layouts` package and partials to share content across your views. In lesson 11, you add a configuration to start your application with a different command and handle errors with new middleware functions.

Try this

Now that you have templates, partials, and a layout in your application, you should use them to create multiple views. Try creating a contact page for your recipe application that uses your application layout and a partial that renders a notification box called `notificationBox.ejs`. Add this partial to your `index.ejs` view as well.

QC 10.3 answer The `include` keyword looks for a partial in the relative path provided and renders it in place.

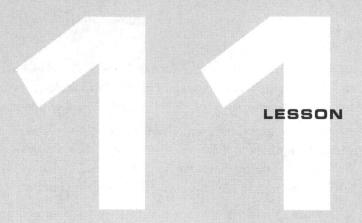

CONFIGURATIONS AND ERROR HANDLING

In lesson 10, you added Embedded JavaScript (EJS) to your application views. In this lesson, you add finishing touches to your application by modifying your package.json file to use a start script. This script changes the way that you start your application from terminal. Then you add error handling middleware functions to log errors and respond with error pages.

This lesson covers

- Changing your application start script
- Serving static pages with Express.js
- Creating middleware functions for error handling

Consider this You're in full swing developing your recipe application. As is common in programming, you run into many errors, but you have no clear indication of those errors in your browser.

In this lesson, you explore ways to serve error pages to your browser window when appropriate.

11.1 Modifying your start script

To start this lesson, you modify a file that you haven't touched in a while. The package
.json file is created every time you initialize a new Node.js application, but you've
changed hardly any of its values manually. In lesson 4, I talked about using the npm
start command to start your application when that script is configured in your project's
package.json.

Make a copy of your express_templates application folder from lesson 10. In your
package.json file, locate the scripts property; you should see a placeholder for a test
script. Add a comma to the end of that test script, and add "start": "node main.js". This
script allows you to run npm start to start your application and abstracts the need to
know the name of your main application file. That part of your package.json file should
look like the next listing. Within the scripts object, you can use the key—start—to start
your application by running npm start, npm run start, or npm run-script start.

> **Listing 11.1 Add the npm start script to your package.json**

```
"scripts": {
  "test": "echo \"Error: no test specified\" && exit 1",
  "start": "node main.js"
},                            Add a start script
                              to package.json.
```

Save your file, and run your application with npm start. Functionally, nothing else
should change in your application, which should start as usual.

> **TIP** If you experience any issues restarting your application, try reverting to node main to
> rule out any accidental changes made in your main.js file.

In the next section, you improve the way that you handle errors in your application.

> **Quick check 11.1** What's the purpose of the scripts object in your package.json file?

QC 11.1 answer   The scripts object allows you to define aliases for commands that you want to
run with npm.

11.2 Handling errors with Express.js

So far, Express.js has been a great improvement on the development process. One perk is that the application doesn't hang forever when a request is made to a path for which no route exists. When you make a request to the home page, however, if there's no route to handle that request, you see an unfriendly Cannot GET / in your browser.

You can take a few approaches to error handling with Express.js. The first approach is logging to your console whenever an error occurs. You can log errors the same way that you logged the requested path in lesson 10. Because I'm dealing with a topic that's separate from serving normal informational pages, I recommend that you create a new controller and install the http-status-codes package by running npm install http-status-codes --save in the project's terminal window.

Create errorController.js in your controllers folder, and add the function shown in listing 11.2. This function contains one more argument than the normal middleware function. If an error occurs in the request-response cycle, it appears as the first argument. As with console.log, you can use console.error to log the error object's stack property, which tells you what went wrong. As in the previous middleware functions, the next argument calls the next function or route in the chain, this time passing the error object in case it needs to be processed further.

> **NOTE** You need to accept four arguments in this error handler, with the first argument always representing the error object. Without all four arguments, the function will not be interpreted as error handling middleware, but instead as a normal middleware function..

Listing 11.2 Adding a function to your error controller, errorController.js

```
exports.logErrors = (error, req, res, next) => {
  console.error(error.stack);
  next(error);
};
```

Add middleware to handle errors.

Pass the error to the next middleware function.

Log the error stack.

> **TIP** Using console.log is great for general debugging, but as your application gets more involved, you'll want to vary your log messages. Tools such as the Chrome browser's console window can color-coordinate these messages for you to distinguish between general log messages and error messages.

Next, you need to tell Express.js to use this middleware function by requiring errorController.js and adding app.use(errorController.logErrors) to your main.js file. You can invoke an error by commenting out the line that defines the paramsName variable in the respondWithName function. Then, when you visit http://localhost:3000/name/jon, your logErrors function will run. Remember to uncomment that line when you're done.

> **WARNING** Make sure to add the middleware line in main.js after the rest of your normal route definitions.

By default, Express.js handles any errors at the end of processing a request. If you want to respond with a custom message, however, you can add a catch-all route at the end of your routes to respond with a 404 status code if the page is not found or a 500 status code if your application got an error in the process. That code should look like listing 11.3 in errorController.js.

In errorController.js, the first function responds with a message to let the user know that the request page wasn't found in your routes. The second function notifies the user of an internal error that prevented the request from being processed. Here, you use the http-status-codes module in place of the code values themselves.

Listing 11.3 Handle missing routes and errors with custom messages in errorController.js

```
const httpStatus = require("http-status-codes");

exports.respondNoResourceFound = (req, res) => {      // Respond with
  let errorCode = httpStatus.NOT_FOUND;               // a 404 status
  res.status(errorCode);                              // code.
  res.send(`${errorCode} | The page does not exist!`);
};
exports.respondInternalError = (error, req, res, next) => {
  let errorCode = httpStatus.INTERNAL_SERVER_ERROR;
  console.log(`ERROR occurred: ${error.stack}`)
  res.status(errorCode);
  res.send(`${errorCode} | Sorry, our application is
experiencing a problem!`);                            // Catch all errors
};                                                    // and respond with a
                                                      // 500 status code.
```

In main.js, order matters. respondNoResourceFound will catch requests made with no matching routes, and respondInternalError will catch any requests where errors occurred. Add these middleware functions to main.js, as shown in the following listing.

Listing 11.4 Handle missing routes and errors with custom messages: main.js

```
app.use(errorController.respondNoResourceFound);
app.use(errorController.respondInternalError);
```

Add error-handling middleware to main.js.

If you want to customize your error pages, you can add a 404.html and a 500.html page in your public folder with basic HTML. Then, instead of responding with a plain-text message, you can respond with this file. This file won't use your templating engine to process the response. Your respondNoResourceFound function in your error controller looks like the next listing. In this code, res.sendFile allows you to specify an absolute path to your error page, which is helpful if your normal templating renderer isn't working.

Listing 11.5 Handle missing routes and errors with custom messages

```
exports.respondNoResourceFound = (req, res) => {
  let errorCode = httpStatus.NOT_FOUND;
  res.status(errorCode);
  res.sendFile(`./public/${errorCode}.html`, {
    root: "./"
  });
};
```

Respond with a custom error page.

Send content in 404.html.

Now that you have error messages being served to your users and logged to your terminal, you should make sure that your application is set up for serving static files like your 404.html page.

> **Quick check 11.2**   Why does your middleware that handles missing routes go after your normal application routes?

QC 11.2 answer   The middleware function that responds with 404 status codes acts like an else in and if-else code block. If no other route paths match the request, this function responds with the message to your user.

11.3 Serving static files

This last section is a short one. In your application from unit 1, serving all different types of static files and assets would require hundreds of lines of code. With Express.js, these file types are accounted for automatically. The only thing you need to do is tell Express.js where to find these static files.

> **NOTE** Static files include your assets and custom error pages, such as 404.html and 500.html. These HTML pages don't go through a templating engine because they don't contain any EJS values.

To set up this task, you need to use the `static` method from the `express` module. This method takes an absolute path to the folder containing your static files. Then, as with any other middleware function, you need to tell the Express.js app instance to use this feature. To enable the serving of static files, add `app.use(express.static("public"))` to main.js. This line of code tells your application to use the corresponding public folder, at the same level in the project directory as main.js, to serve static files.

With this code in place, you can visit http://localhost:3000/404.html directly. You can also place an image or another static asset in your public folder and access it by filename after the main domain in your URL. If you add an image, such as cat.jpg, within another subdirectory called images, you can view that image alone by visiting http://localhost:3000/ images/cat.jpg.

> **Quick check 11.3** What important static files live in your public folder?

 ## Summary

In this lesson, you learned how to change your application's start script. You also learned how to log and manage some of the errors that occur in your Express.js application. At the end of the lesson, you set up Express.js to serve static assets from your public folder. Now you have quite a few tools at your disposal to use in building your recipe

> **QC 11.3 answer** Your public folder contains static HTML files for your error pages. If something goes wrong in your application, these files can be served back to the client.

application. In lesson 12, you put what you've learned to the test by restructuring the Confetti Cuisine application.

....

Try this

Now that you have the ability to serve static files, build a creative HTML page for 404 and 500 errors in your application. These files don't use the normal layout file that you use for templating, so all your styling must live inside the HTML page.

CAPSTONE: ENHANCING THE CONFETTI CUISINE SITE WITH EXPRESS.JS

After some consideration, I decided that it would be easier to rely on a web framework to assist me in building a web application for Confetti Cuisine. Building custom routes and application logic has become a tedious task, so I'm converting my application to use Express.js.

I still want the application to have home, courses, and sign-up pages. I need to convert the routes to use keywords and syntax found in Express.js. I need to make sure that I serve my static assets out of the public directory and have all necessary package.json configurations set up for launching the application locally. When I feel ready to make this transformation, I'll start by initializing the project with `npm init`.

 ## 12.1 Initializing the application

To begin this site redesign, I'm going to create a new project directory called confetti_cuisine and enter that folder. Within the project folder in terminal, I'll initialize the application package.json with `npm init`.

Remembering the configurations that I previously set, I'll keep the default settings for the project name and use entry point main.js.

Now that my package.json is set up, I'm going to add a start script under "scripts", which will allow me to run the application by using `npm start` instead of `node <filename>`. I add "start": "node main.js" to my list of scripts.

TIP   Don't forget to separate multiple script items with a comma.

The last step in the initialization process is adding the main Express.js web framework, EJS templating, a layout, and `http-status-codes` packages to this project. To do so, I run `npm install express ejs express-ejs-layouts http-status-codes --save` in the command line.

NOTE   The `--save` flag saves the `express` package as a dependency in this project's package.json. This way, any future work on this project will ensure that Express.js is installed before anything is able to work.

My resulting package.json file looks like the following listing.

Listing 12.1   Project configurations in package.json

```json
{
  "name": "confetti_cuisine",
  "version": "1.0.0",
  "description": "A site for booking classes for cooking.",
  "main": "main.js",
  "scripts": {
    "test": "echo \"Error: no test specified\" && exit 1",
    "start": "node main.js"
  },
  "author": "Jon Wexler",
  "license": "ISC",
  "dependencies": {
    "ejs": "^2.6.1",
    "express": "^4.16.4",
    "express-ejs-layouts": "^2.5.0",
    "http-status-codes": "^1.3.0"
  }
}
```

List dependencies installed for this project.

Before I add any new files, I'm going to set up my application's directory structure. The final project structure will look like listing 12.2. I'll add the following:

- A views folder to hold my HTML pages
- A controllers folder to hold any routing functions
- A public folder with css, js, and images folders within to hold my client-side assets

Listing 12.2 Confetti Cuisine project file structure

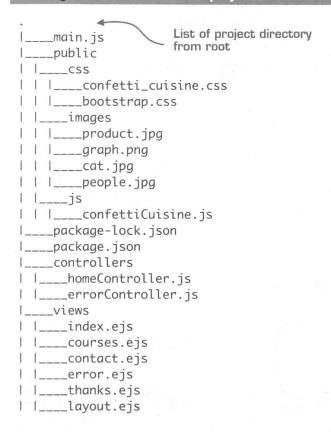

```
.
|____main.js          ← List of project directory
|____public             from root
| |____css
| | |____confetti_cuisine.css
| | |____bootstrap.css
| |____images
| | |____product.jpg
| | |____graph.png
| | |____cat.jpg
| | |____people.jpg
| |____js
| | |____confettiCuisine.js
|____package-lock.json
|____package.json
|____controllers
| |____homeController.js
| |____errorController.js
|____views
| |____index.ejs
| |____courses.ejs
| |____contact.ejs
| |____error.ejs
| |____thanks.ejs
| |____layout.ejs
```

Great. Now I'm ready to add application logic.

 ## 12.2 Building the application

Now that the application is set up with Express.js installed, I'll create my main.js application file. Although this file will resemble my http module version, writing it from scratch will eliminate a ton of headaches in converting line by line. My main.js will look like the code in listing 12.3.

The first line of main.js requires the contents of the Express.js package, assigning them to a constant called express. As with the app constant in the first version of this application, I'll instantiate the express object, representing this project's main application framework as another constant called app. The app constant will have the ability to set up a GET route, listening for requests made to the root URL (/) and responding with the Express.js send function called on the response. I can finally set up the server to listen on port 3000 and log a message to my console when it's up and running.

Listing 12.3 Setting up the main application logic in main.js

```
const express = require("express"),     ◄——— Require express.
  app = express();     ◄———
                                        Instantiate the
app.set("port", process.env.PORT || 3000);     express application.

app.get("/", (req, res) => {     ◄———
  res.send("Welcome to Confetti Cuisine!");     Create a route for
});                                              the home page.

app.listen(app.get("port"), () => {     ◄———
  console.log(                                  Set the
    `Server running at http://localhost:${app.get(     application up
      "port"                                     to listen on
    )}`                                          port 3000.
  );
});
```

With this logic in place, I can start the application by running npm start in my command line.

The json and urlencoded Express.js middleware functions will be used as middleware that interpret incoming request bodies for me. In main.js, I'll add the code in the next listing.

Listing 12.4 Adding body parsing to the top of main.js

```
app.use(
  express.urlencoded({     ◄———
    extended: false                   Tell the Express.js app to use
  })                                  body-parser for processing URL-
);                                    encoded and JSON parameters.
app.use(express.json());
```

Now my application is ready to analyze data within incoming requests. Next, I need to create routes to reach views in my application.

12.3 Adding more routes

Now that my application has a starting point, I'm going to create routes for the courses and sign-up pages. Additionally, I'll add a POST route to handle submissions made from the form on the sign-up page.

First, I create a home controller in my controllers folder, which is where I'll store the functions my routes will use. I need to require this controller by adding const homeController =

`require("./controllers/homeController")` in main.js. I add the code in the next listing to my home controller, below my application's first route. All three of these functions respond with an EJS page reflecting the requested route. I need to create the following views: `courses.ejs`, `contact.ejs`, and `thanks.ejs`.

Listing 12.5 Adding route actions to my home controller in homeController.js

```
exports.showCourses = (req, res) => {
  res.render("courses");
};
exports.showSignUp = (req, res) => {
  res.render("contact");
};
exports.postedSignUpForm = (req, res) => {
  res.render("thanks");
};
```

Add callback functions for specific routes.

In my main.js, I add the following routes and modify my original home-page route to use my home controller too, as shown in listing 12.6. The first route handles GET requests made to view course listings. For the most part, this route behaves similarly to the home page. The route for the contact page also listens for GET requests, as most people will be expecting a sign-up form on this page when the /contact URL is requested. The last route is for POST requests targeting the /contact URL. The GET route is used internally to view who submitted a request to get in contact. The POST route is used by the sign-up form on the contact page.

Listing 12.6 Adding routes for each page and request type in main.js

```
app.get("/courses", homeController.showCourses);
app.get("/contact", homeController.showSignUp);
app.post("/contact", homeController.postedSignUpForm);
```

Add routes for the courses page, contact page, and contact form submission.

Now that all the routes are defined, I'm still missing the bulk of the content. It's time to add and render some views.

12.4 Routing to views

With Express.js, my views are going to be cleaner and easier to render. I need to create the views listed in table 12.1.

Table 12.1   Confetti Cuisine views

Filename	Purpose
layout.ejs	Serves as the application's main styling and navigation foundation
index.ejs	Produces the home page's content
courses.ejs	Displays course content
contact.ejs	Displays the contact form
thanks.ejs	Displays a thank-you message upon form submission
error.ejs	Displays an error message when a page isn't found

I'll start by generating my application's layout view, which will handle what the navigation and general site structure looks like from page to page.

For the layout to work, I need to include it in my main application file, right below my initialization of the Express.js module, as shown in listing 12.7. First, I require the express-ejs-layouts module to allow me to use the layout.ejs file. Then, I set the application server to use the ejs rendering template. Last, I set the application server to use the recently required layouts module. This way, when a new view is rendered, it goes through the layout.ejs file.

Listing 12.7   Enable EJS layout rendering in main.js

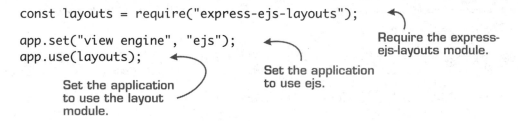

```
const layouts = require("express-ejs-layouts");

app.set("view engine", "ejs");
app.use(layouts);
```

Require the express-ejs-layouts module.

Set the application to use ejs.

Set the application to use the layout module.

I'll add this file, called layout.ejs, to my views folder. The key component of this file includes <%- body %>, which will be replaced by my target route's rendered content.

Each of the following views will use this layout to provide visual consistency (and to avoid repetition of code between files). Within the views folder, I'm going to create index.ejs, courses.ejs, contact.ejs, thanks.ejs, and error.ejs files. Like the layout file, these views render as Embedded JavaScript, allowing me to dynamically feed content to the pages from the server file. After creating index.ejs, I change my home-page route (/) to render the index page in place of sending plain text.

The one view I need to focus on is contact.ejs, where I'll have prospective students fill out a form, submitting a POST request to my application's /sign-up route. That form will look like the HTML in the next listing. Notice that the form action is /contact and the form method is POST. When the form is submitted, it will make a POST request to the /contact route.

Listing 12.8 Contact form in contact.ejs

```
<form action="/contact" method="post">
  <label for="name">Name</label>
  <input type="text" name="name">
  <label for="email">Email</label>
  <input type="email" name="email">
  <input type="submit" value="Submit">
</form>
```

Display example contact form.

I should be all set. If I named my routes to match and render their corresponding views, I should be able to launch my app and see those views rendered within the layout I built. The only thing missing is my app's ability to serve images and other static files, which I cover next.

> **NOTE** The layout file is rendered on every page I visit. Try adding new HTML content above and below the <%- body %> marker. Notice that these elements are applied to every page.

 ## 12.5 Serving static views

In my first take of this application using http, serving static assets became a big mess. With every new asset I added to my project directory, I needed to create a new route and handle it appropriately. Luckily, Express.js handles this task nicely, requiring virtually no effort on my part to handle any and all static files I want my application to serve. To enable static assets, I'll use Express.js' static function by adding app.use(express.static ("public")) below the initialization of Express.js in my application file. This addition allows individual assets in the application to be served directly.

The last major step in converting the app to an Express.js app is using dynamic content in the views.

12.6 Passing content to the views

Confetti Cuisine often modifies its course listings, so the application is better off not showing those courses on a static web page. With Express.js, passing content from the server logic to the view is a piece of cake.

For this app, I need to display an array of course offerings as a JavaScript object. Then I can send the object to my rendered view. I add the code in listing 12.9 to homeController.js. By assigning the courses variable to an array of JavaScript objects, I can use this list and target specific keys in my view. The res.render method allows me to pass the courses object to the view and refer to it as offeredCourses on that page.

> **NOTE** Within the view, I can access this array by using the variable name offered-Courses. Within the home controller, that array goes by the name courses.

Listing 12.9 Set up content on server and pass into rendered view in homeController.js

```
var courses = [
  {
    title: "Event Driven Cakes",
    cost: 50
  },
  {
    title: "Asynchronous Artichoke",
    cost: 25
  },
  {
    title: "Object Oriented Orange Juice",
    cost: 10
  }
];              ◄────── Define an array of courses.

exports.showCourses = (req, res) => {
  res.render("courses", {
    offeredCourses: courses
  });                         ◄── Pass the courses
};                              array to the view.
```

To benefit from this feature, I need to add some EJS and HTML to loop through the offeredCourses list in courses.ejs and print the relevant content, as shown in listing 12.10.

> **Listing 12.10 Loop through and display dynamic content in view in courses.ejs**

```
<h1>Our Courses</h1>
<% offeredCourses.forEach(course => { %>
  <h5> <%= course.title %> </h5>
  <span>$ <%= course.cost %> </span>
<% }); %>
```

Loop through the array of courses in the view.

Now the application is complete. My courses page looks like figure 12.1. Instead of modifying my courses.ejs view every time a modification is made to the course offerings, I can change the array in my main application file. Running the application is the easy part now.

Figure 12.1 View of courses page

I should anticipate that things won't go exactly as planned, so it's always smart to prepare for certain errors and handle them accordingly. Soon, when this array of courses is replaced by contents from a persistent database, I won't need to make any code changes to update the course listing.

12.7 Handling the errors

An application handling most expected outcomes ensures a fairly consistent and good experience for its users. I know that my application may be missing some foolproof logic, though, and I prefer to send my own custom error messages to my client's audience when those errors occur.

For error handling, I'll create an error controller, errorController.js, to store my functions, as shown in listing 12.11. The first function handles all requests not previously handled, which fits the category of URLs visited without an active route and results in a 404 error, serving error.ejs. The last function handles any internal server errors that occur. Instead of necessarily crashing and scaring the audience away, I prefer a friendlier message.

Listing 12.11 Adding error handling routes in errorController.ejs

```
const httpStatus = require("http-status-codes");

exports.pageNotFoundError = (req, res) => {        // Handle all requests not previously handled.
  let errorCode = httpStatus.NOT_FOUND;
  res.status(errorCode);
  res.render("error");
};

exports.internalServerError = (error, req, res, next) => {   // Handle any internal server errors.
  let errorCode = httpStatus.INTERNAL_SERVER_ERROR;
  console.log(`ERROR occurred: ${error.stack}`)
  res.status(errorCode);
  res.send(`${errorCode} | Sorry, our application is taking a nap!`);
};
```

Then I add routes to correspond to these functions. I'll add the routes in listing 12.12 to trigger the functions in my error controller if no proceeding routes respond to a request.

NOTE The order of routes matters. These routes must go below any preexisting routes, as they act as a catch-all and override any routes below them.

Listing 12.12 Adding error handling routes in main.js

```
app.use(errorController.pageNotFoundError);
app.use(errorController.internalServerError);    // Add error handlers as middleware functions.
```

I need to require this controller by adding const errorController = require("./controllers/errorController") to the top of my main.js file. Now my application is ready to handle errors and launch. When a URL is visited without a corresponding route, users see my cat, Hendrix, relaxing on the error page (figure 12.2).

Figure 12.2   View of error page

 Summary

Through this project, I redefined the Node.js project file structure to fit a web frame-work. I used npm to install three external packages. Then I rebuilt the main application file, using Express.js syntax. To create a path for specific URLs, I set up new routes, using Express.js keywords. For a consistent user interface, I used layouts with EJS. Using Express.js' static library, I set up static assets to be served to the client through my public folder. Last, I added content to the main project application file and set up that content to be served dynamically to one of my views.

With consistent practice of these techniques and proper error handling, I can use Express.js to build future applications in a few steps. With new features such as layouts and dynamic content, I can try to send content to other views in my application or try modifying the layout as it's used throughout the app.

In unit 3, I discuss how to organize application code around persistent data with Express.js.

Connecting to a database

Unit 2 taught you how to set up a Node.js application with Express.js. By this point, you should feel comfortable building a basic web application with Express.js routing and templating. This unit is about taking the application you built in unit 2 and connecting it to a database. A *database* is where values can be stored permanently, as opposed to the data in earlier lessons, which was reset every time your application restarted.

In this book, you learn to use MongoDB, a popular database for Node.js. First, you download and install Mongo on your computer. Then you explore the MongoDB shell, a database environment similar to the Node.js REPL shell. Next, you learn some database theory behind structuring your database and the data within it. You see how models fit into the model-view-controller (MVC) architecture and how they interact with your application's database via a package called Mongoose. Last, you explore how a database schema—an outline of your structured data—helps you relate data objects to one another.

With the goal of building a Node.js application that can store user information and display that information back on your screen, this unit covers the following topics:

- Lesson 13 introduces MongoDB, a NoSQL database that stores data in a JSON structure. In this lesson, you learn how MongoDB works with Express.js and install the database program on your computer. You also create a database and insert some data by using the MongoDB shell.

- Lesson 14 shows how to connect your MongoDB database to an Express.js application. After initial setup, you learn how object-oriented programming (OOP) can help you build reliable models for an MVC-structured Node.js application. For your models, you install and use the Mongoose package, an object-document mapper (ODM).

- Lesson 15 discusses the types of query commands you can use with your MongoDB database from within the Node.js application. You also implement JavaScript promises to work with Mongoose to build a more streamlined, ES6-friendly application.

- Finally, lesson 16 shows how to put your skills to the test by implementing a MongoDB database for the Confetti Cuisine cooking-school application. In this capstone exercise, you save user data and newsletter emails.

Get ready to collect and store data in lesson 13.

SETTING UP A MONGODB DATABASE

In unit 2, you built web applications with Express.js. Structuring your applications to use the model-view-controller (MVC) architecture, you can now handle requests through your controllers and serve views. The third essential piece is models, with which you'll organize data that you plan to store permanently. In this lesson, you install MongoDB, the database system that you'll use to store persistent data. You also explore what makes document database structure in MongoDB particularly convenient for Node.js applications. By the end of the lesson, you'll have a database set up and connected to your application.

This lesson covers

- Installing MongoDB
- Reading and entering data within the MongoDB shell
- Connecting MongoDB to a Node.js application

> **Consider this**   You want to start saving data from your application into a database, but you're unsure which database to use. With Node.js, you can work with practically any common database, such as MySQL, PostgreSQL, Cassandra, Redis, and Neo4j. You can get a sense of the most supported and popular database management systems by exploring their associated packages on npm.   ▐▶

> MongoDB, however, offers a unique style of data storage that resembles JSON—a JavaScript-friendly format that may make working with databases easier for you as you delve into saving data with Node.js for the first time.

13.1 Setting up MongoDB

Storing data is arguably the most important part of application development. Without long-term storage, you're limited in the way you can interact with your users. The data in every application you've built to this point disappeared each time you restarted the application. If data from a social network were to disappear every time a user closed his browser or every time you restarted that application, users would have to create new accounts and start from scratch.

A *database* is an organization of your data designed for easy access and efficient changes made by your application. A database is like a warehouse: the more items you need to store, the happier you'll be with an organized system that helps you find those items. Like a web server, your application connects to a MongoDB database and requests data.

Throughout this unit, I discuss how to save information to a database for long-term storage. Your data will persist, even if the application is shut down.

MongoDB is an open-source database program that organizes data by using documents. MongoDB *documents* store data in a JSON-like structure, allowing you to use key-value pairing to associate data objects with properties.

This system of storage follows a familiar JavaScript syntax. Notice in figure 13.1 that a document's contents resemble JSON. In fact, MongoDB stores documents as BSON (a

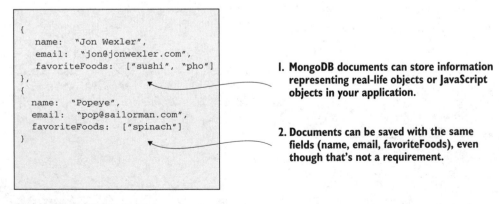

Figure 13.1 Example document

binary form of JSON). Unlike relational databases used by the majority of applications, MongoDB's nonrelational database system leads the Node.js application community.

A look at relational databases

This book focuses on MongoDB and on how its documents complement a JavaScript-based application platform like Node.js. It's worth noting what MongoDB is not, however, as well as how the rest of the programming world is working with databases.

Most databases used by software and web applications use a different model of data storage from the document structure used in MongoDB. Most databases are *relational*, meaning that they associate data via tables, like a standard spreadsheet. Within these tables, columns define the type of data that should be stored, and rows store the values that correspond to the columns. In the following figure, data representing people, courses, and which people are enrolled in certain courses is displayed in separate tables.

People table

id	first	last	enroll
1	Jon	Wexler	true
2	William	Wonka	true
3	Cookie	Monster	true
4	Alfredo	Linguini	true

Courses table

id	title	topic	max
1	Wheaties	Bread	3
2	Sweeties	Chocolate	15
3	Tortellinies	Pasta	10
4	Meaties	Steak	7

People-courses association table

id	personId	courseId
1	4	3
2	2	2
3	1	1
4	3	1

In this example, the table in the middle represents the IDs of associated people and courses. Each association has its own unique ID.

Example relational database structure

> **(continued)**
>
> In this example, two tables are associated by their ID values. To connect a person with their desired cooking course, the IDs of the items from the `people` and `courses` tables are added to new rows in a join table. The *join table* generally holds only IDs of associated items to define a relationship among those items. This relationship designed through reference IDs is where the database system gets its name. Databases that use this structure are often SQL-based, making MongoDB a NoSQL database system.
>
> You could set up a relational database with Node.js—in fact, many applications do—but to best make use of a SQL database, it helps to know how to write in the SQL language. The MongoDB query language is simpler to understand for people who have a JavaScript background.
>
> For more information on relational databases, I recommend reading the overview by Oracle at https://docs.oracle.com/javase/tutorial/jdbc/overview/database.html.

In this section, you install MongoDB and look at some data. The installation process is a bit different for Windows and Macintosh. For the Mac, the recommended approach is a terminal command-line tool called Homebrew. You can install Homebrew by entering the command shown in the next listing.

Listing 13.1 Command to install Homebrew on a Mac in terminal

```
mkdir homebrew && curl -L
  https://github.com/Homebrew/brew/tarball/master |
  tar xz --strip 1 -C homebrew
```

Run the command in terminal to install Homebrew on MacOS machines.

> **NOTE** Homebrew is a tool that helps you install software and other low-level tools such as database management systems. For more information, visit https://brew.sh.

When Homebrew is installed, you should be able to enter `brew` in any new terminal window and see a list of available Homebrew commands, one of which is `brew install`. Install MongoDB by running `brew install mongodb`.

> **TIP** If your computer throws an error or complains about permissions issues at any point in the installation, you may need to run the command as a superuser by appending `sudo` to the command. Then you'll be prompted to enter your computer's login password.

Next, create a folder called db within another folder called data at your computer's root level (as far back as you can cd .. in a terminal window). You can create this folder by entering `mkdir -p /data/db` in a terminal window.

You may need to give permissions to your user account to use this folder. To do so, run `sudo chown <your_username> /data/db`, and enter your computer's password. For Windows, the steps are as follows:

- Go to https://www.mongodb.com/download-center#community in your browser.
- Download MongoDB for Windows (.msi).
- When the download is complete, open the file, and click through the default installation steps.
- When the installer completes, go to your C:\ drive, and create a new folder called data and a folder within it called db.

> **NOTE** In Windows, you may need to add the MongoDB folder path to your environment's PATH variable. To add it, right-click Computer, choose Properties⏎Advanced system settings⏎Environment variables⏎Edit environment variables⏎PATH, and add your MongoDB executable path to this string. Your MongoDB path might look something like `C:\Program Files\MongoDB\Server\3.6.2\bin\mongod.exe`.

For more installation instructions, including those for Ubuntu Linux machines, go to https://docs.mongodb.com/v3.0/tutorial/install-mongodb-on-ubuntu.

So far, you've gotten MongoDB installed on your computer. Like a web server, MongoDB needs to be started to create new databases for your applications. You can start MongoDB by running `mongod` in a terminal window. This command assigns MongoDB a port and establishes the location of its databases at `data/db`.

> **NOTE** To start and stop MongoDB with Homebrew on a Mac, run `brew services start mongodb` or `brew services stop mongodb`. Homebrew runs the database server in the background, so if `mongod` doesn't work, you may have started MongoDB with Homebrew elsewhere.

You can test whether Mongo was installed successfully by typing `mongo` in a new terminal window. This command brings up the MongoDB shell, an environment within which you can run MongoDB commands and view data. This shell environment is similar to REPL because it isolates your terminal window to allow you to interact purely with MongoDB syntax. When you have some data to work with, you can further explore this environment.

Quick check 13.1   What data structure does MongoDB use to store data?

 ## 13.2 Running commands in the MongoDB shell

Now that MongoDB is running, it's ready to receive commands to add, view, delete, or otherwise change data. Before you connect MongoDB to your application, you can test some commands in the MongoDB shell.

> **WARNING**   Commands that you run in the MongoDB shell are permanent. If you delete data (or an entire database), there's no going back.

Run mongo in a new terminal window. This command should prompt the shell to start. You'll be greeted by your MongoDB version number, potentially a few warnings (which you can ignore for now), and the familiar > to indicate that the shell is active and ready for commands.

MongoDB can store multiple databases; it's a management system for all your applications' databases. To start, the MongoDB shell places you in the test database. You can see this test database by entering db, to list your current database, after the prompt (figure 13.2).

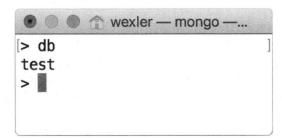

Figure 13.2   MongoDB shell viewing current test database

To view all available databases, run show dbs. With a clean install of MongoDB, your shell's response should look like the next listing. Your test database is one of three that comes prepackaged with MongoDB. To the right of the database name is the size of the database. Because you haven't stored any data yet, the databases are understandably empty.

QC 13.1 answer   MongoDB uses documents to store data.

Listing 13.2 Show all databases in terminal

```
admin          0.000GB
local          0.000GB
test           0.000GB   ◄──────  View local databases.
```

You can create a new database and simultaneously switch into it by entering use `<new_database_name>`. Try switching to a new database for the recipe application by entering use `recipe_db`. Then run `db` again to see that you're within the `recipe_db` database.

> **NOTE** You won't see your new database in the list of databases until data is added.

To add data to your database, you need to specify a collection name with which that data is associated. A MongoDB *collection* is representative of your data model, storing all documents related to that model within the same grouping. If you want to create a contact list for the recipe application, for example, create a new collection and add a data item with the command shown in the following listing. The `insert` method runs on a MongoDB collection to add elements of a JavaScript object to a new document.

Listing 13.3 Add data to a new collection in terminal

```
db.contacts.insert({
  name: "Jon Wexler",
  email: "jon@jonwexler.com",       Insert new data into the
  note: "Decent guy."               database.
})
```

At this point, there's no strict collection structure; you can add any values to new documents without needing to follow previous data patterns. Insert another item into the contacts collection with these properties: {first_name: "Jon", favoriteSeason: "spring", countries_visited: 42}. MongoDB lets you add these seemingly conflicting data elements.

> **NOTE** Just because MongoDB lets you store inconsistent data doesn't mean that you should. In lesson 14, I discuss ways of organizing data around your application's models.

To list the collection's contents, you can enter `db.conntacts.find()`. You should see a response that looks like the next listing. Both inserted items are present, with an extra property added by MongoDB. The `id` property stores a unique value that you can use to differentiate and locate specific items in your database.

Listing 13.4 Find all data response in terminal

```
{"_id": ObjectId("5941fce5cda203f026856a5d"), "name": "Jon
➥Wexler", "email": "jon@jonwexler.com", "note":
```

```
⇒"Nice guy." }
{"_id": ObjectId("5941fe7acda203f026856a5e"), "first_name":
⇒"Jon", "favoriteSeason": "spring", "countries_visited": 42}
```

Display results of
database documents.

ObjectId

To keep your data organized and unique, MongoDB uses an ObjectId class to record some meaningful information about its database documents. ObjectId("5941fe7ac-da203f026856a5e"), for example, constructs a new ObjectId representing a document in your database. The hexadecimal value passed into the ObjectId constructor references the document, a timestamp of the record's creation, and some information about your database system.

The resulting ObjectId instance provides many useful methods that you can use to sort and organize data in your database. As a result, the _id property becomes a more useful feature in MongoDB than a string representation of the document ID.

Try searching for a specific item in the contacts collection by entering db.contacts .find({_id: ObjectId("5941fce5cda203f026856a5d")}).

> **NOTE**   Replace the ObjectId in this example with one from your own database results.

MongoDB Compass

As you become familiar with MongoDB, you may want a more user-friendly window into your MongoDB databases than the MongoDB shell in terminal. The people at MongoDB agreed and have produced a MongoDB graphical user interface called MongoDB Compass for all major operating systems.

MongoDB Compass is straightforward to use. To view the database that you set up for your recipe application, follow these steps:

1 Download the software from https://www.mongodb.com/download-center# compass.
2 Follow the installation steps to add MongoDB Compass to your applications folder.
3 Run MongoDB Compass and accept the default connection settings to your existing MongoDB setup.
4 See your databases (including recipe_db) listed with options to view the collections and documents within them, as in figure 13.3.

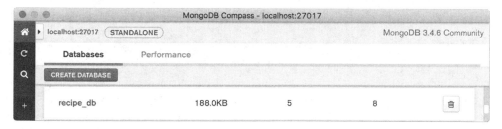

Figure 13.3   Database view in MongoDB Compass

> **Database view in MongoDB Compass**
> I recommend using MongoDB Compass as a supplemental tool while you work with MongoDB in your application.

You can use many MongoDB commands. Table 13.1 lists a few that you should know about.

Table 13.1   MongoDB Shell Commands

Command	Description
`show collections`	Displays all the collections in your database. Later, these collections should match your models.
`db.contacts.findOne`	Returns a single item from your database at random or a single item matching the criteria passed in as a parameter, which could look like findOne({name: 'Jon'}).
`db.contacts.update({name: "Jon"}, {name: "Jon Wexler"})`	Updates any matching documents with the second parameter's property values.
`db.contacts.delete({name: "Jon Wexler"})`	Removes any matching documents in the collection.
`db.contacts.deleteMany({})`	Removes all the documents in that collection. These commands can't be undone.

For more practice, view the command cheat sheet at https://docs.mongodb.com/manual/reference/mongo-shell/.

In the next section, you see how to add MongoDB to your Node.js application.

Quick check 13.2   What MongoDB command can you use to view existing collections within a database?

13.3   Connecting MongoDB to your application

To add MongoDB to your Node.js recipe application, enter your project folder (or create a newly initialized project) in terminal, and install the mongodb package by running npm i mongodb -S. This command saves the mongodb package to your project's package.json dependencies.

> **NOTE**   In the corresponding code repository for this lesson, some views and styling rules have been added from the last capstone project.

At the top of your main.js file, add the code shown in listing 13.5. Require the MongoDB module to use the MongoClient class. MongoClient sets up a connection to your local database at its default port. The callback function returns your connection to the MongoDB server. Then get the database called recipe_db from your connection to the server. If there's no database by the name provided, MongoDB creates one for use in the app.

> **NOTE**   Remember to run mongod to ensure that your MongoDB server is running before you try to connect to it.

Next, ask the database to find all records in the contacts collection and return them in an array. The resulting data is returned in the callback function. Then you can log the results to the console.

Listing 13.5   Add MongoDB connection to Express.js in main.js

Require the
MongoDB module.

```
const MongoDB = require("mongodb").MongoClient,
  dbURL = "mongodb://localhost:27017",
  dbName = "recipe_db";

MongoDB.connect(dbURL, (error, client) => {
  if (error) throw error;
```

Set up a connection
to your local
database server.

QC 13.2 answer   show collections lists the collections within the active database in your MongoDB shell.

```
let db = client.db(dbName);
db.collection("contacts")
  .find()
  .toArray((error, data) => {
    if (error) throw error;
    console.log(data);
  });
});
```

Get the recipe_db database from your connection to the MongoDB server.

Find all records in the contacts collection.

Print the results to the console.

NOTE The find query method here works differently from a find query in a traditional functional programming language. If you get no match when you use find in MongoDB, you get an empty array.

You can use the same commands within your Node.js application that you did in the MongoDB shell. To add a new item to the database, for example, you can add the code in listing 13.6 within your MongoDB connection callback function.

As when you query all the items in the database, you connect to the contacts collection and insert an item. If the new data was inserted successfully, you log that database message to the console.

Listing 13.6 Insert data from your Node.js application into terminal

```
db.collection("contacts")
  .insert({
    name: "Freddie Mercury",
    email: "fred@queen.com"
  }, (error, db) => {
    if (error) throw error;
    console.log(db);
  });
```

Insert a new contact into the database.

Log the resulting errors or saved item.

In lesson 14, you explore a package called Mongoose, which works with MongoDB to provide a bit more organization to your application's storage.

> **Quick check 13.3**   True or false: If you try to connect to a database that doesn't exist, MongoDB throws an error.

 **Summary**

In this lesson, you learned how to set up MongoDB and how to use certain commands to manage databases on your computer. At the end of the lesson, you inserted collections and documents into your own database and connected that database to your Node.js application. In lesson 14, you build models to represent the types of data that you want to store in your application.

Try this

Imagine that you're creating an application to track ice-cream-truck statistics. Create an appropriately named database with a collection called ice_cream_flavors. Try inserting some flavors and include fields that would help with your statistics analysis.

BUILDING MODELS WITH MONGOOSE

In lesson 13, you got up and running with MongoDB. With a database connected to your Node.js application, you're ready to save and load data. In this lesson, you apply a more object-oriented approach to your data. First, you install the Mongoose package, a tool that provides a syntactic layer between your application logic and your database. Mongoose allows you to convert your application data to fit a model structure. Later in the lesson, you build your first model and schema to represent newsletter subscribers to your recipe application.

This lesson covers

- Installing and connecting Mongoose to your Node.js application
- Creating a schema
- Building and instantiating Mongoose data models
- Loading and saving data with custom methods

Consider this   You finally have a database connected to your application, but data can change over time. One day, you may want to require all recipes to follow the same format. How can you determine such a structure and make sure that all saved data follows that structure's rules?

In this lesson, you explore Mongoose, a library used to create model schema. When you use these schemas, your data begins to follow strict rules that only you can customize.

14.1 Setting up Mongoose with your Node.js application

You've already experienced Express.js and seen how it helps you handle HTTP requests and responses. Similarly, other packages are available to assist with the communication between your Node.js application and its database. The tool you're going to use is called Mongoose. *Mongoose* is an object-document mapper (ODM) that allows you to run MongoDB commands in a way that preserves the object-oriented structure of your application. With MongoDB alone, for example, it's difficult to keep one saved document consistent with the next. Mongoose changes that situation by offering tools to build models with schemas defining what type of data can be saved.

I discussed model-view-controller (MVC) architecture in unit 2 and described how controllers communicate with both views and models to ensure that the correct data flows through the application. A *model* is like a class for a JavaScript object that Mongoose uses to organize your database queries. In this section, you install Mongoose and see what a model looks like in your application (figure 14.1).

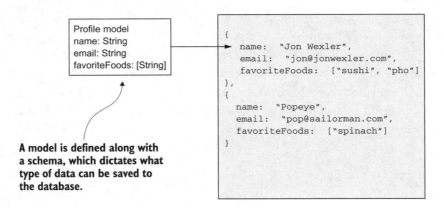

Figure 14.1 Models created with Mongoose map to documents in MongoDB.

To install Mongoose, run `npm i mongoose -S` within your project folder in terminal. With Mongoose, you no longer need to require `mongodb` at the top of main.js or use any of the MongoDB code from lesson 13. Add the code in listing 14.1 to main.js. Require `mongoose` into the application file. Set up the application's connection to your MongoDB database. (The same rules apply here as in a normal MongoDB connection.) Then assign the database connection to the `db` variable, which you can use later in the file for data changes or database state changes.

Listing 14.1 Configuring Mongoose with your Node.js application in main.js

```
const mongoose = require("mongoose");        ◄────── Require mongoose.
mongoose.connect(
  "mongodb://localhost:27017/recipe_db", ◄┐  Set up the connection
  {useNewUrlParser: true}                  └─ to your database.
);
const db = mongoose.connection; ◄┐ Assign the database
                                 └─ to the db variable.
```

> **NOTE** Remember to have the MongoDB server running in the background. To run MongoDB, enter mongod in a terminal window.

That's all you need to do to set up Mongoose. You can log a message as soon as the database is connected by adding the code in the next listing to main.js. The database connection runs the code in the callback function (the log message) only once upon receiving an "open" event from the database.

Listing 14.2 Log a message when the database is connected in main.js

```
                              Log a message when the
                              application connects to
                              the database.
db.once("open", () => {  ◄────
  console.log("Successfully connected to MongoDB using Mongoose!");
});
```

In the next section, you explore how to model your data to make best use of Mongoose.

Quick check 14.1   What is an ODM?

14.2 Creating a schema

A schema is like a class definition in some languages or, more broadly, a blueprint for how you want data to be organized for specific objects in your application. To avoid

QC 14.1 answer   ODM is an object-document mapper, which is the role of Mongoose in your application development. ODM (like an object-relational mapper) makes it easier to think purely in terms of objects in your application and not worry about how your data is structured in the database.

inconsistent data, where some documents have an email field and others don't, for example, you can create a schema stating that all contact objects need to have an email field to get saved to the database.

Because you want to add a newsletter subscription form to the recipe application, create a schema for the subscriber. Add the code from listing 14.3 to main.js. mongoose.Schema offers a constructor that allows you to build a schema object with the given parameters. Then add object properties to state the name of the object's field and its data type. Someone's name can't be a number, for example.

Listing 14.3 Subscriber schema in main.js

```
const subscriberSchema = mongoose.Schema({
  name: String,
  email: String,
  zipCode: Number
});
```

Create a new schema with mongoose.Schema.

Add schema properties.

> **NOTE** MongoDB isn't enforcing your schema; Mongoose is. For more information about Mongoose schema data types, visit http://mongoosejs.com/docs/schematypes.html.

Now that the schema is defined, you need to apply it to a model by using const Subscriber = mongoose.model("Subscriber", subscriberSchema). The model is what you'll use to instantiate new Subscriber objects, and the schema you created can be used for that model. The model method takes a model name of your choosing and a previously defined schema (in this case, the subscriberSchema).

You can instantiate new objects from this model by referring to Subscriber. You have two ways to generate new objects, as shown in listing 14.4. You can construct a new instance of the Subscriber model by using the new keyword and by passing properties that abide by the subscriberSchema earlier in the section. To get this newly created Subscriber object into the database, you can call save on it and handle any errors or returned data through a callback function.

An error may have to do with data that doesn't match the schema types you defined earlier. The saved item returns data that you can use elsewhere in the application. You may want to thank the subscriber by name for signing up, for example. create does what new and save do in one step. If you know that you want to create and save the object right away, use this Mongoose method.

> **NOTE** Instantiating objects from your Mongoose models is similar to instantiating JavaScript objects. The new keyword can be used with JavaScript Array and other data types.

Listing 14.4 Statements to create and save models in main.js

```
var subscriber1 = new Subscriber({
  name: "Jon Wexler",
  email: "jon@jonwexler.com"
});
```
Instantiate a new subscriber.

Save a subscriber to the database.

```
subscriber1.save((error, savedDocument) => {
  if (error) console.log(error);
  console.log(savedDocument);
});
```
Log saved data document.

Pass potential errors to the next middleware function.

```
Subscriber.create(
  {
    name: "Jon Wexler",
    email: "jon@jonwexler.com"
  },
  function (error, savedDocument) {
    if (error) console.log(error);
    console.log(savedDocument);
  }
);
```
Create and save a subscriber in a single step.

Add the code from the listings in this section to your main.js file. As soon as you start the application with node main.js, you should see your MongoDB recipe_db database populate with a new subscriber.

> **Quick check 14.2** True or false: Using new Subscriber({ name: "Jon", email: "jon@jonwexler.com" }) saves a new record to your database.

 ## 14.3 Organizing your models

Now that you have a way of saving data in the form of Mongoose models, you'll want to organize your models so that they don't clutter your main.js file. As you do for your views and controllers, create a models folder at the root level of your application. Within that folder, create a new file called subscriber.js.

QC 14.2 answer False. This code only creates a new virtual object. If you store the value of this line to a variable and call save on that variable, the new subscriber is stored in the database.

This file is where you'll move your model's code. Move all the schema and model definition code to this file and the model to the file's exports object. (See the following listing.) Any module that requires subscriber.js will have access to the Subscriber model. The schema doesn't need to be made accessible outside the file.

Listing 14.5 Moving the schema and model to a separate module

```
const mongoose = require("mongoose"),
  subscriberSchema = mongoose.Schema({
    name: String,                          Export the
    email: String,                         Subscriber model
    zipCode: Number                        as the only module
  });                                      export.

module.exports = mongoose.model("Subscriber", subscriberSchema);
```

NOTE   You need to require mongoose in this module because both the schema and model use Mongoose methods to work. Node.js loads a module into the project only once, so requiring it here shouldn't slow your application; you're telling Node.js that you want to use an already-loaded module.

Next, require this model in your main.js by adding const Subscriber = require("./models/subscriber") below your other required modules. Now you should be able to use the model the same way as before.

In main.js, find documents in your database by using Mongoose's findOne and where query methods. As an example, you can use Subscriber.findOne({ name: "Jon Wexler" }) .where("email", /wexler/) to find and return one document that matches the criteria name where the email contains the string "wexler".

This example custom query shows how flexible your queries can be to get the data you need. Mongoose lets you chain parts of a query and even store queries in a variable. You could create a variable var findWexlers and assign it to the code querying for emails with the word wexler. Then you could run the query later by using findWexlers.exec(). (For more on exec, see lesson 15.)

If you plan to run a query immediately without the exec method, you need a callback function with two arguments. The first argument represents any errors that occur, and the second argument represents any data returned by the database, as shown in the following listing. Try creating your own queries by following some of the example queries at http://mongoosejs.com/docs/queries.html.

Listing 14.6 Example query to run in main.js

```
var myQuery = Subscriber.findOne({
    name: "Jon Wexler"
  })
  .where("email", /wexler/);
myQuery.exec((error, data) => {
  if (data) console.log(data.name);
});
```

Run a query with a callback function to handle errors and data.

NOTE For queries indicating that multiple items will be returned from the database, you should expect an array. If no documents are found, you get an empty array.

Now you have the freedom to create more modules and save them by using their names instead of the MongoDB collection names.

In unit 4, you learn how to make a more-robust model whose values can be created, read, updated, and deleted—the four core model functions in a CRUD application. I discuss this approach in detail in that unit.

Quick check 14.3 What two components are required for each field specified in a Mongoose schema?

 Summary

In this lesson, you learned how to set up Mongoose and use your MongoDB connection to map data to your database. You also learned about some Mongoose syntax and methods. Through the steps in this lesson, you learned how to create a schema and model for storing persistent data. Last, you organized your models, clearing your main.js for new tools to come. In lesson 15, you clean up some of the functionality that you built in this lesson by implementing JavaScript promises in your database queries.

QC 14.3 answer The schema requires a property name and data type.

Try this

Eventually, you'll create more models for your recipe application. Start to think about what those models will look like. You may need a model to represent the different types of courses offered through the program, for example. Try creating a schema and model for a recipe item.

CONNECTING CONTROLLERS AND MODELS

So far, you've set up your Node.js application to handle data and store that data in a MongoDB database. With the help of Mongoose, you've structured your data with a model and schema. In this lesson, you connect your routes to your controllers and to these models so that you can start to save meaningful data based on your user's URL requests. First, you build a new controller for subscriber routes. Then you will convert those routes to use JavaScript ES6-enabled promises. Adding promises gives more flexibility to your database calls now and as your application grows. Finally, you wrap up this lesson with new views and a form where subscribers can post their information.

This lesson covers

- Connecting controllers to models
- Saving data through a controller action
- Implementing database queries with promises
- Handling posted form data

Consider this   Your recipe application is taking shape with Mongoose models to represent data in your database. JavaScript, however, is asynchronous in your application, so database calls require callbacks to run upon completion. Callbacks can be messy, though, especially with complicated queries.

Luckily, you can use multiple other types of syntax to wrap your callbacks and handle returned data or errors in a more elegant way. Promises are a way to do that, and Mongoose offers support for using the promise syntax within your application.

 ## 15.1   Creating a controller for subscribers

Recall that controllers are the glue between your models (the data) and your views (the web page). Now that you have a model set up, you need a controller that handles external requests specifically looking for data related to your model. If someone requests the home path /, you can return a view following logic in the home controller. Now that someone may request to register as a subscriber, you need to implement a subscriber controller. Create a new file in your controllers folder called subscribersController.js.

> **NOTE**   Conventionally, controllers are named in the plural version of your model. There's no strict rule, and as you can see, you already have a homeController.js, but this controller doesn't represent a model in the application.

This file needs access to mongoose and your Subscriber model, both of which can be required at the top of the file. Next, you can create a controller action for when a request is made to view all subscribers in your database. The code would look like listing 15.1. You require mongoose so that you have access to the tools needed to save your model to the database. Next, require the Subscriber model from your subscriber module so that you can integrate the model into your code logic; you no longer need any reference to the Subscriber model in main.js. getAllSubscribers will be accessible to any file that requires this module. You can use this exported callback function to return data from the database.

In this controller action, you use the Mongoose find method on the Subscriber model to tell MongoDB that you want an array of all the subscribers in your database.

> **NOTE**   Using the find query method without any arguments is the same as an empty object [{}]. Here, you using the empty object to make it clear that you want to get all subscribers with no conditions attached.

If an error occurs while reading from the database, send it to the next middleware function. Otherwise, set the data that comes back from MongoDB to the request object. Then this object can be accessed by the next function in the middleware chain.

Listing 15.1 Building your subscribers controller in subscribersController.js

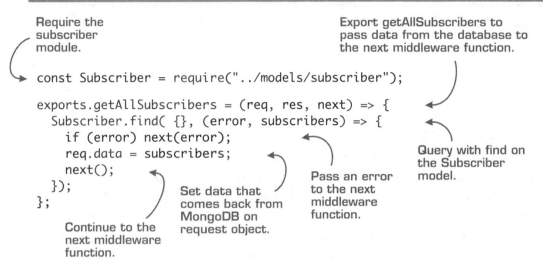

Require the subscriber module.

Export getAllSubscribers to pass data from the database to the next middleware function.

```
const Subscriber = require("../models/subscriber");

exports.getAllSubscribers = (req, res, next) => {
  Subscriber.find( {}, (error, subscribers) => {
    if (error) next(error);
    req.data = subscribers;
    next();
  });
};
```

Query with find on the Subscriber model.

Pass an error to the next middleware function.

Set data that comes back from MongoDB on request object.

Continue to the next middleware function.

> **NOTE** Because the model is in a different folder, you need to use .. to indicate stepping out of your current folder before entering the models folder and requiring it.

Make sure that you still have Express.js installed and working properly. The next step is setting up the route in main.js. First, make sure to require the subscribers controller in main.js by using `const subscribersController = require("./controllers/subscribers Controller")`. The route you use looks like the code in listing 15.2.

In this code, you're looking for GET requests made to the /subscribers path. Upon getting a request, pass the request to your `getAllSubscribers` function in subscribersController .js. Because you aren't doing anything with the data in that function, attach the results of your query to the request object, and pass it to the next middleware function. In this case, that function is a custom callback created to render the data in the browser.

Listing 15.2 Using the subscribers controller in main.js

```
app.get("/subscribers", subscribersController.getAllSubscribers,
  (req, res, next) => {
  console.log(req.data);
  res.send(req.data);
});
```

Pass the request to the getAllSubscribers function.

Log data from the request object.

Render the data on the browser window.

Test this code by running npm start to relaunch your application. If everything worked as planned, you can visit http://localhost:3000/subscribers and see a list of all the subscribers in your database by name and email (figure 15.1).

Figure 15.1   Example browser response with subscriber data

You could immediately improve this action by responding with the data in a view instead of returning the data. Modify the action's return statements and replace them with res.render from Express.js. The line to render a view called subscribers.ejs could look like res.render("subscribers", {subscribers: req.data}). The response makes a call to render a view called subscribers.ejs and passes the subscribers from the database to that view in a variable called subscribers. Now you need to build the view to display these subscribers.

> **NOTE**   Ultimately, this page will be used by administrators of the application to see who has signed up for the recipe application. But right now, this page is public to anyone who visits its associated route.

Create a file in your views folder called subscribers.ejs, and add the code in listing 15.3. Using the EJS template syntax, loop through the subscribers array passed in from the action you just created. For each subscriber, s, you can print some information. You print the name and email address of the subscriber in a paragraph tag.

Listing 15.3   Looping and printing subscribers in a subscribers.ejs

```
<% subscribers.forEach(s => { %>          Loop through
  <p><%= s.name %></p>                    subscribers.
  <p><%= s.email %></p>          Insert subscriber
<% }); %>                        data into the view.
```

Your view at http://localhost:3000/subscribers should list your subscribers, as shown in figure 15.2.

Figure 15.2   Example browser view with listed subscriber data

In the next section, you add two more routes to handle information posted with a form.

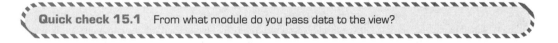

Quick check 15.1   From what module do you pass data to the view?

 ## 15.2   Saving posted data to a model

So far, you should have data flowing in one direction when a request is made to your application's web server. The next step is saving user-submitted data in the form of a subscriber object. Figure 15.3 shows the flow of information from a form to your database.

Recall that according to its schema, a subscriber object must contain name, email, and zipCode fields, so you should have a view with a form that contains these input fields. Change the form in contact.ejs to use the form shown in the next listing. The form will submit data to the /subscribe path via an HTTP POST request. The inputs of the form match the fields of the subscriber model.

QC 15.1 answer   You can pass data to the view from your controller. Within subscribersController.js, you pass an array of subscribers within the rendered `subscribers.ejs`.

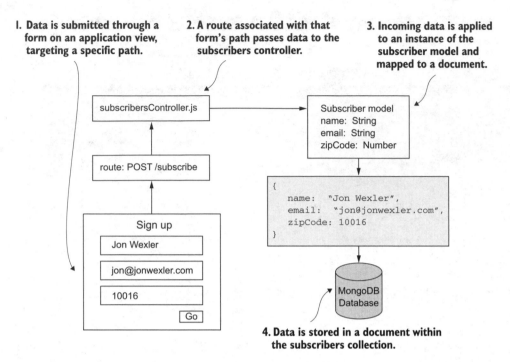

1. Data is submitted through a form on an application view, targeting a specific path.

2. A route associated with that form's path passes data to the subscribers controller.

3. Incoming data is applied to an instance of the subscriber model and mapped to a document.

subscribersController.js

route: POST /subscribe

Sign up

Jon Wexler

jon@jonwexler.com

10016

Go

Subscriber model
name: String
email: String
zipCode: Number

```
{
    name:    "Jon Wexler",
    email:   "jon@jonwexler.com",
    zipCode: 10016
}
```

MongoDB Database

4. Data is stored in a document within the subscribers collection.

Figure 15.3   Flow from a web page form to your database

Listing 15.4 Form to post subscriber data in contact.ejs

```
<form action="/subscribe" method="post">    ⟵── Add a subscription form.
  <input type="text" name="name" placeholder="Name">
  <input type="text" name="email" placeholder="Email">
  <input type="text" name="zipCode" placeholder="Zip Code"
➥ pattern="[0-9]{5}">
  <input type="submit" name="submit">
</form>
```

Because this form will display when contact.ejs is rendered, create a route to render this view when requests are made to the /contact path from the subscribers controller. You need to build a GET route for the /subscribe path and modify the existing POST route for the /contact path. These routes look like the code in listing 15.5.

The first route listens for requests made to /subscribe and uses the getSubscriptionPage callback in the subscribersController. The second route uses the saveSubscriber callback function only for requests made with the POST method.

NOTE After these changes, you no longer need the contact form route handlers in home-Controller.js or their routes in main.js.

Listing 15.5 Routes for the subscriptions in main.js

```
app.get("/contact", subscribersController.getSubscriptionPage);
app.post("/subscribe", subscribersController.saveSubscriber);
```

Add a GET route for the subscription page.

Add a POST route to handle subscription data.

To complete your work here, create the getSubscriptionPage and saveSubscriber functions. Within subscribersController.js, add the code in listing 15.6. The first action renders an EJS page from the views folder. saveSubscriber collects data from the request and allows the body-parser package (installed in unit 2) to read the request body's contents. A new model instance is created, mapping the subscriber's fields to the request body parameters. As a final step, try to save the subscriber. If it fails, respond with the error that occurred. If it succeeds, respond with thanks.ejs.

Listing 15.6 Controller actions for subscription routes in subscribersController.js

```
exports.getSubscriptionPage = (req, res) => {
  res.render("contact");
};
```

Add an action to render the contact page.

```
exports.saveSubscriber = (req, res) => {
  let newSubscriber = new Subscriber({
    name: req.body.name,
    email: req.body.email,
    zipCode: req.body.zipCode
  });
```

Add an action to save subscribers.

Create a new subscriber.

```
  newSubscriber.save((error, result) => {
    if (error) res.send(error);
    res.render("thanks");
  });
};
```

Save a new subscriber.

NOTE MongoDB returns the _id of the newly created subscriber. The result variable in the example contains this information.

You can try this code by filling out your own form at http://localhost/contact. Then visit http://localhost:3000/subscribers to see the list of subscribers, including your new post. In the next section, you add one more touch to your database queries by using JavaScript promises.

15.3 Using promises with Mongoose

ES6 made popular the idea of using promises to facilitate a chain of functions, usually callback functions, in asynchronous queries. A *promise* is a JavaScript object that contains information about the state of a function call and what the next call in the chain needs to see. Similar to middleware, promises can allow a function to start and patiently wait for it to complete before passing it off to the next callback function. Ultimately, promises offer a cleaner way of representing nested callbacks, and with database queries now introduced to your applications, your callback functions can get long.

Luckily, Mongoose is built to work with promises. All you need to do to get set up is let Mongoose know that you want to use native ES6 promises by adding `mongoose.Promise = global.Promise` near the top of main.js. Now with each query made, you can choose to return the normal database response or a promise containing that response. In listing 15.7, for example, a query to get all subscribers from the database returns a new promise with the database's response.

Rewriting this action with a promise still allows querying of all subscribers in the database. Within the query, instead of rendering a view immediately, return a promise that contains data on whether to resolve by rendering a view or reject by logging an error. By using the exec call following `find`, you're invoking your query to return a promise.

> **NOTE**   Without using `exec`, you're still able to use `then` and `catch` to handle follow-up commands. Without `exec`, however, you won't have an authentic promise—only Mongoose's version of a promise query. Some Mongoose methods, however, such as `save`, return a promise and won't work with `exec`. You can read more about the distinctions at http://mongoosejs.com/docs/promises.html.

If an error occurs in the process, the error propagates down the promise chain to the catch block. Otherwise, data returned from the query passes on to the next then block. This promise-chain procedure follows the promise convention of rejecting or resolving code in a promise block to determine what code should be run next (figure 15.4).

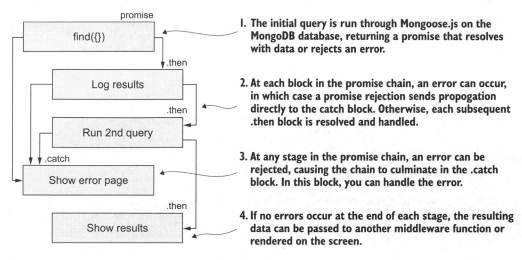

1. **The initial query is run through Mongoose.js on the MongoDB database, returning a promise that resolves with data or rejects an error.**

2. **At each block in the promise chain, an error can occur, in which case a promise rejection sends propogation directly to the catch block. Otherwise, each subsequent .then block is resolved and handled.**

3. **At any stage in the promise chain, an error can be rejected, causing the chain to culminate in the .catch block. In this block, you can handle the error.**

4. **If no errors occur at the end of each stage, the resulting data can be passed to another middleware function or rendered on the screen.**

Figure 15.4   Promise chain in Mongoose.js

When the promise is complete, it calls next to use any following middleware in Express.js. You chain on a then method to tell the promise to perform this task immediately after the database responds. This then block is where you render your view. Next, the catch method is chained to handle any errors rejected in the promise.

> **NOTE**   then is used only in the context of promises. next is used in a middleware function. If both are used, as in listing 15.7, you're waiting for a promise to resolve with then and later calling next to go to another middleware function.

You can add as many then chains as you like, ultimately telling your promise to run the code within that block when everything else is complete. The final then block logs a message to your console to let you know that the promise completed.

Listing 15.7   Using promises to get all subscribers in subscribersController.js

```
exports.getAllSubscribers = (req, res) => {        Rewrite the
  Subscriber.find({})                              getAllSubscribers
    .exec()      Return a promise                  action.
             from the find query.
```

```
  .then((subscribers) => {            ←——  Send saved data to the
    res.render("subscribers", {             next then code block.
      subscribers: subscribers
    });            ←————————————————  Serve results from
  })                                  the database.
  .catch((error) => {      ←——
    console.log(error.message);         Catch errors that
    return [];                          are rejected in the
  })                                    promise.
  .then(() => {          ←——
    console.log("promise complete");    End the promise
  });                                   chain with a log
};                                      message.
```

You may also modify your save command in saveSubscriber to use promises as shown in the following listing. In this example, exec isn't needed.

Listing 15.8 Modifying saveSubscriber to use promises in subscribers-Controller.js

```
newSubscriber.save()
  .then(result => {        ←——
    res.render("thanks");       Save a new
  })                            subscriber with a
  .catch(error => {             promise return.
    if (error) res.send(error);
  });
```

Last, if you want to add data in bulk to your application in development instead of tediously entering new subscribers through the contact form, you can create a module for that purpose. Create seed.js in your project directory, and add the code in listing 15.9. This file makes a connection to your local database and loops through an array of subscribers to create. First, clear the existing subscriber database with remove. Then the promise library's Promise.all waits for all new subscriber documents to be created before printing log messages.

Listing 15.9 Creating new data in seed.js

```
const mongoose = require("mongoose"),
  Subscriber = require("./models/subscriber");
```

```
mongoose.connect(
  "mongodb://localhost:27017/recipe_db",        ←── Set up the connection
  { useNewUrlParser: true }                          to the database.
);

mongoose.connection;

var contacts = [
  {
    name: "Jon Wexler",
    email: "jon@jonwexler.com",
    zipCode: 10016
  },
  {
    name: "Chef Eggplant",
    email: "eggplant@recipeapp.com",
    zipCode: 20331
  },
  {
    name: "Professor Souffle",
    email: "souffle@recipeapp.com",
    zipCode: 19103
  }
];

Subscriber.deleteMany()
  .exec()                    ←────── Remove all existing data.
  .then(() => {
    console.log("Subscriber data is empty!");
  });
                                        Loop through
var commands = [];                      subscriber objects
                                        to create promises.
contacts.forEach((c) => {        ←
    commands.push(Subscriber.create({
      name: c.name,
      email: c.email
    }));                          Log confirmation after
});                               promises resolve.

Promise.all(commands)        ←
  .then(r => {
    console.log(JSON.stringify(r));
    mongoose.connection.close();
  })
  .catch(error => {
```

```
    console.log(`ERROR: ${error}`);
});
```

You can run this file by entering node seed.js in terminal in each subsequent lesson to avoid having an empty or inconsistent database. I talk more about how to use seed data in unit 8.

> **Quick check 15.3**   True or false: using exec on a Mongoose query is the same as running a query that returns a new promise.

 **Summary**

In this lesson, you learned how to connect your models with controller actions. You also made a complete connection between models, views, and controllers by loading a list of subscribers from your database. At the end of the lesson, you were introduced to promises used with Mongoose and Node.js. In lesson 16, you take everything you learned in this unit and build a database for an application in the capstone exercise. In unit 4, you'll take these steps further by building more-robust models and actions for doing more than saving and viewing data.

Try this

Try converting your other controller actions to use promises. You can also chain other Mongoose query methods, such as where and order. Each method passes a promise to the next command.

QC 15.3 answer   True. exec is designed to run a query and return a promise if promises are configured with your Mongoose setup.

CAPSTONE: SAVING USER SUBSCRIPTIONS

I presented the Express.js application to Confetti Cuisine, and they love it. They tell me that they're ready to start promoting their cooking courses and want people who visit the site to subscribe to the school's newsletter. The subscribers to this newsletter are potential customers, so Confetti Cuisine wants me to save each subscriber's name, email address, and ZIP code.

When I have a database in place, Confetti Cuisine is comfortable with moving to the next stages of building user accounts. To accomplish this task, I need to build an application with

- A MongoDB database
- The Mongoose package
- A data schema with three fields
- A form for subscribing on the site
- A route to handle POST requests and save the subscriber data model

16.1 Setting up the database

Now that Confetti Cuisine is ready to save user data, I need to install MongoDB and Mongoose for this project. First, I install MongoDB with Homebrew on my Mac by running brew install mongodb. Then I start the MongoDB server locally by running mongod.

In a new terminal window, in my project directory, I install the mongoose package by entering npm i mongoose -S in a new terminal window within my project folder.

Next, I open the project's main.js file and require mongoose along with my database configuration by using the code in listing 16.1. I require mongoose in this project to use the module's methods for building a connection to my MongoDB database. Then I set up a connection to the confetti_cuisine database on my local computer. If this database doesn't exist yet, it's created when I first run this application.

Listing 16.1 Setting up Mongoose in the Node.js application in main.js

Require mongoose.

Set up the database connection.

```
const mongoose = require("mongoose");
mongoose.connect(
  "mongodb://localhost:27017/confetti_cuisine",
  {useNewUrlParser: true}
);
```

Next, I need to build out how my data should look before it goes into the database.

 ## 16.2 Modeling data

Because Confetti Cuisine wants me to store three fields for new subscribers, I'll create a Mongoose schema defining those fields. First, I create a new models folder and a new subscriber.js file with the schema from listing 16.2.

I need to require mongoose into this file so that I have access to that module's tools and methods. This Mongoose schema defines what a subscriber model should contain. In this case, every subscriber object should have name and email fields that are both Strings and a zipCode field that's a Number.

Listing 16.2 Defining a subscriber schema in subscriber.js

Require mongoose.

```
const mongoose = require("mongoose"),
  subscriberSchema = mongoose.Schema({
```

```
    name: String,
    email: String,
    zipCode: Number
});          ←──────── Define schema properties.
```

Now that the schema is defined, I need to define a model to use this schema. In other words, I've defined a set of rules, and now I need to create a model to use those rules.

The subscriber model also lives in the subscriber.js file, but unlike the schema, the model should be accessible by other modules in the application. For that reason, I add the model to the module's exports object, as shown in listing 16.3.

I assign my subscriber model to the module.exports object. Other modules will need to require this file to access the Subscriber model.

Listing 16.3 Creating an exported subscriber model in subscriber.js

```
module.exports = mongoose.model("Subscriber",
  subscriberSchema);       ←──────── Export the model.
```

Because I know that I'll need to save subscribers who submit a form on the site, I'll prepare a route and some logic to create and save new subscribers to the database. All my code is related to subscribers, so I'll create a new subscribersController.js file within the controllers folder where my actions will exist to respond to a POST route. The code in that controller appears in listing 16.4.

First, I require the subscriber.js module. Because the module lives within another local folder, the require line looks for the models folder relative to the controllers folder. Node.js looks for the subscriber.js file within the models folder and assigns that module's exports content to a local constant called Subscriber. Right now, this module is the only one in which I need to use the Subscriber model. Now I can create instances of the Subscriber module or make calls on that model within the main application file.

The first action uses find to run a query finding all subscribers in the database and returning a promise. I use then to continue the query chain and render a view upon successfully receiving data or catching an error with catch. The second action doesn't require a promise; it renders a view. The third action creates an instance of Subscriber and saves to the database. This behavior automatically returns a promise through Mongoose and allows me to chain more functionality or catch errors. I add mongoose.Promise = global.Promise to main.js so that Mongoose will support my promise chains.

Listing 16.4 Controller actions for subscribers in subscribersController.js

```javascript
const Subscriber = require("../models/subscriber");

exports.getAllSubscribers = (req, res) => {
  Subscriber.find({})
    .exec()
    .then((subscribers) => {
      res.render("subscribers", {
        subscribers: subscribers
      });
    })
    .catch((error) => {
      console.log(error.message);
      return [];
    })
    .then(() => {
      console.log("promise complete");
    });
};

exports.getSubscriptionPage = (req, res) => {
  res.render("contact");
};

exports.saveSubscriber = (req, res) => {
  let newSubscriber = new Subscriber( {
    name: req.body.name,
    email: req.body.email,
    zipCode: req.body.zipCode
  });

  newSubscriber.save()
    .then( () => {
      res.render("thanks");
    })
    .catch(error => {
      res.send(error);
    });
};
```

Require the subscriber model.

Retrieve all subscribers.

Render the contact page.

Save subscribers.

At this point, my application can launch normally with npm start, but I haven't created the routes to connect to my new controller actions. First, I create a form to correspond with my getSubscriptionPage function.

16.3 Adding subscriber views and routes

The last piece of the puzzle is adding my views and a form that visitors can use to submit their information. The subscribers.ejs view contains a loop within the HTML tags to display all the subscribers in the database, as shown in listing 16.5. EJS allows basic JavaScript to run side by side with HTML content. Here, I'm looping through the subscribers I got from the getAllSubscribers action in the subscribers controller.

Listing 16.5   Looping through subscribers in subscribers.ejs

```
<% subscribers.forEach(s => {%>        ◄────   Loop through the
  <p><%= s.name %></p>                          subscribers array.
  <p><%= s.email %></p>
<% })%>
```

The other view I need is for the subscription form, which replaces my form in contact.ejs. The form posts to the /subscribe route and looks like listing 16.6. This form contains input fields with names that match the fields in the Subscriber schema. When the form is submitted, data can easily be extracted by the model's field names and saved within a new Subscriber instance.

> **NOTE** I'm deprecating my postedContactForm in the home controller. The old route and action can be removed.

Listing 16.6   For new subscribers in contact.ejs

```
<form action="/subscribe" method="post">        ◄────   Add a
  <label for="name">Name</label>                        subscription
  <input type="text" name="name" placeholder="Name">    form.
  <label for="email">Email</label>
  <input type="email" name="email" placeholder="Email">
  <label for="zipCode">Zip Code</label>
  <input type="text" pattern="[0-9]{5}" name="zipCode"
   placeholder="Zip Code">
  <input type="submit" name="submit">
</form>
```

To get these views to display, I need to add and modify some routes in main.js, as shown in listing 16.7. First, I require subscribersController.js to the top of the file. Then I add a new route to view all subscribers; this route uses the getAllSubscribers function in subscribersController.js (figure 16.1).

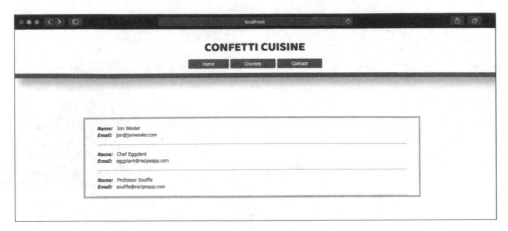

Figure 16.1   Listing subscriber data on the subscribers page

Instead of creating a new route for the subscription view, I modify the /contact route to use my getSubscriptionPage function. When users click the contact button in the site's navigation, they see my subscription form. Last, I add a POST route to let my save-Subscriber function handle submissions from the subscription form.

Listing 16.7   Adding subscriber routes in main.js

Require the
subscribers controller.

```
const subscribersController = require(
  "./controllers/subscribersController");

app.get("/subscribers", subscribersController.getAllSubscribers);
app.get("/contact", subscribersController.getSubscriptionPage);
app.post("/subscribe", subscribersController.saveSubscriber);
```

Add a route to view
all subscribers.

Add a route to view the
contact page.

Add a route to handle
posted form data.

The result is a form accessible from the contact page where new visitors can send me their information (figure 16.2).

The pieces are in place, and the application is ready to launch. I'm going to show this application to Confetti Cuisine. I relaunch my application with npm start and demonstrate the subscription process to see whether the company is interested. This addition could be a good way to gauge interest among subscribers to the newsletter.

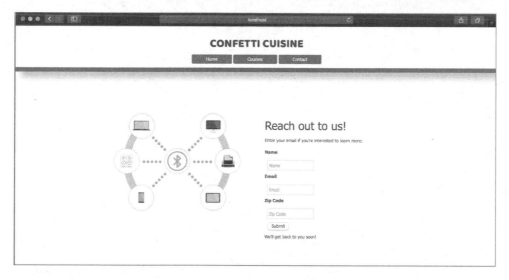

Figure 16.2   Listing subscription form on the contact page

 ## Summary

In this project, I took a largely static Express.js application and modified it to start saving and displaying dynamic data. With these changes and the help of a templating engine and middleware in Express.js, this application is taking shape.

I started by connecting the application with Mongoose and using the schema and modeling tools that come with Mongoose to structure application data. Next, I connected those models with new controllers and routes that handle specific requests to view and save subscriber data. Last, I incorporated a form where users can finally interact with and pass along their information to be processed and reviewed by the Confetti Cuisine team. With the help of promises, the code is clean and ready for errors that may occur.

In unit 4, you learn how to use Mongoose on another level by building a user model. Through this model, you learn about validation and security steps taken when creating, reading, updating, and deleting (CRUD) data.

4

Building a user model

In unit 3, you learned how to connect your application to a database. You also constructed your first schema and model. This unit builds on those lessons by introducing more functionality to your models. First, you learn more about how Mongoose schemas and methods can be used to interact more reliably with your models. You build a model to represent user data and connectivity. Every user needs to create an account, edit, and delete their account. In this unit, I discuss create, read, update, and delete (CRUD) functions in application development and show what you need to create a robust model. By the end of this unit, you'll have an application that supports three models, each associated with one another and manageable from views in your browser.

This unit covers the following topics:

- Lesson 17 dives deeper into Mongoose schemas and models. In this lesson, you add database validations to ensure that data is saved only if it meets the requirements you set. You also learn how to associate models with one another. You start by applying certain techniques to the Subscriber model and then move to the application's other models.

175

- Lesson 18 shows how to construct a user model. This lesson teaches about the core CRUD controller actions to manage model data. You start by building a users-index page.
- Lesson 19 guides you through constructing the create and read routes, actions, and views for your user model. In this lesson, you create everything needed to save user data from browser views.
- Lesson 20 guides you through constructing the update and delete routes, actions, and views for your user model. By the end of this lesson, your CRUD functionality will be complete.
- Lesson 21 wraps up the unit by guiding you through the construction of a user model and the necessary model- associations needed for the Confetti Cuisine application.

Get ready to collect, store, and associate data in unit 4.

LESSON

IMPROVING YOUR DATA MODELS

In this lesson, you take advantage of Mongoose's schema- and model-creation tools. To start, you improve on your simple model and add properties to the models to restrict what data can be saved to the database. Next, you see how to associate data in a NoSQL database such as MongoDB. At the end, you build out static and instance methods for the model. You can run these methods directly on Mongoose model objects, and create the necessary controller actions for them to work with the application.

This lesson covers

- Adding validations to your models
- Creating static and instance methods for your models
- Testing your models in REPL
- Implementing data associations on multiple models

> **Consider this**   You've set up a form for people visiting your recipe application to subscribe to a newsletter. Now you want to populate your application with courses in which users will be able to enroll and learn to cook.
>
> With the help of Mongoose, you'll be able to set up your models so that subscribers can show interest in a particular program before signing up as users.

17.1   Adding validations on the model

So far, you've built a model with Mongoose. The model you created is an abstraction from the data, represented as a document, in your MongoDB database. Because of this abstraction, you can create a blueprint of how you want your data to look and behave using Mongoose schemas.

Take a look at the subscriber data model for your recipe application in listing 17.1. The subscriber's schema lets your application know that it's looking for three properties of a certain data type. It doesn't specify, however, whether the properties can be duplicates, if a size limit exist (the ZIP code could be saved as 15 digits, for example), or whether the properties are even required for saving to the database. It won't be any help to have subscriber records in your database if they're mostly blank. Next, you add some ways to validate that your properties ensure that your data is consistent.

Listing 17.1   Defining a subscriber schema in subscriber.js

```
const mongoose = require("mongoose");
const subscriberSchema = mongoose.Schema({
  name: String,
  email: String,
  zipCode: Number
});
module.exports = mongoose.model("Subscriber", subscriberSchema);
```

> Define a subscriberSchema to contain name, email, and zipCode properties.

The schema defined so far works, but it also allows you to save an instance of the Subscriber model without any meaningful data.

SchemaTypes

Mongoose provides a set of data types that you can specify in your schema; these data types are appropriately called SchemaTypes. The types resemble data types in JavaScript, though they have a particular relationship with the Mongoose library that normal JavaScript data types don't have. Here are some SchemaTypes you should know about:

- String—This type, like Boolean and Number, is straightforward. Specifying a schema property of type String means that this property will save data presented as a JavaScript String (not null or undefined).

- Date—Dates are useful in data documents, as they can tell you when data was saved or modified, or when anything involving that model occurred. This type accepts a JavaScript Date object.

- Array—The Array type allows a property to store a list of items. When specifying the Array type, use the array literal, enclosing square brackets [] instead of its name.
- Mixed—This type is most similar to a JavaScript object, as it stores key-value pairs on a model. To use the Mixed type, you need to specify mongoose.Schema .Types.Mixed.
- ObjectId—Like the ObjectId value for each document in your MongoDB database, this type references that object. This type is particularly important when associating models with one another. To use this type, specify mongoose.Schema.Types.ObjectId.

To start improving your model, add some Mongoose validators. *Validators* are rules that you apply to model properties, preventing them from saving to your database unless those rules are met. See the amended schema in listing 17.2. Notice that each model property can have a type assigned directly or a bunch of options passed as a JavaScript object.

You want to require the name property and make it type String. The email property should be required because no two records can have the same email, and it's also of type String.

> **NOTE** In this example, require means that data must exist for the model instance before it can be saved to the database. It's not the same way I've been using the term to require modules.

You also add the lowercase property set to true to indicate that all emails saved to the database are not case-sensitive. Last, the ZIP code property won't be required, but it has a minimum and maximum number of digits. If a number less than 10000 is entered, the error message "Zip Code too Short" is used. If the number exceeds 99999, or 5 digits in length, you get a generic error from Mongoose, and the data won't save.

Listing 17.2 Adding validators to the subscriber schema in subscriber.js

```
const mongoose = require("mongoose");

const subscriberSchema = new mongoose.Schema({
  name: {
    type: String,          Require the
    required: true         name property.
  },
  email: {
    type: String,          Require the email
    required: true,        property, and add the
                           lowercase property.
```

```
    lowercase: true,
    unique: true                Set up the zipCode
  },                            property with a custom
  zipCode: {                    error message.
    type: Number,
    min: [10000, "Zip code too short"],
    max: 99999
  }
});
```

> **NOTE** The unique option used on the email property isn't a validator, but rather a Mongoose schema helper. Helpers are like methods that perform tasks that behave like a validator in this case.

Because the subscriber's schema defines how instances of the Subscriber model behave, you can also add instance and static methods to the schema. As in traditional object-oriented programming, *instance* methods operate on an instance (a Mongoose document) of the Subscriber model and are defined by subscriberSchema.methods. *Static* methods are used for general queries that may relate to many Subscriber instances and are defined with subscriberSchema.statics.

Next, you add two instance methods from listing 17.3 to your recipe application.

getInfo can be called on a Subscriber instance to return the subscriber's information in one line, which could be useful to get a quick read of the subscribers in your database. findLocalSubscribers works the same way but returns an array of subscribers. This instance method involves a Mongoose query where this refers to the instance of Subscriber on which the method is called. Here, you're asking for all subscribers with the same ZIP code. exec ensures that you get a promise back instead of needing to add an asynchronous callback here.

Listing 17.3 Adding instance methods to the schema in subscriber.js

Add an instance   Add an instance
method to get the full   method to find
name of a subscriber.   subscribers with the
                                                             same ZIP code.

```
subscriberSchema.methods.getInfo = function() {
  return `Name: ${this.name} Email: ${this.email} Zip Code:
  ➥ ${this.zipCode}`;
};

subscriberSchema.methods.findLocalSubscribers = function() {
  return this.model("Subscriber")
```

```
        .find({zipCode: this.zipCode})
        .exec();
};
```

Access the Subscriber model
to use the find method.

> **WARNING** As of the writing of this book, when using methods with Mongoose, you won't
> be able to use ES6 arrow functions without drawbacks. Mongoose makes use of binding
> `this`, which is removed with arrow functions. Inside the function, you can use ES6 again.

> **NOTE** Recall that you need to export the `Subscriber` model by using `module.exports = mongoose.model("Subscriber", subscriberSchema)` after setting up these methods.
> This line allows you to `require` the `Subscriber` model directly by importing this module in
> another file.

Mongoose provides dozens of other query methods. You could add more methods and
validations in subscriber.js, but Mongoose already offers many methods for you to
query documents. Table 17.1 lists a few query methods that you may find useful.

Table 17.1 Mongoose queries

Query	Description
find	Returns an array of records that match the query parameters. You can search for all subscribers with the name "Jon" by running `Subscriber.find({name: "Jon"})`.
findOne	Returns a single record when you don't want an array of values. Running `Subscriber.findOne({name: "Jon"})` results in one returned document.
findById	Allows you to query the database by an `ObjectId`. This query is your most useful tool for modifying existing records in your database. Assuming that you know a subscriber's `ObjectId`, you can run `Subscriber.findById("598695b29ff27740c5715265")`.
remove	Allows you to delete documents in your database by running `Subscriber.remove({})` to remove all documents. Be careful with this query. You can also remove specific instances such as `subscriber.remove({})`.

> **NOTE** Each of these queries returns a promise, so you need to use then and catch to
> handle the resulting data or errors.

For more information about Mongoose queries, visit http://mongoosejs.com/docs/
queries.html.

Before you get to programming the routes and user interface to interact with your new
models, try another way to test whether everything is working: REPL. In the next section, you apply the code from earlier in this lesson to a new REPL session.

Quick check 17.1   When you use promises with Mongoose queries, what should a query always return?

 ## 17.2 Testing models in REPL

To start interacting with your database by using the Subscriber model, you need to go into REPL by typing the node keyword in a new terminal window and adding the lines in listing 17.4. Set up the environment by requiring Mongoose. (You need to be in your project's directory in terminal for this procedure to work.) Next, set up the connection to MongoDB. Enter the name of your database—in this case, recipe_db.

Listing 17.4 Set up subscriber model in REPL in terminal

Require Mongoose in REPL.

Assign the Subscriber model to a variable, using the model name and local project file.

```
const mongoose = require("mongoose"),
  Subscriber = require("./models/subscriber");
mongoose.connect(
  "mongodb://localhost:27017/recipe_db",
  {useNewUrlParser: true}
);
mongoose.Promise = global.Promise;
```

Set up a database connection, using recipe_db.

Tell Mongoose to use native promises as you did in main.js.

Now you're all set to test whether your model and its methods work. In REPL, run the commands and queries in listing 17.5 to see whether you've set up your model correctly.

Create a new subscriber document with the name "Jon" and email "jon@jonwexler.com". Try running this line twice. The first time, you should see the saved document logged back to the console. The second time, you should see an error message saying the email already exists in the database, which means that your email validator is working.

QC 17.1 answer   When using promises with Mongoose, you should expect to get a promise as a result of a database query. Getting back a promise ensures that a result or error can be handled appropriately without having to worry about timing issues with asynchronous queries.

Next, set up a variable to which you can assign the following results of your query. Using Mongoose's findOne query, you're searching for the document you just created. Then assign the resulting record to your subscriber variable. You can test that this code works by logging the subscriber record or, better, the results of your custom getInfo method on this instance.

The resulting text should read: Name: Jon Email: jon@jonwexler.com Zip Code: 12345.

> **NOTE** Because emails must be unique, you may run into a duplicate key error when saving new records with the same information. In that case, you can run Subscriber .remove({}) to clear all subscriber data from your database.

Listing 17.5 Testing model methods and Mongoose queries in REPL in terminal

```
Subscriber.create({
  name: "Jon",
  email: "jon@jonwexler.com",            Create a new
  zipCode: "12345"                       subscriber
})                                       document.
  .then(subscriber => console.log(subscriber))
  .catch(error => console.log(error.message));

var subscriber;              Set up a variable to
Subscriber.findOne({         hold query results.
  name: "Jon"
}).then(result => {          Search for the document
  subscriber = result;       you just created.
  console.log(subscriber.getInfo());      Log the subscriber record.
});
```

Your terminal console window should resemble the one in figure 17.1.

```
recipe_app — node — node — node — 85×14
> Subscriber.findOne({
...     name: 'Jon'
... }).then(result => {subscriber = result; console.log(subscriber.getInfo());});
Promise {
  <pending>,
  domain:
   Domain {
     domain: null,
     _events: { error: [Function: debugDomainError] },
     _eventsCount: 1,
     _maxListeners: undefined,
     members: [] } }
> Name: Jon Email: jon@jonwexler.com Zip Code: 12345
```

Figure 17.1 Example response for Mongoose REPL commands

Try to create new records with different content. Check that your validators for the zip-Code property are working by creating a new Subscriber with ZIP code 890876 or 123. Then try to delete one or all of your subscriber records directly from REPL.

Next, I show you how to associate this new model with other new models.

> **TIP** The code in this section can be saved and reused. Add your REPL code to a file called repl.js in your project directory. The next time you open REPL, you can load the contents of this file into the environment. Remember: Node.js runs asynchronously, so if you try to create a record in one command and query for that record immediately afterward, those two commands run virtually at the same time. To avoid any errors, run the commands individually, or nest queries within each other's then blocks.

> **Quick check 17.2**   Why do you need to require the database connection and Mongoose models into REPL to test your code?

17.3 Creating model associations

In unit 3, I discussed how data is structured with MongoDB and how Mongoose acts as a layer over the database to map documents to JavaScript objects. The Mongoose package saves you a lot of time in development by offering methods that make it easy to query the database and generate results quickly in an object-oriented way.

If your background is relational databases, you may be familiar with the ways you can associate data in your applications, as shown in figure 17.2.

Because you're working with a document-based database, you have no tables—and definitely no join tables. But you do have fairly simple ways to use Mongoose to set up the data relationships laid out in table 17.2.

> **QC 17.2 answer**   Until you build views to interact with your database, REPL is a great tool to run CRUD operations on your models. But you need to require the modules with which you'd like to test so that your REPL environment will know which database to save to and which Subscriber model you're creating.

Model associations

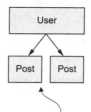
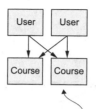

1. A user may be associated with a single profile. This relationship prevents users from adding multiple profile IDs to their profile property.

2. A user may have authored many posts on a social media site. These posts may be represented as an array of post IDs within the user model. In this case, no other user may share authorship of a post.

3. Users may enroll in many courses in which other users are also enrolled. This many-to-many relationship permits the user model to store an array of course IDs that may exist for more than one user.

Figure 17.2   Relational database associations

Table 17.2   Data relationships

Relationship	Description
One-to-one	When one model can have an association to another model. This association could be a User with one Profile; that profile belongs only to the user.
One-to-many	When one model can have many associations to another model, but the other model can have only a single association back to the first model. This association could be a Company with many instances of Employee. In this example, the employees work for only one company, and that company has many employees.
Many-to-many	When many instances of one model can have multiple associations to another model, and vice versa. Many Theatre instances could show the same Movie instances, and each Movie can be traced to many Theatre instances. Typically, a join table is used to map records to one another in a relational database.

If two models are associated in some way—a user has many pictures, an order has a single payment, many classes share multiple enrolled students—you add a property with the associated model's name, where the type is Schema.Types.ObjectId, the ref attribute is set to the associated model's name, and Schema is mongoose.Schema. The following code might represent a schema property for users with many pictures: pictures: [{type: Schema.Types .ObjectId, ref: "Picture"}].

Add another model to this recipe application called Course, and associate it with Subscriber. This course model represents recipe courses to choose from in the application. Each course has different food offerings in different locations. Add the code from listing 17.6 to a new model file called course.js in your models folder.

Courses have titles that are required and must not match another course's title. Courses have a description property to inform users of the site of what the course offers. They also have an items property, which is an array of strings to reflect items and ingredients they include. The zipCode property makes it easier for people to choose the courses that are nearest them.

Listing 17.6   Creating a new schema and model in course.js

```javascript
const mongoose = require("mongoose");

const courseSchema = new mongoose.Schema({
  title: {
    type: String,                      ← Add properties to the
    required: true,                      course schema.
    unique: true
  },
  description: {
    type: String,
    required: true
  },
  items: [],
  zipCode: {
    type: Number,
    min: [10000, "Zip code too short"],
    max: 99999
  }
});

module.exports = mongoose.model("Course", courseSchema);
```

You could add a subscribers property to the Course model that stores a reference to the subscribers by each subscriber's ObjectId, which comes from MongoDB. Then you'd reference the Mongoose model name, Subscriber, like so: subscribers: [{type: mongoose .Schema.Types.ObjectId, ref: "Subscriber"}]. Technically, though, you don't need the models to reference each other; one model referencing the other is enough. Therefore, add the association on the Subscriber model.

Head back over to subscriber.js, and add the following property to the subscriberSchema: courses: [{type: mongoose.Schema.Types.ObjectId, ref: "Course"}]

Add a courses property to subscribers that stores a reference to each associated course by that course's ObjectId. The ID comes from MongoDB. Then reference the Mongoose model name, Course.

NOTE Notice how the property's name is plural to reflect the potential to have many associations between subscribers and courses.

If you wanted to restrict subscribers to one course at a time, you could remove the brackets around the property. The brackets signify an array of multiple referenced objects. If a subscriber could sign up for only a single course, the course property would look like the following: `course: {type: mongoose.Schema.Types.ObjectId, ref: "Course"}`.

In this case, each subscriber could be associated with only a single course. You can think of this as allowing subscribers to sign up for only one course at a time. In a way, this database limitation can also behave like a feature, preventing subscribers from signing up for multiple courses at a time. Nothing prevents different subscribers from signing up for the same course, however, as long as each subscriber has one course association.

To associate two instances of separate models in practice, rely on JavaScript assignment operators. Suppose that you have a subscriber assigned to the variable `subscriber1` and a course instance represented as `course1`. To associate these two instances, assuming the subscriber model can have many course associations, you need to run `subscriber1.courses.push(course1)`. Because `subscriber1.courses` is an array, use the push method to add the new course.

Alternatively, you can push the `ObjectId` into `subscriber.courses` instead of using the whole course object. If `course1` has `ObjectID` `"5c23mdsnn3k43k2kuu"`, for example, your code would look like the following: `subscriber1.courses.push("5c23mdsnn3k43k2kuu")`.

To retrieve course data from a subscriber, you can use the course's `ObjectID` and query on the `Course` model or use the `populate` method to query the subscriber along with the contents of its associated courses. Your `subscriber1` MongoDB document would come with the `course1` document nested within it. As a result, you get the `ObjectIDs` of associated models only.

In the next section, you explore the `populate` method a little further.

Quick check 17.3 How do you distinguish between a model that's associated to one instance of another model versus many instances?

QC 17.3 answer When defining a model's schema, you can specify that model's relationship as one-to-many by wrapping the associated model in brackets. The brackets indicate an array of associated records. Without the brackets, the association is one-to-one.

17.4 Populating data from associated models

Population is a method in Mongoose that allows you to get all the documents associated with your model and add them to your query results. When you populate query results, you're replacing the ObjectIds of associated documents with the documents' contents. To accomplish this task, you need to chain the populate method to your model queries. Subscriber.populate(subscriber, "courses"), for example, takes all the courses associated with the subscriber object and replaces their ObjectIds with the full Course document in the subscriber's courses array.

> **NOTE**   You can find some useful examples at http://mongoosejs.com/docs/populate .html.

With these two models set up, go back to REPL, and test the model associations. See the commands in listing 17.7. First, require the Course model for use in the REPL environment. Set up two variables outside the promise chain scope so that you can assign and use them later. Create a new course instance with values that meet the Course schema requirements. Upon creation, you're assigning the saved course object to testCourse. Alternatively, if you've already created a course, you can get it from the database with Course.findOne({}).then(course => testCourse = course);.

Assuming that you created a subscriber earlier in the lesson, this line pulls a single subscriber from the database and assigns it to testSubscriber. You push the testCourse course into the testSubscriber array of courses. You need to make sure to save the model instance again so that changes take effect in the database. Last, use populate on the Subscriber model to locate all the subscriber's courses and fill in their data in the subscriber's courses array.

Listing 17.7 Testing model associations using REPL in terminal

```
const Course = require("./models/course");        ← Require the
var testCourse, testSubscriber;        ←              Course model.
Course.create( {
  title: "Tomato Land",                     Set up two variables
  description: "Locally farmed tomatoes only",   outside the promise
  zipCode: 12345,                              chain.
  items: ["cherry", "heirloom"]
}).then(course => testCourse = course);   ←
Subscriber.findOne({}).then(                     Create a new
  subscriber => testSubscriber = subscriber   ←  course instance.
);
                        Find a subscriber.
```

```
 testSubscriber.courses.push(testCourse);
testSubscriber.save();
 Subscriber.populate(testSubscriber, "courses").then(subscriber =>
   console.log(subscriber)
 );
```

Save the model instance again.

Use populate on the model.

Push the testCourse course into the courses array of testSubscriber.

> **NOTE** For these examples, you're not handling potential errors with `catch` to keep the code short, though you'll want to add some error handling while you test. Even a simple `catch(error => console.log(error.message))` can help you debug if some error occurs in the promise pipeline.

After running these commands, you should see the results in listing 17.8. Notice that the testSubscriber's courses array is now populated with the Tomato Land course's data. To reveal that course's items, you can log `subscriber.courses[0].items` in the last REPL populate command you ran.

Listing 17.8 Resulting console log from REPL in terminal

```
{ _id: 5986b16782180c46c9126287,
  name: "Jon",
  email: "jon@jonwexler.com",
  zipCode: 12345,
  __v: 1,
  courses:
   [{ _id: 5986b8aad7f31c479a983b42,
      title: "Tomato Land",
      description: "Locally farmed tomatoes only",
      zipCode: 12345,
      __v: 0,
      subscribers: [],
      items: [Array]}]}
```

Display results for a populated object.

Now that you have access to associated model data, your queries have become more useful. Interested in creating a page to show all subscribers subscribed for the Tomato Land course with ObjectId 5986b8aad7f31c479a983b42? The query you need is `Subscriber.find({courses: mongoose.Types.ObjectId("5986b8aad7f31c479a983b42")})`.

If you want to run all the examples from this lesson in sequence, you can add the code in listing 17.9 to repl.js, restart your REPL environment by entering `node`, and load this file by running `.load repl.js`.

The code in repl.js clears your database of courses and subscribers. Then, in an organized promise chain, a new subscriber is created and saved to an external variable called test-Subscriber. The same is done for a course, which is saved to testCourse. At the end, these two model instances are associated, and their association is populated and logged. The commands, in order, demonstrate how powerful REPL can be for testing code.

Listing 17.9 Series of commands in REPL.js

```
const mongoose = require("mongoose"),
  Subscriber = require("./models/subscriber"),
  Course = require("./models/course");

var testCourse,
  testSubscriber;

mongoose.connect(
  "mongodb://localhost:27017/recipe_db",
  {useNewUrlParser: true}
);

mongoose.Promise = global.Promise;

Subscriber.remove({})                                       Remove all subscribers and courses.
  .then((items) => console.log(`Removed ${items.n} records!`))
  .then(() => {
    return Course.remove({});
  })
  .then((items) => console.log(`Removed ${items.n} records!`))
  .then(() => {
    return Subscriber.create( {                             Create a new subscriber.
      name: "Jon",
      email: "jon@jonwexler.com",
      zipCode: "12345"
    });
  })
  .then(subscriber => {
    console.log(`Created Subscriber: ${subscriber.getInfo()}`);
  })
  .then(() => {
    return Subscriber.findOne( {
      name: "Jon"
    });
  })
  .then(subscriber => {
    testSubscriber = subscriber;
```

```
      console.log(`Found one subscriber: ${subscriber.getInfo()}`);
  })
  .then(() => {                        ◄────── Create a new course.
      return Course.create({
        title: "Tomato Land",
        description: "Locally farmed tomatoes only",
        zipCode: 12345,
        items: ["cherry", "heirloom"]
      });
  })
  .then(course => {
    testCourse = course;
    console.log(`Created course: ${course.title}`);
  })
  .then(() => {                        ◄────────────  Associate the
      testSubscriber.courses.push(testCourse);                course with
    testSubscriber.save();                                    subscriber.
  })
  .then( () => {                       ◄────────────  Populate course
      return Subscriber.populate(testSubscriber, "courses");  document in subscriber.
  })
  .then(subscriber => console.log(subscriber))    Query subscribers
  .then(() => {                        ◄───────     where ObjectId is
      return Subscriber.find({ courses: mongoose.Types.ObjectId(  same as course.
➡ testCourse._id) });
  })
  .then(subscriber => console.log(subscriber));
```

> **TIP** Querying with Mongoose and MongoDB can get complicated. I recommend exploring the sample queries for Mongoose and practicing some of the integrated MongoDB query syntax. You'll discover the queries that make the most sense to you as you need them in the development process.

In lesson 18, you expand on these associations. You add some controller actions to manage how you interact with your data.

> **Quick check 17.4** Why wouldn't you want to populate every associated model on every query?

QC 17.4 answer The `populate` method is useful for collecting all associated data for a record, but if it's misused, it can increase the overhead time and space needed to make a query for a record. Generally, if you don't need to access the specific details of associated records, you don't need to use `populate`.

 ## Summary

In this lesson, you learned how to create more-robust Mongoose models. You also created instance methods for your models that can be run from elsewhere in your application on specific model instances. Later, you tested your models for the first time in REPL and created a new Course model with a many-to-many association to your existing Subscriber model. This relationship allows subscribers on the site to show interest in specific recipe courses, allowing you to target your users better by location and interest. In lesson 18, you build a user model along with the CRUD methods that any application needs to manage its data.

Try this

Now that you have two models set up, it's time to step up your Mongoose methods game. First, practice creating a dozen subscribers and half a dozen courses. Then run a line of code to randomly associate each subscriber in your database to a course. Remember to save your changes after pushing courses into your subscribers' courses array.

When you're done, log each subscriber to your console in REPL, using populate to see which courses you've associated each subscriber with.

BUILDING THE USER MODEL

In lesson 17, you improved your models by adding validators and instance methods. You also made your first model associations and populated data from referenced models. In this lesson, you apply some of those techniques to the user model. In doing so, you also interact with these models through their respective controllers and routes. Last, you build some forms and tables to make it easier to visualize all the data in the application.

This lesson covers

- Creating model associations with a user model
- Using virtual attributes
- Implementing a CRUD structure on the user model
- Building an index page to view all users in your database

Consider this   You have two models working with your recipe application: Subscriber and Course. You'd still like visitors to create accounts and start signing up for recipe programs. The user model is in nearly every modern application, along with a system to create, read, update, and delete (CRUD) data from the database. With the help of Mongoose, Express.js, and CRUD, your users will soon have a way to sign in to your application.

18.1   Building the user model

Now that you have models that protect against unwanted data in your database, you need to do the same for the most important model in the application: user. Your recipe application currently has a subscriber model and a course model to allow prospective users to show interest in certain recipe programs. The next step is allowing users to sign up for and enroll in these courses.

Like the subscriber model, the user model needs some basic information about each person who signs up. The model also needs an association with the course and subscriber models. (If a former subscriber decides to sign up as a user, for example, you want to connect the two accounts.) Then you want to track all the courses in which the user decides to participate.

To create the user model, add the code in listing 18.1 to a new file in your models folder called user.js. The user schema contains many overlapping properties from the subscriber schema. Instead of a name property that's one String, here, the name is an object containing first and last. This separation can help if you want to address the user by first name or last name only. Notice that the trim property is set to true to make sure that no extra whitespace is saved to the database with this property. Email and zipCode are the same as in the subscriber schema. The password property currently stores the user's password as a string and is required before an account is created.

> **WARNING**   For this unit only, you'll be saving passwords to the database in plain text. This approach isn't secure or recommended, however, as you'll learn in unit 5.

As in the subscriber schema, you associate the user to many courses. The user may also be connected to a single subscriber's account. You can name the property subscribed-Account and remove brackets to signify that only one object is associated. A new set of properties, createdAt and updatedAt, populates with dates upon the creation of a user instance and any time you change values in the model. The timestamps property lets Mongoose know to include the createdAt and updatedAt values, which are useful for keeping records on how and when data changes. Add the timestamps property to the subscriber and course models, too.

> **NOTE**   Notice the use of object destructuring for the Mongoose Schema object. {Schema} assigns the Schema object in mongoose to a constant by the same name. Later, you'll apply this new format to other models.

Listing 18.1 Creating a User model in user.js

```
const mongoose = require("mongoose"),
  {Schema} = mongoose,                          Create the user
                                                schema.
  userSchema = new Schema({
  name: {
    first: {                          Add first and last
      type: String,                   name properties.
      trim: true
    },
    last: {
      type: String,
      trim: true
    }
  },
  email: {
    type: String,
    required: true,
    lowercase: true,
    unique: true
  },
  zipCode: {
    type: Number,
    min: [1000, "Zip code too short"],
    max: 99999
  },                                                      Add a courses
                                                          property to
  password: {                                             connect users
    type: String,        Add a password                  to courses.
    required: true       property.
  },
  courses: [{type: Schema.Types.ObjectId, ref: "Course"}],
  subscribedAccount: {type: Schema.Types.ObjectId, ref:
➥ "Subscriber"}
}, {                                 Add a subscribedAccount
  timestamps: true                   to connect users to
                                     subscribers.
});
            Add a timestamps property
            to record createdAt and
            updatedAt dates.
```

Given that the first and last name may occasionally be useful in one line, you can use a
Mongoose virtual attribute to store that data for each instance. A *virtual attribute* (also

known as a *computed attribute*) is similar to a regular schema property but isn't saved in the database. To create one, use the `virtual` method on your schema, and pass the property and new virtual attribute name you'd like to use. A virtual attribute for the user's full name resembles the code in listing 18.2. This virtual attribute won't be saved to the database, but it will behave like any other property on the user model, such as `user.zip-Code`. You can retrieve this value with `user.fullName`. Below that is a line to create the user model.

Listing 18.2   Adding a virtual attribute to the user model in user.js

```
userSchema.virtual("fullName")
  .get(function() {
    return `${this.name.first} ${this.name.last}`;
  });

module.exports = mongoose.model("User", userSchema);
```

Add a virtual attribute to get the user's full name.

> **NOTE**   As of the writing of this book, you won't be able to use arrow functions here because Mongoose methods use lexical `this`, on which ES6 arrow functions no longer depend.

Test this model right away in REPL. Remember to require Mongoose and everything needed for this environment to work with your new model. With a new REPL session, you need to require Mongoose again, specify Mongoose to use native promises, and connect to your database by typing `mongoose.connect("mongodb://localhost:27017/recipe_db", {useNewUrlParser: true})`. Then require the new user model with `const User = require("./models/user")`.

Create a new user instance in REPL, and log the returned user or error to see whether the model was set up correctly. Listing 18.3 shows a working line to create a sample user. In this example, a user is created and saved to the database with all the required properties. Notice the extra space in the `last` field, which should be trimmed through Mongoose before saving to the database.

> **TIP**   You can add the REPL commands in these examples to your REPL.js file for future use.

Listing 18.3   Creating a new user in REPL in terminal

```
var testUser;
User.create({
  name: {
    first: "Jon",
    last: "Wexler"
```

```
    },
    email: "jon@jonwexler.com",
    password: "pass123"
})                                          Create a new user.
    .then(user => testUser = user)
    .catch(error => console.log(error.message));
```

> **NOTE** If you get an error complaining about unique email addresses, it probably means that you're trying to create a user with the same information as one in your database (which isn't permitted, due to the rules you set in the user schema). To get around this restriction, create a user with a different email address or use the find() method instead of create, like so: User.findOne({email: "jon@jonwexler.com"}).then(u=> testUser = u) .catch(e => console.log(e.message));.

The user variable should now contain the document object shown in the next listing. Notice that the courses property for this user is an empty array. Later, when you associate this user with courses, that property will populate with ObjectIds.

Listing 18.4 Showing the results of a saved user object in terminal

```
{ _id: 598a3d85e1225d0bbe8d88ae,
  email: "jon@jonwexler.com",
  password: "pass123",
  __v: 0,                                  Display of query response
  courses: [],
  name: { first: "Jon", last: "Wexler" } }
```

Now you can use the information from this user to link any subscribers in the system with the same email. To link a subscriber, see the code in listing 18.5. You're setting up a targetSubscriber variable scoped outside of the query and assigning it the results of the query on the subscriber model. This way, you can use your targetSubscriber variable after the query completes. In this query, you're using the user's email from the create command earlier to search over subscribers.

Listing 18.5 Connecting a subscriber to the user in REPL in terminal

```
var targetSubscriber;
Subscriber.findOne({                     Set the targetSubscriber
    email: testUser.email                variable to a subscriber found
})                                       with the user's email address.
    .then(subscriber => targetSubscriber = subscriber);
```

After you run these commands, your targetSubscriber variable should contain the value of the subscriber object that shares the user's email address. You can console.log(target Subscriber); to see that content in your REPL environment.

With promises, you can condense these two operations into one, as shown in listing 18.6. By nesting the call to find associated subscribers, you get a promise chain that can be moved as a whole into a controller action. First, create the new user. You get back the new user whose email you use to search for subscribers with the same email. The second query returns any subscribers that exist. When you find the subscriber with the same email, you can link it with the user by its attribute name on the user model, subscribedAccount. Finally, save the change.

Listing 18.6 Connecting a subscriber to the user in REPL in terminal

```
var testUser;
User.create({
  name: {
    first: "Jon",
    last: "Wexler "
  },
  email: "jon@jonwexler.com",
  password: "pass123"
})
  .then(user => {
    testUser = user;
    return Subscriber.findOne({          Find a subscriber
      email: user.email                  with the user's email.
    });
  })
  .then(subscriber => {                        Connect a subscriber
    testUser.subscribedAccount = subscriber;   and user.
      testUser.save().then(user => console.log("user updated"));
  })
  .catch(error => console.log(error.message));
```

Now that you can create a user and connect it to another model in REPL, the next step is moving this interaction to the controllers and views.

> **NOTE** You've moved to REPL to test your database queries, so you can remove the required subscriber module from main.js, where it's no longer needed.

Quick check 18.1   How are virtual attributes different from normal model attributes?

 ## 18.2 Adding CRUD methods to your models

In this section, I discuss the next steps you need to take with the user, subscriber, and group models. All three models have schemas and associations that work in REPL, but you're going to want to use them in the browser. More specifically, you want to manage the data for each model as an admin of the site and allow users to create their own user accounts. First, I'll talk about the four major functions in database operations: create, read, update, and delete (CRUD). Figure 18.1 illustrates these functions.

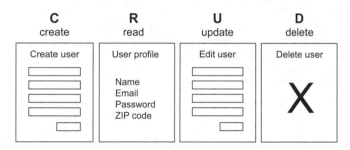

Figure 18.1   Views for each CRUD action

In web development, a CRUD application lays the groundwork for any larger or more evolved application, because at the root and in some way, you always need to perform the actions listed in table 18.1 on each model.

QC 18.1 answer   Virtual attributes aren't saved in the database. These attributes, unlike normal schema attributes, exist only while the application is running; they can't be extracted from the database or found directly through MongoDB.

Table 18.1   CRUD actions

Action	Description
Create	The create function has two parts: new and create. new represents the route and action taken to view the form with which you'll create a new instance of your model. To create a new user, for example, you might visit http://localhost:3000/users/new to view a user-creation form located in new.ejs. The create route and action handle any POST requests from that form.
Read	The read function has only one route, action, and view. In this book, their names are show to reflect that you're showing that model's information, most likely as a profile page. Although you're still reading from the database, the show action and show.ejs view are more conventional names used for this operation.
Update	The update function has two parts: edit and update. edit, like new, handles GET requests to the edit route and edit.ejs view, where you'll find a form to change a model's attribute values. When you modify the values and submit the form by using a PUT request, the update route and action handle that request. These functions depend on some instance of the model preexisting in your database.
Delete	The delete function can be the simplest of the functions. Although you can create a view to ask a user whether he's sure that he wants to delete a record, this function is usually implemented with a button that sends a DELETE request to a route with a user's ID. Then the delete route and action remove the record from your database.

For the new.ejs and edit.ejs forms, you need to route the form submissions to create and update routes, respectively. When you submit a form to create a new user, for example, the form data should be posted to the user/create route. The following examples walk you through the creation of CRUD actions and views for the user model, but you should apply the same technique to the course and subscriber models.

> ## CRUD HTTP methods
>
> Earlier in this book, you learned about the GET and POST HTTP methods, which account for most of the requests made across the internet. Many other HTTP methods are used in specific cases, and with the update and delete functions, you can introduce two more, as shown in table 18.2.
>
> **Table 18.2**   PUT and DELETE HTTP methods
>
> | HTTP method | Description |
> |---|---|
> | PUT | The method used to indicate that you're submitting data to the application server with the intention of modifying or updating an existing record. PUT usually replaces the existing record with a new set of attributes, even if some haven't changed. Although PUT is the leading method for updating records, some people prefer the PATCH method, which is intended to modify only the attributes that have changed. To handle update routes in Express.js, you can use app.put. |

Table 18.3	PUT and DELETE HTTP methods *(continued)*
HTTP method	**Description**
DELETE	The method used to indicate that you're removing a record from your database. To handle delete routes in Express.js, you can use `app.delete`.

Although you can get away with using GET and POST to update and delete records, it's best to follow these best practices when using HTTP methods. With consistency, your application will run with fewer problems and better transparency when problems arise. I discuss these methods further in lesson 19.

Before you get started, take a look at your controllers, and prepare them for a renovation. So far, you've created new controller actions by adding them to the module's exports object. The more actions you create, the more you repeat that `exports` object, which isn't particularly pretty in the controller module. You can clean up your controller actions by exporting them all together with `module.exports` in an object literal. Modify your home controller to the code in listing 18.7.

In this example, your actions are now comma-delimited, which makes the names of the actions much easier to identify. After you apply this change in the controller, you don't need to change any other code for the application to function as it did before.

Listing 18.7   Modifying your actions in homeController.js

```
var courses = [
  {
    title: "Event Driven Cakes",
    cost: 50
},
  {
    title: "Asynchronous Artichoke",
    cost: 25
},
  {
    title: "Object Oriented Orange Juice",
    cost: 10
}];
module.exports = {           ⟵  Export object literal with
  showCourses: (req, res) => {        all controller actions.
```

```
    res.render("courses", {
      offeredCourses: courses
    });
  }
};
```

Apply this structure to your other controllers (errorController.js and subscribers-Controller.js) and to all controllers moving forward. These modifications will start to become important as you build out your CRUD actions and structure your middleware within your routes.

> **NOTE** Also create coursesController.js and usersController.js in your controllers folder so that you can create the same actions for the course and user models over the next few lessons.

In the next section, you build the forms you need for the user model. First, though, create an often-overlooked view for the application: index.ejs. Also create this index page for each application model. The purpose of the index route, action, and view is to fetch all records and display them on a single page. You build the index page in the next section.

> **Quick check 18.2** What CRUD functions don't necessarily need a view?

18.3 Building the index page

To start, create the index.ejs view by creating a new users folder inside the views folder and adding the code in listing 18.8.

In this view, you're looping through a users variable and creating a new table row listing each user's attributes. The same type of table can be used for subscribers and courses. You need to populate the users variable with an array of users at the controller level.

> **NOTE** You should apply the same approach to other models in your application. The subscriber model views will now go in the subscribers folder within the views folder, for example.

> **QC 18.2 answer** Although every CRUD function can have its own view, some functions could live in modals or be accessed through a basic link request. The delete function doesn't necessarily need its own view because you're sending a command to delete a record.

Listing 18.8 Listing all users in index.js

```
<h2>Users Table</h2>
  <table class="table">
    <thead>
      <tr>
        <th>Name</th>
        <th>Email</th>
        <th>Zip Code</th>
      </tr>
    </thead>
    <tbody>
      <% users.forEach(user => { %>         ⟵  Loop through an array of
      <tr>                                      users in the view.
        <td><%= user.fullName %></td>
        <td><%= user.email %></td>
        <td><%= user.zipCode %></td>
      </tr>
      <% }); %>
    </tbody>
  </table>
```

To test this code, you need a route and controller action that will load this view. Create a usersController.js in the controllers folder with the code in listing 18.9.

You need to require the user model in usersController.js to have access to it in this controller. First, you receive a response from the database with your users. Then you render your list of users in your index.ejs view. If an error occurs, log the message to the console and redirect the response to the home page.

Listing 18.9 Creating the index action in usersController.js

```
const User = require("../models/user");    ⟵
                                               Require the user model.
module.exports = {
  index: (req, res) => {                  Render the index page
    User.find({})                         with an array of users.
      .then(users => {
        res.render("users/index", {
          users: users
        })
                                        Log error messages and
    })                                  redirect to the home page.
      .catch(error => {
```

```
            console.log(`Error fetching users: ${error.message}`)
        res.redirect("/");
      });
  }
};
```

> **NOTE** In the subscribers controller, the index action replaces your `getAllSubscribers` action. Remember to modify the action's corresponding route in main.js to point to `index` and to change the subscribers.ejs file to index.ejs. This view should now live in a subscribers folder within views.

The last step is introducing the `usersController` to main.js and adding the `index` route by adding the code in listing 18.10 to main.js.

First, require the `usersController` into main.js. Add this line below where your `subscribers-Controller` is defined. Creating your first user route, take incoming requests to /users, and use the `index` action in `usersController`.

Listing 18.10 Adding `usersController` **and a route to main.js**

```
const usersController = require("./controllers/usersController");
app.get("/users", usersController.index);
```

Require usersController.   Create the index route.

Fire up your application in terminal, and visit http://localhost:3000/users. Your screen should resemble figure 18.2.

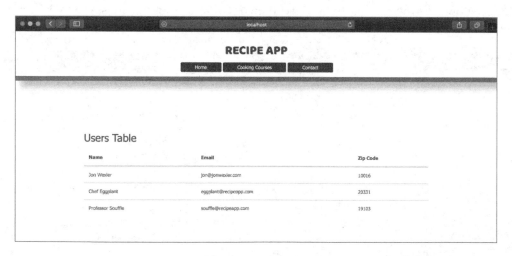

Figure 18.2   Example of users index page in your browser

This list is your window into the database without revealing any sensitive data to the public. Before you continue, though, make one more modification to your routes and actions.

Quick check 18.3   What is the purpose of the index view?

 ## 18.4 Cleaning up your actions

Right now, your index action is designed to serve only an EJS template view with data from your database. You may not always want to serve your data in a view, however, as you learn in unit 6. To make better use of your actions, break them into an action to run your query and an action to serve results through your view.

Modify the users controller to the code shown in listing 18.11. In this revised code, you have the index action, which calls the find query on the user model. If you successfully produce results, add those results to the res.locals object—a unique object on the response that lets you define a variable to which you'll have access in your view. By assigning the results to res.locals.users, you won't need to change your view; the variable name users matches locally in the view. Then call the next middleware function. If an error occurs in the query, log the error, and pass it to the next middleware function that will handle the error. In this case, that function is the internalServerError action in the errors controller. The indexView action renders the index view.

Listing 18.11 Revisiting the index action in usersController.js

```js
const User = require("../models/user");

module.exports = {
  index: (req, res, next) => {        Run query in index
    User.find()                       action only.
      .then(users => {
        res.locals.users = users;     Store the user data on the
          next();                     response and call the next
      })                              middleware function.
```

QC 18.3 answer   The index view displays all documents for a particular model. This view can be used internally by a company to see the names and email addresses of everyone who subscribed. It can also be visible to all users so that everyone can see who signed up.

```
        .catch(error => {
          console.log(`Error fetching users: ${error.message}`);
          next(error);
      });                          Catch errors, and pass to
    },                             the next middleware.
    indexView: (req, res) => {
      res.render("users/index");
    }                            Render view in
  };                             separate action.
```

To get your application to load your users on the index page as before, add the indexView
action as the middleware function that follows the index action in your route. To do
so, change the /users route in main.js to the following code: app.get("/users", users
Controller.index, usersController.indexView). When usersController.index completes
your query and adds your data to the response object, usersController.indexView is
called to render the view. With this change, you could later decide to call a different
middleware function after the index action in another route, which is exactly what
you'll do in unit 6.

Now you have a way, other than REPL and the MongoDB shell, to view the users,
courses, and subscribers in your database. In lesson 19, you pull more functionality into
the views.

> **Quick check 18.4**   Why do you need to log error messages to the console if you're working
> mainly in the browser?

 **Summary**

In this lesson, you learned how to create a user model and where to get started with
CRUD functions. You also learned about two new HTTP methods and saw how to create an index page to display all your users. With this index page, you started to interact
with your application from the browser. Finally, you modified your controller and

> **QC 18.4 answer**   Although you're moving more data and functionality into the views, your terminal is
> still the heart of your application. Your console window is where you should expect to see application
> errors, requests made, and custom error messages you create so that you'll know where to look to fix
> the problem.

routes to make better use of middleware functions and interactivity among your actions. In lesson 19, you apply the create and read functions to your three models.

· ·

Try this

With your index page set up, try to think about how an administrator of your application might use this page. You created the table to display user data, but you may want other columns in this table. Create new user instance methods to give you the number of characters in each user's name and then create a new column in this table to show that number for each user.

Try creating a new virtual attribute for the user model.

CREATING AND READING YOUR MODELS

In lesson 18, you constructed your user model and built an index page to display users on the same page. In this lesson, you add more functionality to your application by focusing on the create and read functions of CRUD. You start by creating an EJS form that handles a user's attributes as inputs. Then you create the routes and actions to handle that form data. Last, you build a show page to act as the user's profile page.

This lesson covers

- Constructing a model creation form
- Saving users to your database from the browser
- Displaying associated models in a view

Consider this With a new way to create courses for your recipe application, you're finding it tedious to add individual documents to your database on REPL. You decided to create dedicated routes to create new model instances, edit them, and display their data. These routes are the foundations of CRUD methods that allow interaction with your data to flow through your application views.

19.1 Building the new user form

To create a new user instance in your database, you need some way of retrieving that user's data. So far, you've been entering that data directly in REPL. Because you're moving all your data interactions to the browser, you need a form through which new users can create their accounts. In CRUD terms, that form lives in a view called new.ejs.

To start, build that form by adding the code in listing 19.1 to new.js in the views/users folder. The resulting form looks like figure 19.1. This form makes a POST request to the /users/create route upon submission. You need to make sure to create that route before you try to submit anything; otherwise, your application will crash.

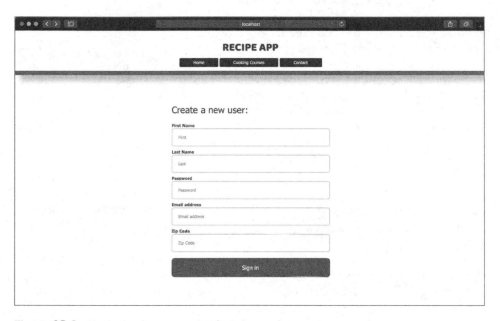

Figure 19.1 Example of user-creation form in your browser

The form is embellished with bootstrap, but the major takeaways are that each user attribute is represented as a form input and that the attribute's name is set to that input's name property—in the case of the first name, name="first". You'll use these name attributes later to identify values in the controller. Notice that the password, email, and zip-Code fields have some unique properties. These HTML validations are some ways that you can prevent invalid or insecure information from entering your application from the web page.

Listing 19.1   Building a user creation form in new.ejs

Build a form to create
user accounts.

```
<div class="data-form">
  <form action="/users/create" method="POST">
    <h2>Create a new user:</h2>
    <label for="inputFirstName">First Name</label>
    <input type="text" name="first" id="inputFirstName"
 placeholder="First" autofocus>
    <label for="inputLastName">First Name</label>
    <input type="text" name="last" id="inputLastName"
 placeholder="Last">
    <label for="inputPassword">Password</label>
    <input type="password" name="password" id="inputPassword"
 placeholder="Password" required>
    <label for="inputEmail">Email address</label>
    <input type="email" name="email" id="inputEmail"
 placeholder="Email address" required>
    <label for="inputZipCode">Zip Code</label>
    <input type="text" name="zipCode" id="inputZipCode" pattern="\d*"
 placeholder="Zip Code" required>
    <button type="submit">Sign in</button>
  </form>
</div>
```

Add user
properties as
inputs to the form.

Apply HTML
attributes to
protect password
and email fields.

Now that you have a new view, you need a route and controller actions to serve that view. You also add the create routes and actions to handle data from that view in the next section.

> **Quick check 19.1**   Which form input attribute must have a value for controller actions to identify form data?

> **QC 19.1 answer**   The name attribute must be filled in on the form to create a new record. Whatever value is mapped to the name attribute is what the controller uses to compare against the model schema.

19.2 Creating new users from a view

The form for new users collects data as it pertains to the user schema. Next, you need to create actions for this form. To get your form to render and process data, add the code for the user actions in listing 19.2 to usersController.js.

The new action takes incoming requests to create a new user and render the form in new.ejs. The create action receives incoming posted data from the form in new.ejs and passes the resulting created user to the next middleware function through the response object. The next middleware function, redirectView, determines which view to show based on the redirect path it receives as part of the response object. If a user is created successfully, redirect to the index page.

In the create action, assign a userParams variable to the collected incoming data. Then call User.create and pass those parameters, redirecting the user to the /users index page upon success and to the error page in case of a failure.

> **NOTE** For the subscribers controller, the new and create actions effectively replace the getSubscriptionPage and saveSubscriber actions you created earlier in the book. After swapping in these new actions, you need to change the action names in the main.js routes to match.

Listing 19.2 Adding a create action to usersController.js

```
new: (req, res) => {
  res.render("users/new");          Add the new action
},                                  to render a form.

create: (req, res, next) => {       Add the create action
  let userParams = {                to save the user to
    name: {                         the database.
      first: req.body.first,
      last: req.body.last
    },
    email: req.body.email,
    password: req.body.password,
    zipCode: req.body.zipCode
  };
                                    Create users with
  User.create(userParams)           form parameters.
    .then(user => {
      res.locals.redirect = "/users";
      res.locals.user = user;
```

```
      next();
    })
    .catch(error => {
      console.log(`Error saving user: ${error.message}`);
      next(error);
    });
},
redirectView: (req, res, next) => {
  let redirectPath = res.locals.redirect;
  if (redirectPath) res.redirect(redirectPath);
  else next();
}
```

Render the view in a separate redirectView action.

To see this code work, add the new and create routes to main.js, as shown in listing 19.3. The first route takes incoming GET requests to /users/new and renders new.ejs in the usersController. The second route accepts POST requests to /users/create and passes that incoming request body to the create action, followed by the view redirect with the redirectView action in usersController.js. These routes can go below your user's index route.

NOTE The addition of the new and create actions to the subscribers controller means that you can remove the getAllSubscribers and saveSubscriber actions in favor of the new CRUD actions. Likewise, the only action you need in the home controller is to serve the home page: index.ejs.

Now that you're starting to accumulate the number of routes you're using in main.js, you can use the Router module in Express.js by adding const router = express .Router() to your main.js file. This line creates a Router object that offers its own middleware and routing alongside the Express.js app object. Soon, you'll use this router object to organize your routes. For now, modify your routes to use router instead of app. Then add app.use("/", router) to the top of your routes in main.js. This code tells your Express.js application to use the router object as a system for middleware and routing.

Listing 19.3 Adding new and create routes to main.js

```
router.get("/users/new", usersController.new);
router.post("/users/create", usersController.create,
  usersController.redirectView);
```

Handle requests to view the creation form.

Handle requests to submit data from the creation form, and display a view.

Restart your application, fill out the form on http://localhost:3000/users/new, and submit the form. If you were successful, you should see your newly created user on the index page.

When you have users successfully saving to your database, add a finishing touch. You've already designed the User schema with an association to the Subscriber model. Ideally, whenever a new user is created, you'd like to check for an existing subscriber with the same email address and associate the two. You do so with a Mongoose pre("save") hook.

Mongoose offers some methods, called *hooks*, that allow you to perform an operation before a database change, such as save, is run. You can add this hook to user.js by adding the code in listing 19.4 after the schema is defined and before the model is registered. You need to require the Subscriber model into user.js for this hook to work. Use const Subscriber = require("./subscriber").

This hook runs right before a user is created or saved. It takes the next middleware function as a parameter so that when this step is complete, it can call the next middleware function. Because you can't use arrow functions here, you need to define the user variable outside the promise chain.

> **NOTE** As of the writing of this book, arrow functions don't work with Mongoose hooks.

You perform this function only if the user doesn't already have an associated subscriber, which saves an unneeded database operation. Search for one subscriber account, using the user's email address. If a subscriber is found with a matching email address, assign that subscriber to the user's subscribedAccount attribute. Unless an error occurs, continue saving the user in the next middleware function. You also need to add a reference to the subscriber model in user.js by adding const Subscriber = require("./subscriber") to the top.

Listing 19.4 Adding a pre('save') hook to user.js

Set up the pre('save') hook.

Use the function keyword in the callback.

Add a quick conditional check for existing subscriber connections.

```
userSchema.pre("save", function (next) {
  let user = this;
  if (user.subscribedAccount === undefined) {
    Subscriber.findOne({
      email: user.email
    })
      .then(subscriber => {
```

Query for a single subscriber.

```
      user.subscribedAccount = subscriber;          Connect the user
      next();                                        with a subscriber
   })                                                account.
   .catch(error => {
      console.log(`Error in connecting subscriber:
${error.message}`);
      next(error);                Pass any errors to the
   });                            next middleware function.
 } else {
   next();              Call next function if user
 }                      already has an association.
});
```

Give this new code a shot by creating a new subscriber in REPL (or through the subscriber's new page, if you've created that already) and then creating a new user in your browser with the same email address. Going back to REPL, you can check whether that user's subscribedAccount has a value reflecting the associated subscriber's ObjectId. This value will come in handy in the next section, when you build the user's show page.

> **Quick check 19.2** Why does the Mongoose pre("save") hook take next as a parameter?

 ## 19.3 Reading user data with show

Now that you can create users, you want a way to display a user's information on dedicated pages (such as the user's profile page). The only operation you need to perform on the database is to read data, finding a user by a specific ID and displaying its contents in the browser.

Start by creating a new view called show.ejs. Call the view and action show, making it clear that your intention is to show user data. In show.ejs, create a table similar to the one in index.ejs, except that you won't need the loop. You want to show all the user's attributes. Add the code in listing 19.5 to show.ejs within the views/users folder.

> **QC 19.2 answer** The pre("save") hook is Mongoose middleware, and as with other middleware, when the function completes, it moves on to the next middleware function. next here indicates the next function in the middleware chain to be called.

This form uses the user variable's attributes to populate each table data box. At the end, check whether that user has a subscribedAccount. If not, nothing is displayed. If a subscriber is associated, display some text and link to the subscriber's show page.

Listing 19.5 User show table in show.ejs

```
<h1>User Data for <%= user.fullName %></h1>

<table class="table">              Add a table to
  <tr>                             display user data.
    <th>Name</th>
    <td><%= user.fullName %></td>
  </tr>
  <tr>
    <th>Email</th>
    <td><%= user.email %></td>
  </tr>
  <tr>
    <th>Zip Code</th>
    <td><%= user.zipCode %></td>
  </tr>
  <tr>
    <th>Password</th>
    <td><%= user.password %></td>
  </tr>
</table>                            Check for linked
                                   subscriber
<% if (user.subscribedAccount) { %>   accounts.
    <h4 class="center"> This user has a
    <a href="<%=`/subscribers/${user.subscribedAccount}` %>">
    subscribed account</a>.
    </h4>
<% } %>
```

> **NOTE** You will need to follow the same steps in creating CRUD functions and views for the subscriber simultaneously for this linked page to work. The anchor tag href path is /subscribers/${user.subscribedAccount}, which represents the subscriber's show route.

To make it easier to get to a user's show page, in index.ejs, wrap the user's name in an anchor tag that links to users/ plus the user's ID. The table data there should look like the next listing. You embed JavaScript in the anchor tag's href as well as in the table data content.

Listing 19.6   Updated name data in index.ejs

```
<td>
  <a href="<%= `/users/${user._id}` %>">
    <%= user.fullName %>
  </a>
</td>
```
Embed the user's
name and ID in HTML.

If you refresh the users index page, you'll notice that the names have turned into links (figure 19.2). If you click one of those links now, though, you'll get an error because there isn't a route to handle the request yet.

Figure 19.2   Users' index page with linked names in your browser

Next, add the show action to usersController.js, as shown in listing 19.7. First, collect the user's ID from the URL parameters; you can get that information from req.params.id. This code works only if you define your route by using :id (see listing 19.7).

Use the findById query, and pass the user's ID. Because each ID is unique, you should expect a single user in return. If a user is found, add it as a local variable on the response object, and call the next middleware. Soon, you'll set up the next function to be showView, where you render the show page and pass the user object to display that user's information. If an error occurs, log the message, and pass the error to the next middleware function.

Listing 19.7 Show action for a specific user in usersController.js

```
show: (req, res, next) => {
  let userId = req.params.id;        ←——   Collect the user ID from
  User.findById(userId)      ←——              the request params.
      .then(user => {             └——  Find a user by its ID.
        res.locals.user = user;   ←
          next();                     ┌——  Pass the user through the
      })                             └──   response object to the
      .catch(error => {                    next middleware function.
        console.log(`Error fetching user by ID: ${error.message}`);
        next(error);      ←
      });                  ┌——  Log and pass errors
    },                     └——  to next function.

showView: (req, res) => {
  res.render("users/show");   ←——  Render show view.
}
```

Last, add the show route for users in main.js with the following code: router.get
("/users/:id", usersController.show, usersController.showView). This show route uses
the /users path along with an :id parameter. This parameter will be filled with the
user's ID passing in from the index page when you click the user's name in the table.

> **NOTE** You can group routes that are related to the same model in main.js for better orga-
> nization.

Restart your application, and click a user's name. You should be directed to that user's
show page, as shown in figure 19.3.

You now have the ability to create data in your application and view it on a few web
pages. In lesson 20, you explore ways of updating and deleting that data.

> **Quick check 19.3** True or false: the URL parameter representing the user's ID must be
> called :id.

QC 19.3 answer False. The :id parameter is essential for getting the ID of the user you're trying to
display, but this parameter can be referenced by any name you choose. If you decide to use :userId,
make sure that you use that name consistently throughout your code.

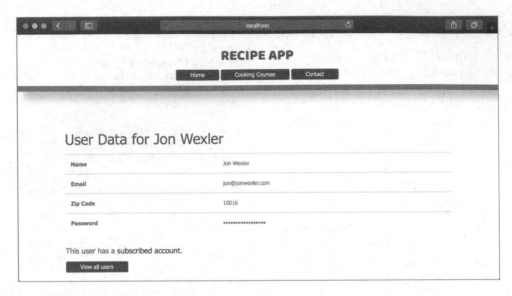

Figure 19.3   Users show page in your browser

 **Summary**

In this lesson, you learned how to create index, new, and show pages for your models. You also created routes and actions to process user data and create new accounts. Finally, you customized the user show page to show user data and an indicator for linked subscriber accounts. You have two of the four CRUD building blocks in place. In lesson 20, you apply the update and delete functions to your three models.

Try this

Your user-account creation form is ready to create new accounts, but you've implemented certain validations on the user model that may allow a form to be submitted with no data saved. Try to test some of your validations to ensure that they're working correctly, as follows:

1 What happens when you enter an email address with capital letters?
2 What happens when a required field is missing?

It's good that you get redirected to the new page again, but you have improvements to make in the error messages shown on the screen.

UPDATING AND DELETING YOUR MODELS

In lesson 19, you built create and read functionality for your models. Now it's time to complete the CRUD methods. In this lesson, you add the routes, actions, and views for the update and delete functions. First, you create a form to edit the attributes of existing users. Then you manage the modified data in an update action. At the end of the lesson, you implement a quick way to delete users from your users index page. To start, make sure that your MongoDB server is running by entering mongod in a terminal window.

This lesson covers

- Constructing a model edit form
- Updating user records in your database
- Deleting user records

Consider this   Your recipe application is ready to accept new users, but you're getting complaints that multiple unnecessary accounts were made and that some users accidentally typed the wrong email address. With the update and delete CRUD functions, you'll be able to clear unwanted records and modify existing ones to persist in your application.

20.1 Building the edit user form

To update a user's information, you use some Mongoose methods in a specific update action. First, though, you create a form to edit user information. The form looks like the one in create.js, but the form's action points to users/:id/update instead of users/create because you want your route to indicate that the form's contents are updating an existing user, not creating a new one.

You also want to replace the values in each form input with the user's existing information. The input for the user's first name might look like the next listing, for example. The value attribute here uses the existing user's first name. This code works only if a user object is being passed into this page.

Listing 20.1 Input example with user's data in edit.ejs

```
<input type="text" name="first" id="inputFirstName" value="<%=
    user.name.first %>" placeholder="First" autofocus>
```

Apply the existing user's
attribute values in edit form.

To ensure that an existing user's data populates this form, add another column to the table in the users index page. Your index page should resemble figure 20.1.

Figure 20.1 Users index page with edit links in your browser

This column has a link for editing each specific user. You can add an anchor tag, as shown in the next listing. The href value for the edit link tag makes a GET request to the /users plus the user's Id plus /edit route.

Listing 20.2 Modified table with link to edit users in index.ejs

```
<td>
  <a href="<%=`/users/${user._id}/edit` %>">
    Edit
  </a>              Embed the user's ID in
</td>                the edit tag link.
```

Next, you want to modify the form in edit.ejs to submit a PUT request with modified user data, but your HTML form element supports only GET and POST requests. It's important to begin using the intended HTTP methods with your CRUD functions so that there's no future confusion about whether a request is adding new data or modifying existing data.

One problem you need to address is how Express.js will receive this request. Express.js receives your HTML form submissions as POST requests, so you need some way to interpret the request with the HTTP method you intended. Several solutions to this problem exist. The solution you use in this lesson is the method-override package.

method-override is middleware that interprets requests according to a specific query parameter and HTTP method. With the _method=PUT query parameter, you can interpret POST requests as PUT requests. Install this package by running npm i method-override -S in your project's terminal window, and add the lines in listing 20.3 to main.js.

First, require the method-override module into your project. Tell the application to use methodOverride as middleware. Specifically, you're telling this module to look for the _method query parameter in the URL and to interpret the request by using the method specified as the value of that parameter. A POST request that you want processed as a PUT request, for example, will have ?_method=PUT appended to the form's action path.

Listing 20.3 Adding method-override to your application in main.js

```
const methodOverride = require("method-override");
router.use(methodOverride("_method", {
  methods: ["POST", "GET"]
}));
```

Require the method-override module.

Configure the application router to use methodOverride as middleware.

You want to modify the form in edit.ejs to submit the form with a POST method to the /users/:id/update?_method=PUT route. The opening form tag will look like listing 20.4.

The action is dynamic, depending on the user's ID, and points to the /users/:id/update route. Your method-override module interprets the query parameter and helps Express.js match the request's method with the appropriate route.

Listing 20.4 Pointing the edit form to the update route in edit.ejs

```
<form method="POST" action="<%=`/users/${user._id}/update
➥ ?_method=PUT`%>">
```

⎫ Add a form to
⎭ update user data.

You can reference the complete user edit form in the next listing, which should look like figure 20.2 in your browser for an existing user.

Listing 20.5 Complete user edit form in edit.ejs

Display the user
edit form.

```
<div class="data-form">
  <form method="POST" action="<%=`/users/${user._id}/update
➥ ?_method=PUT`%>">
    <h2>Edit user:</h2>
    <label for="inputFirstName">First Name</label>
    <input type="text" name="first" id="inputFirstName" value="<%=
➥ user.name.first %>" placeholder="First" autofocus>
    <label for="inputLastName">Last Name</label>
    <input type="text" name="last" id="inputLastName" value="<%=
➥ user.name.last %>" placeholder="Last">
    <label for="inputPassword">Password</label>
    <input type="password" name="password" id="inputPassword"
➥ value="<%= user.password %>" placeholder="Password" required>
    <label for="inputEmail">Email address</label>
    <input type="email" name="email" id="inputEmail" value="<%=
➥ user.email %>" placeholder="Email address" required>
    <label for="inputZipCode">Zip Code</label>
    <input type="text" name="zipCode" id="inputZipCode"
➥ pattern="\d*" value="<%= user.zipCode %>" placeholder="Zip
➥ Code" required>
    <button type="submit">Update</button>
  </form>
</div>
```

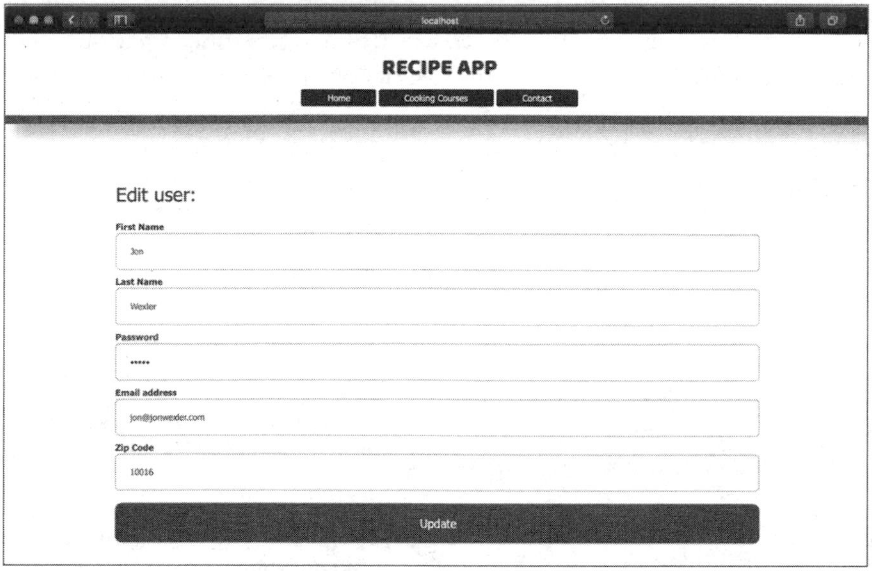

Figure 20.2   User edit page in your browser

In the next section, you add the routes and actions that get this form to work, as well as the data from the form processed.

Quick check 20.1   Why do you use the PUT method for the edit form and POST for the new form?

20.2 Updating users from a view

Now that the user edit form is in its own view, add the controller action and route to complement the form. The edit route and action send users to view edit.ejs. The update route and action are used internally to make changes to the user in the database. Then the redirectView action acts as the action following update, redirecting you to a view that you specify. Add the actions in listing 20.6 to usersController.js.

The edit action, like the show action, gets a user from the database by the user's ID and loads a view to //edit the user. Notice that if a user isn't found by the ID parameter, you

QC 20.1 answer   The edit form is updating data for an existing record. By convention, the request to submit data to your server should use an HTTP PUT method. To create new records, use POST.

pass an error to the error-handling middleware function. The update action is called when the edit form is submitted; like the create action, it identifies the user's ID and userParams, and passes those values into the Mongoose findByIdAndUpdate method. This method takes an ID followed by parameters you'd like to replace for that document by using the $set command. If the user updates successfully, redirect to the user's show path in the next middleware function; otherwise, let the error-handling middleware catch any errors.

Listing 20.6 Adding edit and update actions to usersController.js

```
edit: (req, res, next) => {                     ←  Add the edit action.
  let userId = req.params.id;
  User.findById(userId)                              Use findById to locate a user
                                                     in the database by their ID.
    .then(user => {
      res.render("users/edit", {                 Render the user edit
        user: user                               page for a specific user
      });                                         in the database.
    })
    .catch(error => {
      console.log(`Error fetching user by ID: ${error.message}`);
      next(error);
    });
},

update: (req, res, next) => {          ←——— Add the update action.
  let userId = req.params.id,
    userParams = {
      name: {
        first: req.body.first,
        last: req.body.last
      },
      email: req.body.email,           Collect user parameters
      password: req.body.password,     from request.
      zipCode: req.body.zipCode
    };

  User.findByIdAndUpdate(userId, {     Use findByIdAndUpdate to
    $set: userParams                   locate a user by ID and
  })                                   update the document
                                       record in one command.
    .then(user => {
      res.locals.redirect = `/users/${userId}`;
```

```
    res.locals.user = user;
    next();                    ◀──────        Add user to response as a
  })                                           local variable, and call the
  .catch(error => {                            next middleware function.
    console.log(`Error updating user by ID: ${error.message}`);
    next(error);
  });
}
```

Last, you need to add the routes in listing 20.7 to main.js. The path to edit a user is a straightforward route with an id parameter. The POST route to update the user from the edit form follows the same path structure but uses the update action. You're also going to reuse the redirectView action to display the view specified in your response's locals object.

Listing 20.7 Adding edit and update routes to main.js

```
router.get("/users/:id/edit", usersController.edit);
router.put("/users/:id/update", usersController.update,
 ➥ usersController.redirectView);          ◀─
                                                  Process data from the
Add routes to handle viewing.                     edit form, and display
                                                  the user show page.
```

Relaunch your application, visit the users index page, and click the edit link for a user. Try to update some values, and save.

With the ability to create, read, and update user data, you're missing only a way to remove records that you don't want anymore. The next section covers the delete function.

> **Quick check 20.2** True or false: findByIdAndUpdate is a Mongoose method.

QC 20.2 answer True. findByIdAndUpdate is a Mongoose method used to make your query more succinct and readable in your server's code. The method can't be used unless the Mongoose package is installed.

20.3 Deleting users with the delete action

To delete a user, you need only one route and a modification to your users index page. In index.ejs, add a column titled delete. As you did with the edit column, link each user to a users/:id/delete route (figure 20.3).

Figure 20.3   Users index page with delete links in your browser

> **NOTE**   You can add some basic security with an HTML onclick="return confirm('Are you sure you want to delete this record?')"

Recall that you need to use the _method=DELETE query parameter so that your application can interpret GET requests as DELETE requests. Add the code for the delete column in the users index page, as shown in listing 20.8. With the appended query parameter to send a DELETE request, this link passes the user's ID in search of an Express.js route handling DELETE requests. The confirmation script displays a modal to confirm that you want to submit the link and delete the record.

Listing 20.8 Delete link in users index.ejs

```
<td>
  <a href="<%= `users/${user._id}/delete?_method=DELETE` %>"
➥ onclick="return confirm('Are you sure you want to delete
➥ this record?')">Delete</a>    ◄──── Add a link to the delete
</td>                                      action on the index page.
```

Next, add the controller action to delete the user record by its ID. Add the code in listing 20.9 to usersController.js.

You're using the Mongoose findByIdAndRemove method to locate the record you clicked and remove it from your database. If you're successful in locating and removing the document, log that deleted user to the console and redirect in the next middleware function to the users index page. Otherwise, log the error as usual, and let your error handler catch the error you pass it.

Listing 20.9 Adding the delete action to usersController.js

```
delete: (req, res, next) => {
  let userId = req.params.id;
  User.findByIdAndRemove(userId)         Deleting a user with the
      .then(() => {                       findByIdAndRemove
        res.locals.redirect = "/users";   method
        next();
      })
      .catch(error => {
        console.log(`Error deleting user by ID: ${error.message}`);
        next();
      });
}
```

The only missing piece is the following route, which you add to main.js: router.delete ("/users/:id/delete", usersController.delete, usersController.redirectView). This route handles DELETE requests that match the path users/ plus the user's ID plus /delete. Then the route redirects to your specified redirect path when the record is deleted.

Try this new code by running the application again and visiting the users index page. Click the delete link next to one of the users, and watch it disappear from your page.

Last, to make it easier to use your new CRUD actions from a user's profile page, add the links in the following listing to the bottom of show.ejs.

Listing 20.10 Adding links for user CRUD actions to show.ejs

```
<div>
  <a href="/users">View all users</a>
</div>
<div>
  <a href="<%=`/users/${user._id}/edit`%>">
```

```
    Edit User Details
  </a>
</div>
<div>
  <a href="<%= `/users/${user._id}/delete?_method=DELETE` %>"
➡  onclick="return confirm('Are you sure you want to delete
➡  this record?')">Delete</a>
</div>
```

Add links to edit and delete a user's
account from their profile page.

The user's show page should resemble figure 20.4.

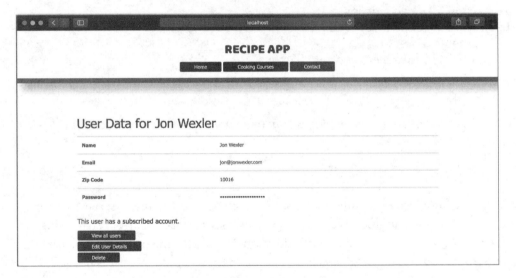

Figure 20.4   User's show page with links to edit and delete

Summary

In this lesson, you learned how to edit records and delete records from your database. You also saw how to use the `method-override` package to assist with HTML limitations in submitting certain request methods. With your CRUD functionality complete, it's time to build an application with associated models and a user interface to save meaningful data to your database. In the next capstone exercise (lesson 21), try to apply everything you've learned in this unit to build the Confetti Cuisine application.

Try this

Now that you have each CRUD function working for user accounts, make sure that the same setup is in place for groups and subscribers. Before you move on to the capstone exercise (lesson 21), make sure that all three models have working index, new, edit, and show pages. Then, as in lesson 19, try to incorporate associated models into each record's show page.

CAPSTONE: ADDING CRUD MODELS TO CONFETTI CUISINE

Confetti Cuisine is satisfied with the progress I made connecting their application to a database and setting it up to process subscriber information. They've sent me a list of cooking courses that they'd like to begin to advertise on their site. Essentially, they want subscribers to pick the courses they're most interested in attending. Then, if a subscriber later creates a user account, the business wants those two accounts to be linked.

To accomplish this task, I need to improve the Subscriber model and build the User and Course models. I need to keep the relationships between these models in mind and populate data from associated models when necessary. Last, I need to generate all the functionality needed to allow the creation, reading, updating, and deletion (CRUD) of model records. In this capstone, I'm going to create a user login form that allows a user to create an account and then edit, update, and delete the account. I'll repeat most of the process for courses and subscribers to Confetti Cuisine's newsletter.

When I'm done, I'll have an application to show the team at Confetti Cuisine that allows them to sign up new users and monitor their courses before officially launching the program.

For this purpose, I need the following:

- Schemas for the user, subscriber, and course models
- CRUD actions for all models in the application
- Views showing links between models

 ## 21.1 Getting set up

Picking up where I left off, I have a MongoDB database connected to my application, with the Mongoose package driving communication between my Subscriber model and raw documents. I'll need the same core and external packages moving forward. Additionally, I need to install the method-override package to assist with HTTP methods not currently supported by HTML links and forms. I can install this package by running the following code in my project directory in a new terminal window: npm i method-override -S. Then I require the method-override module into main.js by adding const method Override = require("method-override") to the top of the file. I configure the application to use method-override to identify GET and POST requests as other methods by adding the following line: app.use(methodOverride("_method", {methods: ["POST", "GET"]})).

Next, I need to think about how this project's directory structure will look by the time I'm done. Because I'm adding CRUD functionality to three models, I'm going to create three new controllers, three new folders within views, and three model modules. The structure resembles figure 21.1.

Notice that I'm creating only four views: index, new, show, and edit. Although delete can have its own view as a deletion confirmation page, I'll handle deletion through a link on the index page for each model.

Next, I start by improving the Subscriber model and simultaneously build out my User and Course models.

 ## 21.2 Building the models

My Subscriber model collected meaningful data for Confetti Cuisine, but they want more security on the data layer. I need to add some validators on the Subscriber schema to ensure that subscriber data meets the client's expectations before entering the database. My new schema looks like listing 21.1.

I start by requiring Mongoose into this module and pulling the Mongoose Schema object into its own constant. I create my subscriber schema by using the Schema constructor and passing some properties for the subscriber. Each subscriber is required to enter a

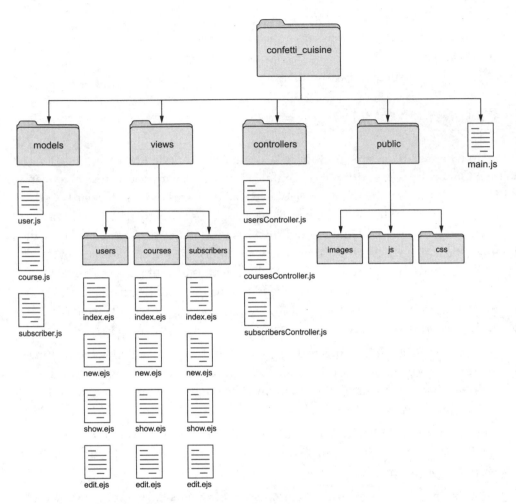

Figure 21.1   Capstone file structure

name and an email address that doesn't already exist in the database. Each subscriber can opt to enter a five-digit ZIP code. The timestamps property is an add-on provided by Mongoose to record the createdAt and updatedAt attributes for this model.

Each subscriber may subscribe to show interest in multiple courses, so this association allows subscribers to associate with an array of referenced courses. I need to create the Course model for this feature to work. getInfo is an instance method added to the subscriber schema to quickly pull any subscriber's name, email, and zipCode in one line. Exporting the Subscriber model with this new schema makes it accessible to other modules in the application.

Listing 21.1 Improved Subscriber **schema in subscriber.js**

```
const mongoose = require("mongoose"),
  { Schema } = mongoose,                    ←——— Require mongoose.
  subscriberSchema = new Schema({
  name: {
    type: String,                    Add schema
    required: true                   properties.
  },
  email: {
    type: String,
    required: true,
    lowercase: true,
    unique: true
  },
  zipCode: {
    type: Number,                              Associate
    min: [10000, "Zip code too short"],        multiple
    max: 99999                                 courses.
  },
  courses: [{type: Schema.Types.ObjectId, ref: "Course"}]
}, {
  timestamps: true
});

subscriberSchema.methods.getInfo = function () {    ←
  return `Name: ${this.name} Email: ${this.email}          Add a getInfo
 Zip Code: ${this.zipCode}`;                               instance
};                                                         method.

module.exports = mongoose.model("Subscriber",
 subscriberSchema);    ←
                            Export the
                            Subscriber model.
```

This model looks good, so I'll apply some of the same techniques to the Course and User model in course.js and user.js, respectively. Every course is required to have a title and description with no initial limitations. A course has maxStudents and cost attributes that default to 0 and can't be saved as a negative number; otherwise, my custom error messages appear.

The Course schema contains the properties in the following listing.

Listing 21.2 Properties for the Course **schema in course.js**

```
const mongoose = require("mongoose"),
  { Schema } = require("mongoose"),
  courseSchema = new Schema(
    {
      title: {
        type: String,             ←──        Require title
        required: true,                      and description.
        unique: true
      },
      description: {
        type: String,
        required: true                       Default maxStudents and
      },                                     cost to 0, and disallow
      maxStudents: {                 ←──     negative numbers.
        type: Number,
        default: 0,
        min: [0, "Course cannot have a negative number of students"]
      },
      cost: {
        type: Number,
        default: 0,
        min: [0, "Course cannot have a negative cost"]
      }
    },
    {
      timestamps: true
    }
  );
module.exports = mongoose.model("Course", courseSchema);
```

The User model contains the most fields and validations because I want to prevent a new user from entering invalid data. This model needs to link to both the Course and Subscriber models. The User schema is shown in listing 21.3.

Each user's name is saved as a first and last name attribute. The email and zipCode properties behave the same way as in Subscriber. Each user is required to have a password. As for subscribers, users are linked to multiple courses. Because subscribers may eventually create user accounts, I need to link those two accounts here. I also add the timestamps property to keep track of changes to user records in the database.

Listing 21.3 Creating the User **model in** user.js

```
const mongoose = require("mongoose"),
  { Schema } = require("mongoose"),
  Subscriber = require("./subscriber"),
  userSchema = new Schema(
    {
      name: {
        first: {                    ◄        Add first and last
          type: String,                     name attributes.
          trim: true
        },
        last: {
          type: String,
          trim: true
        }
      },
      email: {
        type: String,
        required: true,
        unique: true
      },
      zipCode: {
        type: Number,
        min: [10000, "Zip code too short"],
        max: 99999
      },
      password: {
        type: String,
        required: true        ◄    Require password.
      },
      courses: [
        {
          type: Schema.Types.ObjectId,
          ref: "Course"                  Associate users with
        }                         ◄       multiple courses.
      ],
      subscribedAccount: {
        type: Schema.Types.ObjectId,
        ref: "Subscriber"            Associate users
      }                       ◄      with subscribers.
    },
    {
      timestamps: true    ◄──────  Add timestamps property.
```

```
    }
  );
module.exports = mongoose.model("User", userSchema);
```

Two more additions I make to the user model are a virtual attribute to return the user's full name and a Mongoose pre("save") hook to link subscribers and users with the same email address. Those additions can be added directly below the schema definition in user.js and are shown in listing 21.4.

This first virtual attribute allows me to call fullName on a user to get the user's first and last names as one value. The pre("save") hook runs right before a user is saved to the database. I'm passing the next parameter so that when this function is complete, I can call the next step in the middleware chain. To link to the current user, I save the user to a new variable outside the scope of my next query. I run the query only if the user doesn't already have a linked subscribedAccount. I search the Subscriber model for documents that contain that user's email address. If a subscriber exists, I set the returned subscriber to the user's subscribedAccount attribute before saving the record and calling the next function in the middleware chain.

Listing 21.4 Adding a virtual attribute and pre("save") hook in user.js

```
userSchema.virtual("fullName").get(function() {        // Add the fullName virtual attribute.
  return `${this.name.first} ${this.name.last}`;
});

userSchema.pre("save", function (next) {               // Add a pre('save') hook to link a subscriber.
  let user = this;
  if (user.subscribedAccount === undefined) {          // Check for a linked subscribedAccount.
    Subscriber.findOne({
      email: user.email
    })                                                 // Search the Subscriber model for documents that contain that user's email.
      .then(subscriber => {
        user.subscribedAccount = subscriber;
        next();                                        // Call the next middleware function.
      })
      .catch(error => {
        console.log(`Error in connecting subscriber:
  ${error.message}`);
        next(error);
      });
  } else {
    next();
  }
});
```

With this model set up, I need to build the CRUD functionality. I start by creating the views: index.ejs, new.ejs, show.ejs, and edit.ejs.

 ## 21.3 Creating the views

For the Subscriber model, index.ejs lists all the subscribers in the database through an HTML table like the one shown in listing 21.5. This view is a table with five columns. The first three columns display subscriber data, and the last two columns link to edit and delete pages for individual subscribers. For my subscribers index page, I added some new styling (figure 21.2).

Figure 21.2   Subscribers index page in the browser

> **NOTE** Because these views have the same names across different models, I need to organize them within separate folders by model name. The views/users folder has its own index.ejs, for example.

To generate a new row for each subscriber, I loop through the subscribers variable, an array of Subscriber objects, and access each subscriber's attributes. The subscriber's name is wrapped in an anchor tag that links to that subscriber's show page by using the user's _id. The delete link requires the ?_method=DELETE query parameter appended to the path so that my method-override middleware can process this request as a DELETE request. I must remember to close my code block in EJS.

Listing 21.5 Listing subscribers in index.ejs

```
<h2 class="center">Subscribers Table</h2>
  <table class="table">                    ← Add a table to the
    <thead>                                    index page.
      <tr>
        <th>Name</th>
        <th>Email</th>
        <th>Edit</th>
        <th>Delete</th>
      </tr>
    </thead>
    <tbody>                                  Generate a new
      <% subscribers.forEach(subscriber => { %>   row for each
      <tr>                                        subscriber.
       <td>
       <a href="<%= `/subscribers/${subscriber._id}` %>">
         <%= subscriber.name %>            ←
       </a>                                  Wrap the subscriber's
       </td>                                 name in an anchor tag.
        <td><%= subscriber.email %></td>
        <td>
        <a href="<%=`subscribers/${subscriber._id}/edit` %>">
          Edit
        </a>
        </td>
        <td>
          <a href="<%=`subscribers/${subscriber._id}/delete?_method=DELETE` %>"
    onclick="return confirm('Are you sure you want to delete this
    record?')">Delete</a>                   ←
        </td>                                Add a delete link.
      </tr>
      <% }); %>
    </tbody>
  </table>
```

I'll follow this exact same structure for the course and user index pages, making sure to swap out the variable names and attributes to match their respective models.

With this index page in place, I need a way to create new records. I start with the subscriber's new.ejs form in listing 21.6. This form will submit data to the /subscribers/create path, from which I'll create new subscriber records in the subscriber's controller. Notice that the form submits data via POST request. Each input reflects the model's attributes. The name attribute of each form input is important, as I'll use it in the controller to collect the data I need to save new records. At the end of the form is a submit button.

Listing 21.6   Creating the new subscriber form in new.ejs

```
<div class="data-form">
  <form action="/subscribers/create" method="POST">    ◄── Add a form to
    <h2>Create a new subscriber:</h2>                        create new
    <label for="inputName">Name</label>                      subscribers.
    <input type="text" name="name" id="inputName" placeholder="Name"
➥ autofocus>
    <label for="inputEmail">Email address</label>
    <input type="email" name="email" id="inputEmail"
➥ placeholder="Email address" required>
    <label for="inputZipCode">Zip Code</label>
    <input type="text" name="zipCode" id="inputZipCode"
➥ pattern="[0-9]{5}" placeholder="Zip Code" required>
    <button type="submit">Create</button>
  </form>
</div>
```

I re-create this form for users and courses, making sure to replace the form's action and inputs to reflect the model I'm creating. My subscriber edit form looks like the one in figure 21.3.

Figure 21.3   Subscriber edit page in the browser

While I'm working on forms, I create the edit.ejs view, whose form resembles the one in new.ejs. The only changes to keep in mind are the following:

- *The edit form*—This form needs access to the record I'm editing. In this case, a subscriber comes from the subscriber's controller.
- *The form action*—This action points to /subscribers/${subscriber._id}/ update?_method=PUT instead of the create action.
- *Attributes*—Each input's value attribute is set to the subscriber variable's attributes, as in <input type="text" name="name" value="<%= subscriber.name %>">.

These same points apply to the edit.ejs forms for users and courses. The next listing shows my complete subscriber edit page.

Listing 21.7 The edit page for a subscriber in edit.ejs

```
<form action="<%=`/subscribers/${subscriber._id}/update
?_method=PUT` %>" method="POST">          Display the edit form
  <h2>Create a new subscriber:</h2>        for a subscriber.
  <label for="inputName">Name</label>
  <input type="text" name="name" id="inputName" value="<%=
subscriber.name %>" placeholder="Name" autofocus>
  <label for="inputEmail">Email address</label>
  <input type="email" name="email" id="inputEmail" value="<%=
subscriber.email %>" placeholder="Email address" required>
  <label for="inputZipCode">Zip Code</label>
  <input type="text" name="zipCode" id="inputZipCode"
pattern="[0-9]{5}" value="<%= subscriber.zipCode %>"
placeholder="Zip Code" required>
  <button type="submit">Save</button>
</form>
```

Last, I build the show page for each model. For subscribers, this page acts like a profile page, detailing each subscriber's information in their row on the index page. This page is fairly straightforward: I show enough data to summarize a single subscriber record. The subscribers show page has a table, created with the EJS template elements shown in the following listing. This page uses attributes from a subscriber variable to display the name, email, and zipCode.

Listing 21.8 The show page for a subscriber in show.ejs

```
<h1>Subscriber Data for <%= subscriber.name %></h1>
<table>
  <tr>
    <th>Name</th>
    <td><%= subscriber.name %></td>
  </tr>
  <tr>
    <th>Email</th>
    <td><%= subscriber.email %></td>
  </tr>
  <tr>
    <th>Zip Code</th>
    <td><%= subscriber.zipCode %></td>
  </tr>
</table>
```

Display subscriber attributes.

> **NOTE** For some of these views, I'll add links to navigate to other relevant pages for that model.

Something else I want to add to the show page is code that shows whether the record is associated with any other records in the database. For a user, that code showing an associated record could display using an additional tag at the bottom of the page to show whether the user has a subscribedAccount or associated courses. For subscribers, I'll add a line to show the number of subscribed courses, as shown in listing 21.9.

This one line gives Confetti Cuisine insight into the number of courses to which people are subscribing. I could take this line a step further by using the Mongoose populate method on this subscriber to show the associated course details.

Listing 21.9 Show the number of subscribed courses in show.ejs

```
<p>This subscriber has <%= subscriber.courses.length %> associated
  course(s)</p>
```

Display the number of associated courses.

The last step is bringing the models and views together with the controller actions and routes.

21.4 Structuring routes

The forms and links for Confetti Cuisine are ready to be displayed, but there's still no way to reach them via a browser. In main.js, I'm going to add the necessary CRUD routes and require the controllers needed to get everything working.

First, I add the routes for subscribers from listing 21.10 to main.js. To make sure that the subscribersController is required near the top of the file alongside my other controllers, I add const subscribersController = require("./controllers/subscribersController"). I also introduce the Express.js Router to my project to help distinguish application routes from other configurations in main.js by adding const router = express.Router(). With this router object in place, I change every route and middleware handled by my app object to use the router object. Then I tell my application to use this router object by adding app.use("/", router) to main.js.

GET requests to the /subscribers path lead me to the index action on the subscribers-Controller. Then I render the index.ejs page through another action called indexView. The same strategy applies to the other GET routes. The first POST route is for create. This route handles requests from forms to save new subscriber data. l need to create the logic to save new subscribers in the create action. Then I use an action called redirectView that will redirect to one of my views after I successfully create a subscriber record.

The show route is the first case in which I need to get the subscriber's ID from the path. In this case, :id represents the subscriber's ObjectId, allowing me to search for that specific subscriber in the database in the show action. Then I use a showView to display the subscriber's data in a view. The update route works like the create route, but I'm specifying the router to accept only PUT requests, indicating that a request is being made specifically to update an existing record. Similarly, I use the redirectView action after this to display a view. The last route, delete, accepts only DELETE requests. Requests will be made from the link on index.ejs and use the redirectView to link back to the index page.

Listing 21.10 Adding subscriber CRUD routes to main.js

Add GET routes to show views.

Add the first POST route for create.

```
router.get("/subscribers", subscribersController.index,
⇨ subscribersController.indexView);
router.get("/subscribers/new", subscribersController.new);
router.post("/subscribers/create", subscribersController.create,
⇨ subscribersController.redirectView);
```

```
router.get("/subscribers/:id", subscribersController.show,
  ⇒ subscribersController.showView);
router.get("/subscribers/:id/edit", subscribersController.edit);
router.put("/subscribers/:id/update", subscribersController.update,
  ⇒ subscribersController.redirectView);
router.delete("/subscribers/:id/delete",
  ⇒ subscribersController.delete,
  ⇒ subscribersController.redirectView);
```

Add a route to show
a subscriber based
on ObjectId.

Add a route to
update subscribers.

Add a route to delete
subscribers.

The same seven routes need to be made for users and courses. I'll also update the navigation links: the contact link will point to the subscribers' new view, and the course-listings link will point to the courses' index view.

> **NOTE** At this point, I can remove some of my deprecated routes, such as the ones that point to getAllSubscribers, getSubscriptionPage, and saveSubscriber in the subscribers controller, as well as showCourses in the home controller. I can also move my home-page route to the home controller's index action. Finally, I want to make sure that I update my navigation links to point to /subscribers/new instead of /contact.

All I have left to do is create the corresponding controllers.

21.5 Creating controllers

The routes I created in main.js require a subscribersController, coursesController, and usersController. I start by creating those files in the controllers folder.

> **NOTE** I've also cleaned up my error controller to use http-status-codes and an error.ejs view, as in previous application examples.

Next, for the subscriber's controller, I add the actions shown in listing 21.11 to handle requests made to my existing routes. After requiring the Subscriber model into this file, I create the index action to find all subscriber documents in my database and pass them through the subscribers variable into index.ejs via the indexView action. The new and edit actions also render a view to subscribe and edit subscriber data.

The create action collects request body parameters in my custom getSubscriberParams function, listed as the second constant in the code listing, to create a new subscriber record. If I'm successful, I'll pass the user object through the locals variables object in my response. Then I'll specify to redirect to the index page in the redirectView action.

The show action pulls the subscriber's ID from the URL with req.params.id. This value is used to search the database for one matching record and then pass that record to the next middleware function through the response object. In showView, the show page displays the contents of this subscriber variable. The update action behaves like create and uses the findByIdAndUpdate Mongoose method to set new values for an existing subscriber document. Here, I also pass the updated user object through the response object and specify a view to redirect to in the redirectView action.

The delete action uses the subscriber's ID in the request parameters to findByIdAndRemove a matching document from the database. The getSubscriberParams function is designed to have less repetition in my code. Because the create and update actions use form parameters, they can call this function instead. The redirectView action is also intended to reduce code repetition by allowing multiple actions, including the delete action, to specify what view to render when the main function is complete.

> **Listing 21.11** Adding subscriber controller actions in subscribersController.js

```
const Subscriber = require("../models/subscriber"),
  getSubscriberParams = (body) => {          ← Create a custom function
    return {                                    to pull subscriber data
      name: body.name,                          from the request.
      email: body.email,
      zipCode: parseInt(body.zipCode)
    };
  };

module.exports = {                             Create the index
  index: (req, res, next) => {                 action to find all
    Subscriber.find()                          subscriber documents.
      .then(subscribers => {
        res.locals.subscribers = subscribers;
        next();
      })
      .catch(error => {
        console.log(`Error fetching subscribers: ${error.message}`);
        next(error);
      });
  },
  indexView: (req, res) => {
    res.render("subscribers/index");
  },
```

```
new: (req, res) => {
  res.render("subscribers/new");
},

create: (req, res, next) => {
  let subscriberParams = getSubscriberParams(req.body);
  Subscriber.create(subscriberParams)
    .then(subscriber => {
      res.locals.redirect = "/subscribers";
      res.locals.subscriber = subscriber;
      next();
    })
    .catch(error => {
      console.log(`Error saving subscriber:${error.message}`);
      next(error);
    });
},

redirectView: (req, res, next) => {
  let redirectPath = res.locals.redirect;
  if (redirectPath) res.redirect(redirectPath);
  else next();
},
show: (req, res, next) => {
  var subscriberId = req.params.id;
  Subscriber.findById(subscriberId)
    .then(subscriber => {
      res.locals.subscriber = subscriber;
      next();
    })
    .catch(error => {
      console.log(`Error fetching subscriber by ID:
${error.message}`)
      next(error);
    });
},

showView: (req, res) => {
  res.render("subscribers/show");
},

edit: (req, res, next) => {
  var subscriberId = req.params.id;
  Subscriber.findById(subscriberId)
    .then(subscriber => {
```

Create the create action to create a new subscriber.

Create the show action to display subscriber data.

```
      res.render("subscribers/edit", {
        subscriber: subscriber
      });
    })
    .catch(error => {
      console.log(`Error fetching subscriber by ID:
${error.message}`);
      next(error);
    });
  },

  update: (req, res, next) => {
    let subscriberId = req.params.id,
      subscriberParams = getSubscriberParams(req.body);

    Subscriber.findByIdAndUpdate(subscriberId, {
      $set: subscriberParams
    })
      .then(subscriber => {
        res.locals.redirect = `/subscribers/${subscriberId}`;
        res.locals.subscriber = subscriber;
        next();
      })
      .catch(error => {
        console.log(`Error updating subscriber by ID:
${error.message}`);
        next(error);
      });
  },

  delete: (req, res, next) => {
    let subscriberId = req.params.id;
    Subscriber.findByIdAndRemove(subscriberId)
      .then(() => {
        res.locals.redirect = "/subscribers";
        next();
      })
      .catch(error => {
        console.log(`Error deleting subscriber by ID:
${error.message}`);
        next();
      });
  }
};
```

Create the update action to set new values for an existing subscriber document.

Create the delete action to remove a subscriber document.

With these controller actions in place for each model, the application is ready to boot and manage records. I load the views for each model and then create new subscribers, courses, and users. In unit 5, I improve Confetti Cuisine's site by adding user authentication and a login form.

 ## Summary

In this capstone exercise, I improved Confetti Cuisine's application by adding CRUD functionality to three new models. These models allow subscribers to sign up for Confetti Cuisine's upcoming course offerings and create user accounts to get involved with the cooking class product. In unit 5, I clean up these views by adding flash messaging, password security, and user authentication with the passport module.

Authenticating user accounts

In unit 4, you built CRUD functions for the models in your application. You also learned how Mongoose and some external packages can help you define associations between your models and display data from referenced models in your browser.

In this unit, you learn about flash messaging with sessions and cookies, data encryption, and user authentication. You start by implementing basic session storage to handle small messages called *flash messages* between requests. Then you modify your User model to handle password encryption with the bcrypt package. After setting up your first login form, you use bcrypt to authenticate users by comparing their login data with their encrypted passwords in your database. In the last lesson, you reimplement user authentication—the process of confirming that an account is valid before allowing users access to the application. You explore methods of authenticating accounts, encrypting passwords for security, and offering tools for normal users to move around in your application with tools provided by Passport.js. By the end of the unit, you'll be able to sign up new users and even begin building logic based on user data in your database.

This unit covers the following topics:

- Lesson 22 discusses sessions and shows how to preserve your users' login status by storing information on the client side. You learn how to apply flash messages; these short messages, passed between pages, let you know whether some server operation was successful.

- Lesson 23 guides you through the process of building a sign-up form. You've built forms before in this book, but this form handles a user's email and password, so you need to take a slightly different approach to ensure that your data is safe and consistent. With the help of the bcrypt package, an encryption algorithm makes sure that no plain-text passwords are saved to your database. At the end of the lesson, you apply additional validation middleware with express-validator.

- Lesson 24 teaches you how to add application authentication for your users. With the help of the Passport.js middleware and some helpful npm packages, this lesson adds a layer of security to your application and the User model. You also modify your view layout to access your login form quickly, display any currently logged-in users, and provide a way to log out quickly.

- Lesson 25 wraps up the unit by guiding you through the construction of necessary user encryption and authentication for the Confetti Cuisine application. You apply flash messages, validation middleware, encryption, and a robust authentication process.

Start cooking in lesson 22 by adding cookies to your application.

ADDING SESSIONS AND FLASH MESSAGES

In this lesson, you clean up the flow between CRUD functions by passing messages between pages to find out whether the server operations were successful or certain types of errors occurred. Currently, error messages are logged to the console, and users of the application have no way to know what they could do differently. You use sessions and cookies alongside the `connect-flash` package to deliver these messages to your views. By the end of the lesson, you'll have an application that gives you a visual description of the success or failure of operations.

This lesson covers

- Setting up sessions and cookies
- Creating flash messages in your controller actions
- Setting up validation middleware on incoming data

Consider this   Your recipe application is starting to collect data through the view forms you created in unit 4. Users are beginning to get frustrated, though, because they don't know what validations you have in place, and if they fail to meet your validator expectations, they're redirected to a different page without notice.

With some helpful packages, you can incorporate flash messaging into your application to inform your users of specific errors that occur in your application.

22.1 Setting up flash message modules

Flash messages are semipermanent data used to display information to users of an application. These messages originate in your application server and travel to your users' browsers as part of a session. *Sessions* contain data about the most recent interaction between a user and the application, such as the current logged-in user, length of time before a page times out, or messages intended to be displayed once.

You have many ways to incorporate flash messages into your application. In this lesson, you use the `connect-flash` middleware module by typing `npm i connect-flash -S` in terminal to install its package to your application as a dependency.

> **NOTE** Sessions used to be a dependency of Express.js, but because not everyone uses every Express.js dependency and because it's difficult to keep dependencies up to date with the main package, independent packages `cookie-parser` and `express-session` must be installed.

Now you need to install two more packages by running `npm i cookie-parser express-session -S` in terminal. Then require these three modules—`connect-flash`, `cookie-parser`, and `express-session`—in your main.js file, along with some code to use the modules (listing 22.1).

You need the `express-session` module to pass messages between your application and the client. These messages persist on the user's browser but are ultimately stored in the server. `express-session` allows you to store your messages in a few ways on the user's browser. Cookies are one form of session storage, so you need the `cookie-parser` package to indicate that you want to use cookies and that you want your sessions to be able to parse (or decode) cookie data sent back to the server from the browser.

Use the `connect-flash` package to create your flash messages. This package is dependent on sessions and cookies to pass flash messages between requests. You tell your Express.js application to use `cookie-parser` as middleware and to use some secret passcode you choose. `cookie-parser` uses this code to encrypt your data in cookies sent to the browser, so choose something that's hard to guess. Next, you have your application use sessions by telling `express-session` to use `cookie-parser` as its storage method and to expire cookies after about an hour.

You also need to provide a secret key to encrypt your session data. Specify that you don't want to send a cookie to the user if no messages are added to the session by setting `saveUninitialized` to false. Also specify that you don't want to update existing session data on the server if nothing has changed in the existing session. Last, have the application use `connect-flash` as middleware.

> **NOTE** In this example, the secret key is shown in plain text in your application server file. I don't recommend displaying your secret key here, however, because it opens your application to security vulnerabilities. Instead, store your secret key in an environment variable, and access that variable with `process.env`. I discuss this topic further in unit 8.

Listing 22.1 Requiring flash messaging in main.js

```
const expressSession = require("express-session"),
  cookieParser = require("cookie-parser"),            Require the three
  connectFlash = require("connect-flash");            modules.
router.use(cookieParser("secret_passcode"));
router.use(expressSession({                            Configure your
  secret: "secret_passcode",                           Express.js application
  cookie: {                                            to use cookie-parser
    maxAge: 4000000                                    as middleware.
  },
  resave: false,                                       Configure express-
  saveUninitialized: false                             session to use
}));                                                   cookie-parser.
router.use(connectFlash());                            Configure your application
                                                       to use connect-flash as
                                                       middleware.
```

All together, these three packages provide middleware to help you process incoming requests and outgoing responses with necessary cookie data.

Cookie parsing

With each request and response made between the server and client, an HTTP header is bundled with the data sent across the internet. This header contains a lot of useful information about the data being transferred, such as the size of the data, the type of data, and the browser the data is being sent from.

Another important element in the request header is the cookies. *Cookies* are small files of data sent from the server to the user's browser, containing information about the interaction between the user and the application. A cookie might indicate which user accessed the application last, whether the user logged in successfully, and even what requests the user made, such as whether he successfully, created an account or made multiple failed attempts.

In this application, you use encrypted cookies with a secret passcode encryption key to store information about each user's activity on the application and whether the user is still logged in, as well as short messages to display in the user's browser to let them know if any errors occurred on their most recent request.

NOTE   Because requests are independent of one another, if one request to create a new user fails and you're redirected to the home page, that redirect is another request, and nothing is sent in the response to the user to let them know that their attempt to create an account failed. Cookies prove to be helpful in this case.

As you create your custom secret keys, remember to make them a bit more difficult for someone else to guess. Next, you use these added modules by setting up flash messaging on your controller actions.

> **Quick check 22.1**   How does a cookie's secret key change the way that data is sent and stored on a browser?

22.2 Adding flash messages to controller actions

To get flash messages working, you need to attach them to the request made before you render a view to the user. Generally, when a user makes a GET request for a page—say, to load the home page—you don't need to send a flash message.

Flash messages are most useful when you want to notify the user of a successful or failed request, usually involving the database. On these requests, such as for user creation, you're typically redirecting to another page, depending on the outcome. If a user is created, you redirect to the /users route; otherwise, you can redirect to /user/new. A flash message is no different from a local variable being made available to the view. For that reason, you need to set up another middleware configuration for express to treat your connectFlash messages like a local variable on the response, as shown in listing 22.2.

By adding this middleware function, you're telling Express to pass a local object called flashMessages to the view. The value of that object is equal to the flash messages you create with the connect-flash module. In this process, you're transferring the messages from the request object to the response.

Listing 22.2 **Middleware to associate** connectFlash **to flashes on response**

```
router.use((req, res, next) => {
  res.locals.flashMessages = req.flash();
  next();
});
```

Assign flash messages to the local flashMessages variable on the response object.

With this middleware in place, you can add messages to req.flash at the controller level and access the messages in the view through flashMessages. Next, add a flash message to the create action in your usersController by changing the action's code to match listing 22.3.

In this action, you're modifying the way that you handle errors in the catch block. Instead of passing the error to the error-handler action, set the error flash message, and allow the redirectView action to display the user's new.ejs page again. The first flash message is of type success and delivers the message that the user's account was created. The flash message delivered when the account isn't created is of type error.

> **NOTE** getUserParams has been borrowed from the last capstone exercise (lesson 21). This function is reused throughout the controller to organize user attributes in one object. You should create the same functions for your other model controllers.

Listing 22.3 **Adding flash messages to the create action in usersController.js**

```
create: (req, res, next) => {
  let userParams = getUserParams(req.body);
  User.create(userParams)
    .then(user => {
      req.flash("success", `${user.fullName}'s account created
  successfully!`);
      res.locals.redirect = "/users";
      res.locals.user = user;
      next();
    })
    .catch(error => {
      console.log(`Error saving user: ${error.message}`);
      res.locals.redirect = "/users/new";
      req.flash(
        "error",
        `Failed to create user account because: ${error.message}.`
      );
      next();
    });
},
```

Respond with a success flash message.

Respond with a failure flash message.

> **NOTE** Although you use the request object here to store the flash messages temporarily, because you connected these messages to a local variable on the response, the messages ultimately make it to the response object.

As soon as the page is redirected to /users or /users/new, your flash message is available to the view.

> **NOTE** error and success are two flash-message types that I made up. You can customize these types however you like. If you want a flash message of type superUrgent, you can use req.flash("superUrgent", "Read this message ASAP!"). Then superUrgent will be the key used to get whatever message you attach.

The last step in getting flash messages working is adding some code to the view to receive and display the messages. Because you want every view to show potential success or failures, add the code in listing 22.4 to layout.ejs. You may also want to add custom styles in your public/css folder so that the messages can be differentiated from normal view content.

First, check whether any flashMessages exist. If success messages exist, display the success messages in a div. If error messages exist, display those messages with a differently styled class.

Listing 22.4   Adding flash messages in layout.ejs

```
<div class="flashes">
  <% if (flashMessages) { %>                    Check whether
    <% if (flashMessages.success) { %>          flashMessages exist.    Display success
      <div class="flash success"><%= flashMessages.success %></div>     messages.
    <% } else if (flashMessages.error) { %>
      <div class="flash error"><%= flashMessages.error %></div>
    <% } %>
  <% } %>                                        Display error
</div>                                           messages.
```

> **TIP** If you don't see any messages on the screen at first, try removing all styling surrounding the message to get the plain-text message in the view.

Test the new code to display flash messages by starting the Node.js application, visiting /users/new, and filling out the form to create a new user. If you create a new user successfully, your page on redirect should look like figure 22.1.

Figure 22.1 Successful flash message shown on the /users page

If you try to create a new user with an existing email address, your redirect screen should resemble figure 22.2.

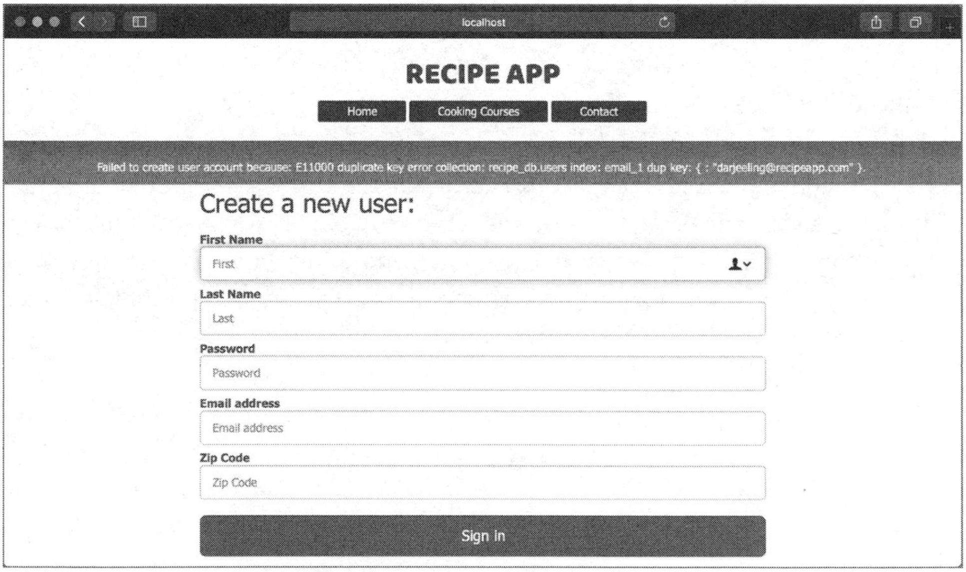

Figure 22.2 Error flash message shown on the home page

When you refresh the page or create any new request, this message disappears. Because you may choose to send multiple success or error messages, you may find it useful to loop through the messages on the view instead of displaying everything mapped to the error and success keys.

If you need to show a flash message on a view you're rendering, pass the message directly as a local variable. The next listing shows how to add a success message to the user's index page. When you pass the flashMessages object directly to the view, you don't need to wait for a redirect or use connect-flash.

Listing 22.5   Adding a flash message to the rendered index view

```
res.render("users/index", {
  flashMessages: {
    success: "Loaded all users!"
  }
});              Pass the flash messages
                with a rendered view.
```

Quick check 22.2   What two arguments are needed for the req.flash method?

 Summary

In this lesson, you learned about sessions and cookies, and saw why they're integral parts of how data is transferred between the server and client. You also set up connect-flash to use cookies and temporarily show success and failure messages on certain views. In lesson 23, you see how to encrypt more than cookie data by implementing encryption on user passwords.

QC 22.2 answer   req.flash needs a flash-message type and a message.

. . . .

Try this

Now that you have flash messaging set up, it's time to add it to all your CRUD actions. You want your users to see whether their attempt to subscribe, create an account, delete an account, or update user information was successful. Add flash messages for each action involving your database for all three models.

BUILDING A USER LOGIN AND HASHING PASSWORDS

In lesson 22, you added flash messages to your controller actions and views. In this lesson, you dive deeper into the User model by creating a sign-up and login form. Then you add a layer of security to your application by hashing users' passwords and saving your users' login state. Next, you add some more validations at the controller level with the help of the express-validator package. By the end of this lesson, a user should be able to create an account, have their password saved securely in your database, and log in or log out as they like.

This lesson covers

- Creating a user log-in form
- Hashing data in your database with bcrypt

Consider this You deliver a prototype of your recipe application in which users can create accounts and store their unencrypted passwords in your database. You're reasonably concerned that your database might get hacked or (even more embarrassing) that you might show user passwords in plain text to all users. Luckily, security is a big concern in the programming world, and tools and security techniques are available to protect sensitive data from being exposed. bcrypt is one such tool you'll use to mask passwords in your database so that they can't be hacked easily in the future.

23.1   Implementing the user login form

Before you dive into the logic that will handle users logging into the recipe application, establish what their sign-up and login forms will look like.

The sign-up form will look and behave like the form in new.ejs. Because most users will create their own accounts through a sign-up form, you'll refer to the create view and create action for new user registrations. The form you need but don't have yet is the user login form. This form takes two inputs: email and password.

First, create a basic user login view, and connect it with a new route and controller actions. Then create a new login.ejs view in the users folder with the code from the next listing. Notice the important addition here: the /users/login action in the form tag. You need to create a route to handle POST requests to that path.

Listing 23.1   Creating a user login form in login.ejs

```
<form action="/users/login" method="POST">
  <h2>Login:</h2>
  <label for="inputEmail">Email address</label>
  <input type="email" name="email" id="inputEmail"
  placeholder="Email address" required>
  <label for="inputPassword">Password</label>
  <input type="password" name="password" id="inputPassword"
  placeholder="Password" required>
  <button type="submit">Login</button>
</form>
```

Add a form for user login.

Next, add the login route by adding the code in listing 23.2 to main.js. The first route allows you to see the login form when a GET request is made to the /users/login path. The second route handles POST requests to the same path. In this case, you route the request to the authenticate action, followed by the redirectView action to load a page.

> **NOTE**   You'll want to add these routes above the lines where you have your show and edit routes; otherwise, Express.js will mistake the word login in the path for a user ID and try to find that user. When you add the route above those lines, your application will identify the full path as the login route before looking for a user ID in the URL.

Listing 23.2 Adding the login route to main.js

```
router.get("/users/login", usersController.login);
router.post("/users/login", usersController.authenticate,
➥ usersController.redirectView);
```

> Add a route to handle POST requests to the same path.

> Add a route to handle GET requests made to the /users/login path.

Create the necessary controller actions in your users controller to get the login form working. Add the code from listing 23.3 to usersController.js.

The login action renders the login view for user login. The authenticate action finds one user with the matching email address. Because this attribute is unique in the database, it should find that single user or no user at all. Then the form password is compared with the database password and redirected to that user's show page if the passwords match. As in previous actions, set the res.locals.redirect variable to a path that the redirect-View action will handle for you. Also set a flash message to let the user know they've logged in successfully, and pass the user object as a local variable to that user's show page. By calling next here, you invoke the next middleware function, which is redirect-View. If no user is found, but no error occurred in the search for a user, set an error flash message, and set the redirect path to take the user back to the login form to try again.

If an error occurs, log it to the console, and pass the error to the next middleware function that handles errors (in your errors controller).

Listing 23.3 Adding login and authenticate actions to usersController.js

```
login: (req, res) => {
  res.render("users/login");
},
authenticate: (req, res, next) => {
  User.findOne({
    email: req.body.email
  })
      .then(user => {
        if (user && user.password === req.body.password){
          res.locals.redirect = `/users/${user._id}`;
          req.flash("success", `${user.fullName}'s logged in successfully!`);
          res.locals.user = user;
          next();
```

> Add the login action.

> Add the authenticate action.

> Compare the form password with the database password.

```
    } else {
        req.flash("error", "Your account or password is incorrect.
➥ Please try again or contact your system administrator!");
        res.locals.redirect = "/users/login";
        next();
    }
  })
    .catch(error => {
        console.log(`Error logging in user: ${error.message}`);
        next(error);
    });
}
```

Log errors to the
console, and redirect.

At this point, you should be able to relaunch your Node.js application and visit the users/login URL to see the form in figure 23.1. Try logging in with the email address and password of a user in your database.

Figure 23.1   Example of user login page in your browser

If you type an incorrect email or password, you're redirected to the login screen with a flash message like the one in figure 23.2. If you log in successfully, your screen will look like figure 23.3.

You have a problem, though: the passwords are still being saved in plain text. In the next section, I talk about ways to hash that information.

Figure 23.2   Failed user login page in your browser

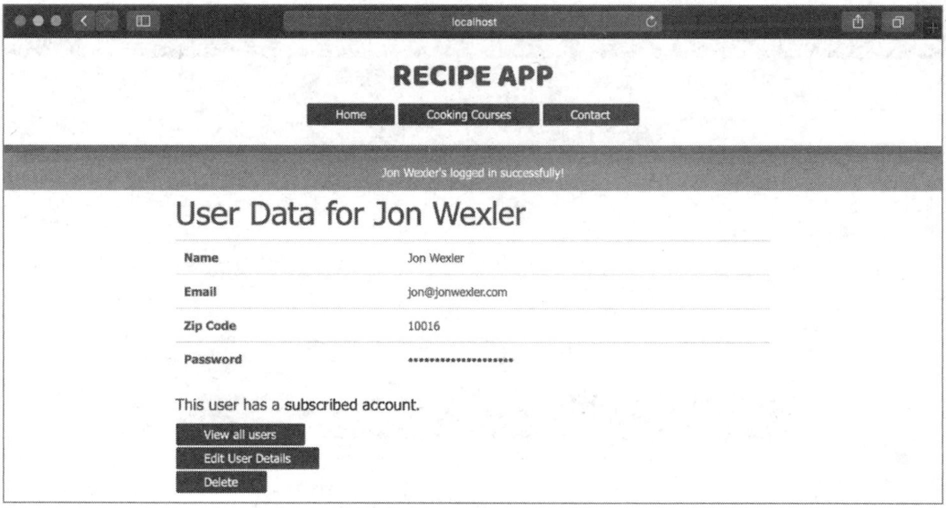

Figure 23.3   Successful user login page in your browser

Quick check 23.1   Why does the placement of the /users/login route matter in main.js?

QC 23.1 answer   Because you have routes that handle parameters in the URL, if those routes (such as /users/:id) come first, Express.js will treat a request to /users/login as a request to the user's show page, where login is the :id. Order matters: if the /users/login route comes first, Express.js will match that route before checking the routes that handle parameters.

23.2 Hashing passwords

Encryption is the process of combining some unique key or passphrase with sensitive data to produce a value that represents the original data but is otherwise useless. The process includes hashing data, the original value of which can be retrieved with a private key used for the hashing function. This *hashed* value is stored in the database instead of the sensitive data. When you want to encrypt new data, pass that data through the encryption algorithm. When you want to retrieve that data or compare it with, say, a user's input password, the application can use the same unique key and algorithm to decrypt the data.

bcrypt is a sophisticated hashing function that allows you to combine certain unique keys in your application to store data such as passwords in your database. Fortunately, you can use a few Node.js packages to implement bcrypt hashing. First, install the bcrypt package by typing npm i bcrypt@3.0.0 -S in a new terminal window. Next, require bcrypt into the module where you'll perform the hashing. Hashing can occur in the usersController, but a better approach is to create a Mongoose pre-save hook in the User model. Require bcrypt in user.js with const bcrypt = require("bcrypt"). Then add the code in listing 23.4 to your User model, above the module.exports line but after your schema definition.

> **NOTE** You'll only be hashing passwords, not encrypting them, because you technically don't want to retrieve the original value of a password. In fact, your application should have no knowledge of a user's password. The application should be able only to hash a password. Later, hash password attempts, and compare the hashed values. I talk more about this topic later in this section.

The Mongoose pre and post hooks are great ways to run some code on the User instance before and after the user is saved to the database. Attach the hook to the userSchema, which (like other middleware) takes next as a parameter. The bcrypt.hash method takes a password and a number. The number represents the level of complexity against which you'd like to hash your password, and 10 is generally accepted as a reliable number. When the hashing of the password is complete, the next part of the promise chain accepts the resulting hash (your hashed password).

Assign the user's password to this hash, and call next, which saves the user to the database. If any errors occur, they'll be logged and passed to the next middleware.

> **NOTE** Because you lose context within this pre-hook when you run bcrypt.hash, I suggest preserving this in a variable that can be accessed within the hashing function.

passwordComparison is your custom method on the userSchema, allowing you to compare passwords from a form's input with the user's stored and hashed password. To perform this check asynchronously, use the promise library with bcrypt. bcrypt.compare returns a Boolean value comparing the user's password with the inputPassword. Then return the promise to whoever called the passwordComparison method.

Listing 23.4 Adding a hashing pre hook in user.js

```
userSchema.pre("save", function(next) {          ← Add a pre hook to
  let user = this;                                  the user schema.

  bcrypt.hash(user.password, 10).then(hash => {   ← Hash the user's
    user.password = hash;                            password.
    next();
  })
    .catch(error => {
      console.log(`Error in hashing password: ${error.message}`);
      next(error);
    });                              Add a function to compare
});                                  hashed passwords.

userSchema.methods.passwordComparison = function(inputPassword){  ←
  let user = this;
  return bcrypt.compare(inputPassword, user.password);   ←
};
                                     Compare the user
                                     password with the
                                     stored password.
```

> **NOTE**   A pre hook on save is run any time the user is saved: on creation and after an update via the Mongoose save method.

The final step is rewriting the authenticate action in usersController.js to compare passwords with bcrypt.compare. Replace the code block for the authenticate action with the code in listing 23.5.

First, explicitly query for one user by email. If a user is found, assign the result to user. Then check whether a user was found or null is returned. If a user with the specified email address is found, call your custom passwordComparison method on the user instance, passing the form's input password as an argument.

Because passwordComparison returns a promise that resolves with true or false, nest another then to wait for a result. If passwordsMatch is true, redirect to the user's show page. If a user with the specified email doesn't exist or the input password is incorrect, return to the login screen. Otherwise, throw an error, and pass it in your next object. Any errors thrown or occurring during this process are caught and logged.

Listing 23.5 Modifying the `authenticate` action in usersController.js

```
authenticate: (req, res, next) => {                      Query for one user by email.
  User.findOne({email: req.body.email})
      .then(user => {                                    Check whether
        if (user) {                                      a user is found.
          user.passwordComparison(req.body.password)     Call the password
              .then(passwordsMatch => {                  comparison method
                if (passwordsMatch) {                    on the User model.
                  res.locals.redirect = `/users/${user._id}`;
                  req.flash("success", `${user.fullName}'s logged in
  successfully!`);
                  res.locals.user = user;
                } else {
                  req.flash("error", "Failed to log in user account:
  Incorrect Password.");
                  res.locals.redirect = "/users/login";
                }
                next();                                  Call the next middleware
              });                                         function with redirect path
        } else {                                          and flash message set.
          req.flash("error", "Failed to log in user account: User
  account not found.");
          res.locals.redirect = "/users/login";
          next();
        }
      })                                                 Log errors to console and
      .catch(error => {                                  pass to the next
        console.log(`Error logging in user: ${error.message}`);   middleware error handler.
        next(error);
      });
}
```

Check whether the passwords match.

Relaunch your Node.js application, and create a new user. You'll need to create new accounts moving forward because previous account passwords weren't securely hashed with bcrypt. If you don't, bcrypt will try to hash and compare your input password with a plain-text password. After the account is created, try logging in again with the same password at /users/login. Then change the password field in the user's show page to display the password on the screen. Visit a user's show page to see the new hashed password in place of the old plain-text one (figure 23.4).

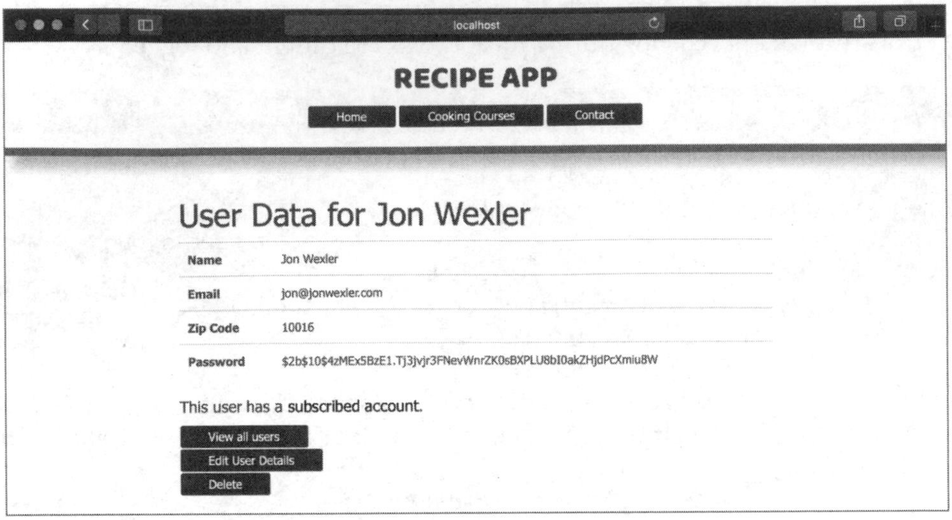

Figure 23.4   Show hashed password in user's show page in browser

> **NOTE**   You can also verify that passwords are hashed at the database level by entering the MongoDB shell with `mongo` in a new terminal window and then typing `use recipe_db` and `db.users.find({})`. Alternatively, you can use the MongoDB Compass software to see the new records in this database.

Now when you log in for a user with a hashed password, you should be redirected to that user's show page upon successful authentication. If you type an incorrect password, you get a screen like figure 23.5.

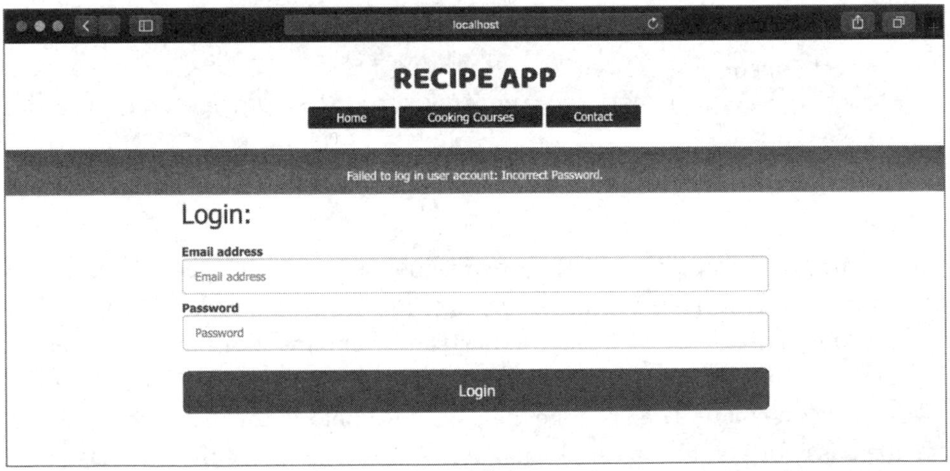

Figure 23.5   Incorrect password screen in browser

In the next section, you add some more security to the create and update actions by adding validation middleware before those actions are called.

> **Quick check 23.2** True or false: bcrypt's `compare` method compares the plain-text password in your database with the plain-text value from the user's input.

 ## 23.3 Adding validation middleware with express-validator

So far, your application offers validation at the view and model levels. If you try to create a user account without an email address, your HTML forms should prevent you from doing so. If you get around the forms, or if someone tries to create an account via your application programming interface (API), as you see in unit 6, your model schema restrictions should prevent invalid data from entering your databases—though more validation can't hurt. In fact, if you could add more validation before your models are reached in the application, you could save a lot of computing time and machine energy spent making Mongoose queries and redirecting pages.

For those reasons, you'll validate middleware, and as is true of most common needs in Node.js, some packages are available to help you build those middleware functions. The package you'll install is `express-validator`, which provides a library of methods you can use to check whether incoming data follows a certain format and methods that modify that data to remove unwanted characters. You can use `express-validator` to check whether some input data is entered in the format of a U.S. phone number, for example.

You can install this package by typing `npm i express-validator -S` in your project folder in terminal. When this package is installed, require it with `const expressValidator = require("express-validator")` in main.js, and tell your Express.js app to use it by adding `router.use(expressValidator())`. You need to add this line after the line where `express.json()` and `express.urlencoded()` middleware is introduced, because the request body must be parsed before you can validate it.

QC 23.2 answer False. The only password value in the database is a hashed password, so there's no plain-text value to compare against. The comparison works by hashing the user's new input and comparing the newly created hashed value with the stored hash value in the database. This way, the application still won't know your actual password, but if two hashed passwords match, you can safely say that your input matched the original password you set up.

Then you can add this middleware to run directly before the call to the create action in the usersController. To accomplish this task, you need to create a validate action between the path and create action in the POST route to /users/create in main.js, as shown in listing 23.6. Between the path, /users/create, and the usersController.create action, you introduce a middleware function called validate. Through this validate action, you'll determine whether data meets your requirements to continue to the create action.

Listing 23.6 Adding the validate middleware to the users create route in main.js

```
router.post("/users/create", usersController.validate,
➥ usersController.create, usersController.redirectView);
```

Add the validate middleware to the users create route.

Finally, create the validate action in usersController.js to handle requests before they reach the create action. In this action, you add the following:

- *Validators*—Check whether incoming data meets certain criteria.
- *Sanitizers*—Modify incoming data by removing unwanted elements or casting the data type before it enters the database.

Add the code in listing 23.7 to your usersController.js.

The first validation function uses the request and response, and it may pass on to the next function in the middleware chain, so you need the next parameter. Start with a sanitization of the email field, using express-validator's normalizeEmail method to convert all email addresses to lowercase and then trim whitespace away. Follow with the validation of email to make sure that it follows the email-format requirements set by express-validator.

The zipCode validation ensures that the value isn't empty and is an integer, and that the length is exactly five digits. The last validation checks that the password field isn't empty. req.getValidationResult collects the results of the previous validations and returns a promise with those error results.

If errors occur, you can collect their error messages and add them to your request's flash messages. Here, you're joining the series of messages with " and " in one long String. If errors have occurred in the validations, set req.skip = true. Here, set is the new custom property you're adding to the request object. This value tells your next middleware function, create, not to process your user data because of validation errors and instead to skip to your redirectView action. For this code to work, you need to add if (req.skip) next() as the first line in the create action. This way, when req.skip is true, you continue to the next middleware immediately.

In the event of validation errors, render the new view again. Your flashMessages also indicate to the user what errors occurred with her input data.

Listing 23.7 Creating a `validate` **controller in usersController.js**

Add the validate function.

```
validate: (req, res, next) => {
  req.sanitizeBody("email").normalizeEmail({
    all_lowercase: true
  }).trim();
  req.check("email", "Email is invalid").isEmail();
  req.check("zipCode", "Zip code is invalid")
.notEmpty().isInt().isLength({
    min: 5,
    max: 5
  }).equals(req.body.zipCode);
  req.check("password", "Password cannot be empty").notEmpty();

  req.getValidationResult().then((error) => {
    if (!error.isEmpty()) {
      let messages = error.array().map(e => e.msg);
      req.skip = true;
      req.flash("error", messages.join(" and "));
      res.locals.redirect = "/users/new";
      next();
    } else {
      next();
    }
  });
}
```

Remove whitespace with the trim method.

Validate the zipCode field.

Validate the password field.

Collect the results of previous validations.

Set skip property to true.

Set redirect path for the new view.

Add error messages as flash messages.

Call the next middleware function.

> **NOTE** You can take many creative approaches to repopulating form data. You may find that some packages are helpful in assisting with this task. When you find the technique that works best for you, change all the forms in your application to handle repopulating data.

You're ready to give these validations a shot. Launch your application, and create a new user in ways that should fail your validations. You may need to remove the required tags from your HTML forms first if you want to test the notEmpty validations. Your failed password and zipCode validations should send you to a screen resembling figure 23.6.

Because express-validator uses the validator package, you can get more information about the sanitizers to use at https://github.com/chriso/validator.js#sanitizers.

Figure 23.6   Failed `express-validator` validation messages

Quick check 23.3   What's the difference between a sanitizer and a validator?

 **Summary**

In this lesson, you implemented a hashing function for your users' passwords. Then you created a login form and action by using the `bcrypt.compare` method to match hashed passwords against user input on login. At the end, you added more validations on input data through an additional middleware function to sanitize data before it's saved to your database. In lesson 24, you take another look at encryption and authentication through Passport.js tools, which make setting up secure user accounts much easier.

QC 23.3 answer   A sanitizer cleans data by trimming whitespace, changing the case, or removing unwanted characters. A validator tests data quality to ensure that the way it was entered meets your database requirements.

- -

Try this

Hashing user passwords is probably the leading scenario for using hashing functions, but you can use hashing functions on other fields on your models. You might hash a user's email address to prevent that data from getting into the wrong hands, for example. After all, getting access to a user's email is getting halfway to hacking that user's account. Try adding hashing to user emails in addition to passwords.

> **NOTE** When you hash a user's email address, you won't be able to display it in any views. Although you may choose to keep user emails in plain text, this practice is good to follow when other sensitive data enters your application.

ADDING USER AUTHENTICATION

In lesson 23, you learned about manual hashing of passwords and the importance of securing user data. In this lesson, you explore some popular and useful tools that make the hashing process less messy. You modify your hashing methods to use the `passport-local-mongoose` package, which uses `passport` and `mongoose` together to perform hashing for you behind the scenes. Next, you learn how to use Passport.js to authenticate user accounts on your application. This process involves session cookies, similar to the way that flash messages use them. By the end of this lesson, you'll have a sign-up and login form that permits only true users of your application to have access.

This lesson covers

- Using the `passport` package to authenticate users throughout your application
- Implementing the `passport-local-mongoose` plugin on your user model
- Creating authentication actions before user login

Consider this   You've added a popular hashing method to your application, but you'd like to simplify the code or, better, put it behind the scenes. It's great to know how hashing works, and tools are available to perform the hashing you want without the need to manually set up your own criteria for hashing. Packages such as `passport.js` hash and authenticate user interactions without your needing to specify a password field in the schema. In this lesson, you look at the quickest and most efficient implementations of the `passport` package.

24.1   Implementing Passport.js

Passport.js is middleware used by Node.js to hash new user passwords and authenticate their activity on an application. Passport.js uses different methods to create and log in user accounts, ranging from basic login with username and password to login with third-party services such as Facebook. These login methods are called *strategies*, and the strategy you'll use for your recipe application is a local strategy because you aren't using external services.

These strategies check whether incoming data is authentic by managing hashing and comparison of passwords and data relating to the user's login state. For more information about the Passport.js strategies, visit www.passportjs.org.

To start, install the necessary packages for your application. You need to install the passport package along with the passport-local-mongoose packages by running npm i passport passport-local-mongoose -S in your project's terminal window. The modules from these packages work together to provide hashing and authentication methods and support to communicate directly with your Mongoose schemas. After you install these packages as dependencies, require them where needed in the application. Add the following lines from listing 24.1 to main.js.

Start by requiring the passport module. Passport.js uses methods called strategies for users to log in. The local strategy refers to the username and password login method. You initialize the passport module and have your Express.js app use it. Now you have passport ready as middleware in your application. passport.session tells passport to use whatever sessions you've already set up with your application. In this case, before this line, you have express-session set up for flash messaging.

Listing 24.1   Requiring and initializing passport in main.js

Require the
passport module.

```
const passport = require("passport");
router.use(passport.initialize());            Initialize passport.
router.use(passport.session());
```

Configure passport
to use sessions in
Express.js.

Next, you need to set up your login strategy on the user model and tell passport to handle the hashing of user data in sessions for you. passport-local-mongoose makes this process simple and pretty much automatic. Add the lines in listing 24.2 to main.js.

> **NOTE** passport.session tells passport to use any previously used Express.js sessions defined. Sessions must be defined before this line.

You need to make sure that your user model is made available in main.js before you continue to connect it with passport. Normally, you'd need to set up some configurations to create a login strategy for a model, but because you're using the default local login strategy, you only need to tell passport to use the strategy created for the user model. The next two lines tell passport to serialize and deserialize your users through the User model. These lines direct the process of encrypting and decrypting user data stored in sessions.

Listing 24.2 Setting up passport serializing in main.js

```
                                              Require the
                                              User model.
const User = require("./models/user");   ◄─        Configure the user's
passport.use(User.createStrategy());     ◄────     login strategy.
passport.serializeUser(User.serializeUser());   ◄─
passport.deserializeUser(User.deserializeUser());  )
                                         Set up passport to
                                         serialize and deserialize
                                         your user data.
```

Passport serializes and deserializes user data to pass into a session. The session stores this serialized data—a condensed form of user information, which is sent back to the server to verify the user as the last one logged in from the client. Deserializing extracts the user data from its condensed version so that you can verify the user's information.

> **Serializing data**
>
> When working with objects in an application, you want to preserve the data structure that allows you to access and modify properties easily. Your user objects, for example, allow you to retrieve information such as email or even to use the User model's virtual attribute fullName. Although the model is particularly useful within your application, you have no straightforward way to send this user object, along with its methods and Mongoose object-document mapper (ODM) tools, to a client. As a result, you need to serialize the user data.

Serialization is the process of converting data from some data structure to a compact readable format. This data can take on many formats, such as JSON, YAML, and XML. The user data is flattened, often into strings, so that it can be sent within an HTTP transaction.

Passport.js performs the serialization process and encrypts your user's data so that it can be stored as part of the session cookie on the client's browser. Because this cookie contains information about the user, it lets your application server know, the next time a request occurs, that this user has logged in before, which is your way of validating someone's state in your application.

When the same user makes another request to your application, Passport.js deserializes the data to restore the user to its original model object form. When that process completes and you verify that the user is valid, you can use the user object again as before, applying model methods and using Mongoose queries.

The last step before building the authentication action to log users into your application is to connect your user model to the passport-local-mongoose module. Add const passportLocalMongoose = require("passport-local-mongoose") to the top of user.js, which is where you'll add a Passport.js plugin to the user schema, as shown in listing 24.3. Using the Mongoose plugin method, you're telling your userSchema to use passportLocalMongoose for password hashing and storage. You're also telling passportLocalMongoose to use the email field as the user's login parameter instead of a username because username is the default field for this module.

NOTE This line must appear before you register your User model.

Listing 24.3 Adding the passport-local-mongoose plugin to the user schema

```
userSchema.plugin(passportLocalMongoose, {
  usernameField: "email"
});
```
Apply the passport-local-mongoose module as a plugin to the user schema.

When this line is in place, Passport.js automatically takes care of password storage, so you can remove the password property from userSchema. This plugin modifies your schema behind the scenes to add hash and salt fields to your User model in place of the normal password field.

Hash and salt

You learned about hashing in lesson 24, but you let bcrypt perform the hashing process through an algorithm that you didn't need to understand. Exactly how do bcrypt and Passport.js hash user passwords?

Modern hashing takes the user's input password and converts it into an undecipherable hash. This hash is a jumble of characters and numbers, making it safer to store in a database than the plain-text password. If anyone hacks the database, he has only the hashed passwords. The best he can do at that point is enter his own guesses at a password into his own hashing function to see whether the resulting hash matches yours. That task is a tedious one, but it's not impossible for hackers to find a way to crack your hashed passwords. Salts were introduced to battle this vulnerability.

Salts are short strings of random characters that are added to a plain-text password before the password is hashed. This way, if someone maliciously guessed your password, they would also need to know the salt associated with it and where to place it in the original password. Hacking has become a lot more difficult.

Passport.js stores both the hashed password and salt in your database so that you can perform hashing consistently within your application. When you register your first users with Passport.js, take a look at their data in MongoDB to see those values by following these steps:

- In a new terminal window, run mongo.
- Run use `recipe_db` to load your recipe database.
- Run db.users.find({}, { password: 1}) to view all user passwords.
- Compare the hashed and nonhashed passwords.

NOTE   Make sure that any reference to the `password` attribute in your application is removed. Because `passport-local-mongoose` adds new password fields to the User model, you won't be using it anymore.

In the next section, you use the `passport` package to simplify the authentication process even more.

Quick check 24.1   True or false: A `salt` is needed to hash passwords.

QC 24.1 answer   False. Salts help make the hashing of passwords stronger by mixing random text with plain-text passwords before they're hashed, but salts aren't required.

24.2 Modifying the create action to use passport registration

Using Passport.js has already simplified your code and made it easier to specify which models you'd like to hash and authenticate. The next step is modifying your create action, so instead of using your bcrypt hashing function before creating a user account, you'll use Passport.js. By incorporating the Passport.js modules, you have access to a library of methods to streamline the account registration process. Change the create action in usersController.js to use the register method, as shown in listing 24.4.

> **NOTE** You must comment out or remove the userSchema.methods.passwordComparison and pre("save") hook for bcrypt in the User model. If you don't remove these hooks, bcrypt will still try to hash user passwords before passport is able to, which also results in an unhandled promise error.

The register method comes with Passport.js. Because you're using passport-local-mongoose as a plugin for the User model, you can use this method to register users. If you successfully save a new user, create a flash message and redirect to the /users route. Otherwise, handle any errors that occur by redirecting to the users/new route so that another attempt to create a user account can be made.

Listing 24.4 Registering new users in the create action in main.js

```
create: (req, res, next) => {
  if (req.skip) next();                                    Register new users.

  let newUser = new User( getUserParams(req.body) );

  User.register(newUser, req.body.password, (error, user) => {
    if (user) {
      req.flash("success", `${user.fullName}'s account created
successfully!`);
      res.locals.redirect = "/users";           Set redirect for successful
      next();                                    user creation.
    } else {
      req.flash("error", `Failed to create user account because:
${error.message}.`);
      res.locals.redirect = "/users/new";
      next();
    }                          Set redirect and log
  });                          errors in flash
}                              messages.
```

With this action in place, you can use the form in /users/new.ejs to create user accounts through Passport.js. Try launching your application and creating a new user. You shouldn't notice a change in behavior; your user account will be created, and you'll see the success flash message.

If you look at the raw documents in MongoDB by typing mongo in a new terminal window, then type use recipe_db and db.users.find({}) to see the users in your database. Any users saved with bcrypt still have their password field with a hashed password saved. Your latest user has two properties added by Passport.js: salt and hash.

> **TIP** Update your seed.js file to register user accounts with passport instead of the Mongoose create method. This practice makes it easier to repopulate your database as your application grows in development.

Update your seed.js file to register user accounts with Passport instead of the Mongoose create method, which will make it easier to repopulate your database as your application grows in development.

Your users are still secure, but you still need a way to log them in. In the next section, you modify the login form to use Passport.js.

> **Quick check 24.2** Why does Passport.js need you to save the hash and the salt in your database?

 ## 24.3 Authenticating users at login

The final step in allowing users to log in to the application is replacing the bcrypt authentication method with passport middleware. Modify your authenticate action in usersController.js with the new action, as shown in listing 24.5. You also need to require passport into the users controller by adding const passport = require("passport") to the top of the file.

This authenticate action is set to call passport.authenticate method directly with passport redirect and flash-message options. When you call usersController.authenticate, you're calling passport.authenticate. In this function, passport attempts to compare the incoming

> **QC 24.2 answer** Passport.js saves the salt and the hash so that each user can have their own unique hashing factors. It's possible to use the same salt for every user account and only store the hash in the database, but this approach is less secure.

request data, describing a user, with the database records. If a user account is found and the input password aligns with the hashed password, you redirect from this action.

Listing 24.5 Adding passport authentication middleware in usersController.js

```
authenticate: passport.authenticate("local", {
    failureRedirect: "/users/login",
    failureFlash: "Failed to login.",
    successRedirect: "/",
    successFlash: "Logged in!"
}),
```

Call on passport to authenticate a user via the local strategy.

Set up success and failure flash messages and redirect paths based on the user's authentication status.

The login route no longer needs your usersController.redirectView action as a follow-up function. With your router.post("/users/login", usersController.authenticate); route set up from lesson 23, your application is ready to authenticate existing users. Restart your application, and log in with a user account you've created at /users/login. If you're successful, you should see the success flash message.

It would be nice to have a visual indication that you're logged in and maybe a way to log out. Add the code from listing 24.6 to your navigation bar in layout.ejs. You're checking whether the local variable loggedIn is set to true. If so, display the text Signed in as followed by the user's fullName, which you get from the currentUser local variable. This list item is wrapped in an anchor tag that, when clicked, takes you to the currently logged-in user's show page. If the loggedIn status is false, show a link to Sign In, taking you to the /users/login route.

Listing 24.6 Adding login status to navigation bar in layout.ejs

Check whether a user is logged in.

```
<% if (loggedIn) { %>
  Logged in as  <a href="<%=`/users/${currenLUser._id}`%>">
  <%= currentUser.fullName %></a>
<%} else {%>                            Display a link to log in.
  <a href="/users/login">Log In</a>
<% } %>
```

If you refresh your application, you may not see anything change in the navigation bar yet. You need to create the loggedIn and currentUser variables so that they appear locally in each view. To do so, add some custom middleware so that on every new request, you add these variables to the response. Because you've already created a middleware function to set up flashMessages as a local object, you can add the code in listing 24.7 within that middleware function in main.js.

isAuthenticated is a method provided by Passport.js, which you can call on the incoming request to see whether an existing user is stored in the request's cookies. loggedIn is either true or false. If a user is in the request, you can pull it out and assign it to your own currentUser variable. After adding this code, you gain access to both of these variables, along with flashMessages, on every page.

Listing 24.7 Adding local variables to custom middleware

Set up the loggedIn
variable to reflect
passport login status.

```
res.locals.loggedIn = req.isAuthenticated();   ←
res.locals.currentUser = req.user;  ←
```

Set up the currentUser to
reflect a logged-in user.

Restart your application to see whether your name appears in the navigation bar. Your screen may look like figure 24.1.

This figure includes a logout link in the navigation bar. To create this link, add <a href="/users/logout">Log out</a> below the line where the name of the currentUser appears. To get this link working, you need to create a route and action for logging out.

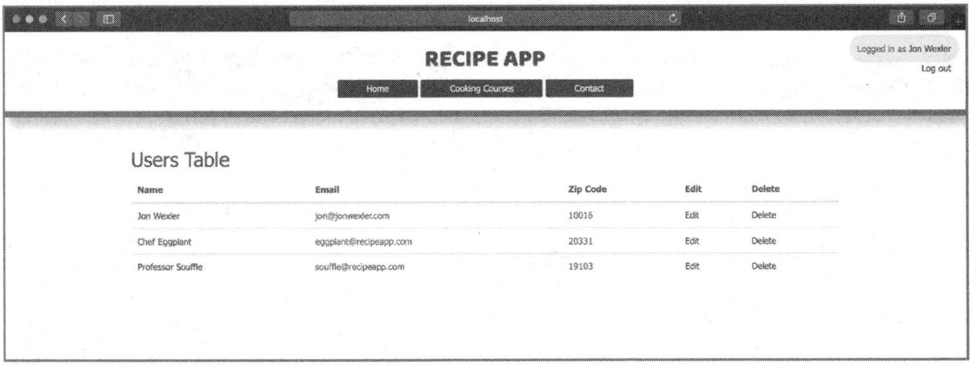

Figure 24.1   Example of a successful login in the browser

First, add router.get("/users/logout", usersController.logout, usersController.redirect-View) to main.js next to where your login routes are located. Then add the logout action from listing 24.8 to usersController.js.

This action uses the logout method provided by Passport.js on the request to clear the user's session. During the next pass through your custom middleware, isAuthenticated returns false, and there'll no longer be a current user. Follow this operation with a flash message to indicate that the user has been logged out and a redirect to the home page through the redirectView action.

Listing 24.8 Adding a logout action in usersController.js

```
logout: (req, res, next) => {          Add an action to
  req.logout();                        log users out.
  req.flash("success", "You have been logged out!");
  res.locals.redirect = "/";
  next();
}
```

With this action in place, it's time to test the full login process. Restart your application, log in, and then click the logout link in the navigation bar (figure 24.2). Your session should be cleared and your account successfully logged out.

In lesson 25, you apply user authentication to the capstone project.

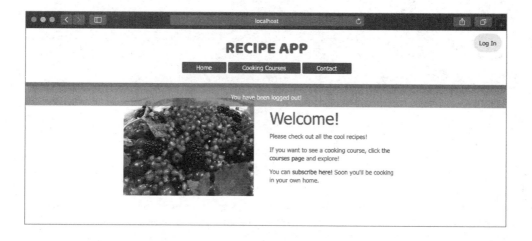

Figure 24.2 Example of a successful user logout in the browser

Quick check 24.3   How do you have access to Passport.js methods on the request through-out the application?

 **Summary**

In this lesson, you added a few Passport.js packages to assist in the encryption and authentication of user data. By connecting an additional validation action to your user-login middleware chain, you can ensure that user passwords are secure and the login experience is consistent. In the next capstone lesson (lesson 25), you apply these valida-tion, hashing, encryption, and authentication techniques to improve the Confetti Cui-sine application experience.

Try this

You've successfully implemented Passport.js to work with your User model and Mon-goose ODM. Because Passport.js does a lot of the heavy lifting for you, it may seem that there isn't much else to add to the login process, but you always have room for more middleware. Add a middleware function, called logEmail, between validation and encryption. This middleware should log to console the user's email address domain (such as gmail, yahoo, or live) and pass to the next middleware function.

CAPSTONE: ADDING USER AUTHENTICATION TO CONFETTI CUISINE

My contacts at Confetti Cuisine are delighted with the progress on their application. They've already started to add new course offerings, manage new subscribers, and spread the word about creating new user accounts. I warn them that although user accounts can be created, the application isn't ready to handle users securely.

The client and I agree that data encryption and proper user authentication are the way forward, so for my next improvements to the application, I'm going to add a couple of packages that use Passport.js to assist in setting up a secure user-login process. I'll also add flash messaging so that users can tell after a redirect or page render whether their last operation was successful. Then I'll add some additional validations with the help of the express-validator middleware package.

By the end of this stage of development, I can comfortably encourage Confetti Cuisine to sign users up for their application. Because the application isn't yet live online, though, the client will have to run it locally on their machines when users sign up.

For this capstone exercise, I'll need to do the following:

- Add sessions and cookies between page requests
- Add new custom middleware for validations and setting up local variables in the views

- Create a login form
- Add passport authentication and encryption for the User model
- Add a visual indicator to show which user is logged in

 ## 25.1   Getting set up

Working off the code I wrote in the last capstone exercise (lesson 21), I currently have three models implemented with CRUD actions for each. To move forward with the improvements to Confetti Cuisine's application, I need to install a few more packages:

- express-session allows me to store temporary data about the user interaction with the application. The resulting sessions let me know whether a user has logged in recently.
- cookie-parser allows me to store session data on the client. The resulting cookies are sent with each request and response, carrying within them messages and data reflecting the user who last used that client.
- connect-flash allows me to use sessions and cookies to generate flash messages in the user's browser.
- express-validator allows me to add a layer of validations to incoming user data through a middleware function.
- passport allows me to set up a painless encryption and authentication process for the User model.
- passport-local-mongoose allows me to integrate passport even further by simplifying the code I need to write through a plugin I can use on the User model.

To install these packages, I'll run npm i express-session cookie-parser connect-flash express-validator passport passport-local-mongoose -S in my projects terminal window. I've already set up the create action and new form for users. I need to modify those soon, but first, I'll create the login form needed for users to log in to the application.

 ## 25.2   Creating a login form

I want this form to contain two straightforward inputs: email and password. I'll create a new login.ejs view in the users folder and add the code in the next listing. This form will submit a POST request to the /users/login route. The inputs of this form will handle the user's email and password.

```
<form class="form-signin" action="/users/login" method="POST">
  <h2 class="form-signin-heading">Login:</h2>
  <label for="inputEmail" class="sr-only">Email</label>
  <input type="text" name="email" id="inputEmail" class="form-
  control" placeholder="Email" autofocus required>
  <label for="inputPassword" class="sr-only">Password</label>
  <input type="password" name="password" id="inputPassword"
    class="form-control" placeholder="Password" required>
  <button class="btn btn-lg btn-primary btn-block" type="submit">
  Login</button>
</form>
```

Create a login form.

Before this form can work or be viewed, I'll add the login routes and actions. The login will accept GET and POST requests, as shown in the following listing.

> **NOTE** I add all routing-specific code on the router object.

Listing 25.2 Adding a login route to main.js

```
router.get("/users/login", usersController.login);
router.post("/users/login", usersController.authenticate);
router.get("/users/logout", usersController.logout,
  usersController.redirectView );
```

Route to the login action.

Add a route to logout and redirect to a view.

Send posted data to an authenticate action.

With these routes in place, I need to create their corresponding actions before my form is viewable at /users/login. First, I'll add the login action from the next listing to users-Controller.js.

Listing 25.3 Adding the login action to usersController.js

```
login: (req, res) => {
  res.render("users/login");
}
```

Add an action to render my form for browser viewing.

In the next section, I use the passport package to start encrypting user data so that this login form will have a purpose.

25.3 Adding encryption with Passport.js

To start using Passport.js, I need to require the passport module in main.js and in users-Controller.js by adding const passport = require("passport") to the top of both files. These files are ones within which I'll set up hashing and authentication. Next, I need to initialize and use passport within Express.js as middleware. Because passport uses sessions and cookies, I also need to require express-session and cookie-parser to main.js, adding the lines in listing 25.4 to that file.

To start using passport, I need to configure cookieParser with a secret key to encrypt the cookies stored on the client. Then I'll have Express.js use sessions as well. This stage in the setup process is where passport starts to store information about active users of the application. passport officially becomes middleware by telling Express.js to initialize and use it on this line. Because sessions were set up before this line, I instruct Express.js to have passport use those preexisting sessions for its user data storage.

I set up the default login strategy, provided through the passport-local-mongoose module that I'll soon add to the User model, to enable authentication for users with passport. The last two lines allow passport to compact, encrypt, and decrypt user data as it's sent between the server and client.

Listing 25.4 Adding passport with Express.js in main.js

```
const passport = require("passport"),
  cookieParser = require("cookie-parser"),
  expressSession = require("express-session"),
  User = require("./models/user");

router.use(cookieParser("secretCuisine123"));
router.use(expressSession({
  secret: "secretCuisine123",
  cookie: {
    maxAge: 4000000
  },
  resave: false,
  saveUninitialized: false
}));
router.use(passport.initialize());
router.use(passport.session());
passport.use(User.createStrategy());
```

Configure cookieParser with a secret key.

Configure Express.js to use sessions.

Configure Express.js to initialize and use passport.

Instruct passport to use sessions.

Set up the default login strategy.

```
passport.serializeUser(User.serializeUser());
passport.deserializeUser(User.deserializeUser());
```

Set up passport to compact, encrypt, and decrypt user data.

NOTE I need to make sure that the User model is required in main.js before I can use the createStrategy method. This method works only after I set up the User model with passport-local-mongoose.

With this configuration set up, I can move to the User model in user.js to add passport-local-mongoose. I need to require passport-local-mongoose in my User model by adding const passportLocalMongoose = require("passport-local-mongoose") to the top of user.js.

In this file, I attach the module as a plugin to userSchema, as shown in listing 25.5. This line sets up passportLocalMongoose to create salt and hash fields for the User model in my database. It also treats the email attribute as a valid field for logging in an authenticating. This code should be placed just above the module.exports line.

Listing 25.5 **Adding** passport-local-mongoose **as a plugin to the User model**

```
userSchema.plugin(passportLocalMongoose, {
  usernameField: "email"
});
```

Add the passport-local-mongoose module as a user schema plugin.

NOTE With this addition to my User model, I no longer need the plain-text password property in the user schema. I'll remove that property now, as well as the password table row on the user show page.

In the next section, I modify the create action in usersController.js to use passport for registering new users, and I set up flash messaging so that the user will know whether account creation is successful.

 ## 25.4 Adding flash messaging

With sessions and cookies ready to attach data to the request and respond to the user, I'm ready to integrate flash messaging by using connect-flash. To configure connect-flash, I need to require it in main.js as a constant, called connectFlash, by adding the following line: const connectFlash = require("connect-flash"). Then I tell my Express.js app to use it as middleware by adding router.use(connectFlash()) to main.js.

Now that the middleware is installed, I can call `flash` on any request in my application, which allows me to attach messages to the request. To get these request flash messages to my response, I add some custom middleware in main.js, as shown in listing 25.6. By telling the Express.js app to use this custom middleware, I'm able to assign a local variable called `flashMessages` to objects containing flash messages created in my controller actions. From here, I'll be able to access the `flashMessages` object in my views.

Listing 25.6 Adding custom middleware to use flash messaging in main.js

```
router.use((req, res, next) => {
  res.locals.flashMessages = req.flash();    ← Assign flash
  next();                                        messages to a
});                                              local variable.
```

Because I want flash messages to appear on every page, I'll add some code to my layout .ejs file to look for `flashMessages` and display them if they exist. I'll add the code in listing 25.7 to layout.ejs above the `<%- body %>`.

I intend to show only success and error messages. First, l check whether `flashMessages` is defined; then I display success messages or error messages that are attached to the object.

Listing 25.7 Adding logic to use flash messaging in layout.ejs

```
                                           Display flash
                                           messages in the view.
<div class="flashes">
<% if (flashMessages) { %>  ←
  <% if (flashMessages.success) { %>
    <div class="flash success"><%= flashMessages.success %></div>
  <% } else if (flashMessages.error) { %>
    <div class="flash error"><%= flashMessages.error %></div>
  <% } %>
<% } %>
</div>
```

Finally, I test this newly added code by modifying my user's `create` action to use `passport` and flash messaging by adding the code in listing 25.8 to usersController.js. The `create` action uses the `register` method provided by Passport.js to create a new user account. The result is a user document in my database with a hashed password and salt. If the user is saved successfully, I add a `success` flash message to be displayed in the `index` view. Otherwise, I show an `error` message on the user creation page.

> **Listing 25.8 Adding passport registration and flash messaging in the create action**

```
create: (req, res, next) => {          ← Add the create action
  if (req.skip) next();                    to register users.

  let newUser = new User(getUserParams(req.body));

  User.register(newUser, req.body.password, (e, user) => {
    if (user) {
      req.flash("success", `${user.fullName}'s account
  created successfully!`);
        res.locals.redirect = "/users";        ← Respond with
      next();                                      flash messages.
    } else {
      req.flash("error", `Failed to create user account
  because: ${e.message}.`);
      res.locals.redirect = "/users/new";
      next();
    }
  });
}
```

With this action in place, I'm ready to demo my new Passport.js registration process with flash messaging. Next, I add some custom validations before users are created.

 ## 25.5   Adding validation middleware with express-validator

The express-validator module provides useful methods for sanitizing and validating data as it enters this application. I start by requiring the module in main.js by adding const expressValidator = require("express-validator") and telling my Express.js application to use this module as middleware by adding router.use(expressValidator()) to the same file.

I know that I want data to pass through some middleware validation function before it reaches the create action in the usersController, so I change my /users/create route to take that requirement into consideration, as shown in listing 25.9. This validate action lives in usersController and runs before the create action, which ensures that my custom validation middleware filters bad data before it gets a chance to reach my User model.

Listing 25.9   Adding a validation action before create in main.js

```
router.post("/users/create", usersController.validate,
    usersController.create, usersController.redirectView);
```
Add validation
middleware to the
user create route.

Then I create the `validate` action in usersController.js by using the code in listing 25.10. This `validate` action parses incoming requests and cleans the data in the request body. In this case, I'm trimming whitespace from the `first` and `last` name fields.

I use some other methods provided by `express-validator` to keep the emails in my database consistent and the ZIP codes at the required length. I'll also check to make sure that users entered some password when they signed up. I collect any errors that may have occurred during the validation steps. Then I concatenate the error messages into a single string. I set a property on the request object, `req.skip = true`, so that I skip the `create` action and go directly back to the view. All flash messages display in the users/new view. If there are no errors, I call `next` to move to the `create` action.

Listing 25.10   Adding a `validate` action in usersController.js

```
validate: (req, res, next) => {        Add the validate action.
  req
    .sanitizeBody("email")
    .normalizeEmail({
      all_lowercase: true
    })
    .trim();
  req.check("email", "Email is invalid").isEmail();
  req
    .check("zipCode", "Zip code is invalid")
    .notEmpty()
    .isInt()
    .isLength({
      min: 5,
      max: 5                          Sanitize and check
    })                                input field data.
    .equals(req.body.zipCode);
  req.check("password", "Password cannot be empty").notEmpty();
  req.getValidationResult().then((error) => {
    if (!error.isEmpty()) {
      let messages = error.array().map(e => e.msg);
```

```
        req.skip = true;
        req.flash("error", messages.join(" and "));
        res.locals.redirect = '/users/new';
        next();
    } else {
        next();
    }
  });
}
```

Collect errors, and
respond with flash
messages.

The application is ready to validate data for user creation. The last step is connecting my login form to an authentication action I set up earlier.

 ## 25.6 Adding authentication with Passport.js

Passport.js makes my life easier by providing some default methods to use as middleware on requests. When I added passport-local-mongoose, my User model inherited even more useful methods than passport offered alone. Because the passport-local-mongoose module was added as a plugin on the User model, a lot of the authentication setup was taken care of behind the scenes.

The register method is one of the most powerful and intuitive methods provided by passport. To use it, I need to call passport.register and pass the login strategy that I plan to use. Because I'm using the default local strategy, I can create my authenticate action in usersController.js to use the passport.authenticate method as shown in listing 25.11.

> **NOTE** I need to make sure that const passport = require("passport") is at the top of my users controller.

This action points directly to the passport.register method. I've already created a local strategy for my User model in main.js and told passport to serialize and deserialize user data upon successful authentication. The options I add here determine which path to take if authentication succeeds or fails, with flash messages to go along.

Listing 25.11 Adding an authenticate **action in usersController.js**

```
authenticate: passport.authenticate("local", {
  failureRedirect: "/users/login",
  failureFlash: "Failed to login.",
  successRedirect: "/",
  successFlash: "Logged in!"
})
```

Add authentication
middleware with
redirect and flash-
message options.

I'm ready to test authentication with my login form at /users/login. Everything should be working at this point to log an existing user into the application. I need only to put some finishing touches on my layout file and add a logout link.

 ## 25.7 Logging in and out

I've already gotten the login process working. Now I'd like to add some visual indication that a user is logged in. First, I set up some variables that help me know whether there's an unexpired session for a logged-in user. To do so, I add the code in listing 25.12 to my custom middleware, where I added the flashMessages local variable, in main.js.

With this middleware function, I have access to loggedIn to determine whether an account is logged in via the client from which the request was sent. isAuthenticated tells me whether there's an active session for a user. currentUser is set to the user who's logged in if that user exists.

Listing 25.12 Adding local variables to the response through middleware

```
res.locals.loggedIn = req.isAuthenticated();        ◀── Set up the loggedIn
res.locals.currentUser = req.user;    ◀──                variable to reflect
                                                         passport login
         Set up the currentUser variable                status.
         to reflect a logged-in user.
```

Now I can use these variables by adding the code in listing 25.13 to the navigation bar in my layout. I check to see whether loggedIn is true, telling me that a user is logged in. If so, I display the fullName of the currentUser linked to that user's show page and a logout link. Otherwise, I display a sign-in link.

Listing 25.13 Adding a login status to my navigation bar in layout.ejs

```
<div class="login">                     Check whether a
  <% if (loggedIn) { %>  ◀──            user is logged in.
    <p>Logged in as
      <a href="<%=`/users/${currentUser._id}`%>">
  <%= currentUser.fullName %></a>
      <a href="/users/logout">Log out</a>
    </p>                      ◀────────────────
  <%} else {%>                                      Display the current user's
    <a href="/users/login">Log In</a>               name and logout link.
  <% } %>
</div>
```

Finally, with my /users/logout route already in place, I need to add the logout action to my usersController, as shown in listing 25.14. This action uses the logout method on the incoming request. This method, provided by passport, clears the active user's session. When I redirect to the home page, no currentUser exists, and the existing user is successfully logged out. Then I call the next middleware function to display the home page.

Listing 25.14 Adding a logout action to usersController.js

```
logout: (req, res, next) => {                    Add an action to
  req.logout();                                  log users out.
  req.flash("success", "You have been logged out!");
  res.locals.redirect = "/";
  next();
}
```

With this last piece working, I can tell my contacts at Confetti Cuisine to advertise user accounts. When they log in successfully, the screen will look like figure 25.1. I'm confident that the registration and login process is safer, more reliable, and more intuitive than it was before.

Figure 25.1   Successful login on Confetti Cuisine

 **Summary**

In this capstone exercise, I improved the Confetti Cuisine application by adding a few packages to make incoming data secure and more transparent to the user. With sessions and cookies installed, I'm able to use packages like passport and connect-flash to share information between the server and client about a user's interaction with the Confetti Cuisine application. I added encryption to user passwords and two new user attributes set up by the passport-local-mongoose plugin on the User model. With stricter validations, my custom validate action serves as middleware to filter unwanted data and make sure form data meets my schema requirements. Last, with authentication in place, passport offers a way to track which users are logged in to my application, allowing me to cater specific content to registered users who are actively involved. In the next unit, I'll add a few features to search content within the application, and in doing so, build an API on the server.

Building an API

In unit 5, you added some new features to allow users to log in to your application securely. This addition allows you to start distinguishing content that you'd like to show only to logged-in users, not the general public. After all, you probably want users to be able to delete only their own content, not that of others. These improvements increase the possibilities of browser interaction by your users. Internet browsers, however, are only one of many types of clients that may want to interact with your data.

In this lesson, I discuss how to make better use of your application programming interfaces (APIs). An *API* is the method through which clients can interact with your application data. Currently, that interaction is through rendered HTML pages, available to only web clients, though you may want to modify your controller actions to respond to different types of requests with various formats of the same data. You can use other data formats through XML or JSON. You may want to access the course listings from within a user's edit page without switching views, for example. Maybe you have unsaved content in the edit form, and you'd like to look quickly at the list of courses without having to update your user data.

In the first lesson, you set up a basic API with RESTful routes to respond with course listings in JSON format. Then you use client-side JavaScript to display the data on the screen. At the end of the unit, you'll apply some security barriers to your API to prevent unwanted requests from getting access to your database.

This unit covers the following topics:

- Lesson 26 introduces you to the way APIs are used in the tech industry and ways of responding with different data formats. In this lesson, you organize your routes for a more maintainable API and use query params to determine the type of data with which you respond.
- Lesson 27 shows how to use AJAX through the client-side JavaScript to load data in a view without refreshing the page. In this lesson, you create a new route and handle incoming requests to a /api namespace.
- Lesson 28 guides you through basic approaches you can take to secure your API when there's no way to sign in users visually.

Lesson 29 wraps up the unit by providing the steps you need to make AJAX requests to load Confetti Cuisine course data from the user's profile page. Then you can enroll a user without leaving the profile page.

ADDING AN API TO YOUR APPLICATION

In this lesson, you take a first look at reorganizing your routing structure and responding with data. First, you create new folders to house the routes you've built in main.js. The new structure follows some of the application programming interface (API) conventions you set up in earlier lessons. Next, you modify some controller actions to respond with Embedded JavaScript (EJS) and JSON, depending on the query parameters. Last, you test your new API connection by creating an Ajax GET request from your client-side JavaScript.

This lesson covers

- Organizing your routes with namespacing
- Creating API endpoints to respond with JSON
- Making Ajax requests from your views

> **Consider this** Your recipe application renders many pages and offers specific functionality on each page. To make the user experience less complicated, you'd like to allow users to view available programs from their profile pages. To do so, you decide to conditionally serve data in JSON format and display that data through JavaScript and HTML on the client. When you modify your controller actions, your application can offer an API that goes beyond serving web pages.

26.1 Organizing your routes

As your application grows, the routes in your main.js file start to overwhelm other middleware and configurations. Routes are important parts of your application, and keeping your routes organized in a way that multiple developers can manage and understand is arguably as important.

To start this lesson, you break down the routing structure you've set up in an easy-to-follow directory structure. In units 4 and 5, you created routes to reflect CRUD functionality in what's called a REST architecture. *Representational state transfer* (REST) is a way of programming your application to represent the involvement of its resources across the web. Your application's resources are the users, subscribers, and courses stored in the database and displayed in the views. You implemented a RESTful structure by constructing your routes to contain the model name, HTTP method, action being performed, and model ID if necessary. `router.get("users/:id/edit"` , `usersController .edit)` tells you that an HTTP GET request was made to the `users/:id/edit` path, for example.

These routes make it easy for users to know exactly what information is needed to get the data they want to see—in this case, an edit form for an existing user. From the path alone, you know that you're trying to edit a specific user record. From there, you can connect to the appropriate action and redirect to another RESTful route.

> **NOTE** Redirecting is often a secondary action when you're creating or updating information in the database. After arriving at the initial controller action to modify data, you redirect to another route to send the user to another page to view.

In this section, you reorganize your routes into individual modules to reflect the models that they use. This structure will be useful when you decide to expand the types of routes and response data you use in the application.

Start by creating a new folder called routes at the root level of your project and create the following new modules within that folder:

- userRoutes.js
- courseRoutes.js
- subscriberRoutes.js
- errorRoutes.js
- homeRoutes.js
- index.js

These six modules will divide the routes that are currently in main.js. For now, focus on the user routes.

Start by requiring the Express.js Router and the usersController at the top of the module. Then import the login routes and CRUD routes, and add them to the local router object. Doing so allows these routes to be handled by the same router. With all the working routes attached to the router, you can export the router object. Notice in this example that you're leaving users out of the path. You'll define that part of the path in index.js later.

Copy all the routes in main.js that pertain to the user (CRUD operations, login, and authentication), and move them into userRoutes.js, as shown in the next listing.

Listing 26.1 Moving user routes to userRoutes.js

Require Express.js Router and users controller.

```
const router = require("express").Router(),
  usersController = require("../controllers/usersController");

router.get("/", usersController.index,                      ← Add CRUD routes.
➥ usersController.indexView);
router.get("/new", usersController.new);
router.post("/create", usersController.validate,
➥ usersController.create, usersController.redirectView);
router.get("/login", usersController.login);
router.post("/login", usersController.authenticate);
router.get("/logout", usersController.logout,               Add login and
➥ usersController.redirectView);                            authentication
router.get("/:id/edit", usersController.edit);              routes.
router.put("/:id/update", usersController.update,
➥ usersController.redirectView);
router.get("/:id", usersController.show,
➥ usersController.showView);
router.delete("/:id/delete", usersController.delete,
➥ usersController.redirectView);

module.exports = router;     ←
```

Export the module router.

Namespaces

Namespacing is a way of defining routes, paths, and other application items under the umbrella of a specific string or path. Instead of defining dozens of routes with the same path prefix, /users, you can make that prefix a namespace for those routes.

Namespacing is particularly helpful in separating routes in your API based on the format of the content returned. If an iOS application wants to access the data in your recipe application, for example, you might create specific routes with the namespace /ios. Then you could define paths such as /ios/courses and /ios/subscribers. Through the routes defined under this namespace, the iOS application can access data.

Follow the same strategy for the other route files. Subscriber routes go in subscriber-Routes.js, and error routes go in errorRoutes.js.

The index.js module requires all route modules to be in one place. This convention makes it easier to identify all the route types in one file and requires only a single file into main.js. As with the route modules, you require the Express.js Router in index.js. Next, require each relative route module. With those modules added, tell the local router object to use those routes with specific namespaces.

For the home and error routes, no namespace is necessary. By adding the /users name-space for the user routes defined in listing 26.1, you return to the original functionality of your routes. The last step is requiring this index.js module in main.js. Add const router = require("./routes/index") to the top of main.js and app.use("/", router) after your middleware functions.

To tie all these routes to the same router used by your application, add the code in the next listing to index.js.

Listing 26.2   Importing all routes into index.js

Require the Express.js Router.

Require all the route modules within the same directory.

Use the routes from the relative route modules with namespaces.

```
const router = require("express").Router(),
  userRoutes = require("./userRoutes"),
  subscriberRoutes = require("./subscriberRoutes"),
  courseRoutes = require("./courseRoutes"),
  errorRoutes = require("./errorRoutes"),
  homeRoutes = require("./homeRoutes");

router.use("/users", userRoutes);
router.use("/subscribers", subscriberRoutes);
router.use("/courses", courseRoutes);
```

```
router.use("/", homeRoutes);
router.use("/", errorRoutes);        Export the router
                                     from index.js.
module.exports = router;
```

> **NOTE** Order matters. Make sure to have the more-detailed routes closer to the top of index.js. Otherwise, the error routes will handle all incoming requests before they can reach the routes you intended.

The Express.js router object operates through middleware. Within it, you can define specific tasks that you want to perform on incoming requests. In this case, you're using router to load routes under different namespaces. As with other middleware, if you want the router middleware to be part of the main application's middleware flow, you need to add it with app.use. In main.js, remove all the controllers' require statements, as well as the require statement for express.Router(). The rest of the middleware in main.js is used by the app object.

> **NOTE** It's important to change all remaining middleware in main.js to be used by app instead of router because you'll want the app to parse requests and use your templating engine before the request reaches your router at the bottom of the file. Order of middleware matters!

Restart your application, and confirm the original functionality of your application is intact. If you get any errors or if some routes aren't found, make sure that all the route namespaces are defined correctly and that the resource name prefixes are stripped from the original paths. Under the new namespace, your user index route, for example, should read router.get("/", usersController.index, usersController.indexView) instead of router.get("/users" , usersController.index, usersController.indexView).

In the next section, you learn how to use your existing routes to return two types of data formats.

Quick check 26.1 Why do you add app.use("/", router) in main.js?

QC 26.1 answer When the router is defined in main.js, you need to tell the Express.js application to use it as middleware.

26.2 Creating an API

An API is a structure set up within your application to allow external sources to access your application data. In effect, you've already built an API by creating your Express.js web server. By serving HTML and EJS, you've provided an avenue through which users of your application can access your data: the web browser. Not every user, however, will want to see your application data exclusively through the browser on a web page with the styling and formatting you've applied.

Think of your current Express.js application as being like a restaurant menu. It's likely that most people will refer to the printed menu to find out what food items a restaurant offers. Getting access to the hard-copy menu requires traveling to the restaurant itself. By providing a phone number to call to inquire about menu items and a website to display the restaurant's menu, you give customers more options to get the information they need. Similarly, a robust API provides application data in different formats that you access in different ways.

In this section, you reconstruct some of your application routes and actions to respond with data in JSON format in addition to rendered EJS views. Responding with JSON is simple in Express.js. Change the `res.render("courses/index")` line in the `indexView` action of coursesController.js to `res.json(res.locals.courses)`. When you restart your application and visit http://locatlhost:3000/courses, your browser should display all the courses in your database in JSON format (figure 26.1).

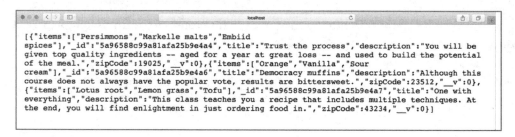

Figure 26.1   Display of JSON course results in browser

This output should resemble the output from your MongoDB server when you run `mongo` in a new terminal window: use `recipe_db` and `db.courses.find({})`, as shown in figure 26.2. Running these commands starts your MongoDB environment and lists all the courses in your recipe database. In the application, you're essentially showing the full database documents in the browser.

```
● ● ●                    ⌂ wexler — mongo — mongo — mongo — 84×14
> db.courses.find({})
{ "_id" : ObjectId("5a96588c99a81afa25b9e4a4"), "title" : "Trust the process", "desc
ription" : "You will be given top quality ingredients — aged for a year at great lo
ss — and used to build the potential of the meal.", "items" : [ "Persimmons", "Mark
elle malts", "Embiid spices" ], "zipCode" : 19025, "__v" : 0 }
{ "_id" : ObjectId("5a96588c99a81afa25b9e4a6"), "title" : "Democracy muffins", "desc
ription" : "Although this course does not always have the popular vote, results are
bittersweet.", "items" : [ "Orange", "Vanilla", "Sour cream" ], "zipCode" : 23512, "
__v" : 0 }
{ "_id" : ObjectId("5a96588c99a81afa25b9e4a7"), "title" : "One with everything", "de
scription" : "This class teaches you a recipe that includes multiple techniques. At
the end, you will find enlightment in just ordering food in.", "items" : [ "Lotus ro
ot", "Lemon grass", "Tofu" ], "zipCode" : 43234, "__v" : 0 }
> ▮
```

Figure 26.2   Display of courses in MongoDB

You can further improve the index action by responding with JSON only when requested. You can accomplish this task in many ways. One way is to use query params. In this code, you perform a check for the format query param. If it exists and equals json, respond with the course data in JSON format. Otherwise, respond with a rendered EJS view as usual. Change the courses indexView action to the code in the next listing.

Listing 26.3   Responding with JSON when query param exists in usersController.js

```
indexView: (req, res) => {
  if (req.query.format === "json") {        Respond with JSON if the
    res.json(res.locals.courses);           format query param
  } else {                                  equals json.
    res.render("courses/index");            Respond with an EJS view
  }                                         if the format query param
}                                           doesn't equal json.
```

Restart your application, and visit http://localhost:3000/courses to ensure that your original EJS index view is still rendering. To display JSON data instead of the normal view, append ?format=json to the end of your URL: visit http://localhost:3000/courses?format=json. This additional query parameter tells your courses controller to render data in JSON format instead of EJS.

With this change in place, if an external application wants to access the list of courses, it can make a request to the URL with the query parameter. External applications are only one group of consumers that can benefit from this implementation, though. You can use this data endpoint from within your own application in many ways. (An API *endpoint* is a reference to one or more application paths whose routes accept web requests.)

> **Quick check 26.2**   What method do you use on the response to send data as JSON back to the client?

 ## 26.3 Calling your API from the client

In the restaurant analogy, a menu's items could be made available through different media: print, phone, or web. This variety makes it easier for customers to learn more about the food served in the restaurant and also could make it easier for restaurant staff to access the menu items more quickly. After all, pulling up a web page is a convenient alternative to finding a menu on a busy night.

In many places within your application, you could benefit from application routes that return JSON data. Primarily, you could benefit by making Ajax requests from the client to access data from pages you don't want to refresh. What if you want users to be able to view the course listings without having to change their current page, for example?

Implement a solution by populating a *modal* (a window that overlays the main browser screen with some instruction or content) with course data via an Ajax request. To start, create a partial view called _coursesModal.ejs in the views/courses folder. Use a simple bootstrap modal, as shown in the next listing.

In this modal, you have a button that triggers a modal to appear. The modal has a tag with the modal-body class. Target this class to populate course data.

Listing 26.4 Simple bootstrap modal in _coursesModel.ejs

```
<button id="modal-button" type="button" data-toggle="modal"
   data-target="#myModal">Latest Courses</button>

<div id="myModal" class="modal fade" role="dialog">
  <div class="modal-dialog">
    <div class="modal-body">  ←——— Add a modal where you'll
                                    populate modal-body.
```

QC 26.2 answer   In Express.js, you can use res.json followed by the parameters you'd like to send in JSON format.

```
        </div>
        <div class="modal-footer">
          <button type="button" data-dismiss="modal">Close</button>
        </div>
      </div>
    </div>
```

Include this partial view in your layout.ejs file so that you can access it from anywhere in your application by adding `<li><%- include courses/_coursesModal %></li>` as an item in your layout's navigation. To get this modal to work, you also need to have the bootstrap client-side JavaScript as well as jQuery. You can get the minified code for jQuery.min.js at https://ajax.googleapis.com/ajax/libs/jquery/3.2.1/jquery.min.js and bootstrap.min.js at https://maxcdn.bootstrapcdn.com/bootstrap/3.3.7/js/bootstrap.min.js.

> **NOTE** I recommend copying the code from this content delivery network and saving the code locally to files with the same name in public/js.

Then, in layout.ejs, link to these JavaScript files, as shown in the following listing.

Listing 26.5 Import jquery and bootstrap into layout.ejs

```
<script type="text/javascript" src="/js/jquery.min.js"></script>
<script type="text/javascript" src="/js/bootstrap.min.js"></script>
```

Add local JavaScript
files from public/js.

With a few styling changes, you can restart your application. You should see a button in your top navigation bar that opens a modal, as shown in figure 26.3.

To give this modal some data, create recipeApp.js in your public folder's js folder. This JavaScript file will run on the client side. Make sure that this file is linked in your layout .ejs file below bootstrap and jQuery by adding `<script type="text/javascript" src="/js/recipeApp.js"></script>`.

Within recipeApp.js, add the code in listing 26.6. You wrap the code block in `$(document).ready` to ensure that no JavaScript is run until the DOM is loaded and ready. Then you add a click listener on the `modal-button` ID. When that button is clicked in the navigation bar, perform an Ajax GET request, using `$.get` to the `/courses?format=json` path. With the added query param, you expect the response to include data as an array in JSON. Then you loop through that array to access individual course records and use `$(".modal-body").append` to add some HTML with each course's title and description.

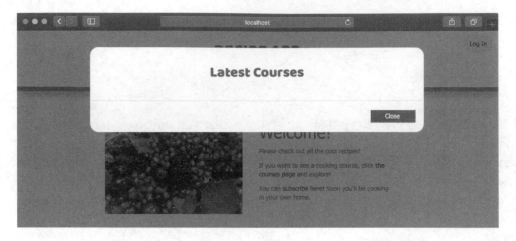

Figure 26.3   Simple modal button in navigation bar

Listing 26.6 Ajax function to load data in modal in recipeApp.js

Wait for DOM to load.

Listen for a click event on the modal button.

Clear the modal from any previous content.

Request data from /courses?format=js on asynchronously.

Loop through array of data in the response.

```
$(document).ready(() => {
  $("#modal-button").click(() => {
    $(".modal-body").html('');
    $.get("/courses?format=json", (data) => {
      data.forEach((course) => {
        $(".modal-body").append(
          `<div>
          <span class="course-title">
          ${course.title}
          </span>
          <div class="course-description">
          ${course.description}
          </div>
          </div>`
        );
      });
    });
  });
});
```

Append each course to the modal.

With this Ajax request in place, restart the application and load course data into the modal. Clicking the modal button fetches new data from the server, as shown in figure 26.4.

Figure 26.4   Populating course data within modal

Now users can view the list of courses from any page. Even if new courses are added to the database, clicking the modal button fetches that new list.

Ajax

Asynchronous JavaScript and XML [Ajax] is a technology that allows client-side requests to be made asynchronously without interfering with any behavior or display of the application page. Ajax uses JSON and XML to format data and requests to be sent to a server. By managing only the data layer of an application on your browser, Ajax allows you to make a request asynchronously and handle data in the resulting response through a callback function.

Because of the way that Ajax interacts with a backend server without the need to reload your web page, it's widely used to update content dynamically in real time. Through multiple Ajax requests, a web page theoretically might never have to reload.

> **Quick check 26.3**   What do you expect will happen if there are no courses in the database when you make an Ajax request?

 **Summary**

In this lesson, you learned about modifying your application route structure to make room for an extensive API. First, you reorganized your routes into individual modules. Next, you added a way to respond with JSON data from your controller action. Last, you added client-side JavaScript to make asynchronous requests to your server from within a view. In lesson 27, you explore namespacing further and see ways in which you can enroll users in courses from the modal itself.

Try this

With one action modified to respond with JSON data, try applying the same technique to other actions. Start by adding the query param condition to the other model index actions; then implement it for the show actions.

Keep in mind that the show actions return individual records, not arrays.

QC 26.3 answer   The Ajax request returns an array of items from the database. If there are no records, the response contains an empty array.

ACCESSING YOUR API FROM YOUR APPLICATION

In this lesson, you change the way that you access JSON-formatted data by adding an API namespace. Then you modify your AJAX function to allow users to join courses directly from a modal. Last, you create the action to link users and courses through a new route.

This lesson covers

- Creating an API namespace
- Building a UI modal to fetch data asynchronously
- Connecting models with MongoDB methods

Consider this   Users can now view course listings from any page on your application, but they want to do more than view that list. With AJAX requests, you can not only pull data asynchronously into the page, but also perform other actions, such as creating new records and editing existing records.

In this lesson, you explore ways in which you can make better use of your API and how AJAX can help.

27.1 Applying an API namespace

I discussed namespacing in lesson 26. Now you're going to implement a namespace for API endpoints that return JSON data or perform actions asynchronously. To get started, create a new route module called apiRoutes.js in your routes folder. This module will contain all the API routes with JSON response bodies. Require this new module in index.js by adding const apiRoutes = require("./apiRoutes"). Then tell your router to use this module under the api namespace with router.use("/api", apiRoutes).

> **NOTE** You must add this new route above the home and error routes. Those routes are namespaced for /, meaning that any URL entered that doesn't match a route name before reaching the error or home routes defaults to an error page.

Create your first route, and have it point to your coursesController.js. Add the code in listing 27.1 to apiRoutes.js. Require the Express.js router along with your courses controller at ../controllers/coursesController. Then point GET requests to the /courses path to the index action of coursesController.js and export the router, followed by respond-JSON. As with your other error-handling middleware, tell this router to use errorJSON in case actions run earlier don't return a response.

> **NOTE** If an action doesn't explicitly respond to the client, the connection is still open, and the request continues to flow through the chain of middleware functions. Typically, this situation means that an error has occurred, and that error will propagate through until error-handling middleware catches it.

Listing 27.1 Adding a route to show all courses in apiRoutes.js

```
const router = require("express").Router(),          Require courses
  coursesController =                                 controller.
➥ require("../controllers/coursesController");  ⟵

router.get("/courses", coursesController.index,
➥ coursesController.respondJSON);          ⟵          Add the API route
router.use(coursesController.errorJSON);    ⟵          to the Express.js
                                                       Router.
module.exports = router;          Add API error-handling
                                  middleware.
```

To get this code to work, create the respondJSON and errorJSON actions in courses-Controller.js. Add the code in listing 27.2 to the courses controller for this action.

The index action in coursesController.js already attaches courses to the response's locals object. Take that locals object and display it in JSON format instead of rendering the data in EJS. If an error occurs in the courses query, pass the error to your errorJSON action. Your normal errors controller actions respond only with browser views. If an error occurs, instead of redirecting to another page, respond with a status code of 500, indicating that an internal error has occurred.

Listing 27.2 Adding JSON responses for courses in coursesController.js

```
respondJSON: (req, res) => {         ← Handle the request from
  res.json({                            previous middleware,
    status: httpStatus.OK,              and submit response.
    data: res.locals
  });                                  ← Respond with the
},                                       response's local data
                                         in JSON format.
errorJSON: (error, req, res, next) => {   ←
  let errorObject;
                                         Respond with a 500
  if (error) {                            status code and
    errorObject = {                       error message in
      status: httpStatus.INTERNAL_SERVER_ERROR,   JSON format.
      message: error.message
    };
  } else {
    errorObject = {
      status: httpStatus.INTERNAL_SERVER_ERROR,
      message: "Unknown Error."
    };
  }

  res.json(errorObject);
},
```

> **NOTE** You will also need to add const httpStatus = require("http-status-codes") to the top of coursesController.js.

Restart your application, and visit http://localhost:3000/api/courses in your browser to see course data in JSON. Having these routes and controllers separate from your web application routes and controllers prevents you from making mistakes in the future. As things stand now, you always want to render EJS or redirect if you visit /courses, and you always expect a JSON response from /api/courses.

With this new API namespace, route, and controller action in place, change the AJAX GET request in recipeApp.js to call /api/courses instead of /courses?format=json. Then remove the conditional block checking for the format query param in your courses indexView action. Restart your application, and check whether you can still load the course data in the modal.

Also, because you're now returning your data wrapped in another JavaScript object containing your status code, you need to modify your AJAX call to handle returned data properly. Change the AJAX call in recipeApp.js as shown in the next listing.

Listing 27.3 Modifying AJAX call in recipeApp.js

Set up a local variable
to represent data.

Check that the data
object contains
course information.

```
$.get("/api/courses", (results = {}) => {
  let data = results.data;
  if (!data || !data.courses) return;
  data.courses.forEach((course) => {
    $(".modal-body").append(
      `<div>
      <span class="course-title">
      ${course.title}
      </span>
      <div class='course-description'>
      ${course.description}
      </div>
      </div>`
    );
  });
});
```

Loop through
course data, and
add elements to
modal.

Restart your application, and click the modal button to see that functionality hasn't changed from the last section.

In the next section, you add more functionality to the modal to allow users to join courses.

Quick check 27.1   Why do you create a new folder for API controllers?

QC 27.1 answer   Having a separate folder for API controllers and actions makes it easier to split the application in two. One part of the application serves data with a visual aspect, and the other serves data to sources looking for the raw data.

27.2 Joining courses via modal

Listing the courses in a modal is a great accomplishment. In this section, you improve the modal even more by allowing users to join a course asynchronously through the modal. Add a button that allows users to join the course. Through AJAX, you submit a request to an API endpoint where a controller action attempts to add the user to the course and responds with a success or failure message in JSON.

First, add the link to join the course by adding the HTML code in listing 27.4 to the bottom of the HTML rendered from the original AJAX call in recipeApp.js. This button needs a custom class join-button and can be placed next to the course title in the modal. It also needs the data-id set to ${course._id}, which allows you to know which course listing you selected.

> **NOTE** The data attribute in HTML is helpful in situations like these. You can mark each button with a data-id attribute so that each button's unique ID matches some corresponding course ID.

Listing 27.4 Adding a button to join a course in recipeApp.js

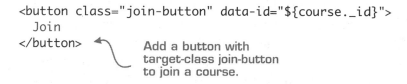

```
<button class="join-button" data-id="${course._id}">
  Join
</button>
```
Add a button with target-class join-button to join a course.

If you restart the application now, you should see a button next to each course item, as shown in figure 27.1. These buttons don't have any functionality yet, though.

To get these buttons to work, change the code in recipeApp.js to use the code in listing 27.5. In this example, you create a function called addJoinButtonListener that sets up a click-event listener for each button with the class join-button. You need to call this function right after the AJAX request completes because you want to attach the listener to the buttons after they're created on the page. To do this, append a then block to the AJAX request.

> **NOTE** AJAX functions use promises, so you can chain then and catch blocks to the end of requests to run code after you get a response. The success block behaves the same way.

In addJoinButtonListener, you grab the target of the click—the button—and then pull the data ID you set earlier with the course's ID. With this information, you can make a new AJAX GET request to the /api/courses/:id/join endpoint. For this request to work, you

Figure 27.1   Adding a join button

need to make sure that the user is logged in. This route allows you to target specific courses to join by using the course ID.

The route and action that handle that request return the JSON value success: true if you're able to add the user to the course. If you're successful, change the text and color of the button to indicate that the user has joined by adding a new joined-button class and removing the old join-button class. This swapping of classes allows you to style each button with different style rules in recipe_app.css and also prevents the click event from triggering another request. If you don't see the color of the button change, make sure that you're targeting the correct button class. If joining the course results in an error, change the button's text to tell the user to try again.

> **NOTE**   The variable $button has only the $ in front to indicate that it represents a jQuery object. This syntax is stylistic and conventional but not required to get your code to work.

Listing 27.5 Adding an event listener to each button in recipeApp.js

```
$(document).ready(() => {
  $("#modal-button").click(() => {
    $(".modal-body").html("");
    $.get("/api/courses", (results = {}) => {
      let data = results.data;
      if (!data || !data.courses) return;
      data.courses.forEach((course) => {
        $(".modal-body").append(
```

```
            `<div>
            <span class="course-title">
            ${course.title}
            </span>
            <button class="join-button" data-id="${course._id}">
            Join
            </button>
            <div class="course-description">
            ${course.description}
            </div>
            </div>`
        );
      });
    }).then(() => {
      addJoinButtonListener();
    });
  });
});


let addJoinButtonListener = () => {
  $(".join-button").click((event) => {
    let $button = $(event.target),
      courseId = $button.data("id");
    $.get(`/api/courses/${courseId}/join`, (results = {}) => {
      let data = results.data;
      if (data && data.success) {
        $button
          .text("Joined")
          .addClass("joined-button")
          .removeClass("join-button");
      } else {
        $button.text("Try again");
      }
    });
  });
}
```

Call addJoinButtonListener to add an event listener on your buttons after the AJAX request completes.

Create the event listener for the modal button.

Grab the button and button ID data.

Make an AJAX request with the course's ID to join.

Check whether the join action was successful, and modify the button.

Now your application is prepared to send an AJAX request and handle its response when the join button is clicked. In the next section, you create the API endpoint to handle this request.

27.3 Creating an API endpoint to connect models

To complete the course modal, you need to create a route to handle requests made for the current user to join a course. To do so, add router.get("/courses/:id/join", courses-Controller.join, coursesController.respondJSON) to apiRoutes.js. This route allows get requests to go through a join action and feed results to your respondJSON action, which returns to the client. At the top of coursesController.js, require the User model with const User = require("../models/user"). Then, in coursesController.js, add the join action in listing 27.6.

In this join action, you get the current logged-in user and the course's ID from the URL params. If a currentUser exists, use the Mongoose findByIdAndUpdate to locate the user object and update its courses array to contain the target course ID. Here, you use the MongoDB $addToSet method, which ensures that the array has no duplicate IDs. If you're successful, add a success property to the response's locals object, which in turn is passed to respondJSON and passed back to the client. In case the user isn't logged in or an error occurs while updating the user's association, pass an error to be handled by your error-handling middleware.

Listing 27.6 Creating an action to join a course in coursesController.js

```
join: (req, res, next) => {
  let courseId = req.params.id,
    currentUser = req.user;

    if (currentUser) {
      User.findByIdAndUpdate(currentUser, {
        $addToSet: {
```

Add the join action to let users join a course.

Get the course id and current user from the request.

Check whether a current user is logged in.

```
      courses: courseId
    }
  })
    .then(() => {
      res.locals.success = true;
      next();
    })
    .catch(error => {
      next(error);
    });
} else {
  next(new Error("User must log in."));
}
}
```

→ Update the user's courses field to contain the targeted course.

← Respond with a JSON object with a success indicator.

← Respond with a JSON object with an error indicator.

Pass an error through to the next middleware function.

With this action in place, restart your application, and try joining courses in the modal. If you're not signed in, you may see the Try Again text appear over the button. Otherwise, depending on your custom styling, your button should turn green and change text for every button you click, as shown in figure 27.2.

Figure 27.2 Example modal after a course has been joined

You can improve the user experience by letting users know whether they're already part of one or more courses in the modal.

Given your application structure and model schemas, you can filter your results by adding the middleware function `filterUserCourses` to coursesController.js, as shown in listing 27.7. In this code, you're checking whether a user is logged in before you continue. If a user is logged in, use the `map` function on your array of courses. Within this function, look at each course and check whether its `_id` is found in your logged-in user's array of courses. The `some` function returns a Boolean value to let you know if a match occurs. If a user has joined a course with ID 5a98eee50e424815f0517ad1, for example, that ID should exist in `currentUser.courses`, and the `userJoined` value for that course is `true`. Last, convert the `courses` Mongoose document object to JSON so that you can append an additional property by using `Object.assign`. This property, `joined`, lets you know in the user interface whether the user previously joined the course. If no user is logged in, call `next` to pass along the unmodified course results.

Listing 27.7 Adding an action to filter courses in coursesController.js

Check whether a user is logged in.

Modify course data to add a flag indicating user association.

```
filterUserCourses: (req, res, next) => {
  let currentUser = res.locals.currentUser;
  if (currentUser) {
    let mappedCourses = res.locals.courses.map((course) => {
      let userJoined = currentUser.courses.some((userCourse) => {
        return userCourse.equals(course._id);
      });
      return Object.assign(course.toObject(), {joined: userJoined});
    });
    res.locals.courses = mappedCourses;
    next();
  } else {
    next();
  }
}
```

Check whether the course exists in the user's courses array.

To use this middleware function, you need to add it to your APU route for /courses before you return the JSON response. The route will look like router.get("/courses", coursesController.index, coursesController.filterUserCourses, coursesController

.respondJSON), where coursesController.filterUserCourses sits after your query for courses in coursesController.index.

The last step is changing the client-side JavaScript in recipeApp.js to check whether the current user has already joined the course and modifying the button in the course listing modal. In listing 27.8, you use a ternary operator in the button's class attribute and main text content. These operators check whether the course data's joined property is true or false. If the property is true, create the button to indicate that the user has already joined. Otherwise, display a button inviting users to join.

Listing 27.8 **Adding dynamic button styling in recipeApp.js**

```
<button class='${course.joined ? "joined-button" : "join-button"}'
  data-id="${course._id}">
  ${course.joined ? "Joined" : "Join"}
</button>
```

Add the appropriate class to reflect join status.

Add the button's text to reflect join status.

After applying these changes, relaunch your application and log in. The color and text of your course-listing buttons will correctly reflect the status of your associations in the database.

> **NOTE** If you experience problems maintaining a logged-in account, make sure to use sessions and cookies prior to initializing passport and your custom middleware.

Quick check 27.3 Why do you need to use the findByIdAndUpdate method?

Summary

In this lesson, you learned how to modify your namespacing structure to accommodate an API for JSON data responses. You also improved your courses modal by allowing users to join specific courses without needing to change pages. Through the AJAX requests and API endpoints you created, more of your application's functionality can

QC 27.3 answer The findByIdAndUpdate Mongoose method combines the find and update methods, so you can conveniently perform a single step to update a user document.

move to a single page and away from individual views for each action. In lesson 28, I discuss some ways in which you can secure your API.

∎∎∎

Try this

With this new API in place, you'll want to create endpoints for every route that might return data. You may want to add every index and show action to the controllers in the api directory, for example.

Create those actions and one additional action to create a user, and return JSON with a confirmation of success or failure instead of a rendered view.

ADDING API SECURITY

In this lesson, you apply a few security strategies to your API routes. Without a browser to store cookies, some external applications may find it difficult to use your API without a way to verify the user's identity. First, you implement some basic security by providing an API token that must be appended to each request. Then you improve that strategy by generating a unique API key for each user upon account creation. Last, you explore JSON Web Tokens (JWT), a system of hashing user data and exchanging tokens to authenticate user accounts without a browser.

This lesson covers

- Adding security-token-verification middleware
- Creating a pre("save") hook to generate API keys
- Implementing JWT header authentication

Consider this You built a robust API for the recipe application. Your endpoints include routes to create new users and update existing users. Because an API endpoint can be accessed from any device that can make an HTTP request, there's no telling who might make a request to your API without first creating an account and storing session data on the server.

Having some form of security on your API routes ensures that your data doesn't fall into the wrong hands.

28.1 Implementing simple security

Unit 5 guided you through user-account creation and authentication. With the help of a few packages, you created a thorough process of validating and encrypting user data and of ensuring that those users were authenticated before getting access to certain pages.

Even without the help of external packages, you can take some simple steps to protect your API. The first method you'll use in this lesson is generating an API token that must be used by users accessing your API. Users need to have a token because they may not be using a browser to access the API, so your current implementation with Passport.js, cookies, and sessions may not work with the client. An additional token reduces this risk, ensuring that only users who make requests with a valid token can see data. You could add `app.set("token", process.env.TOKEN || "recipeT0k3n")` to main.js, for example. Then this application variable would be set to whatever you use as the `TOKEN` environment variable or default to `recipeT0k3n`. The token could be retrieved by using `app.get("token")`.

Because you want to monitor incoming requests to the API in the `apiRoutes` module, set the token as a constant in usersController.js in the api folder, using `const token = process.env.TOKEN || "recipeT0k3n"`. This token will be used by middleware within usersController.js to verify incoming API requests. Create that middleware function by adding the code in listing 28.1 to usersController.js.

This middleware function, `verifyToken`, checks for a query param called `apiToken` that matches the token you set earlier. If the tokens match, call `next` to continue the middleware chain; otherwise, pass an error with a custom message. This error reaches your error-handling middleware and displays the message as JSON.

Listing 28.1 Adding middleware function to verify API token in usersController.js

```
verifyToken: (req, res, next) => {
  if (req.query.apiToken === token) next();
  else next(new Error("Invalid API token."));
}
```

Create the verifyToken middleware function with the next parameter.

Respond with error message if tokens don't match.

Call the next middleware function if tokens match.

To add the usersController.verifyToken middleware so that it runs before every API request is handled, you can add router.use(usersController.verifyToken), as the first function in apiRoutes.js. You also need to require the users controller by adding const usersController = require("../controllers/usersController") to apiRoutes.js.

Restart your application, and when you visit http://localhost:3000/api/courses, notice the following error message: {"status":500, "message":"Invalid API token."}. This message is a good sign. It means that your API validation is working because you didn't make a request by using a valid API token.

To bypass this message, add the apiToken query parameter. Visiting http://localhost:3000/api/courses?apiToken=recipeT0k3n should result in a display of the original course data in JSON format. If you choose to implement your API security this way, you need to share this token with your trusted users. To get your AJAX requests to work, add the ?apiToken=recipeT0k3n query parameter to those URLs as well in recipeApp.js.

This simple security barrier is definitely a start, but you can imagine that it quickly becomes an unreliable system as more users require the token to access your API. The more users who have access to the same token, the more likely it is for that token to fall into the hands of nonusers. When you're quickly building an application that requires a thin layer of security, this approach may be sufficient. When the application is live online, however, you'll want to modify the API security to treat each user request uniquely.

In the next section, you explore ways to keep the token unique for each user.

> **Quick check 28.1**   Why might you store a secret token in process.env.TOKEN?

 ## 28.2 Adding API tokens

You just constructed a middleware function to verify API tokens passed as query parameters in the URL. This method is effective at securing your API, but it doesn't prevent nonusers from getting their hands on the one and only token.

QC 28.1 answer   You can store sensitive or secret data in process.env as environmental variables. These variables are normally stored on the server but don't need to appear in the code. This practice makes it easier to change the token directly on the server (you don't have to change the code each time), and it's a more-secure convention.

To improve this system, add a custom token to each user account. Do this by adding a new apiToken field to the user schema that's of type String. Next, build a pre("save") hook on the User model to generate an API token that's unique to that user upon account creation. Before you get to the code, use a Node.js package to help with the token generation.

The rand-token package provides some simple tools for creating new alphanumeric tokens of your desired length. Run npm install rand-token -S to install the rand-token package in this project, and require it in user.js by adding const randToken = require ("rand-token").

Add the code in the next listing to user.js. This code first checks whether the user's apiToken field is set. If it isn't, generate a new unique 16-character token with rand-Token.generate.

Listing 28.2 Creating a pre("save") hook to generate an API token in user.js

```
userSchema.pre("save", function(next) {
  let user = this;
  if (!user.apiToken) user.apiToken =
    randToken.generate(16);                  Check for an existing
  next();                                    API token and generate
});                                          a new one with
                                             randToken.generate.
```

> **NOTE** You can improve the functionality here by comparing the generated token with other users' tokens to ensure that no duplicity occurs.

Next, add the apiToken field as an item in the table on the user's show page. This way, when a new user visits their profile page, they'll have access to their API token. In figure 28.1, for example, my user account has the token 2plMh5yZMFULOzpx.

To use this token, you need to modify the verifyToken middleware to check the apiToken query param against the tokens in your database. Change verifyToken in /api/users-Controller.js to use the code in listing 28.3.

In this modified middleware function, you grab the token as the query parameter. If a token appears in the URL, search the user database for a single user who has that API token. If such a user exists, continue to the next middleware function. If no user with that token exists, if an error occurs in the query, or if no query parameter was used, pass an error.

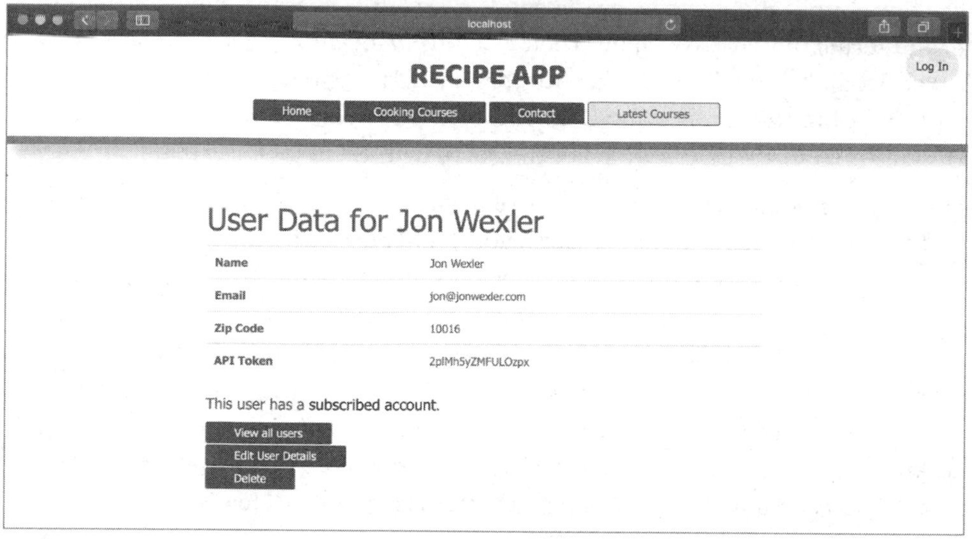

Figure 28.1 Displaying the API token on the user's show page

Listing 28.3 Improving the token verification action in usersController.js

Check whether a token exists
as the query parameter.

Search for a user
with the provided
API token.

Call next if a user
with the API
token exists.

```
verifyToken: (req, res, next) => {
  let token = req.query.apiToken;
  if (token) {
    User.findOne({ apiToken: token })
      .then(user => {
        if (user) next();
        else next(new Error("Invalid API token."));
      })
      .catch(error => {
        next(new Error(error.message));
      });
  } else {
    next(new Error("Invalid API token "));
  }
}
```

Pass an error to
error handler.

Restart your application, and create a new user account. Visit that new user's show page, and locate the apiToken value. Then visit http://localhost:3000/api/courses? apiToken= followed by the API token for that user. The jon@jonwexler.com user, for example, would use the following URL: http://localhost:3000/api/courses?apiToken= 2plMh5yZMFULOzpx. You should see the list of courses in JSON as before.

This new system reduces the vulnerability of having a single API token for all users. With the API token connected to a user account, you could also verify the user's information in your database and keep metrics on the number or quality of that user's API requests. To get your client-side JavaScript to use this token in your API calls, you can add a hidden element to layout.ejs with the current user's token. You could add <div id="apiToken" data-token="<%= currentUser.apiToken %>" style="display: none;"> within the block to check whether a user is logged in, for example. Then, when the document is ready in recipeApp.js, you can locate the token, use it with let apiToken = $("#apiToken").data ("token"), and call your Ajax request on /api/courses?apiToken=${apiToken}.

Still, you can take a more-secure approach to building API authentication in which a web browser isn't necessarily involved. That method uses JSON web tokens (JWT).

Quick check 28.2   What does randToken.generate(16) do?

 ## 28.3   Using JSON web tokens

You can build a secure API by using cookies, but the API's functionality still depends on its clients to support and store those cookies. Consider someone who writes a script to run requests against your API solely from their terminal window, for example. In this case, if you want to apply user authentication on incoming requests, you need some way to keep track of which users are requesting and whether they've recently logged in. Without a visual login page, that task can be difficult. You can try some alternative solutions, one of which is using JSON web tokens.

JSON web tokens (JWT) are signed or encrypted data passed between the server and client as a means of representing an authenticated user request. Ultimately, JWTs are like sessions in a different format and used differently in web communication. You can think

QC 28.2 answer   This method generates a random 16-character alphanumeric token.

of JWTs as being like API tokens that are regenerated on every login. JWTs contain three parts, as defined in table 28.1.

Table 28.1 Parts of JWTs

JWT part	Description
Header	A JSON object detailing how the data in the JWT is prepared and hashed.
Payload	The data stored in the JWT, used to verify the user who previously authenticated. The payload normally includes the user's ID.
Signature	A hashed code using the header and payload values.

> **TIP** The smaller the payload, the smaller the JWT and the faster it's sent with each response.

These three values together offer a unique arrangement of data indicating the recent login status for a specific user. First, the user makes a request and passes their email and password. The server responds with an encoded JWT verifying the user's correct login information. For each subsequent user request, that same JWT must be sent back to the server. Then the server verifies the JWT by decoding its values and locating the user specified in the payload. Unlike in password encryption with Passport.js and bcrypt, JWTs aren't encrypted through hashing and salting. JWTs are encoded, which means that the server can decode the JWT to reveal its contents without needing to know some secret value set by the user.

In this section, you apply JWT API security with the help of the jsonwebtoken package. Install the jsonwebtoken package by running npm i jsonwebtoken -S in terminal. Because you're going to use JWTs for user verification in the API, require jsonwebtoken in usersController.js with const jsonWebToken = require("jsonwebtoken").

To use JWTs, you need to allow the user to log in without a browser. Create a new API login action by adding the code in listing 28.4 to usersController.js.

> **NOTE** You can find more information on the jsonwebtoken package at https://github .com/auth0/node-jsonwebtoken.

This action uses the Passport.js local strategy that you set up in lesson 24. Through the authenticate method, verify that the user email address and password match that of a user in the database. Then, through a callback function, if a user is found with the matching email and password, use jsonWebToken.sign to create a token with the user's ID and an expiration date set to one day from the time of signing. Finally, respond with a JSON object with a success tag and the signed token; otherwise, respond with the error message.

Listing 28.4 Creating a login action for the API in usersController.js

```
apiAuthenticate: (req, res, next) => {
    passport.authenticate("local", (errors, user) => {
        if (user) {
            let signedToken = jsonWebToken.sign(
                {
                    data: user._id,
                    exp: new Date().setDate(new Date().getDate() + 1)
                },
                "secret_encoding_passphrase"
            );
            res.json({
                success: true,
                token: signedToken
            });
        } else
            res.json({
                success: false,
                message: "Could not authenticate user."
            });
    })(req, res, next);
}
```

Authenticate with the passport.authenticate method.

Sign the JWT if a user exists with matching email and password.

Respond with the JWT.

Respond with an error message.

Now this token can be used for 24 hours to make requests to secured API endpoints.

Next, add the following POST route to apiRoutes.js: router.post("/login", usersController .apiAuthenticate). You can generate the token without a browser by making a POST request to the /api/login route with your email and password in the body. To do so, run a curl command in terminal, such as curl -d "email=jon@jonwexler.com&password=12345" http://localhost:3000/api/login. In this example, the -d flag indicates that the user is posting their email and password as data to the provided URL. After running this command, you should expect a response similar to the response in the next listing.

Listing 28.5 Example response for a successful JWT authentication in terminal

```
{"success":true,"token":"eyJhbGciOiJIUzI1NiIsInR5cCI6IkpXVCJ9
➡ .eyJkYXRhIjoiNTljOWNkN2VmNjU5YjMwMjk4YzkzMjY4IiwiZXhwIjox
➡ NTA2NDk2NDMyODc5LCJpYXQiOjE1MDY0MTAwMzJ9.Gr7gPyodobTAXh1p
➡ VuycIDxMEf9LyPsbrR4baorAbw0"}
```

Display of a successful response with a JWT after authentication.

To secure all the API endpoints, add an action to verify incoming JWTs and add that middleware for every API route. Add the code in listing 28.6 to usersController.js.

First, pull the incoming token from the request header. Then, if a token exists, use json-WebToken.verify along with the token and secret passphrase to decode the token and verify its authenticity. The following callback provides any errors that may have occurred, as well as the decoded payload. You can check whether the payload has a value. If so, pull the user's ID from payload.data, and query the database for a user with that ID. If no such user exists, that user's account may have been deleted, or the JWT may have been tampered with, so return an error message. If the user ID matches, call next and move on to the API endpoint. This method of communication continues until the token expires and the user creates a new JWT.

Listing 28.6 Creating a verification action for the API in usersController.js

```
verifyJWT: (req, res, next) => {                      Retrieve the JWT from
  let token = req.headers.token;                      request headers.
  if (token) {
    jsonWebToken.verify(
      token,                                          Verify the JWT, and
      "secret_encoding_passphrase",                   decode its payload.
      (errors, payload) => {
        if (payload) {
          User.findById(payload.data).then(user => {
            if (user) {                                 Check for a user
              next();                                   with the decoded
            } else {                                    user ID from the
              res.status(httpStatus.FORBIDDEN).json({   JWT payload.
                error: true,
                message: "No User account found."
              });
            }
          });
        } else {
          res.status(httpStatus.UNAUTHORIZED).json({
            error: true,
            message: "Cannot verify API token."
          });
          next();                                       Respond with an
        }                                               error message if
      }                                                 the token can't be
    );                                                  verified.
```

Call the next middleware function if a user is found with the JWT ID.

```
  } else {
    res.status(httpStatus.UNAUTHORIZED).json({
      error: true,
      message: "Provide Token"      ◄─────
    });
  }
}
```

Respond with an error
message if no token is found
in the request headers.

The final step is placing this verifyJWT middleware function before any API request is processed. Add router.use(usersController.verifyJWT) to apiRoute.js below the login route and above all other routes. This step ensures that every route needs to use the verifyJWT middleware except for the login route, which is used to generate your JWT.

> **NOTE** At this point, you no longer need your token generator hook on the User model or any remnants of the past two API security techniques to use JWTs. You may want to keep these recently implemented API security techniques in place, however, as a fallback to access your API. More work is needed to get these security approaches to work together.

You can test your JWT by running another curl command in terminal and identifying the token in the request headers. With the token from listing 28.5, that command looks like listing 28.7.

In this command, you use the -H flag to indicate a header key-value pair for your JWT in quotation marks. By making a request and passing a valid JWT, you should gain access to the application's data.

> **NOTE** You need to remove the usersController.verifyToken action to make this new approach work. Otherwise, your application will look for both a JWT header and an apiToken.

Listing 28.7 Creating a verification action for the API in usersController.js

```
curl  -H "token: eyJhbGciOiJIUzI1NiIsInR5cCI6IkpXVCJ9.eyJkY
➥ XRhIjoiNTljOWNkN2VmNjU5YjMwMjk4YzkzMjY4IiwiZXhwIjoxNT
➥ A2NDk2NDMyODc5LCJpYXQiOjE1MDY0MTAwMzJ9.Gr7gPyodobTAX
➥ h1pVuycIDxMEf9LyPsbrR4baorAbw0" http://localhost:3000
➥ /api/courses  ◄──────
```

Make a request with
JWT in the headers.

> **WARNING** The way you're building your API to use JWTs will interfere with the work you've already done in your client-side Ajax request. Consider this section to be an introduction to using JWTs, not necessarily a replacement for the security you've implemented in the recipe application so far.

If your request is successful, you should expect to see the same list of courses as the JSON from the first section of this lesson. If you plan to use JWTs for securing your API, you need to specify to the users of your API exactly how you expect them to authenticate and verify their tokens. One way is to create a view with an additional login form where a user can post their email and password to get an API token in response. That token can be stored temporarily on the User model like the random token in the preceding section.

> **NOTE** Using JWTs requires the client to store the token in some way. Not being able to store the JWT temporarily makes it impossible to create future requests after the token is created on login.

JWTs can help prevent attacks on your application's data and secure access through your API, but this requires more steps to implement. Ultimately, you may find that it makes more sense to start with a simpler approach, such as generating random tokens for each user.

Quick check 28.3 Why do you pass the JWT in the header of the request?

 Summary

In this lesson, you learned how to implement three security tokens on your API. The first strategy is a simple security token that can be used by all clients. The second strategy requires generating a new random token for each user upon creation. In the third approach, you use JWTs to provide the most-secure option for authenticating users to access your API. In lesson 29 (this unit's capstone exercise), you have an opportunity to build an API with some of the functionality introduced in this unit.

Try this

Now that you have some basic security options to choose among, try creating more API routes that require JWTs. You can also exclude certain routes from requiring a token, such as the login route. Pick two routes to exclude from your API security.

QC 28.3 answer You could pass the JWT in the body of the request, but because not all requests will be POST, the headers offer a more convenient place.

CAPSTONE: IMPLEMENTING AN API

Confetti Cuisine raves about the user interaction with the application. To encourage more users to enroll in their courses, however, they'd like me to add more data on individual pages. More specifically, they want me to include a modal on every page that lists the offered courses and a link to enroll in each one.

To accomplish this task, I'm going to make requests to my application server by using Ajax on the client side. By making an asynchronous call to my server behind the scenes, I won't need to load the course data until the user clicks a button to enroll. This change to use Ajax should help with the initial page-load time and ensure that course data is up to date when the user views it.

First, I'm going to need to modify my application layout view to include a partial containing the Embedded JavaScript (EJS) for my modal. Next, I'm going to create the client-side JavaScript code to request for course data. To get this data to appear, I need to create an API endpoint to respond with course data as JSON. When I have that endpoint working, I'll add an action to handle enrolling users in courses and respond with JSON upon completion. This endpoint will allow users to enroll in classes from any page without needing to leave or refresh the page they're on.

Before I begin, I'm going to restructure my routes to pave the way for my new API endpoints.

29.1 Restructuring routes

To start with the application's improvements, I'll move my routes into their own modules to clean up my main application file. As this application grows, the routes will increase as well. I'd like future developers on this project to be able to locate the routes they need easily. Because my routes for each model resource are already RESTful—meaning that the route paths take my application's models and CRUD functions into consideration—the restructuring process is much simpler. My new application structure will separate my routes based on controller name, as shown in figure 29.1.

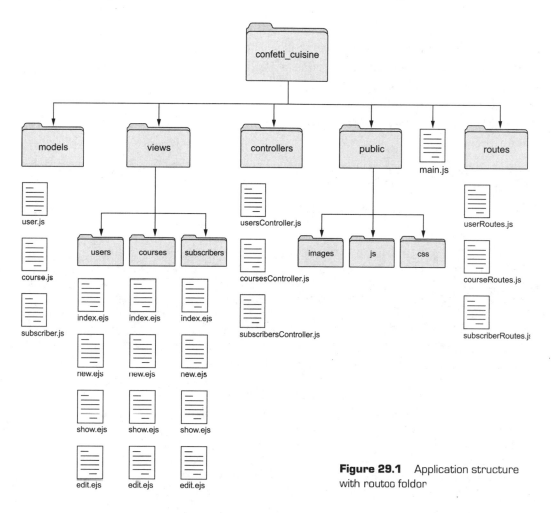

Figure 29.1 Application structure with routes folder

First, I create a new routes folder at the root level of my application directory. Within that folder, I create three modules to hold my models' respective routes:

- userRoutes.js
- courseRoutes.js
- subscriberRoutes.js

Next, I move all the user routes out of main.js and into userRoutes.js. This new routes file resembles the code in listing 29.1.

> **NOTE** I'll also move my home and error routes into their own home: Routes.js and error-Routes.js, respectively.

At the top of this file, I require the Express.js Router and usersController.js. These two modules allow me to attach my routes to the same object across my application and link those routes to actions in the users controller. Then I apply the get, post, put, and delete routes for users, which include the routes for CRUD actions as well as the routes to sign in and log in. Before I continue, I remove all occurrences of the text users in the route path. Instead, I'll apply these routes under the users namespace later. These routes are bound to the router object, which I export with this module to make it available to other modules in the project.

Listing 29.1 User routes in userRoutes.js

```
const router = require("express").Router(),
  usersController = require("../controllers/usersController");

router.get("/", usersController.index,
  usersController.indexView);
router.get("/new", usersController.new);
router.post("/create", usersController.validate,
  usersController.create, usersController.redirectView);
router.get("/login", usersController.login);
router.post("/login", usersController.authenticate);
router.get("/logout", usersController.logout,
  usersController.redirectView);
router.get("/:id/edit", usersController.edit);
router.put("/:id/update", usersController.update,
  usersController.redirectView);
router.get("/:id", usersController.show,
  usersController.showView);
router.delete("/:id/delete", usersController.delete,
  usersController.redirectView);

module.exports = router;
```

Require the Express.js Router and usersController.

Define user routes on the router object.

Export the router object from the module.

Then I apply the same strategy to the other model routes and export the *router* object in each module. Exporting the *router* object allows any other module to require these routes. My routes are better organized, with each module requiring only the controllers it needs to use. To get these routes accessible in main.js, I create a new file called index.js in the routes folder. This file requires all relevant routes so that they can be accessed in one place. Then I'll require index.js in main.js.

> **NOTE** All remaining middleware in main.js should be applied to `app.use` and should no longer use `router`.

I start by requiring the Express.js Router along with all my route modules. In this example, I include model routes and routes for errors and my home controller. `router.use` tells my router to use the first parameter as the namespace and the second parameter as the routes module specific to that namespace. At the end of the file, I export my *router* object, which now contains all the previously defined routes. The code in index.js is shown in the next listing.

Listing 29.2 All routes in index.js

```
const router = require("express").Router(),          ← Require the
  userRoutes = require("./userRoutes"),                 Express.js
  subscriberRoutes = require("./subscriberRoutes"),     Router and
  courseRoutes = require("./courseRoutes"),             route modules.
  errorRoutes = require("./errorRoutes"),
  homeRoutes = require("./homeRoutes");
                                                     ← Define namespaces for
                                                        each route module.
router.use("/users", userRoutes);
router.use("/subscribers", subscriberRoutes);
router.use("/courses", courseRoutes);
router.use("/", homeRoutes);
router.use("/", errorRoutes);                    Export the
                                                 complete
module.exports = router;                      ← router object.
```

With these routes reorganized, I'll still be able to access my index of courses and individual courses at the /courses and /courses/:id paths, respectively. Because my routes are more organized, I have room to introduce new route modules without complicating my code structure. To import these routes into the application, I need to require index.js at the top of main.js by using `const router = require("./routes/index")`. This *router* object replaces the one I had before. Then I tell my Express.js app to use this router in the same way that I told the router to use previously defined routes by making sure that `app.use("/", router)` is in main.js.

> **NOTE** I also need to remove my require lines for all controllers in main.js, as they're no longer referenced in that module.

With this new routing structure in place, my application continues to function as before. I can start implementing my API modifications by creating the modal that will display courses.

 ## 29.2 Adding the courses partial

To create a modal, I use the default bootstrap modal HTML, which provides the code for a button that displays a simple modal in the center of the screen. I add that code to a new file called _coursesModal.ejs in my courses folder. The underscore distinguishes the names of partials from regular views.

This partial, which contains only the modal code shown in the next listing, needs to be included in my layout.ejs file. I include the partial as a list item in my navigation bar, with `<%- include courses/_coursesModal %>`.

Listing 29.3 Code for modal in _coursesModal.ejs

```
<button id="modal-button" type="button"           Add the button
➥ data-toggle="modal"                             to open modal.
➥ data-target="#myModal"> Latest Courses</button> ←

<div id="myModal" class="modal fade" role="dialog"> ←
  <div class="modal-dialog">
    <h4 class="modal-title">Latest Courses</h4>
    <div class="modal-body">                       Add code for the
    </div>                                         modal window.
    <div class="modal-footer">
      <button type="button" data-dismiss="modal">Close</button>
    </div>
  </div>
</div>
```

> **NOTE** I also need to make sure that the JavaScript files for bootstrap and jQuery are added to my public/js folder and imported into my layout.ejs through script tags. Otherwise, my modal won't animate on the screen. I can download the latest jQuery code from https://code.jquery.com and bootstrap code from https://www.bootstrapcdn.com.

When I restart my application, I see a button in my navigation bar, which opens an empty modal when clicked (figure 29.2).

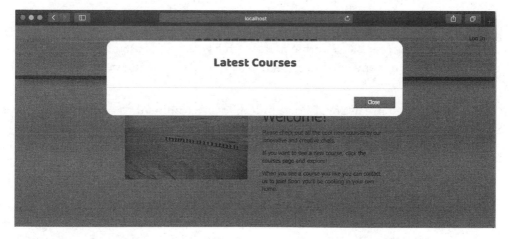

Figure 29.2   Modal button in layout navigation

The next step is populating this modal by using course data with AJAX and a new API endpoint.

 ## 29.3 Creating the AJAX function

One way to access application data without needing to refresh my web page is to make an asynchronous Ajax request to my server. This request occurs behind the scenes on the browser used by the application's clients and originates from the client's JavaScript file in the public folder.

To get this Ajax function to work, I need to ensure that jQuery is added to my project and linked from the layout file, because I'll use some of its methods to populate my modal. Then, through my custom confettiCuisine.js file in my public/js folder, I can add the code in listing 29.4. I can reference this file in layout.ejs using the following script tag: <script type="text/javascript" src="js/confettiCuisine.js"></script>.

This Ajax function runs only when the Document Object Model (DOM) is loaded and the modal button is clicked. I handle the click event by making a GET request to my API endpoint at /api/courses. This request is equivalent to making a GET request to http://localhost:3000/api/courses in my web browser and receiving a page of JSON data. I'll create this route soon.

Next, I handle the results in the response through the results object. Within this object, I expect to see a data object. If there's no data or course object, I return to exit the function. I parse the data object for JSON and loop through its array of contents to populate my modal. For each item in my data object, I display the title, cost, and description within HTML tags.

To the side of each course listing, I link a button to an enrollment route for that course. I create a function called addJoinButtonListener to add an event listener on each course listing after its elements are added to the DOM. That function listens for a click event on the join button, marked with the .join-button class. When that button is clicked, I make another AJAX request through my API namespace to /api/courses/${courseId}/join for the specific course listing I selected. If my server returns a response saying that I was successfully added to the course, I change the color and text of the button. Using the ternary operator ${course.joined ? "joined-button" : "join-button" }, I determine the class of the button's styling, depending on the value of course.joined. I'll create this property on each course object to let my user interface know whether the currently logged-in user has already joined the course.

Listing 29.4 Creating an Ajax function to retrieve course data in confettiCuisine.js

Wait for the DOM to load.   Handle a click event
                                             on the modal button.

                                                         Reset the modal
                                                         body's contents to
                                                         an empty string.

```
$(document).ready(() => {
  $("#modal-button").click(() => {
    $(".modal-body").html("");
    $.get(`/api/courses`, (results = {}) => {
```

Fetch course data
via an AJAX GET
request.

```
      let data = results.data;
      if (!data || !data.courses) return;

      data.courses.forEach((course) => {
        $(".modal-body").append(
          `<div>
            <span class="course-cost">$${course.cost}</span>
              <span class="course-title">
                ${course.title}
              </span>
            <button class="${course.joined ? "joined-button" :
"join-button"} btn btn-info btn-sm" data-id="${course._id}">
                ${course.joined ? "Joined" : "Join"}
```

Loop through
each course, and append
to the modal body.

```
                </button>
                <div class="course-description">
                    ${course.description}
                </div>
            </div>`
        );                    ⟵━━━━━━  Link to enroll the current user.
      });
   }).then(() => {
      addJoinButtonListener();    ⟵
   });
  });
});
```

Call **addJoinButtonListener** to add an event listener on the course listing.

```
let addJoinButtonListener = () => {
  $(".join-button").click((event) => {
    let $button = $(event.target),
      courseId = $button.data("id");
    $.get(`/api/courses/${courseId}/join`, (results = {}) => {  ⟵
      let data = results.data;
      if (data && data.success) {
        $button
          .text("Joined")
          .addClass("joined-button")
          .removeClass("join-button");
      } else {
        $button.text("Try again");
      }
    });
  });
}
```

Make an API call to join the selected course.

To get this code to work, I need to create two new API endpoints. One endpoint retrieves course data as JSON; the other handles my requests to enroll users at /api/course/${courseId}/join. I'll add these endpoints in the next section.

 ## 29.4 Adding an API endpoint

Now that my Confetti Cuisine application is configured to communicate with two new API endpoints, I need to create the routes to handle these requests. The first step is adding the routes to my index.js file in the routes folder. For the AJAX request, I need a specific route under an api namespace because I want requests to go to /api/courses, not only /courses. To accomplish this task, I create apiRoutes.js within the routes folder with the code in listing 29.5.

This file requires the Express.js Router and my coursesController. Then I have that router object handle GET requests made to the /courses path. This route gets the course listing from the index action in the courses controller. Then the course listing goes through a filterUserCourses middleware function to mark the courses that the current user has already joined, and results are sent back through the respondJSON function. Under the api namespace, this path is /api/courses. The second route handles GET requests to a new action called join. I have one more piece of middleware for this API. I make reference to the errorJSON action, which handles all errors resulting from any of the routes in this API. Last, I export the router.

Listing 29.5   Creating an API route in apiRoutes

```
const router = require("express").Router(),          Require the
  coursesController = require("../controllers/        Express.js Router
➥ coursesController");                                and
                                                      coursesController.

router.get("/courses", coursesController.index,       Create a route
➥ coursesController.filterUserCourses,                for the courses
➥ coursesController.respondJSON);                     data endpoint.
router.get("/courses/:id/join", coursesController.join,
➥ coursesController.respondJSON);
router.use(coursesController.errorJSON);              Create a route
                                                      to join a course
module.exports = router;                              by ID.
                        Handle all API errors.
```

Next, I need to add this router to the router defined in index.js. I require apiRoutes.js into index.js by adding const apiRoutes = require("./apiRoutes"). I add router.use ("/api", apiRoutes) to index.js to use the routes defined in apiRoutes.js under the /api namespace. I've already created the index action to fetch the courses from my database. Now I need to create the filterUserCourses, respondJSON, and errorJSON actions in my courses controller so that I can return my data in JSON format. To do so, I add the code in the following listing to coursesController.js.

Listing 29.6 Creating an action to enroll users in courses in coursesController.js

```
respondJSON: (req, res) => {
  res.json({                          Return a courses
    status: httpStatus.OK,            array through the
    data: res.locals                  data property.
  });
},
errorJSON: (error, req, res, next) => {    Return an error
  let errorObject;                         message and status
  if (error) {                             code of 500 if an
    errorObject = {                        error occurs.
      status: httpStatus.INTERNAL_SERVER_ERROR,
      message: error.message
    };
  } else {
    errorObject = {
      status: httpStatus.OK,
      message: "Unknown Error."
    };
  }                                    Check whether the
  res.json(errorObject);              user is logged in and
},                                     return an array of
filterUserCourses: (req, res, next) => {   courses with joined
  let currentUser = res.locals.currentUser;  property reflecting
  if (currentUser) {                    user association.
    let mappedCourses = res.locals.courses.map((course) => {
      let userJoined = currentUser.courses.some((userCourse) => {
        return userCourse.equals(course._id);
      });
      return Object.assign(course.toObject(), {joined: userJoined});
    });
    res.locals.courses = mappedCourses;
    next();
  } else {
    next();
  }
}
```

Figure 29.3   Showing course listing through modal in browser

With these new endpoints in place, I can restart my application and see the course listings populate my modal when the navigation button is clicked (figure 29.3).

> **NOTE**   While testing that this API endpoint works, I need to comment out my route to `join` until the action is added to my courses controller. Otherwise, my application will complain that it's looking for a callback that doesn't exist.

The last phase is creating a route and action to handle users who are looking to enroll in a class and filter the course listing to reflect those users who have already joined.

 ## 29.5 Creating an action to enroll users

To enroll a user in a cooking class, I need the current user's ID and the selected course's ID. I can get the user's ID from the user object on the request, provided by `passport`. I need to use `req.user._id` or the `currentUser` variable I created the last time I worked on this project (lesson 25). I also have easy access to the course ID through the RESTful route. The course ID is the second element in the route's path. My second route, `'/courses/:id/join'` in apiRoutes.js, points to the `join` action in my courses controller.

The last step is adding a controller action to enroll the user in the selected course. I start by creating a new action called join and defining local variables for the course and user IDs. Because I'm referencing the User model in this controller, I need to require that model in coursesController.js by adding const User = require("../models/user"). Then I check whether a user is signed in. If not, I return an error message in JSON format.

> **NOTE** You will also need to add const httpStatus = require("http-status-codes") and const User = require("../models/user") to the top of coursesController.js.

If the user is logged in, I use the Mongoose findByIdAndUpdate query method to search for the user by the user object, the currentUser, and the MongoDB array update operator $addToSet to insert the selected course into the user's courses list. This association signifies an enrollment. I accomplish all these tasks by using the code in listing 29.7.

> **NOTE** $addToSet ensures that no duplicate values appear in the courses array. I could have used the MongoDB $push operator to add the course ID to the user's courses array, but this operator may have allowed users to enroll in the same course multiple times by accident.

Listing 29.7 Creating an action to enroll users in courses in coursesController.js

Define local variables for course and user IDs.

```
join: (req, res, next) => {
  let courseId = req.params.id,          Check whether the
    currentUser = req.user;              user is logged in.

  if (currentUser) {
    User.findByIdAndUpdate(currentUser, {
      $addToSet: {
        courses: courseId
      }                                  Find and update the
    })                                   user to connect the
      .then(() => {                      selected course.
        res.locals.success = true;
        next();                          Continue to next middleware.
      })
      .catch(error => {
        next(error);                     Continue to error middleware
      });                                with an error message if the
  } else {                               user failed to enroll.
    next(new Error("User must log in."));
  }
}
```

Figure 29.4   Trying to enroll before logging in

With this action in place, I can restart the application. When I try to enroll in a course before logging in, I see the message in figure 29.4.

After I successfully log in and click the button to join a course, the screen resembles figure 29.5. Also, after joining a course, I can refresh my window and still see my `joined` status preserved in the modal.

With a new API namespace, I can open this application to more Ajax requests and other applications that want to access Confetti Cuisine's raw JSON data. I could secure the API, but doing so isn't required for this small change.

Now that I've implemented a new feature to allow users to enroll in courses, I'll work on improving other parts of the application that may benefit from single-page asynchronous calls to my API.

Figure 29.5 Successfully enrolling in a course

Summary

In this capstone exercise, I improved the Confetti Cuisine application experience by
introducing an Ajax request to a new API endpoint. I started by reorganizing my application's routes and separating the web routes from the API routes. Then I created an
Ajax function on the client-side JavaScript to populate a modal with course-listing
results from a custom API endpoint. Last, I created a route and action to allow users to
enroll in courses from any page in the application. With this new improvement in place,
Confetti Cuisine's marketing team feels better about informing users and encouraging
them to join their classes.

Adding chat functionality

By this point, the main structure of your application is complete. It's time to think about new features that could improve the overall interaction on your application but aren't necessary for the fundamental functionalities. In earlier lessons, I discussed how particularly useful Node.js is for handling streams of data. If you want to send a big batch of data across the internet, Node.js makes the process simpler by supporting data chunking. Chunks of data are connected as they arrive at the server and processed when there's enough data to do something meaningful with them. This approach is useful in various types of data streams, and it's made possible through the event-emitting and event-handling features of Node.js.

In this unit, you explore how to use Node.js to facilitate a real-time chat application through event-driven communication over web sockets. I discuss how chat applications can be built with the simplest of HTML tools and how web sockets and socket.io are more-efficient, sophisticated options than historic client-server communication. You apply the chat functionality to your existing application to allow existing users to communicate in a group setting. Then you take things a step further by creating a data model for your chat messages and loading messages from the database when you open the application's chat page. Last, you implement an icon in the navigation bar that acts as an indicator when the chat page is active, even when the user is on a different page.

This unit covers the following topics:

- Lesson 30 introduces web sockets and shows how the socket.io package can help you connect users of your application through a real-time chat application. In this lesson, you learn how to create a simple chat page on your existing recipe application.
- Lesson 31 shows you how to take your chat application to the next level by saving the messages to your MongoDB database. In this lesson, you create a message model and connect the message to the sender. This way, you'll be able to identify which messages belong to the user who's logged in.
- Lesson 32 guides you through the implementation of an active chat indicator in the navigation bar. This icon animates as messages are shared on the chat page.

In lesson 33 (the capstone lesson), you use the concepts learned in this unit to build a chat feature for the Confetti Cuisine application.

WORKING WITH SOCKET.IO

Building a web application in Node.js can be exciting. Often, you'll find that the most challenging aspects stem primarily from architecting the application from a web-development perspective. It's easy to forget what Node.js is capable of outside the normal request-response cycle. In this lesson, you explore communication between the client and server via an open TCP connection. This connection is made available by means of the socket.io package, which runs on web sockets and long polling, using normal HTTP requests held for longer periods on the server before responses are returned to facilitate a live-stream of data between client and server. You start by learning how to implement socket.io with Express.js. Then you create a chat box in a new application view. Last, you connect the client-side JavaScript and server code through custom events triggered and handled by socket.io.

This lesson covers

- Implementing socket.io in a Node.js application
- Structuring your socket.io listeners within a controller
- Creating a simple chat feature

> **Consider this**   You built a perfectly functional application with tons of users flocking to sign up. Unfortunately, these users have no way of communicating with one another. Given that you're building an application that's community-driven, communication among members is important. The user data is already in the database. All you need to do is associate that data through a tool that supports real-time communication.
>
> With a little help from socket.io, you'll soon be able to connect users so that they can chat with one another.

30.1 Using socket.io

You've built Node.js web applications that feature client-to-server communication. When the client wants to view a web page or post data, your application generates an HTTP request to the server. This method of communication over the internet has been around for a long time, celebrating its 20th birthday in 2017. In technology years, that's old. Although developers still heavily rely on the request-response cycle, it isn't the most effective method of communication for every use case.

What if you want to view the scores of an NBA basketball game in real time, for example? You can load the page containing scores and statistics, but you'd need to reload the page every time you wanted to see an update in information. For a basketball game, these changes can come as rapidly as every second. Repeatedly creating GET requests to the server is a lot of work to expect from the client. *Polling* is used to generate repeated requests from the client to the server in anticipation of updated server data. Polling uses the standard techniques you've used so far to transfer data between the client and server, but it sends requests so frequently that it creates an illusion of an open channel of communication between both participants (figure 30.1).

To further improve on this technique, long polling was developed to reduce the number of requests needed to get updated data. *Long polling* behaves similarly to polling, in that the client makes repeated requests to the server for updated data, but fewer requests are made. Instead of making hundreds of requests when only dozens of them receive updated data, long polling allows requests to stay open as long as HTTP allows before the requests time out. Within that time—say, 10 seconds—the server can hold on to the request and either respond with updated data when the server receives it or respond with no changes before the request times out. This more-efficient approach has allowed

Long polling

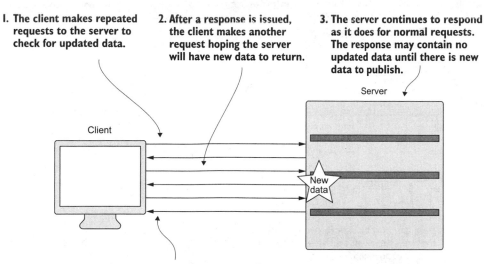

I. **The client makes repeated requests to the server to check for updated data.**

2. **After a response is issued, the client makes another request hoping the server will have new data to return.**

3. **The server continues to respond as it does for normal requests. The response may contain no updated data until there is new data to publish.**

Server

Client

New data

4. **In long polling, each request may wait on the server for a longer period of time before a response is issued. This reduces the number of requests made.**

Figure 30.1   Polling between a client and server

web browsers and devices to experience a sense of real-time informational exchange over a protocol that hasn't changed much for decades.

Although these two methods are widely used, a recent new addition has allowed platforms like Node.js to thrive. *Web sockets* were introduced in 2011 to allow an open stream of communication between clients and server, creating a true open channel that allows information to flow in either direction as long as the server or clients are available. Web sockets use a different internet protocol from HTTP but are supported in use with a normal HTTP server. In most cases, a server running with web sockets enabled allows its open channels to be reached over the same application ports you'd use for a typical request-response exchange (figure 30.2).

Although web sockets are a preferred method for live communication, they're not supported by many older browsers and clients. This relatively new technology allows developers to build applications that stream data in real time, and you can incorporate it into your existing Node.js application: socket.io, a JavaScript library that uses web sockets when it can and polling where web sockets are unsupported.

socket.io is also a package that can be installed within a Node.js application, providing library support for web sockets. It uses the event-driven communication in Node.js and

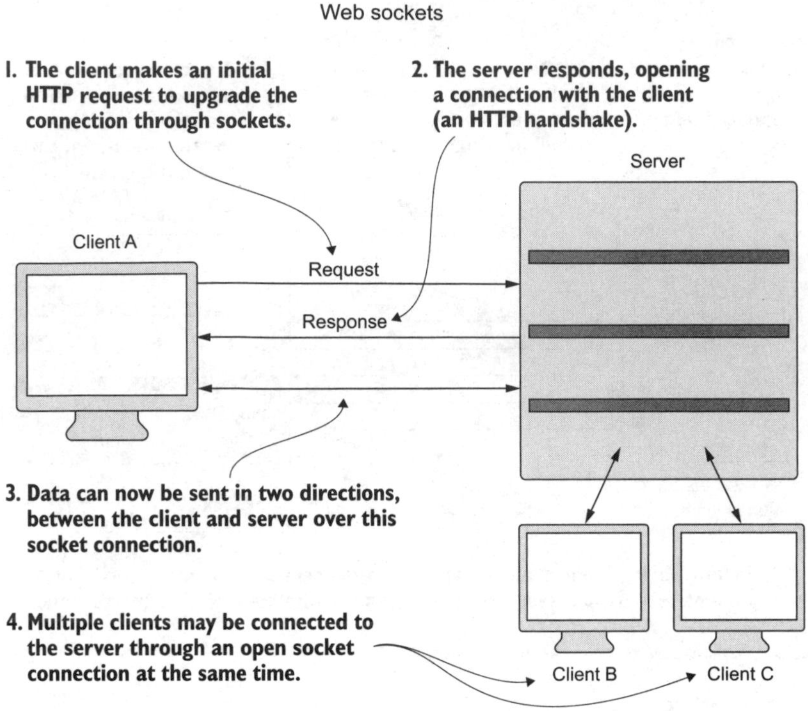

Web sockets

I. **The client makes an initial HTTP request to upgrade the connection through sockets.**

2. **The server responds, opening a connection with the client (an HTTP handshake).**

Server

Client A

Request

Response

3. **Data can now be sent in two directions, between the client and server over this socket connection.**

4. **Multiple clients may be connected to the server through an open socket connection at the same time.**

Client B   Client C

Figure 30.2   Opening a web socket connection between a client and server

web sockets to allow the client and server to send data by triggering events. As a client looking for updated basketball-game statistics, for example, you might have client-side JavaScript listening for an *updated data* event triggered by the server. Then your browser would handle the *updated data* event along with any data passed with it to modify the contents of your web page. These events can come in a continuous stream or hours apart, if needed. If you wanted to signal to the server to send a message to all other listening clients, you could trigger an event that the server knows how to handle. Luckily, you have control of both the client-side and server-side code, so you can implement the firing and handling of any events you want.

To start, install socket.io in your recipe application by running npm i socket.io -S in your project's terminal window. You'll use this library in the following sections to build a live-chat feature for users to communicate.

Quick check 30.1   How is long polling different from polling?

 30.2 Creating a chat box

To get started with a chat feature, you need to build a basic view with a chat box and submit button. As you build the code to allow the client to handle server events, this chat box will populate with data.

Create a new view called chat.ejs in your views folder. Within this view, add the code in listing 30.1. In this code, you have a form that takes an input and a submit button. Below the form code is the tag created for the chat box. With some simple CSS styling, you can add a border and size dimensions to the chat box, prompting users to type the form input and submit it to add the content to the chat window below.

Listing 30.1 Creating a chat box in chat.ejs

```
<div class="container">
  <h1>Chat</h1>                     Add an HTML form
  <form id="chatForm">              for chat input.
    <input id="chat-input" type="text">
    <input type="submit" value="Send">      Add a custom input
  </form>                                    element for chat content.
  <div id="chat"></div>      Create a tag for
</div>                       the chat box.
```

To load this view, add a new route and action. Add `router.get("/chat", homeController.chat)` to homeRoutes.js in your routes folder. This new route will be absorbed by the index.js route file and used by main.js. Now you need to create the chat action in homeController.js, as shown in the next listing. In this action, you simply render the chat.ejs view.

QC 30.1 answer   Long polling works by sending the server requests that are sustained longer than typical requests. Polling depends on many individual GET requests. Long polling is more efficient because it keeps a single GET request alive for a longer period, allowing the server to receive updates and respond before the client makes another request.

Listing 30.2 Adding a chat action in homeController.js

```
chat: (req, res) => {
  res.render("chat");          ⟵——— Render a chat view.
}
```

Relaunch your application, and visit http://localhost:3000/chat to see the chat box shown in figure 30.3.

> **NOTE**   Your chat page will not look exactly like figure 30.3 unless you add custom styling to it.

Figure 30.3   Displaying chat view

With this chat page set up, you need to remember the tag IDs that you used in the HTML. In the next section, you target the #chat box with chat messages and send new messages found in #chat-input to the server.

> **Quick check 30.2**   Why does the HTML element with ID chat not have any content?

> **QC 30.2 answer**   The #chat element starts empty on each page load. You'll use client-side Java-Script to populate the element with content as it's received by the server.

30.3 Connecting the server and client

Now that you have a chat page, you need the guts to get it working. With socket.io installed, you need to require it into your project. Because you want your socket server to run on your existing Express.js HTTP server, require socket.io, and pass it to your Express.js server. Add the require line to main.js below the line where you tell your app to listen on a specified port, as shown in listing 30.3. In this code, you save the running server instance into a constant server so that you can pass the same Express.js HTTP server to socket.io. This process allows socket.io (which I'll refer to as io) to attach to your application server.

Listing 30.3 Adding the server io object in main.js

```
const server = app.listen(app.get("port"), () => {
    console.log(`Server running at http://localhost:
⮡ ${ app.get("port") }`);
  }),                                          Save the server
                                               instance to server.
  io = require("socket.io")(server);   ↖
                                       Pass the server
                                       instance to socket.io.
```

Now you can start using io to build out your socket logic. As with your other code, though, compartmentalize this code into its own controller. Create a new chatController .js in your controllers folder, and require it below where you required socket.io. To require the controller, add require("./controllers/chatController")(io) to main.js. In this line, you're passing the io object to your chat controller so that you can manage your socket connections from there. You don't need to store this module in a constant because you won't be using it further in main.js, so you can require it.

> **NOTE** It's important that you require chatController.js after defining the io object. Otherwise, you won't have socket.io configured for use in your controller.

Within chatController.js, add the code in listing 30.4. In this code block, you're exporting all the controller's contents and taking a single parameter: the io object from main.js. In this file, you use io to listen for certain events. To start, io listens for the connection event, indicating that a client has connected to the socket channel. In handling this event, you can use the specific client socket to listen for when the user disconnects or for custom events, such as the message event you created. If the server receives a message event, it uses io to send a string of data to all connected clients, using its emit method.

Listing 30.4 Handling chat socket connections in chatController.js

```
module.exports = io => {                    ← Export the chat
  io.on("connection", client => {          ←   controller contents.
    console.log("new connection");
                                            ← Listen for new
                                                user connections.
    client.on("disconnect", () => {        ←
      console.log("user disconnected");
    });
                                              Listen for when
                                              the user
    client.on("message", () => {           ←  disconnects.
      io.emit("message", {
        content: "Hello"
      });                                    Listen for a custom
    });                            ←         message event.
  });
};                          Broadcast a
                            message to all
                            connected users.
```

> **NOTE** Notice that you're using the argument name `client` because this code will run
> with each new client connect. `client` represents the connected entity on the other side of
> the socket with the server. Client listeners run only if an initial `io` connection is made.

With this code in place, you need to set up the client-side code to handle data from and
send events to the server. To accomplish this task, add some code to your recipeApp.js
JavaScript code in your public folder.

In this code, initialize `socket.io` on the client side, allowing your server to detect that a
new user has connected. Then, using jQuery, handle the form submission by emitting a
`message` event to the server, and prevent the form from submitting naturally with `return`
`false`. `socket.emit` takes a string argument as the event name and emits the event back to
the server. Using `socket.on`, you listen for the `message` from the server, along with a string
message. You display that message by appending it as a list item in your #chat element.
On the server, you've already set up a handler in chatController.js for the `message` event
to send back the message content `"Hello"` to the client.

Listing 30.5 Adding client-side JavaScript for `socket.io` in recipeApp.js

```
const socket = io();                ←        Initialize socket.io
                                             on the client.
$("#chatForm").submit(() => {       ←
  socket.emit("message");
  $("#chat-input").val("");                  Emit an event
  return false;                              when the form
});                                          is submitted.
```

```
socket.on("message", (message) => {          ⟵  Listen for an event, and
  displayMessage(message.content);               populate the chat box.
});
                                                 Display messages from
let displayMessage = (message) => {          ⟵  the server in the chat box.
  $("#chat").prepend($("<li>").html(message));
};
```

The last step is loading the socket.io library on the client by adding a script tag to the view on which the chat is generated. To simplify this task, add the tag to your layout file. In layout.ejs, add `<script src="/socket.io/socket.io.js"></script>` below your other script and link tags. This tag tells your Node.js application to find the socket.io library in your node_modules folder.

Relaunch your application, visit http://localhost:3000/chat, enter some text in the input box, and click Send. You should see "Hello" in your chat box (figure 30.4). A new line should appear with each new text submission.

Figure 30.4 Displaying text in the chat box

In lesson 31, you improve this chat to allow the application to save these messages to your database.

Summary

In this lesson, you learned about socket.io and saw how to install it in a Node.js application. Then you created your first chat application by using web sockets over your Express.js server to facilitate event and data exchange between client and server. When this chat feature is installed, users can communicate with one another in real time. When a client refreshes the web page, however, the chat history is erased. What's more, you have no indication of which user sent which message. In lesson 31, you create a new data model and associate user accounts so that message authors can be identified and chats can persist across user sessions.

Try this

With a chat feature implemented, try sending more meaningful data between the client and server. The message content allows all clients to see the same messages at the same time, but maybe you want to see more than the message itself. Try sending the date stamp showing when the message was sent to the server. Then, with client-side JavaScript, collect that date stamp and display it next to the message in the chat box.

SAVING CHAT MESSAGES

Your chat feature is coming together, and you can take it in many directions to improve it. Though the chat feature allows for real-time communication, when you refresh your page, all messages disappear. The next step is persisting these messages in your database. In this lesson, you implement a simple model to represent each chat message. Then you connect that model to the user model, allowing senders to associate with their own messages. Last, you query the database for the most recent messages whenever a page is reloaded. When you complete these steps, the chat will start to resemble ones that you've used on familiar websites and in familiar applications.

This lesson covers

- Creating a message model
- Saving messages in a socket.io event handler
- Querying messages upon new socket connections

Consider this You have a chat page working, finally allowing users to talk to one another. As soon as a user refreshes their page, their chat history is gone. Although this feature could be marketed as a security implementation, it's impractical. You want to save the message and do so without interrupting the fast-paced, event-driven system on which your chat application functions. In this lesson, you use Mongoose and your existing application structure to support saving and loading chat messages.

31.1 Connecting messages to users

In lesson 30, you created a chat feature for your application, allowing users to trigger a
message event, prompting the server to respond with the same "Hello" text-message content. You can improve this feature by sending the actual content you type in the chat
input box to the server. To do so, modify your client-side code so that your event handler on form submission looks like listing 31.1.

This small change allows you to grab the text the user typed right after he clicks the submit button. Then you send the text within an object as you emit the message event to the
server.

Listing 31.1 Emitting an event from the client in recipeApp.js

```javascript
$("#chatForm").submit(() => {
  let text = $("#chat_input").val();          Grab text from the
  socket.emit("message", {                    view input field.
    content: text
  });
  $("#chat_input").val("");                   Emit form data to
  return false;                               the server.
});
```

In response, have the server emit this form data to all listening clients. You can do so by
modifying the message event handler in the chat controller to emit the data back to all clients. Change the code around the io.emit line in chatController.js to the code in listing
31.2. Here, you grab the data from the client and emit it back. If you relaunch your
application and try to type a new chat message, that specific message appears in the
chat box. You can also open a second browser window to mimic two users, and these
two browsers allow for multiple socket connections to submit data and display new
messages in the other browser's chat box in real time (figure 31.1).

Listing 31.2 Change emit message to data in chatController.js

```javascript
client.on("message", data => {                        Collect data as
  io.emit("message", { content: data.content });      a parameter.
});
                     Return data in the
                     message event as
                     content.
```

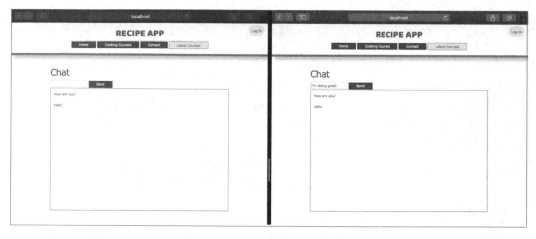

Figure 31.1 Displaying chats with two sockets

The next thing you want to do is add some information about the user who posted the chat message. Currently, you're sending only the message content to the server, but you can send the user's name and ID as well. Modify your chat form to include two pieces of hidden data, as shown in listing 31.3. In this example, you check whether a `currentUser` is logged in, using data on the response provided by `passport`. If there's a user, use that user's `_id` attribute in the form as a hidden field. Then this value can be passed to the server when you submit your message.

Listing 31.3 Adding hidden fields in chat form in chat.ejs

```
<% if (currentUser) { %>          ← Check for a
  <h1>Chat</h1>                      logged-in user.
  <form id="chatForm">
    <input id="chat-input" type="text">
      <input id="chat-user-name" type="hidden"
  value="<%= currentUser.fullName %>">
    <input id="chat-user-id" type="hidden"
  value="<%= currentUser._id %>">   ← Add a hidden field
    <input type="submit" value="Send">   contain user data.
  </form>
  <div id="chat"></div>
<% } %>
```

Now that you've included a user field in your chat form, you'll display the chat box only if a user is signed in. Try loading /chat before logging in. Then try again after logging in with one of your local user accounts. The second try yields the chat-page contents.

Next, modify your custom client-side JavaScript to pull these values when the form is submitted. Replace your form-submission event listener with the code in the next listing. In this modified code, you grab the user's ID and pass the value to the server, using the same local variable name.

Listing 31.4 Pulling hidden field values from chat form in recipeApp.js

```
$("#chatForm").submit(() => {
  let text = $("#chat-input").val(),
    userId = $("#chat-user-id").val();          Pull hidden field
  socket.emit("message", {                       data from the form.
    content: text,
    userId: userId
  });
  $("#chat-input").val("");            Emit an event with
  return false;                        message content
});                                    and user data.
```

Now you can handle this data on the server side by changing your code in the message event handler in chatController.js to collect all the individual attributes passed to the server (listing 31.5). By saving these values to a new object, you can filter out any unwanted values outside what you specify in the messageAttributes object. Then emit those values containing the message contents and user information to the other clients.

> **NOTE** This code must exist within the io.on("connection")... block. You can listen for specific events only from client sockets that are connected.

Listing 31.5 Receiving socket data in chatController.js

```
client.on("message", (data) => {
  let messageAttributes = {
    content: data.content,
    userName: data.userName,          Collect all incoming data.
    user: data.userId
  };
  io.emit("message", messageAttributes);        Emit the message
});                                              with user data.
```

Last, you need to arrange this data and display it appropriately in the view. Back in recipeApp.js, change the code in displayMessage to match the code in listing 31.6. This function adds an HTML class attribute to the messages associated with the logged-in user. By comparing the ID of the user in the form with the ID associated with the chat message, you can filter out the logged-in user's messages.

To accomplish this task, add getCurrentUserClass to determine whether the message in the chat belongs to the user who's currently logged in. If so, add a current-user class, which you can use to distinguish the messages for that user visually. After this change, each message identified as belonging to the current signed-in user will have this style class associated. Because you're using the user's ID and message content in this function, you need to pass the entire message object, not only the message content as you did before, to displayMessage.

> **NOTE** Change your call displayMessage(message.content) to displayMessage (message) so that you can use all properties of the message object.

Listing 31.6 Pulling hidden field values from chat form in recipeApp.js

```
let displayMessage = (message) => {
  $("#chat").prepend(
    $("<li>").html(`
<div class="message ${getCurrentUserClass(message.user)}">
${message.content}                Display the message
</div>`)                           contents along with the
  );                               user name in chat box.
};

let getCurrentUserClass = (id) => {
  let userId = $("#chat-user-id").val();
  return userId === id ? "current-user": "";      Check whether the
};                                                message's user ID
                                                  matches the form's
                                                  user ID.
```

Now add some styling to the current-user class elements and distinguish chat messages from one another. With two browser windows side by side, and two users logged in, the chat can look like figure 31.2.

You've implemented the logic to associate messages with users and distinguish those messages on the view. This chat still seems to lack a few points, however. Although the logged-in user can identify their own messages, they don't know the identity of the other users. In the next section, you add user names to the chat messages.

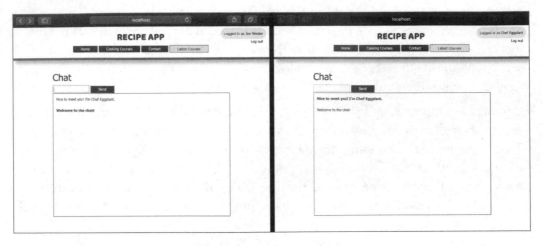

Figure 31.2   Styling user messages with two sockets

Quick check 31.1   Why do you need to compare the chat message's user ID with the user ID on the chat form in the client-side JavaScript?

31.2 Displaying user names in chat

The closer you get to coupling messages with the user accounts that created them, the easier it will be for users to communicate with one another. To eliminate confusion, you want to use the user's name as an identifier on the chat message. To do so, implement a few small changes in your code from section 1.

You've already added a hidden input field on the chat form to submit the user's fullName. When the logged-in user submits their chat message, their name is sent along too.

Next, grab this field value in recipeApp.js by pulling the value from the #chat_user_name input on form submission, and save it to a variable. The new submit event handler looks

QC 31.1 answer   The form's user ID reflects that of the logged-in user. If the user ID in the chat's message matches the one in the form, you can safely mark that message as belonging to the logged-in user and apply styling to indicate that fact.

like the code in the next listing. Then emit that value within the same object paired with the userName key. You'll use this key in the server later.

Listing 31.7 Pulling an additional hidden field value from chat form in recipeApp.js

```
$("#chatForm").submit(() => {
  let text = $("#chat-input").val(),
    userName = $("#chat-user-name").val(),   ←— Pull the user's name.
    userId = $("#chat-user-id").val();
  socket.emit("message", {
    content: text,
    userName: userName,
    userId: userId
  });
  $("#chat_input").val("");     Emit a custom event
  return false;                 with message contents
});                             to the server.
```

On the server, you need to include this user name in the message attributes you collect so that they can be emitted to other client sockets. You could use the user's ID to retrieve their name, but this approach saves you from communicating with the database. In the message event handler in chatController.js, your message attributes variable assignment should read let messageAttributes = {content: data.content, userName: data.userName, user: data.userId}.

Last, arrange this data, and display it appropriately in the view. Back in recipeApp.js, change the code in the displayMessage function to the code in listing 31.8. This change displays the name of the user associated with the posted message. You can still use the getCurrentUserClass function to determine whether the message in the chat belongs to the currently logged-in user.

Listing 31.8 Displaying the user name in the chat in recipeApp.js

```
$("#chat").prepend($("<li>").html(`
<strong class="message ${getCurrentUserClass(
➥ message.user )}">
${message.userName}          Display the user name
</strong>: ${message.content}    in bold and stylize if
`));                             currentUser.
```

After implementing these changes, you can see the names of the users posting in the chat (figure 31.3).

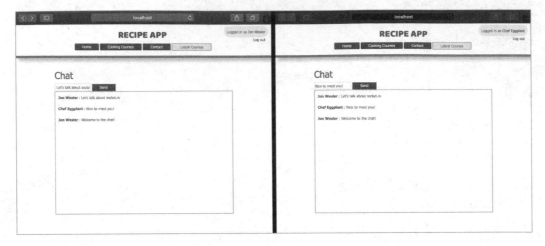

Figure 31.3   Showing user names with two sockets

With this improvement, users can identify the author of specific chat messages by that sender's name. This feature is great, as it reduces the anonymity of chat and allows registered users to connect with one another. You still have the problem of chat messages disappearing with each page load, however. You need to connect these chat messages to your database, and the best way to do so is through a Mongoose data model. In the next section, you explore the model schema needed for a chat message.

> **Quick check 31.2**   Why do you pass the user's name to the server instead of using the user's ID to find the name in your database?

QC 31.2 answer   Using the user's ID to look up their name can work, but it adds another layer of work involving the database. With no immediate need to use your database for this chat, you can pass the extra string values.

31.3 Creating a message model

To make this chat page worth revisiting, you need to save the messages being shared. To do so, you need to save the messages to your database, and you have a few ways to save them:

- You can modify your user schema to save an array of messages. With each new message that any user submits, that message is added to the user's messages array. This approach can work, but you'll quickly end up with long lists that aren't efficient or necessary to store in the user model.
- You could also create a new model to represent the chat and its messages. This approach requires a new model module but ultimately saves you some work and makes it easier to understand exactly what data you're working with and saving.

In this section, you build a Message model to contain the values you've been working with in this lesson. Create a new message.js file in your project's models folder, and add the code in listing 31.9 to that file.

In this code, you're defining a message schema that contains content, userName, and user properties. The content of the chat message is required, as are the user's name and ID. In essence, every message needs some text and an author. If someone tries to save a message somehow without logging in and authenticating, your database won't allow the data to save. You also set timestamps to true so that you can keep track of when the chat message was added to your database. This feature allows you to show the timestamp in the chat box, if you want.

Listing 31.9 Creating the message schema in message.js

```
const mongoose = require("mongoose"),
  { Schema } = require("mongoose");

const messageSchema = new Schema({
  content: {
    type: String,
    required: true          Require content
  },                        in each message.
  userName: {
    type: String,
    required: true          Require the
  },                        user's name with
  user: {                   each message.
```

```
    type: Schema.Types.ObjectId,
    ref: "User",
    required: true                    Require a user ID
  }                                    with each message.
}, { timestamps: true });  ←—— Save the timestamp with each message.

module.exports = mongoose.model("Message", messageSchema);
```

Next, require this new model in chatController.js by adding const Message = require
("../models/message") to the top of the file.

> **NOTE** ../models/message means you're stepping out of the controllers folder and into
> the models folder to find message.js.

To start saving incoming data to message models, you need to use your messageAttributes
as the properties of a new message object. Then try to save that message to your MongoDB
database, and emit the message if you're successful. Modify your code with the code in
the next listing to change the client.on("message") block in chatController.js.

Listing 31.10 Saving a message in chatController.js

```
client.on("message", (data) => {        Create a new
  let messageAttributes = {             message object with
      content: data.content,            messageAttributes.
      userName: data.userName,
      user: data.userId
  },
  m = new Message(messageAttributes);
  m.save()                              ←———— Save the message.
    .then(() => {
      io.emit("message", messageAttributes);
    })
    .catch(error => console.log(`error: ${error.message}`));
});
```

Emit the message values
if the save is successful,
or log any errors.

That's all it takes to start saving your messages. You can relaunch your application, log
in, and send messages to have them save behind the scenes. You won't notice any
changes, because as soon as you refresh the chat page, you still wipe the chat history,
even though messages are saved in your database. To correct this problem, you need to
load some recent chat messages whenever a user reconnects to the chat socket. Within
chatController.js, add the code in listing 31.11 to find the ten most recent chat messages

and emit them with a new custom event. Use sort({createdAt: -1}) to sort your database results in descending order. Then chain limit(10) to limit those results to the ten most recent. When you emit your custom "load all messages" events on the client socket, only newly connected users' chat boxes will refresh with the latest chat messages. Reverse the list of messages with messages.reverse() so that you can prepend them in the view.

Listing 31.11 Loading most recent messages in chatController.js

```
Message.find({})
  .sort({ createdAt: -1 })        Query the ten
  .limit(10)                       most recent
  .then(messages => {             messages.
    client.emit("load all messages", messages.reverse());
  });
                                                Emit a custom event
                                                with ten messages to
                                                the new socket only.
```

The last step is handling this new custom event in your client-side JavaScript. In recipe-App.js, add the event handler in listing 31.12. This code listens for the "load all messages" event emitted to this specific socket. Any data received here is handled by sending each message in the data array to your displayMessage function to prepend the message contents to your chat box.

Listing 31.12 Displaying most recent messages in recipeApp.js

```
socket.on("load all messages", (data) => {
  data.forEach(message => {           Handle 'load all
    displayMessage(message);          messages' by parsing
  });                                 incoming data.
});
              Send each message to
              displayMessage to
              display in the chat box.
```

Try comparing views of two adjacent sockets before and after one of the sockets refreshes its connection. A user's new connection refreshes the chat box with messages from the database. Now it's much easier for users to participate in the chat with a preserved history of messages shared.

Summary

In this lesson, you learned how to curate messages in your chat box to display information about the message's author. You also displayed the names of users alongside their messages to increase transparency in the chat page. At the end of the lesson, you created a Message model and started saving messages to your application's database. This implementation allows messages to persist across multiple socket connections. By loading the most recent messages on every new socket connection, you immediately involve users in the conversation. In lesson 32, you look at one way to use `socket.io` events to notify users of new messages even when they aren't actively on the chat page.

Try this

Now that you have messages saving to your database and associated with user accounts, add another layer of security at the controller layer. Although you're saving user IDs to the message, you aren't making sure that the user ID is valid in your database. Add some code within the promise chain where the message is saved in chatController.js to check the database for a user by the same ID and verify it before you officially save the message. For this task, you need to require the user model in this controller.

ADDING A CHAT NOTIFICATION INDICATOR

Your chat page is coming together. Now users can log in and view the most recent chat messages, whether they were sent moments or weeks ago. The chat page currently facilitates all the visual aspects of your application's chat functionality. The nice thing about socket.io is that it doesn't need to exist on one page. Because your chat works by emitting and handling events, you can use those events in other ways. In this lesson, you build a custom event emitter to notify all active users when chat messages are being submitted. Then you build a small visual indicator in the navigation bar that animates when new messages are being shared. Through this small feat, users get a visual indication of an active chat room even when they're browsing a different page.

This lesson covers

- Broadcasting a custom event
- Animating an icon in response to an event

> **Consider this**   Users are enjoying the chat page in your application, but they'd like to browse other pages in your application instead of waiting for new messages to arrive on the chat page. They don't want to miss out when the chat is active again, however. In this lesson, you rely on a custom event emitted by the server to animate a navigation-bar icon. When this icon is animated, users on any page of the application know that a chat is active.

32.1 Broadcasting to all other sockets

One thing to know about socket.io is that it can be configured to work over multiple specific chat rooms and different namespaces. It can even allow users to be added and removed from specific groups. In addition to these features, messages don't always need to be emitted to every client. In fact, it doesn't always make sense to emit a message to everyone if, for example, the client emitting the message is disconnecting.

In this section, you implement a new feature to notify all other users in the chat when a user's socket disconnects. To do so, add the code in listing 32.1 to chatController.js within the io.on("connect") block.

In this code, you're listening for when a certain client disconnects. You used this code block before to log a message to your console. In addition to logging this information, use client.broadcast.emit("user disconnected") to send a message to every socket aside from the one emitting the message. client.broadcast sends a custom event called 'user disconnected' to the connected chat users.

The reason you're broadcasting the message instead of emitting it is because the client that's emitting the message is disconnected and can no longer handle that custom event. You can use broadcast to emit to all other sockets even when the emitting socket isn't disconnected, though.

Listing 32.1 Broadcasting event to all other users in chatController.js

```
client.on("disconnect", () => {
  client.broadcast.emit("user disconnected");
  console.log("user disconnected");
});
```

 Broadcast a message to all otherconnected sockets.

With this new event being emitted, you need to handle it on the client side. As with your other events, listen for the "user disconnected" event, and print some indication in the chat box. Add the event handler in listing 32.2 to recipeApp.js. In this code, you reuse your displayMessage to post a hardcoded message to let other users know that someone disconnected.

Listing 32.2 Displaying a message when a user disconnects in recipeApp.js

```
socket.on("user disconnected", () => {        Listen for the 'user
  displayMessage({                              disconnected' event, and
    userName: "Notice",                         display a custom message.
    content: "User left the chat"
  });
});
```

Now relaunch your application, and log into multiple accounts by logging in on two different browsers or by using your browser's incognito mode to log in with a new session. With two chat windows open side by side, you should see when one of the users is connected in the other chat box. In figure 32.1, the left chat window shows that a user disconnected when the right window is refreshed. In this case, a page refresh results in an immediate connection thereafter.

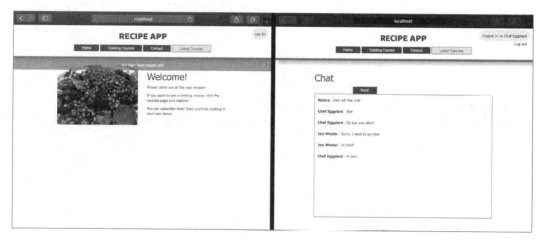

Figure 32.1 Displaying user disconnects in chat

Quick check 32.1   What's the difference between `client.broadcast.emit` and `client`
`.emit`?

 ## 32.2 Creating a chat indicator in navigation

The last addition you'll make to your chat application is a feature to let users on other
pages in the application know when there's activity on the chat page. This feature could
be helpful to users who are viewing their profiles or recipes, or hanging out on the
home page; they might like to know that other users are awake and talking to one
another in the chat room. To add this feature, add an icon to the navigation bar. When a
message is submitted in the chat room, you animate the chat icon in the navigation bar
to let users elsewhere know of chat activity.

First, add the icon to your navigation bar by adding `<a href="/chat" class="chat-icon">`
`@</a>` in layout.ejs. With this icon in place, you should see @ in your navigation bar the
next time you relaunch your application. If you click this icon, it takes you to the /chat
route.

Next, animate the icon by having it flash twice when any user sends a message. To
accomplish this task, use jQuery's `fadeOut` and `fadeIn` methods on the chat icon whenever a `"message"` event is received. Modify your `socket.on("message")` handler in recipe-
App.js to look like the code in the next listing. In this example, you still use the
`displayMessage` function to post the message to your chat view; then, with a simple for
loop, you animate the chat icon to flash twice.

Listing 32.3 Animating chat icon when messages are sent in recipeApp.js

```
socket.on("message", (message) => {
  displayMessage(message);
  for (let i = 0; i < 2; i++) {
    $(".chat-icon").fadeOut(200).fadeIn(200);
  }
});
```

Animate the chat
icon to flash when a
message is sent.

QC 32.1 answer   `client.broadcast.emit` emits an event to all sockets except for itself, and
`client.emit` emits an event to all sockets including itself.

Relaunch your application, and log in to two browsers under two different accounts. Notice that now when one user sends a message, the other user sees the chat icon flash twice in the navigation bar, no matter where in the application they are (figure 32.2).

Figure 32.2 Animating the chat icon in the navigation bar

In lesson 33, you apply these steps and fully implement a chat feature in your capstone project.

Quick check 32.2   True or false: You can handle `socket.io` events on any page in your application.

QC 32.2 answer   True. For the example in this lesson, you imported the `socket.io` library in the layout.ejs file, which is used in every view. Similarly, your client-side JavaScript lives in files also imported to your layout file. If you were to import `socket.io` client only on a specific view, you'd be able to handle events only on that specific page.

 **Summary**

In this lesson, you learned how to customize your socket.io events for use outside the normal chat feature. Because events can be used in any part of the application that has a socket.io client, you can create events for many types of data transfer over an open connection. First, you created a new event to notify other users when a user disconnects. Then you used an existing event to trigger a nonchat feature in your layout's navigation. With this chat feature functioning, it's time to apply the same tools to your capstone project (lesson 33). Then it's time to deploy!

Try this

Now that your chat application has a feature that lets users know when a user has disconnected, it would be useful to know when a user connects. Use io.on("connection") to trigger a new event to your client to let them know that a new user has joined the chat.

When you're done, see whether you can add the user's name in the connection message, as in Notice: Jon Wexler has joined the chat.

CAPSTONE: ADDING A CHAT FEATURE TO CONFETTI CUISINE

At this stage, my application's foundation is complete. I can continue to improve existing functionality or build new features. Before the application is released to production and made available for everyone to use, Confetti Cuisine asked me to add an interesting feature to engage users. Without hesitation, I tell them that this is a perfect opportunity to build a chat feature within their Node.js application. Because I don't want to complicate the application too much before deployment, I'll keep the chat simple.

The chat will allow only users with accounts to communicate with one another. Every time a message is sent, I'll save the message and associate it with the sender behind the scenes. Also, I'll take advantage of socket.io to maintain an open connection between connected clients and the server for real-time communication. Through this library's event-driven tools, I can emit events from the server to individual clients or all clients and from the client to the server. I could also emit events to a select group of clients, but I won't need to implement that feature for this application.

Later, I'll connect a chat icon in the navigation bar to animate whenever a chat message is sent. All users see this icon animate whenever a message is emitted. This icon doubles as a link to the chat page. It's time to put the finishing touches on the Confetti Cuisine application.

33.1   Installing socket.io

First, I need to install the socket.io package. socket.io offers a JavaScript library that helps me build a real-time communication portal through its use of web sockets and long polling to maintain open connections between the client and the server. To install this package as a dependency, I run npm i socket.io -S in my project's terminal window.

With this package installed, I need to require it in my main application file and on the client side.

 ## 33.2   Setting up socket.io on the server

Before I require socket.io, I need to save the server instance I'm creating with Express.js by assigning my app.listen line in main.js to a constant called server. Below this line, I'll require socket.io in my project by adding const io = require("socket.io")(server). In this line, I'm simultaneously requiring the socket.io module and passing it the instance of my HTTP server used by Express.js. This way, the connection used by socket.io will share the same HTTP server as my main application. With my socket.io instance stored in the io constant, I can start using io to build out my chat functionality.

First, I set up a new controller for chat functionality. Though all the socket.io code can exist in main.js, it's easier to read and maintain in its own controller. I start by requiring a new controller in main.js and passing it the io object by adding const chatController = require("./controllers/chatController")(io) to the bottom of main.js. Next, I create chatController.js in my controllers folder. In this file, I add the code from listing 33.1.

I use the same io object created in main.js to listen for specific socket events. io.on ("connection") reacts when a new client connects to my socket server. client.on ("disconnect") reacts when a connected client disconnects. client.on("message") reacts when a client socket sends a custom message event to the server. I can name this event whatever I want. Because I'm working with chat messages, this event name seems to be appropriate. Within that last block, I use io.emit to send a message event back to all connected clients with the same data I received from an individual client. This way, everyone gets the same message that a single user submits.

Listing 33.1 Adding a chat action in chatController.js

```
module.exports = io => {          ←  Export the chat
  io.on("connection", client => {      controller contents.
    console.log("new connection");  ←  Listen for new
                                        user connections.
    client.on("disconnect", () => {   ←
      console.log("user disconnected");
    });                                  Listen for when the
                                         user disconnects.
    client.on("message", (data) => {  ←
      let messageAttributes = {
        content: data.content,           Listen for a custom
        userName: data.userName,         message event.
        user: data.userId
      };
      io.emit("message");
    });
  });                               Broadcast a
};                                  message to all
                                    connected users.
```

The last line of code sends a specific set of message attributes that I expect to receive from the client. That is, I expect the client to emit a message event along with content, user name, and user ID. I need to send those three attributes from the view.

33.3 Setting up socket.io on the client

To build a successful chat connection, I need a view that facilitates the socket connection from the client side. I want to build my chat box in a view called chat.ejs that's reachable at the /chat URL path. I create a new route for this path in my homeRoutes.js by adding `router.get("/chat", homeController.chat)`.

Then I add the controller action to match this route by adding the code in the next listing to homeController.js. This code renders my chat.ejs view.

Listing 33.2 Adding a chat action in homeController.js

```
chat: (req, res) => {
  res.render("chat");    ←——— Render a chat view.
}
```

To render my chat view, I need to build the view. I create a new file in my views folder called chat.ejs and add the code in listing 33.3. In this Embedded JavaScript (EJS) code, I first check for a currentUser in the view. Earlier, I set up the currentUser as a local variable to reflect an active user session through Passport.js. If a user is logged in, I display the chat form. The form contains three inputs. Two of the inputs are hidden but carry the user's name and ID. I'll use these inputs later to send the identity of the message author to the server. The first input is for the actual message content. Later, I'll grab the value of this input as the content that I submit to the server.

Listing 33.3 Adding hidden fields in chat form in chat.ejs

```
<% if (currentUser) { %>      ◄────── Check for a logged-in user.
  <h1>Chat</h1>
  <form id="chatForm">
    <input id="chat-input" type="text">
    <input id="chat-user-id" type="hidden" value="<%=
➥ currentUser._id %>">
    <input id="chat-user-name" type="hidden" value="<%=
➥ currentUser.fullName %>">                          ◄──── Add hidden fields
    <input type="submit" value="Send">                       containing user data.
  </form>
  <div id="chat"></div>
<% } %>
```

The last pieces of this puzzle are adding some client-side JavaScript to monitor user interaction on this chat page and submitting the socket.io events needed to notify the server of new messages. In my public folder, I locate confettiCuisine.js and add to it the code in listing 33.4. In this code, I import socket.io for the client and add logic to interact over web sockets with my server. In the first code block, I use jQuery to handle my form's submission and grab all the values from my form's three inputs. I expect to receive these same three attributes in my server's client.on("message") event handler.

The second block of code uses the socket object to represent the specific client on which this code will run. socket.on("message") sets up the client to listen for the message event, which emits from the server. When that event is emitted, each client takes the message delivered with that event and passes it to a custom displayMessage function that I created. This function locates my chat box in the view and prepends the message to the screen.

Listing 33.4 Adding socket.io on the client in confettiCuisine.js

```
const socket = io();    ◄────── Initialize socket.io on the client.

$("#chatForm").submit(() => {
  let text = $("#chat-input").val(),
    userName = $("#chat-user-name").val(),
    userId = $("#chat-user-id").val();
  socket.emit("message", {
    content: text,
    userName: userName,
    userId: userId
  });
  $("#chat-input").val("");
  return false;
});

socket.on("message", (message) => {
  displayMessage(message);
});

let displayMessage = (message) => {
  $("#chat").prepend( $("<li>").html(message.content));
};
```

Listen for a submit event in the chat form.

Emit an event when the form is submitted.

Listen for an event, and populate the chat box.

Display messages in the chat box.

Before my application can use the io object in this file, I need to require it within my lay-out.ejs by adding the following script tag above my confettiCuisine.js import line: `<script src="/socket.io/socket.io.js"></script>`. This line loads `socket.io` for the client from my node_modules folder.

I'm ready to launch my application and see chat messages stream from one user to the next. With some styling, I can make it easier for users to distinguish their messages from others. I can also use the user's name in the chat box so the sender's name and message appear side by side. To do so, I modify my `displayMessage` function to print the user's name, as shown in the next listing. I check whether the message being displayed belongs to that user by comparing the current user's ID with the ID in the message object.

Listing 33.5 Pulling hidden field values from chat form in confettiCuisine.js

```
let displayMessage = (message) => {
  $("#chat").prepend( $("<li>").html(`
  <div class='message ${getCurrentUserClass(message.user)}'>
```

```
  <span class="user-name">
  ${message.userName}:
  </span>
  ${message.content}
  </div>
    `));
};
```
← Display the user's name along with the message.

```
let getCurrentUserClass = (id) => {
  let userId = $("#chat-user-id").val();
  if (userId === id) return "current-user";
  else return "";
};
```
Check whether the message belongs to the current user.

Next, I need to preserve these messages in my database by creating a Message model.

 ## 33.4 Creating a Message model

To ensure that my chat feature is worth using and a practical tool for users on the Confetti Cuisine application, the messages can't disappear every time a user refreshes the page. To fix this problem, I'll build a Message model to contain the message attributes in the chat form. I create a new message.js file in my project's models folder and add the code in listing 33.6 to that file.

In this code, I'm defining a message schema that contains content, userName, and user properties. The content of the chat message is required, as are the user's name and ID. In essence, every message needs some text and an author. If someone tries to save a message somehow without logging in and authenticating, the database won't allow the data to save. I also set timestamps to true so that I can keep track of when the chat message was added to the database. This feature allows me to show the timestamp in the chat box, if I want.

Listing 33.6 Creating the message schema in message.js

```
const mongoose = require("mongoose"),
  { Schema } = require("mongoose");

const messageSchema = new Schema({
  content: {
    type: String,
    required: true
  },
```
Require content in each message.

```
    userName: {
      type: String,
      required: true
    },
    user: {
      type: Schema.Types.ObjectId,
      ref: "User",
      required: true
    }
  }, { timestamps: true });
```

> Require the user's name with each message.

> Require a user ID with each message.

> Save the timestamp with each message.

```
module.exports = mongoose.model("Message", messageSchema);
```

This Mongoose model is ready for use in my chat controller. Effectively, when a new message arrives in my chat controller, I attempt to save it and then emit it to other users' chats. I require this new model in chatController.js by adding `const Message = require ("../models/message")` to the top of the file. The code in my chatController.js block for `client.on("message")` is shown in listing 33.7. I start by using the same `message-Attributes` from earlier in the controller to create a new `Message` instance. Then I try to save that message. If the message saves successfully, I emit it to all connected sockets; otherwise, I log the error, and the message never gets sent out from the server.

Listing 33.7 Saving a message in chatController.js

```
client.on("message", (data) => {
  let messageAttributes = {
      content: data.content,
      userName: data.userName,
      user: data.userId
    },
    m = new Message(messageAttributes);
  m.save()
    .then(() => {
      io.emit("message",
  messageAttributes);
    })
    .catch(error => console.log(`error: ${error.message}`));
});
```

> Create a new message object with messageAttributes.

> Save the message.

> Emit the message values if save is successful, and log any errors.

This code allows messages to save to my database, but chat message history still doesn't appear for users who are connecting for the first time. I'll correct that problem by loading older messages into my database.

 ## 33.5 Loading messages on connection

The second task in preserving messages in the chat box is maintaining a consistent number of messages from the chat's history in the chat box. I decide to allow the chat box to contain the ten most recent chats at any given moment. To do so, I need to load those ten most recent chats from my database and emit them to every client as soon as they connect to the chat.

Within chatController.js, I add the code in listing 33.8 to find the ten most recent chat messages and emit them with a new custom event. I use sort({createdAt: -1}) to sort my database results in descending order. Then I append limit(10) to limit those results to the ten most recent. By emitting the custom "load all messages" event on the client socket, only newly connected users will have their chat boxes refresh with the latest chat messages. Then, I reverse the list of messages with messages.reverse() so that I can prepend them in the view.

Listing 33.8 Loading most recent messages in chatController.js

```
Message.find({})
  .sort({
    createdAt: -1
  })                              Query the ten most
  .limit(10)                      recent messages.
  .then(messages => {
    client.emit("load all messages",
  messages.reverse());            Emit a custom event
  });                             with ten messages to
                                  the new socket only.
```

To handle the "load all messages" event on the client side, I add the event handler in the next listing to confettiCuisine.js. In this block of code, I listen for the "load all messages" event to occur. When it does emit, I cycle through the messages received on the client and individually display them in the chat box through the displayMessage function.

Listing 33.9 Displaying most recent messages in confettiCuisine.js

```
socket.on("load all messages", (data) => {
  data.forEach(message => {
    displayMessage(message);
  });
});
```

Handle 'load all messages' by parsing incoming data.

Send each message to displayMessage to display in the chat box.

The chat is finally complete and ready to test locally. To mimic two separate users communicating, I relaunch my application and log in on two separate web browsers. I navigate to the chat page and see that my chats are being sent in real time over my Node.js application with socket.io.

 ## 33.6 Setting up the chat icon

I want to make one final addition to this application: an icon that lets users elsewhere in the application know when the chat is active. I can easily add this feature with the existing socket.io event set up. All I need to do is add an icon to the navigation bar in my application by adding `<a href="/chat" class="chat-icon">@</a>` to layout.ejs. With this line alone, I have an icon in my navigation bar that links to the /chat route.

Next, I animate the icon by having it flash twice whenever a chat message is sent. Because I'm already emitting the message event from the server every time a new message is submitted, I can add the icon animation to the client's handler for that event.

In confettiCuisine.js, I modify the socket.on("message") code block to look like the code in the following listing. In this code, I display the message in the chat box as usual and additionally target an element with the chat-icon class. This element represents my chat icon in the navigation bar. Then I rapidly fade the icon out and back in, twice.

Listing 33.10 Animating chat icon when messages are sent in confettiCuisine.js

```
socket.on("message", (message) => {
  displayMessage(message);
  for (let i = 0; i < 2; i++) {
    $(".chat-icon").fadeOut(200).fadeIn(200);
  }
});
```

Animate the chat icon to flash when a message is sent.

With this extra feature, users have some indication that conversations are taking place on the chat page.

I could add to this chat feature in plenty of ways. I could create separate chats for each Confetti Cuisine class, for example, or use socket.io events to notify users when they've been tagged in a chat. I'll consider implementing these features in the future.

 **Summary**

In this capstone exercise, I added a real-time chat feature to my Confetti Cuisine application. I used socket.io to simplify connections between the server and multiple clients. I used some built-in and custom events to transfer data between open sockets. At the end, I added a feature to notify users who aren't in the chat room that others are actively communicating. With this feature added, I'm ready to deploy the application.

Deploying and managing code in production

At just about any stage of your application development, you likely wonder when people can start using what you've built. The eagerness is justified. Luckily, you have many ways to get your application online. Deploying an application is one of the most daunting tasks for new developers building web applications. Part of the struggle is understanding the resources and services that assist with deployment. The deployment process is much more than uploading your application code somewhere, at least during your first attempt. If done correctly, making changes in a production application can be simple. Some problems with making changes in your production application include running into restrictions that limit the database content that you can modify, accidentally removing code used to verify incoming data, and making changes in your local environment that don't work in your production environment, such as configuration changes.

In this unit, you set up your application to deploy on Heroku, a cloud service that hosts and runs your application for you. First, you prepare your application's configuration files to ensure that functionality will work locally and in production. Then you follow a few steps to launch your application on Heroku and set up your MongoDB database. After a

389

short lesson, you'll have your recipe application running under a URL that you can share with family and friends. In a subsequent lesson, you explore ways to improve your code for future refinement. I talk about *linting* your code, a process used to identify inefficient code with the help of an external package. At the end of the unit, you'll get a chance to apply unit and integration testing to your code. These tests provide fundamental protection against accidentally breaking your code in the future. You install the mocha and chai packages to help set up tests for Express.js actions and routes.

This unit covers the following topics:

- Lesson 34 guides you through the preparation steps to complete before your application is production-ready. In this lesson, you set up your application to deploy to Heroku along with a new MongoDB database provided as a plugin on Heroku's services.
- Lesson 35 shows how to catch small bugs in your code through the linting process and how to correct those bugs with the help of a debugging tool. By the end of this lesson, you'll have a set of tricks to pull out of your back pocket whenever you need to clean up your code.
- Lesson 36 introduces testing concepts in Node.js. This lesson touches the surface of test code you can write to ensure that functionality in your application doesn't break over time.

Lesson 37 (the capstone lesson) walks through using the deployment steps you learned in this unit to deploy the Confetti Cuisine application.

DEPLOYING YOUR APPLICATION

At this stage, you've completed a few iterations of your application, and it's time to make it available to the World Wide Web. This lesson introduces application deployment with Heroku. First, you set up your application to work with Heroku's services and plugins. In a few easy steps, you'll have your application live, with a unique URL that you can share with your friends. Next, you see how to set up your MongoDB database and populate your application with content. Last, you learn about tools you can use with Heroku to monitor your application in production, as well as guidelines for making future changes in your production code and Heroku plugins worth exploring further.

This lesson covers

- Configuring a Node.js application for Heroku
- Deploying a Node.js application
- Setting up a remote MongoDB database

Consider this   You've spent countless hours adding features and functionality to your application, only to have it run locally on your personal computer. It's about time that you expose your work on the recipe application to the public. The final step in the development process is deployment. In this lesson, I discuss the necessary steps to get your application ready for production.

34.1 Preparing for deployment

Deployment is the process of taking your application code from your development environment and publishing and running it on the internet to make it accessible to the public. Until this point, you've been developing your application in a local environment. Developers would refer to the application running at http://localhost:3000 as running in your development environment.

One option is to set up a new environment. You need to re-create the system settings and resources that made it possible to run your application on your own machine: a physical computer with Node.js installed, the ability to install any external packages, and a JavaScript engine to run the application. There's no escaping the fact that your application depends on physical hardware to function. For this reason, deploying your application to a *production environment*, somewhere accessible to others online, requires some machine or service to run your application.

You could set up your own computer to run your application and configure your home network to permit users to reach your application via your home's external IP address. The configuration steps are a bit involved, though; they might pose security threats to your home internet network; and they're beyond the scope of this book. Also, if your computer shut down, your application would be unreachable.

The popular alternative is to use one of many cloud services to host and run your application. These services often come at a cost, but for demonstration purposes, you can deploy your application through Heroku's free account services. Heroku is a cloud-based platform that offers servers—the physical processing computers and memory—to run your application. What's more, these computers often come prepackaged with the installation of Node.js that you need and require very little setup on the developer's part.

To get started with deployment, ensure that you have the Heroku command-line interface installed by running `heroku --version` in terminal (`heroku version` in the Windows command line). Also make sure that you have Git installed by running `git --version`. If you see some version of these tools printed on the screen, you can continue to the deployment steps.

> **NOTE** If you haven't yet created your Heroku account, set up the command-line interface (CLI), or installed Git, please follow the instructions in lesson 2.

Before you can deploy to Heroku, you need to make a couple of changes to your application to make it compatible with the services that Heroku provides. Heroku will run your application by using the application's PORT environment variable, so you need to have your application ready to listen at both ports, as shown in the next listing. In this code, you create a constant, port, and assign it to the PORT environmental variable, if it exists. Otherwise, the port defaults to 3000. This port number should remain the same as in previous lessons.

Listing 34.1 Changing the application's port in main.js

```
app.set("port", process.env.PORT || 3000);
const server = app.listen(app.get("port"), () => {
  console.log(`Server running at http://localhost:
${app.get("port")}`);
});
```

Assign the port constant.

Listen at the port assigned to port.

Similar to the way that Heroku specifies the application's port, the database you'll use also can be defined in an environmental variable. In main.js, change the database connection line to mongoose.connect(process.env.MONGODB_URI || "mongodb://localhost:27017/recipe_db", {useNewUrlParser: true}). This line tells Mongoose to connect to the database defined in MONGODB_URI or to default to your local recipe_db database location. (See section 3 for details on why this environmental variable exists.)

Last, create a new file called Procfile at the application's root. This file has no extensions or suffix, and its name is case-sensitive. Heroku uses this file to find out how to launch your application. Add web: node main.js to this file. This single line tells Heroku to create a new server, called a *dyno*, intended for web interaction, and to use node main.js to start the application.

With these three changes in place, you can finally deploy the application.

Quick check 34.1   Why do you need the Procfile in your project folder?

QC 34.1 answer   Heroku uses the Procfile as a configuration file to start your application.

34.2 Deploying your application

With the appropriate configurations in place, you can use Git and the Heroku CLI to deploy your application. Throughout this book, you haven't used Git for version control. Although versioning your code isn't necessary in your development environment, it's good practice, and in the case of deployment, it's required to get your application to its production environment on Heroku. If you're using Git for the first time, go to your project's root directory in terminal, and initialize the project with Git by running `git init`. In the next step, you add the files that you want in your Git repo, but you don't want some files in this repo.

You may recall that the `node_modules` folder gets created when you run `npm install`. This folder can get pretty large, and adding it to your Git repo isn't recommended. To ignore this folder, create a new file called .gitignore at the root of your application directory. Add /node_modules to that file in your text editor, and save. That's all you need to do for Git to know not to add those files within this folder.

To bundle your application code into a specific version, add the rest of the application's files to Git's staging level by running `git add .` (including the period). Then run the command `git commit -m "Initial application commit"` to save and commit this version of your code and receive a feedback message.

> **NOTE** Any other changes you make that aren't added and committed following the same process won't appear in your production environment.

With your code in version control, you can use the `heroku` keyword in terminal to initiate a new application for deployment. Run the command `heroku create` in your project directory in terminal to generate a new URL for your project. The response detailing the name of your Heroku application, its URL, and Git repository should resemble the following listing. This command also creates a connection to Heroku's remote Git repository for your code. You can run the command `git remote -v` to reveal the URL to that repository.

Listing 34.2 Creating a new Heroku app

```
Creating app... done,   crazy-lion-1990
https://crazy-lion-1990.herokuapp.com/ |
  https://git.heroku.com/crazy-lion-1990.git
```

Display the results of creating a new Heroku app.

Next, push your latest versioned code from your computer to the Heroku repository you set up. Publishing your code is the same as uploading your code to a server that will host your application on the internet. You can publish by running the command `git push heroku master`. This step is the most important part of the process because it's where all your code gets uploaded and published on Heroku's services. This step is also when Heroku runs `npm install` to download all your application's package dependencies.

This process may take about a minute, depending on your internet connection. If you experience any issue or notice an error in the process, make sure that you can still run your application locally before trying again.

If your application didn't depend on a database, you could go directly to the URL provided after the `heroku create` command in your browser. If you try visiting your application's `/courses` URL, you may see an error page (figure 34.1). Because your home page doesn't depend on any persistent data, however, that page should load without any errors.

> **NOTE** If you still have remnants of the `bcrypt` package in your project, you might run into issues with deployment to heroku depending on your version of Node.js. Try unninstalling `bcrypt` and replacing it with `bcrypt-nodejs` in usersController.js. In terminal you'll need to run `npm uninstall bcrypt && npm i bcrypt-nodejs -S`.

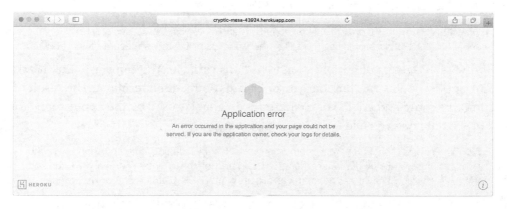

Figure 34.1   Displaying the Heroku error page

This error likely has to do with the fact that you haven't set up your database yet. You can verify, though, by running the command `heroku logs --tail` in your project's terminal window. This command provides a live feed of logs from the application online. You'll find a lot of messages here, and it's the first place I recommend checking if you experience any issue with your application in the future. Suppose that you see an error for a missing database. You can fix the problem by connecting to a MongoDB database.

> **NOTE** If you need some assistance with your Heroku CLI commands, run the command `heroku help` in terminal or visit https://devcenter.heroku.com/articles/heroku-cli-commands.

34.3 Setting up your database in production

Because you don't have direct access to the server on which your production application is running, you can't download, install, and run a MongoDB database on the same server, as you do in development. Heroku provides a free plugin, however, that you can use to set up a small MongoDB database. To add this plugin from terminal, run the command `heroku addons:create mongolab:sandbox`. This line provisions a sandbox database from MongoLab (mLab).

With the help of other cloud services such as Amazon and Google, mLab provides databases and MongoDB servers that can be accessed remotely via a URL. The URL you get is added to your application as the environmental variable `MONGODB_URI`. This variable means that your application can use the variable `MONGODB_URI` to get the URL of the database.

> **WARNING** The URL provided by mLab is a direct link to your application's data. Only your application on Heroku should use this URL; otherwise, you risk database-security vulnerabilities.

You previously set up your application to use this variable. You can verify that it exists in your application by running the `heroku config` command in terminal. The result of running this command is a list of configuration variables used by the application. You should see only one variable for your database at this time.

> **NOTE** You can add new environmental variables by running the command `heroku config:set NAME=VALUE`, where `Name` is the name of the variable you want to set and `VALUE` is its value. I might set `heroku config:set AUTHOR_EMAIL=jon@jonwexler.com`.

After a few minutes, your application should be ready to view. In your web browser, visit the URL provided earlier by Heroku, and add the `/courses` path to see an empty table, as shown in figure 34.2. You should see the home page of your application. Try creating new user accounts, subscribers, and groups through the forms you created in past lessons.

You may be wondering whether there's an easier way to populate your new database online with data than manually entering information in the browser forms. There is! I show you that technique, and some other tools and tips, in lesson 35.

Figure 34.2 Displaying the Heroku courses page

Quick check 34.3 How do you view and set environmental variables on your Heroku application?

 **Summary**

In this lesson, you learned about preparing your application for production and deploying it to Heroku. First, you changed some application configurations to help your Heroku dyno handle and run your application. Next, you deployed the application through your terminal Heroku CLI. Last, you set up a remote MongoDB database by using the mLab plugin through Heroku. In lesson 35, you discover how to manage your application in production, add data, and debug problems.

Try this

With your application on Heroku, test all the functionality to make sure that it works. Everything may seem to work as intended at first, but keep in mind that the environment is different, and sometimes your code may not work as expected. Try opening one terminal window with heroku logs --tail running alongside a browser window with your production application, and watch the log messages that Heroku prints.

QC 34.3 answer To view environmental variables on your Heroku application, run heroku config in your project's terminal window. You can set new variables by using heroku config:set.

MANAGING IN PRODUCTION

Your application is finally online, and you want to ensure that it stays there, fully functional. In this lesson, I discuss ways of getting data into your application even before any forms are used. You may want to add some of the course data you used in development so that your application has a fresh start online with data to view. Adding course data to your live application will reduce the time it takes to make the pages of your site presentable. Then I discuss some ways to improve your code quality and make sure that you don't make mistakes that could cause your application to crash in production. Last, I talk about ways to log, debug, and monitor your application in production to help you investigate when things begin to break.

This lesson covers

- Loading seed data into your production application
- Setting up linting for you code
- Debugging your application

Consider this Your application is finally online, and it's a proud moment, except that your client quickly discovers bugs that went undetected in development. What protocol do you follow to fix your code locally and upload to production?

In this lesson, you learn how to maintain your application in production with a few tools.

35.1 Loading seed data

In lesson 34, you got your database set up, but you may be wondering whether there's a simple way to populate your production application with data. You can upload data into your application on Heroku in a few ways.

Seed data is the database records you feed into your application when you first set it up in a new environment. Other languages and platforms have conventions for loading a file with seed data in different environments. In Node.js, you can create a JavaScript file containing the data you'd like to load. You may want to populate your application with recipe courses before any users even sign up, for example. To do so, you can use an existing seed file or create a new file in your application directory called seed.js. This file defines and creates new records that communicate with your Mongoose plugin. For that reason, you need to require Mongoose and the models you intend to use, as shown in listing 35.1.

To avoid conflict with a preexisting seed file, create courseSeed.js. In this example, you include the necessary modules needed for creating new data objects with Mongoose. Then you create multiple records with values that you'd like to see in your production application. When this file contains the data that you want to use, run the code in this file, using the Heroku command-line interface (CLI).

Listing 35.1 Adding content through seed data in courseSeed.js

```
const mongoose = require("mongoose"),                    Require models
  Course = require("./models/course");                   for seeding data.

mongoose.Promise = global.Promise;
mongoose.connect(
  process.env.MONGODB_URI || "mongodb://localhost:27017/recipe_db",
  { useNewUrlParser: true }                              Remove all existing
);                                                       documents.
Course.remove({})
  .then(() => {                                          Run code to create new
    return Course.create({                               database documents.
      title: "Beets sitting at home",
      description: "Seasonal beets from the guy down
  the street.",
      zipCode: 12323,
      items: ["beets"]
    });
  })
```

```
  .then(course => console.log(course.title))
  .then(() => {
    return Course.create({
      title: "Barley even listening",
      description: "Organic wheats and barleys for bread,
  soup, and fun!",
      zipCode: 20325,
      items: ["barley", "rye", "wheat"]
    });
  })
  .then(course => console.log(course.title))
  .then(() => {
    return Course.create({
      title: "Peaching to the choir",
      description: "Get fresh peaches from the local farm.",
      zipCode: 10065,
      items: ["peaches", "plums"]
    });
  })
  .then(course => console.log(course.title))
  .catch(error => console.log(error.message))
  .then(() => {
    console.log("DONE");
    mongoose.connection.close();
  });
```

> **TIP** As an alternative, you could use the mLab URL to load seed data directly into your production database. Although this approach is quick, I don't recommend it because it exposes your production database to security risks.

Two other alternatives are using Heroku CLI tools to launch your production application's REPL or terminal environment. You may recall that REPL has access to the files and folders in your projects directory, so it's a great way to insert data from terminal. Launch REPL by running the command `heroku run node` in your project's terminal window. With this REPL-like environment for your production application, you can simply copy and paste the contents of courseSeed.js into terminal. The other approach is to run `heroku run bash` in your project's terminal window. This command brings up a prompt where you can run `node courseSeed` to load all the contents directly. First, you'll need to commit your courseSeed.js file to git and push to heroku.

If you're successful, you should see the log outputs of each course created, which also appear immediately on the /courses route in your application online (figure 35.1).

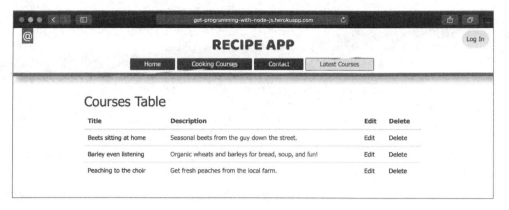

Figure 35.1   Display of the populated courses page

> **NOTE**   To upload new changes to your project, run git add . followed by git commit -m "some commit message" and git push heroku master.

In the next section, I discuss ways to maintain the integrity of your code and ensure that new errors don't pop up.

> **Quick check 35.1**   What happens when you run heroku run node?

🤖 35.2 Linting

Bugs and coding mistakes are part of the development process. What can you do to prevent the inevitable mistakes that halt production? Along with code quality, the process of linting to hold your code to a particular standard is a way to reduce errors. *Linting* involves running a program to read through your code and notify you of bugs or errors that you may not have caught. You also might miss (and some browsers might ignore) syntax errors during development that could break your application in a different environment. To lint your code, globally install a package called eslint by running npm install -g eslint. ESLint is an open-source tool used in terminal to run static analysis

> **QC 35.1 answer**   heroku run node opens a new REPL window for you within the context of your production application. From there, you can run JavaScript commands and load application-specific modules as you would locally, with access to your production database.

on your code. Through this analysis, you can identify code style and structure problems. Other linting libraries that you can use include JSLint and JSHint. You can learn more about ESLint at https://eslint.org/.

> **NOTE** You could also install the package for this project by running npm `install eslint --save-dev` within your project directory in terminal. The `--save-dev` flag signifies that this package doesn't need to be installed in your production environment; it will be marked that way in your application's package.json. To use `eslint` after installing it as a development dependency, you need to access it from `./node_modules/.bin/eslint`.

As you initialized a new package.json file with `npm init`, initialize a .eslintrc.js file by running `eslint --init` in your project's terminal window. Choose to set up your file by answering the questions in terminal, as shown in listing 35.2. You need to let the linter know to look for ES6 syntax and methods because you use them throughout your application. You also tell the linter to analyze your code on the server and client because you've written JavaScript for both.

Listing 35.2 Setting up your .eslintrc.js file in terminal

```
? How would you like to configure ESLint? Answer questions about
  your style
? Are you using ECMAScript 6 features? Yes
? Are you using ES6 modules? Yes
? Where will your code run? Browser, Node
? Do you use CommonJS? No
? Do you use JSX? No
? What style of indentation do you use? Tabs
? What quotes do you use for strings? Double
? What line endings do you use? Unix
? Do you require semicolons? Yes
? What format do you want your config file to be in? JavaScript
```

Answers to questions to set up your linter

Take a look at the .eslintrc.js file that's produced at the end of this prompt in listing 35.3. Notice that you're formatting the linter's configurations in JavaScript, not JSON, like your package.json file. As in your other JavaScript modules, these configurations are assigned to `module.exports`. Most of the configurations that follow are fairly straightforward. Your environments are specified to include node, web browsers, and ES6 syntax. Then there are `eslint` rules, which define when to warn you of inconsistencies. In this case, you throw a linter error when spaces are used instead of tabs, semicolons are missing at the end of statements, or single quotation marks are used around text. You can change these configurations to suit your preferences.

Listing 35.3 Example .eslintrc.js configuration file

```
module.exports = {
  "env": {
    "browser": true,          Specify the
    "es6": true,              environments
    "node": true              to analyze.
  },
  "extends": "eslint:recommended",
  "parserOptions": {
    "sourceType": "module"
  },
  "rules": {
    "indent": [
      "error",                Define eslint rules.
      "tab"
    ],
    "linebreak-style": [
      "error",
      "unix"
    ],
    "quotes": [
      "error",
      "double"
    ],
    "semi": [
      "error",
      "always"
    ]
  }
};
```

Test your linter on the main.js file by running eslint main.js. I hope that you don't see any errors up front. Try deleting a semicolon or defining a variable that you don't use later. Notice how eslint outputs errors with line numbers so that you can correct your code easily. Clean code helps ensure the integrity and readability of your application.

> **NOTE** Keep in mind that some linter rules are stricter than others. The rules are intended to maintain consistency in your code. If you see errors referring to spaces versus tabs, those errors don't mean that your code is bad—only that it could use a cleanup.

The output of errors in your terminal window details which files and line numbers you need to visit to correct your syntax or code structure.

35.3 Debugging your application

You looked at a few ways to debug your application earlier in the book. You used
`console.log` to print custom messages, error messages, and request/response-specific
data in your Express.js middleware functions. Then you used the logs in your terminal
window to determine where to fix certain problems. If an error occurred while saving a
user to the database, for example, you caught the error in your promise chain and
logged it to the console.

Logging is helpful when it's used correctly. Logs provide a recorded history of transac-
tions and interaction with your application. Even if your application is running
smoothly, you want your development logs to tell you more about the application's performance, and you want your production logs to inform you of suspicious activity.

Locally, you can get more information about the request-response cycle by starting your
application in debug mode. In your project's terminal window, type the command
`DEBUG=* node main` to set the `DEBUG` environment variable to logging from all elements of
your application as it runs.

> **NOTE**   On Windows machines, first set the environment variable and then run the applica-
> tion by running the command `set DEBUG=* & node main`.

You'll notice right away that the number of log lines in your terminal window reflects
the operations Express.js performs to register your routes, along with some configurations it makes before your web server launches (listing 35.4). Now when you visit any
page in your application locally, the debug logs stream down your terminal window.
Conveniently, Express.js also tells you how much time each operation takes in its log
messages. During development, this information can help you determine whether some
parts of the application aren't performing well so that you can investigate further.

Listing 35.4 Example of log messages through Express.js in terminal

```
express:router:route new "/new" +0ms
express:router:layer new "/new" +0ms
express:router:route get "/new" +0ms
express:router:layer new "/" +0ms
express:router:route new "/create" +0ms
express:router:layer new "/create" +0ms
```

Log Express.js route registration in debug mode.

If you find it helpful to run your application with debug logs, you can add a start script in your package.json file to avoid writing the whole command each time. Add "debug": "DEBUG=* node main" after your start script. Then, whenever you want to see these logs, run the npm run debug command.

These logs can be valuable in production as well, though you don't want to run your production application in debug mode. Instead, install another package to handle logging the important data that you want to see in production. Install a package called morgan to provide your Node.js application better console log messages.

Install the morgan package by running the command npm i morgan -S. Then, in main.js, require the morgan module by adding const morgan = require("morgan"). Then the process is as simple as telling your Express.js application to use morgan and passing in some formatting options. You can add app.use(morgan(":method :url :status * :response-time ms")) to log the request method, URL, status code, and time taken to process a response, for example.

This output should immediately resemble the logs that Express.js generated in debug mode. Launch your application with npm start, and notice the logs for each request made, as shown in the next listing. I recommend using the morgan("combined") format, in which the combined formatting options provides a lot of the information you'll need to monitor the request-response cycle in your production application.

Listing 35.5 Example of log messages with morgan

```
GET / 200 * 20.887 ms
GET /js/jquery.min.js 304 * 2.504 ms
GET /js/bootstrap.min.js 304 * 1.402 ms
GET /js/recipeApp.js 304 * 0.893 ms
GET /css/recipeApp.css 304 * 1.432 ms
```

Log custom messages with morgan.

With logging set up, the best approach to debugging problems is to pause your application where issues occur and analyze the code surrounding those issues. This practice is easier said than done, but tools are available to help you identify the troubled code. Built into Node.js is a debug tool that lets you step through your code one line at a time. After each line of code, you can evaluate the variables and data to determine whether their values are what you expect.

To run the built-in debugger, run the `node inspect main.js` command in your project's terminal window. After running this command, you'll immediately see the first lines of your main.js file display in your terminal window. The tool pauses as soon as your application starts, stating `Break on start in main.js:1`. You can start evaluating your code by typing n to go to the next line, incrementally jumping over a single line at a time, or typing c to continue running your application. If you type c, your application runs as usual. The debugger becomes particularly useful when you have an idea of where your code isn't working properly. If you think that your code isn't finding users correctly on the user's show page, for example, you may want to pause the code within that controller action. To pause in specific locations, add `debugger;` at that location in your code, as shown in listing 35.6.

By adding this line, running the debugger again in terminal, and typing c to let your application run, you're setting the application up to stop for you when it queries the database for a user in the show action before the view is rendered.

Listing 35.6   Debugging the show **action in usersController.js**

```
User.findById(userId)                    Add a debugger
  .then(user => {                        breakpoint when a user
    debugger;                            is found in the database.
    res.render("users/show", {
      user: user
    });
});
```

As soon as you visit a user's show page in your browser, the page pauses, and your terminal window displays the code where you placed your `debugger;`. From there, you can investigate the variables within this code by entering the REPL environment. By typing `repl` in the debugger window in terminal, you can run normal REPL commands within the context of the code that's being debugged. In this example, you're checking whether the user being retrieved from the database has a valid email address, so run the following statement: `console.log(user.email)`. If you get `undefined` or some value other than the user's email address, you know that the issue has to do with the email, and you can investigate further. When you're done debugging, type c to continue and press Ctrl-D to exit. For more information about this debugger, visit https://nodejs.org/api/debugger.html.

The built-in debugging tool can be a helpful way to analyze the data in your application as it runs. Fully debugging your code this way involves a few steps, however, so I recommend exploring other debugging tools, such as node-inspector, which lets you use the console in Google Chrome to debug. You can also use Node.js with an integrated development environment like TernJS in Atom, which offers debugging tools while you edit your code.

> **Quick check 35.3** What happens when you add debugger to your application code?

 **Summary**

In this lesson, you learned how to add data to your production application through the Heroku console. Then you installed eslint to lint your application for errors or syntactic inconsistencies in your code. Last, I introduced some debugging tips to help you identify production errors and know immediately where to go to fix them.

Try this

Try using the debugger in Node.js to evaluate the values of different variables in your application. Try running your application in debug mode and breaking within the user's create action to evaluate the incoming request parameters.

QC 35.3 answer Adding debugger to your code allows the debugging tool in Node.js to pause at that specific location as your application runs. Outside the debug tool, this addition won't prevent your application from running normally.

TESTING YOUR APPLICATION

Continual maintenance of your application in production requires fixing bugs. Fixing bugs means writing new code. Writing new code has the unforgiving tendency to break existing functionality. In this lesson, you take some steps to prevent the breaking of working code by implementing tests on your Node.js application. Writing tests in Node.js is similar to testing in other platforms and languages. First, you learn how to write simple tests for a function in your application. Then you implement tests for the controller actions and models to cover the bulk of your application's code. By the end of this lesson, you'll have the fundamental skills you need to get started testing your Node.js application.

This lesson covers

- Using core modules to write assertion tests
- Writing a Node.js test with mocha and chai
- Building and running tests for controller actions with chai-http
- Implementing tests for your API

> **Consider this** Your recipe application is looking great in production, and you've gained development support from some local developers. Your application code is being worked on by multiple people, and the new developers don't necessarily know how their implementation of new features will affect the features you've already built.
>
> ⫸

A new developer adds a new index action on the users controller. This new action
doesn't respond with all the user data you originally planned for, which affects your API
and views. If you write tests for your index action specifying what data you expect it to
return, new developers will have a point of reference regarding what functionality is
allowed to change with their modifications.

 ## 36.1 Basic testing with core modules

In the tech industry, application testing is a standard practice. When you write some
code with explicit functionality, you want to make sure that functionality doesn't change
unless it's intended to change. To help ensure that your code isn't accidentally affected
by changes and new features that you implement (or that another developer imple-
ments), you can write tests. Tests contain three components:

- Test data representing sample data that you'd expect to receive in your
  application
- Expectations detailing what a function or series of operations should output,
  given your test data and application code
- A testing framework to run your tests and determine whether your defined
  expectations were met

Before learning about some external tools that you can use to test your application, you
can use a core module that comes with Node.js. The assert module offers some basic
functions that you can use to confirm the equality of two values. You can think of these
functions as being conditional statements wrapped in testing language.

You can use this module by navigating to a new project folder called simple_test and
creating a new file called test.js with the code shown in listing 36.1. In this example, you
require the assert module. Then you write an assertion test by using assert.equal to
determine whether the first value, the result of a call to your custom add function, equals
the second argument, 0. Last, you write the add function to take two values and return
their sum. In this example, you expect the addition of 5 and 4 to equal 0. As you'd
expect, this test should fail, and when it fails, the message in the final argument should
appear in terminal.

Run this file to see the assertion error in terminal by entering node test within the
simple_test project directory. That error should read AssertionError [ERR_ASSERTION]: 5
plus 4 should equal 9.

Listing 36.1 Simple assertion test in test.js

```
const assert = require("assert");          ⟵  Require the
                                               assert module.

assert.equal(add(5, 4), 0, "5 plus 4 should equal 9");  ⟵ Write the
                                                            assertion test.
let add = (x, y) => {      ⟵
  return x + y;
};                    Implement the
                      function specified
                      in your test.
```

To correct this test, you need to change 0 to 9. You could also add another assertion test here to specify what your *add* function shouldn't return. You could write assert.notEqual (add(5, 4), 0), for example. If this test ever fails, you'll know that something is wrong with your *add* function that needs modification.

The assert module is a great way to start writing tests for Node.js. For your application, however, you'll benefit from external packages that test more-complicated functionality. For more information about the assert module, visit https://nodejs.org/api/assert.html.

Test-driven development

Test-driven development (TDD) is an application development strategy in which tests specifying the expectations of your code are written first, followed by the feature implementation designed to pass your initial tests.

You want to make sure that your tests comprehensively cover your application's functionality, which means writing tests that specify how your application should work when it's provided valid and invalid data. Sometimes, when you write your tests after you've already implemented the application code, it's easy to miss edge cases that aren't accounted for in your test suite. For this reason, TDD can offer a more wholesome development experience.

TDD involves the following steps:

1 Write your tests with sample data and expectations of the results, using that sample data through some method or function that you'll build later.

2 Run your tests. At this point, all your tests should fail.

3 Implement code for your testing to behave according to the expectations you defined in your tests.

4 Run your tests again. At this point, all your tests should pass.

If your tests don't pass after you've written your application's code, it could mean that your application code isn't perfected yet.

If you were using TDD to implement a function called reverse that takes a string as a parameter and reverses it, for example, you might follow these steps:

1 Write a test for the reverse function, using a test string, var s = "Hello", such that when you run reverse(s), you expect the result to be "olleH".
2 Run the tests, and expect them to fail.
3 Write the code to reverse strings.
4 Rerun the tests until all of them pass.

Quick check 36.1   What is an assertion test?

 ## 36.2 Testing with mocha and chai

To start testing your application, install the mocha and chai packages in your recipe-application terminal window by running the command npm i mocha -g and npm i chai -S. mocha is a testing framework. Much like Express.js, mocha offers a structure and methods that can be used in conjunction to test your application code. You install mocha globally because you need to use the mocha keyword in terminal, and you'll likely test other projects. chai should be installed as a development dependency because you'll be testing your code only locally; you don't need this package to be installed in your production environment.

To use the mocha module, run mocha in your project's directory in terminal. Running this command directs mocha to look for a test folder within your project folder. As with any framework, a conventional directory structure is used to keep your tests organized and separate from your other code files, so you need to create that test folder at the root of your application directory.

> **NOTE**   Visit https://mochajs.org for more information about the mocha framework, from installation to use in terminal.

QC 36.1 answer   An *assertion test* is code that you write to express your expectations of how some sample data might change, equal, or otherwise relate to another value. This test could be a comparison of two pieces of raw data or a comparison of data resulting from a function call or series of operations.

mocha helps you describe and run tests, but it doesn't provide the tools you need to determine whether the outcomes of your code are what you expected. For that purpose, you need an assertion engine to run assertions, which describe how code should output a specified value.

chai is the assertion engine that you'll use in this lesson. To use chai, require it in each test file you plan to run. Then, like the assert method from your core module, you can use expect, should, or assert as function verbs to check whether your code returns the intended results in your tests. For the following examples, use the expect function. chai also has descriptive functions to help you explain your tests before the assertions themselves. You'll use the describe function to specify the module and function you're testing.

> **NOTE** describe functions can be nested.

For the actual tests, use the it function to explain what you expect to happen in the test. Semantically, this function allows your test to read this way: In a specific module, for a specific function, your code (it) should behave in a certain way when it's provided with some specific data. You take a closer look at this semantic structure in the next example.

The last steps in using these packages are creating the test file, requiring any custom modules with methods you want to test, and providing sample data within your tests. Write a simple test for your recipe application, using mocha and chai. Create a new file called usersControllerSpec.js in the test folder within your project's directory. Per development convention, Spec is used in filenames to indicate a test suite.

Within this file, test the getUserParams function used in your user's controller from the capstone exercise in lesson 25. For testing purposes, add the getUserParams function to usersController.js, as shown in listing 36.2.

> **NOTE** You can make use of this function in the create action by creating a new User instance with the following line: let newUser = new User(module.exports.getUser-Params(req.body)). You can reference the getUserParamsthrough module.exports.

Unless you export this function, there's no way for any other module to access the function.

Listing 36.2 Exporting the getUserParams function

```
getUserParams: (body) => {
  return {
    name: {
      first: body.first,
      last: body.last
    },
```

Export getUserParams in usersController.js.

```
      email: body.email,
      password: body.password,
      zipCode: body.zipCode
   };
 }
```

In usersControllerSpec.js, require chai along with usersController.js. The code for your test file resembles the code in listing 36.3. Because you use the expect assertion function, you can require it directly from the chai module; you won't need chai for anything else. Then define your first describe block by stating the module you're testing. The following describe block specifies the function you're testing. Within that nested describe, you can run multiple tests that pertain to getUserParams. In this case, you're testing whether getUserParams returns data that includes your name properties when provided a sample request body. The second test ensures that a blank request body results in an empty object. You use deep.include to compare the contents of one JavaScript object with another. For more information about chai assertion methods, visit http://chaijs.com/api/bdd/.

Listing 36.3 Exporting the getUserParams function in usersControllerSpec.js

```
const chai = require("chai"),                      Require the expect function.
  { expect } = chai,
  usersController = require("../controllers/usersController");

describe("usersController", () => {
  describe("getUserParams", () => {                Define the focus
    it("should convert request body to contain    of your test in a
  the name attributes of the user object", () => { describe block.
      var body = {
        first: "Jon",                              Detail your test
        last: "Wexler",                            expectations.
        email: "jon@jonwexler.com",
        password: 12345,
        zipCode: 10016                             Provide sample
      };                                           input data.
      expect(usersController.getUserParams(body))
        .to.deep.include({
          name: {
            first: "Jon",
            last: "Wexler"
          }                        Expect some object to be
        });                        included in the results.
```

```
  });
  it("should return an empty object with empty request
➡ body input", () => {
    var emptyBody = {};
    expect(usersController.getUserParams(emptyBody))
      .to.deep.include({});
  });
 });
});
```

To run this test, enter the mocha command in your project's terminal window. You should see an indication that both tests passed (figure 36.1). If you get an error or if a test fails, make sure that your modules are accessible from each other and that your code matches the code listings.

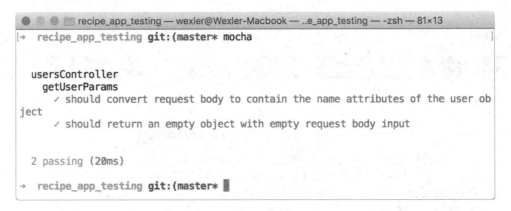

Figure 36.1   Displaying passing tests in terminal

NOTE   To exit your mocha test in terminal, press Ctrl-D.

In the next section, you implement a test that covers more than a single function.

Quick check 36.2   What's the difference between describe and it?

QC 36.2 answer   describe wraps the tests that relate to a particular module or function, which makes it easier to categorize your test results as they appear in terminal. it blocks contain the actual assertion tests that you write.

36.3 Testing with a database and server

To test a web framework, you need more than some sample data and access to the modules you're testing. Ideally, you want to re-create the environment in which your application normally runs, which means providing a functioning web server, database, and all the packages your application uses.

You aim to set up an environment in addition to your development environment. You can define a test environment through the process.env.NODE_ENV environment variable. At the top of any test file, add process.env.NODE_ENV = "test" to let Node.js know that you're running your application in a testing environment. This distinction can help you differentiate between databases and server ports. If you're running your application in the test environment, you can tell the application to use a recipe_test_db database and run on port 3001, for example. This way, you can test saving and retrieving data from a database without interfering with your development data or development server.

Now indicate to your application to use the recipe_test_db test database in the test environment and to otherwise default to the production and development databases, as shown in the next listing. In this example, you define a db variable earlier in the code and assign it to a local database. If the environmental variable, process.env.NODE_ENV, tells you that you're in the test environment, the db variable points to your test database URL.

Listing 36.4 Separating environment databases in main.js

```
if (process.env.NODE_ENV === "test") "mongoose.
➥  connect(mongodb://localhost:27017/recipe_test_db", {
➥  useNewUrlParser: true});
else mongoose.connect(process.env.MONGODB_URI ||
➥  "mongodb://localhost:27017/recipe_db",{ useNewUrlParser: true });
```

Assign to your test database while in the test environment.

Default to the production and development databases.

> **NOTE**   MongoDB creates this test database for you if it doesn't exist.

You apply the same logic to your server port, as shown in the following listing. Here, you use port 3001 if you're in the test environment. Otherwise, you use the normal ports that you've used so far.

Listing 36.5 Setting up a test server port in main.js

```
if (process.env.NODE_ENV === "test")
    app.set("port", 3001);
else app.set("port", process.env.PORT || 3000);
```

Assign the port to 3001 (test),
default to port 3000 (production).

Last, you need to export your application contained in `app` by adding `module.exports = app` to the bottom of main.js. Exporting your application allows you to access it from the test files you write. Also, in your controller tests, you need the help of another package to make requests to your server. Install the `chai-http` package by running the `npm i chai-http -S` command to save this package as a development dependency.

With these changes in place, you're ready to write a comprehensive test on your models and controllers. In the following examples, you test the user's controller actions and User model. First, test the User model by creating a file called userSpec.js in your test folder with the code in listing 36.6.

In this file, you can create multiple tests on the User model. The first tests you write are to ensure that users can be created and saved to your database. You need to require the User module, `mongoose`, and `chai`. From `chai`, pull the expect function into its own constant so that your tests are more readable.

Next, implement the `beforeEach` function provided by `mocha` to remove any and all users from your test database before you run each test. This function ensures that the results of previous tests don't affect other tests in this file. Your `describe` block indicates that you're testing the save functionality on the User model. Your `it` block contains two expectations to determine whether you can successfully save a single user to the database. First, provide some sample data that your application might naturally receive as input data. Then set up two promises to save the user and find all users in the database. The inner nested promise is where you run your expectations.

Last, create two assertions where you expect the results of your promises to yield an array, where the second item contains all the users in your database. Because you created a single user, you expect the size of the array of users to be 1. Similarly, you expect the only user in that array to have an `_id` property, indicating that it has been saved to your MongoDB database. When your test is complete, call `done` to indicate that the tests are complete and promises are resolved.

Listing 36.6 Testing saving a Mongoose user in userSpec.js

```
process.env.NODE_ENV = "test";                          ←——  Require necessary
                                                              modules and set the
const User = require("../models/user"),                       environment as test.
  { expect } = require("chai");        ←——
                                             Assign a variable
require("../main");                          to the chai.expect
                                             function.
beforeEach(done => {          ←——
  User.remove({})                   Remove all users
    .then(() => {                   from the database
      done();                       before each test.
    });
});                                          Describe a series of
                                             tests for saving users.
describe("SAVE user", () => {     ←——
  it("it should save one user", (done) => {   ←——
    let testUser = new User({
      name: {                                  Define a test for
        first: "Jon",                          saving a single user.
        last: "Wexler"
      },
      email: "Jon@jonwexler.com",
      password: 12345,
      zipCode: 10016
    });                          ←——  Set up promises to save
    testUser.save()                   a user with sample data,
      .then(() => {                   and fetch all users from
        User.find({})                 the database thereafter.
          .then(result => {
            expect(result.length)
              .to.eq(1);        ←——   Expect one user with
            expect(result[0])         an ID to exist in the
              .to.have.property("_id");   database.
            done();       ←——
          });                    Call done to complete
      });                        the test with promises.
  });
});
});
```

Run your tests by running the mocha command in your project's terminal window. This command starts your MongoDB test database and saves a test user. If your test doesn't pass, make sure that your modules are connected correctly and that users are saving in your application in the browser. It's helpful to know that the user model works correctly, and you can add more tests to this file. You can use sample data that shouldn't save or try saving two users with the same email address, for example. Your validations should prevent both users from saving.

Next, test a controller action. After all, the controller action connects your models and views, providing a lot more of the experience you'd like to preserve in your application. In the following example, you test the user index action, which fetches all the users in the database and sends those users to your view in the response body.

For this test file, you need to require chai-http by adding const chaiHTTP = require ("chai-http") and your main app module by adding const app = require("../main"). Then tell chai to use chaiHTTP by adding chai.use(chaiHTTP), and you're ready to make server requests. In the following example, you use chai.request(app) to communicate with the server. To test the index action specifically, add the code in listing 36.7 to users-ControllerSpec.js in your test folder.

You can wrap your tests with a describe block indicating that the tests are for users-Controller. Another describe block specifies that the tests are for GET requests to /users.

> **NOTE**   The first argument in describe is any string of your choice that explains what the tests are testing. You don't need to follow the text shown in this example.

Your test to show all users in the database uses chai.request to communicate with your application, which in turn sets up a web server running at port 3001. Then you chain a get request with a chai helper method to reach the /users route. In your application, this should take you to the users index action in the users controller. You end your request with end and write your expectations on the response that's returned from the server. You expect the response to have a status code of 200 and no errors.

Listing 36.7 Testing the users index action

Describe your test block for the users index action.

```
describe("/users GET", () => {
  it("it should GET all the users", (done) => {
    chai.request(app)
      .get("/users")
      .end((errors, res) => {
        expect(res).to.have.status(200);
        expect(errors).to.be.equal(null);
```

Make a GET request to your test server.

End the request with a callback to run your expectations.

Expect your application's response status to be 200.

```
        done();
      });
    });
  });
```

Call done to complete
the server interaction
in your test.

Run this test by entering mocha in your project's terminal window to see two tests pass.
Your test suite contains all the tests contained in files in the test folder. If you want to test
only usersControllerSpec, you can run mocha test/usersControllerSpec.

Quick check 36.3   What does chai.request do?

Summary

In this lesson, you learned about testing your Node.js application. You started with the
assert core module and quickly jumped into testing your models and controllers with
chai, mocha, and chai-http. With these tools and others, you'll be able to re-create most of
the actual experiences that users have with your application. If you can stay ahead by
predicting user experiences and edge cases, and testing them before they go to production, you'll face far fewer production crashes.

Try this

Writing a test suite isn't a simple task, because you can write an endless number of tests.
You want to make sure that you cover most scenarios in your application, using a variety of sample data.

Create a test module for each controller and model in your application. Then try to
build describe blocks and tests for each action.

QC 36.3 answer   chai.request takes a Node.js web server and allows your test environment to
make requests. These requests mimic the ones in your production application, allowing for a more integrated, comprehensive test of your code.

CAPSTONE: DEPLOYING CONFETTI CUISINE

It's time to move my application to production. I've coordinated with Confetti Cuisine on original expectations and feature changes along the way. The result is a Node.js application running with Express.js, MongoDB, and a variety of packages to connect users with the Confetti Cuisine cooking school. I've had multiple opportunities to deploy this application without a database or the ability to save meaningful data. Now that I've cleaned up my code and written a few tests, I turn to Heroku to demo the effect of my application on the world.

Although the steps are short and don't involve much more coding, I want to be careful not to make any mistakes in the deployment process. Troubleshooting in development is a lot simpler than in production.

I'll start by preparing my application for Heroku. Then I'll create a new Heroku application through the Heroku command-line interface (CLI) in terminal. After using Git to save and version my changes locally, I'll push my code up to Heroku.

Next, I'll set up my application's MongoDB database, and add some seed data to start. When those tasks are complete, I'll use a couple of production tools to monitor my application's logs and prepare for meaningful user data and interaction with my application to roll in.

37.1 Linting and logging

Before I deploy my application, I want to ensure that I'm not submitting code with any bugs or inefficiencies. Although I've made a point to code consciously, there's always the possibility that a mistake could affect my application in production. To prevent potential issues in the deployment process, I install `eslint` globally to lint my code by running `npm install -g eslint`.

Linting my code provides me a list of lines in my application code that could be fixed, which range from removing unused variables to not properly handling promises and asynchronous functions. I initialize `eslint` by running the command `eslint --init` in my project's terminal window. Following the prompts in terminal, I choose to lint for ES6 syntax and both server-side and client-side JavaScript. Running `eslint` in terminal creates a .eslintrc.js configuration file that `eslint` uses to evaluate my code. I run the global `eslint` keyword in my project's terminal window to see where my code can be improved.

I'd also like to have better logging in my application before it goes to production. I decide to use `morgan` to log request and response information. First, I install the package locally by running `npm i morgan -S` to save it as an application dependency. Then I require `morgan` in main.js by adding `const morgan = require("morgan")`. Last, I want to use a specific configuration of `morgan` that combines meaningful data from the request in the logs. I add `app.use(morgan("combined"))` to main.js to let my Express.js application know to use `morgan` with the `combined` logging format.

With my code cleaned up, I run my application one last time in development to make sure that no persistent errors prevent my application from launching. Then I move on to prepare my application for deployment.

 ## 37.2 Preparing for production

Confetti Cuisine has given me the choice of production platform to use. Because I'm comfortable with Heroku, I decide to begin preparing my application to live on Heroku's servers.

> **NOTE** The following steps allow me to work with Heroku, but they don't prevent my application from working with other services.

I start by verifying that Heroku CLI and Git are installed on my machine. Running `heroku --version` and `git --version` in terminal should let me know whether they're installed and what versions they are. I need Heroku to allow the server's port to use an environmental variable in production, not just port 3000. I'll make sure in main.js that my port is set by `app.set("port", process.env.PORT || 3000)`. The port number will initially be assigned to the port number at `process.env.PORT` if such a value exists. Otherwise, the port will default to 3000.

Next, I modify my database connect to use the `MONGO_URI` environmental variable if it's present. I add `mongoose.connect(process.env.MONGODB_URI || "mongodb://local-host:27017/confetti_cuisine",{ useNewUrlParser: true })` to main.js. Later, when I provision a database for my production application, `MONGODB_URI` appears as one of the application's configuration variable set to the database's external URL.

The last step is creating a Procfile, a file that Heroku uses as a starting point to launch my application. Heroku can work with a few internet protocols. I'll be setting this application to work over HTTP, so I add `web: node main.js` to the Procfile. This line of code tells Heroku to run my application as a web server that should expect requests and responses over HTTP. Additionally, I'm telling Heroku to use main.js to start the application.

My code is almost ready to deploy. I need to save my changes and follow a few more steps to send my code to production.

37.3 Deploying to Heroku

Now that I'm happy with the state of my code, I'll add and commit my changes to Git. First, I want to run `git init` to initialize my project with Git. If I've already performed this line, Git harmlessly reinitializes the project; none of my previous changes are affected. Git bundles all my code together, so I want to make sure that nothing gets bundled that I don't want to send across the internet, including passwords, sensitive data of any kind, and my node_modules folder. I've kept sensitive data out of my application, so I want to keep my node_modules folder from going to production; the folder can get pretty large, slowing my deployment process. Also, Heroku runs `npm install` for me, once deployed. I create a file called .gitignore and add node_modules to that file.

Next, I run `git add .` to add all my files to a staging area, ready to be committed. I run `git status` to confirm the files that will be committed and run `git commit -m "first production deployment"` to indicate this version of my code before going to production.

With my code saved, I use the heroku keyword in terminal to register my application with Heroku. From my project's directory in terminal, I run heroku create confetti-cuisine.

> **WARNING** If the name confetti-cuisine isn't already used by another application on Heroku, this command generates a URL through which I'll be able to access my application. Anyone following my steps will need to choose a different name for their heroku app in this command.

That URL is https://confetti-cuisine.herokuapp.com. This command also creates a remote Git repository on Heroku for me. This configuration allows me to submit my local Git repository to that address; from there, Heroku will install and run my application. I can verify the URL of the remote repository by running git remote -v. I see that my remote repository is referenced by the name heroku, so when I'm ready, I can use the name heroku to push my code to production.

Making sure that I have a reliable internet connection, I run git push heroku master. master is the name of the container holding my code within Git, and I'm uploading the code in that container to a similarly named container at the URL associated with heroku. Running this command initiates a series of operations that Heroku uses to set up the application and install its package dependencies. The whole process takes less than a minute for my application. When it's complete, I can run heroku open to launch my production URL in a web browser.

Right away, I notice that the application isn't working (figure 37.1) because my database isn't set up yet, and my application depends on a database for any page to load.

In the next section, I set up a MongoDB database for my production application.

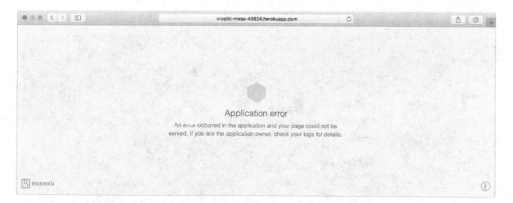

Figure 37.1 Application not loading on Heroku

37.4 Setting up the database

I chose to use MongoDB as my application's database for a few reasons. One reason is that it's so simple to set up in production. Setting up a development and test database is an effortless task. Now I need to add a Heroku plugin to associate a database service, and in a single step, my application will start working.

I run `heroku addons:create mongolab:sandbox` in my project's terminal window to create an mLab MongoDB database for my application. Because I've associated my local project with my registered Heroku application, I can continue to use the Heroku CLI in terminal to manage my production application. This command provides a free-tier database hosted by mLab. This sandbox database isn't recommended for use in production, however, because of its size and availability limitations.

> **NOTE**   If Confetti Cuisine likes the way that my application looks and behaves on Heroku, I can increase my mLab plan at a cost by running `heroku addons:create mongolab:shared-cluster-1`.

> **WARNING**   I don't want to upgrade my database account until I'm sure that I need the extra space. Upgrading from terminal may incur fees in my Heroku account.

Alternatively, I can set up my MongoDB database at any external location and set the `MONGODB_URI` variable to that external database's URL.

I verify the database URL setup with Heroku by running `heroku config:get MONGODB_URI`. This command responds with my mLab database URL, along with the security credentials I need to use to access the database. If I want to view the contents of my database on a web browser, I can run `heroku addons:open mongolab` to open a new web page pointing to my database on mLab's site through Heroku (figure 37.2).

![Displaying contents of mLab database showing Collections tab with courses, subscribers, and users collections]

Figure 37.2   Displaying contents of mLab database

Figure 37.3   Loading the home page

Now when I visit https://confetti-cuisine.herokuapp.com/, I finally see my home page load (figure 37.3).

With my application in production, I'd like to make it more presentable by preloading it with some data. I have a few ways to load seed data into my application, including linking directly to my mLab database and pushing data into my database. Instead, I'm going to run `heroku run node` in my project's terminal window to enter the production REPL environment. As with REPL in development, I can interact with my Node.js application here and even save to my database. I've prepared some courses that I want to save, so I copy the lines of code where those courses are created and paste them into this REPL shell. First, I need to copy the lines requiring the modules I need, such as `mongoose` and the Course model itself. I enter the code in listing 37.1 into my terminal window and watch as courses are populated into my application. I can click my Ajax courses modal to see those new listings.

> **NOTE**   It may help to first format the code into your text editor before pasting into your terminal window.

Listing 37.1   Adding seed data to my production application

```
const mongoose = require("mongoose"),
  Course = require("./models/course");

mongoose.Promise = global.Promise;
mongoose.connect(
process.env.MONGODB_URI ||
  "mongodb://localhost.2701//confetti_cuisine",
```

Require the necessary modules and database connection for REPL.

```
  { useNewUrlParser: true }
);
Course.remove({})
  .then(() => {
    return Course.create({
      title: "Chocolate World",
      description: "Dive into the divine world of sweet
⇒ and bitter chocolate making.",
      cost: 22,
      maxStudents: 14
    });
  })
  .then(course => console.log(course.title))
  .then(() => {
    return Course.create({
      title: "Pasta Boat",
      description: "Swim through original recipes and
⇒ paddle your way through linguine",
      cost: 43,
      maxStudents: 8
    });
  })
  .then(course => console.log(course.title))
  .then(() => {
    return Course.create({
      title: "Hot Potato",
      description: "Potatoes are back and they are hot!
⇒ Learn 7 different ways you can make potatoes
⇒ relevant again.",
      cost: 12,
      maxStudents: 28
    });
  })
  .then(course => console.log(course.title))
  .catch(error => console.log(error.message))
  .then(() => {
    console.log("DONE");
    mongoose.connection.close();
  });
```

Create new courses
for my production
database.

With this data loaded, I can finally show the finished application to Confetti Cuisine. I need to keep an eye on the logs, though, in case any new users experience an issue with the live application.

37.5 Debugging in production

My role has transitioned from developer to bug-fixer and maintainer. I need to make sure that the code I've written preserves the functionality I've promised, and I'll quickly repair the code that doesn't uphold that promise.

Because my code isn't running from my personal computer, I need to access the logs from Heroku by running `heroku logs --tail` in my project's terminal window. This command communicates with Heroku to provide a live stream of logs. The logs tell me when an error occurs, whether my application crashes, and everything I need to know about the incoming requests and outgoing responses.

As I make sense of the log messages, if I come across an issue, I can try to reproduce it locally on my computer. I can run `heroku local web` in my project's terminal window to launch my application code that's in production locally. This command runs my application at http://localhost:5000/. If I see the error occur while testing here, I can get a better sense of what needs to be fixed. Last, I can use the Node.js debug tool by adding a breakpoint on the line of code that I suspect is causing the error. By adding `debugger` to my code, I can step through my running application, pause, and analyze the values in specific functions.

I'm confident that this application will experience few issues and offer Confetti Cuisine a great new way to interact with its audience. Meanwhile, I'll be around in case the company needs my help. I'm only a `git add .`, `git commit -m "<some message>"`, and `git push heroku master` away from deploying an update.

 Summary

In this final capstone exercise, I deployed my application to be accessible to the public. With the right configurations in place and a working Node.js application, I was able to upload my application to a production server. From this server, incoming requests will be handled and queries made to an external database. My application now depends on a variety of resources that may incur fees as my application collects more data and popularity. As traffic and demand increase on my application, more resources will be required, and I'll need to consider the costs of hosting my Node.js application somewhere that can support its growing database and popularity. Scalability, high availability, and performance improvements are all topics of my next iteration with this application, and I hope that Confetti Cuisine will be happy to collaborate as I implement future improvements.

JAVASCRIPT SYNTAX INTRODUCED IN ES6

In this appendix, I cover JavaScript syntax introduced in ES6 as it applies to Node.js. I start with variable definitions and the new style of String interpolation. Then I talk about arrow functions.

A.1 New in ES6

Since 2015, ECMAScript 6 has offered new syntax and conventions for developing with JavaScript. For that reason, this book covers some of the ES6 keywords and formats you'll use. *Keywords* are terms that have a reserved meaning in JavaScript and are used to provide the syntax and interpretability of your code.

A.1.1 The let keyword

You're probably used to declaring variables with the var keyword. With ES6, it's more appropriate to use the let keyword to define variables as they apply to a specific scoped block. Until a variable is defined within a particular block of code, you can't access it.

A let variable defined in an if block can't be accessed outside the block, for example, whereas a var variable is scoped to the function within which it's defined, as shown in the next listing.

Listing A.1 Example use of the `let` keyword

```
function sample() {
  var num = 60;
  if (num > 50){
    let num = 0;
  }
  console.log(num);
}
```

Because let variables are scoped to code blocks beyond functions, they could be global variables to a module or an entire application. As a result, let gives variable definition more security and is preferred to var.

> **NOTE** When using `"use strict"`; you can't redefine the same `let` variable, whereas you can with var.

A.1.2   The const variable

A const variable can't be reassigned. Typically, you should use this keyword in place of let for variables whose values you don't expect to manipulate in your code. This guideline can also apply to loading libraries or modules in Node.js, as you see in unit 1. If you try to reassign a const variable, you get a `Duplicate Declaration Error`.

The code in the next listing crashes because a new let variable is being declared with the name of an existing constant.

Listing A.2 Example use of the `const` variable

```
function applyDiscount(discountPrice) {
  const basePrice = 1000;
  let basePrice = basePrice - discountPrice;
  console.log(basePrice);
}
```

A.1.3   String interpolation

Until ES6, to print or log a variable's value within a string, you had to append the string around the variable, as shown in the following listing.

Listing A.3 **Example of string concatenation**

```
var x = 45;
console.log("It is " + x + " degrees outside!");
```

With ES6, you can use backticks (`) and ${} to interpolate variables into a string, as shown in the next listing.

Listing A.4 **Interpolating strings with backticks**

```
var x = 45;
console.log(`It is ${x} degrees outside!`);
```

The resulting code is cleaner, easier to read, and easier to edit.

A.1.4   Arrow functions

Arrow functions are one way that ES6 is making code more succinct and easier to read. With the => arrow symbol and a change in the conventional function syntax, you can turn a multiline function into one line. Take the example in the following listing.

Listing A.5 **Defining a function with the** function **keyword**

```
function printName(name) {
  console.log(`My name is ${name}`);
}
```

You can rewrite this code as shown in the next listing.

Listing A.6 **Defining an arrow function**

```
let printName = name => console.log(`My name is ${name}`);
```

More important, arrow functions in ES6 preserve the this variable from its outer scope, as shown in the following listing.

Listing A.7 **Example use of the** this **keyword within functions**

```
let dog = {
  name: "Sparky",
  printNameAfterTime: function() {
```

```
    setTimeout(function() {
      console.log(`My name is ${this.name}`);
    }, 1000);
  }
}
```

In this example, dog.printNameAfterTime() prints My name is undefined because this
.name is out of the setTimeout function scope despite the assumption that this refers to
the dog object. With arrow functions, however, this persists within the setTimeout function, as shown in the next listing.

Listing A.8 Example use of the `this` keyword with arrow functions

```
let dog = {
  name: "Sparky",
  printNameAfterTime() {
    setTimeout(() => {
      console.log(`My name is ${this.name}`);
    }, 1000);
  }
}
```

Now you can print My name is Sparky, and the code is more compact!

To succeed with Node.js, you need to succeed with JavaScript in general. Because
Node.js requires sufficient knowledge of some core JavaScript and programming concepts, this lesson reviews what you need to know to get started. If you haven't had
much experience with JavaScript, I recommend reading *Secrets of the JavaScript Ninja,
Second Edition* by John Resig and Bear Bibeault (Manning, 2016).

A.2   REPL

When you have Node.js installed, your first stop in running your code is in the Read-
Evaluate-Print Loop (REPL). This interactive environment is similar to the console window in a Chrome web browser. In REPL, you're able to run any JavaScript code. You can
also require Node.js modules to test aspects of your application.

A.2.1   Running JavaScript in REPL

To start REPL, navigate to any terminal window on your computer and enter node. This
command immediately returns a prompt (>), after which you may enter any JavaScript

statements. You can think of REPL as a running Node.js application that responds to your commands instantaneously. That is, you don't need to write your JavaScript code in a separate file and then run it; you can type that JavaScript code directly in the REPL window. Try defining a couple of variables, as shown in the next listing. You'll notice that with each JavaScript statement you run, REPL outputs the return value of that statement. For variable assignment, the return value is undefined.

Listing A.9 Defining variables in REPL

```
> let x = 42;
undefined
> let sentence = "The meaning of life is ";
undefined
```

Now perform some operation on these variables. You can concatenate the two values, for example, as shown in the following listing.

Listing A.10 Concatenating variables in REPL

```
> sentence + x;
The meaning of life is 42
```

There's no limit to the ways you can use the REPL environment to behave like any Node.js application you've used or seen before. You can also use the tab key to autocomplete variable or function names and list object properties. If you defined a string by the variable name sentence, for example, but you're unsure what functions you can call on that string, you can add a dot (.) to the end of the variable name and press Tab to list that variable's available functions and properties, as shown in the next listing.

Listing A.11 Listing variable properties in REPL

```
> sentence.
sentence.anchor              sentence.big
sentence.blink               sentence.bold
sentence.charAt              sentence.charCodeAt
sentence.codePointAt         sentence.concat
sentence.endsWith            sentence.fixed
sentence.fontcolor           sentence.fontsize
sentence.includes            sentence.indexOf
sentence.italics             sentence.lastIndexOf
```

You can find additional REPL commands in lesson 1.

A.2.2   Using REPL in application development

One other useful way to use REPL is through the repl module within your Node.js application code. As you build more custom modules in your project, you'll notice that it's tedious to load all those files into REPL to test the functionality of the code you've written. If you wrote a module called multiply.js (listing A.12) that contains a function to multiply two numbers, you'd need to require that module into REPL by entering require("./multiply") along with every other module you created. What's more, you'd need to enter these lines for every new REPL session.

Listing A.12 Creating a single-function module in multiply.js

```
module.exports = {
  multiply: (x, y) => {
    return x * y;
  }
};
```

Instead of requiring your modules into each REPL session, you could bring REPL into your modules. Listing A.13 shows how you could use the repl module within your project. You can create a module within your project directory called customRepl.js that requires all the modules you want to test at the same time. This file shows the repl module being required and then a REPL server starting. Like a Node.js HTTP server, this REPL server has a context within which you can load custom variables. After the REPL server is started, add a name variable and your multiply module.

Listing A.13 Using the repl module in customRepl.js

```
const repl = require("repl"),
  replServer = repl.start({
    prompt: "> ",
  });

replServer.context.name = "Jon Wexler";
replServer.context.multiply = require("./multiply").multiply;
```

All you need to do now is navigate to your project directory in terminal and enter node customRepl. You'll see the REPL prompt, only this time, the context of your REPL session contains all the modules you want to test. This technique comes in handy when you want to test creating or modifying records in your database without having to copy and paste the code to require your database configurations.

Summary

This appendix provided an overview of the JavaScript keywords and syntax you should be aware of in this book. With ES6 now widely used in the development community, it's important to start writing code that reflects the latest and greatest JavaScript changes. The more familiar you get with using REPL and JavaScript commands, the easier it will be to develop your applications quickly.

LOGGING AND USING NODE.JS GLOBAL OBJECTS

B.1 Logging

Logging helps you understand what functions and middleware are being run, shows you what errors your application is producing, and provides better insight into what's going on in your application.

The `console` module is a core Node.js module and a global object, which means that you can access the console keyword anywhere in your application code. When you run `console.log()`, passing some message as a string of text, the output typically is printed in a terminal window or a file. For the purposes of this book, the `console` module offers the right logging tools for dissecting your application code. Aside from the logging tips in lesson 2, a few logging commands are important to keep in mind.

The `console` module has two outputs: standard and error. Although both of these outputs show text in your terminal window, they behave differently in a browser console. The next listing shows some of the other logging functions you can use with `console`.

Listing B.1 Using logging functions

```
console.log("Standard output log message");
console.error("Error output log message");
console.info("Standard output log message");
console.warn("Error output log message");
```

Prints a log message to your console

Prints a log message as an alias for console.log

Prints a log message using the error output

Prints a log message as an alias for console.error

In a Node.js application, these four functions behave similarly on the server. When you use these logging functions in client-side JavaScript, you'll notice that your browser's console window prints your log messages in formats that correspond to the message type. Warning messages have an orange background, for example, and error messages appear in red.

Two other functions that you may find useful are console.time and console.timeEnd. These two functions can be used in tandem to log the time it takes between the beginning and end of certain operations in your code. The text within these functions needs to match for the timer to work. In the next listing, function xyz takes one second and then logs a message. The resulting time for this operation logs slightly more than one second.

Listing B.2 Logging time of an operation

```
console.time("function xyz");
(function xyz() {
  setTimeout(function() {
    console.log("prints first");
    console.timeEnd("function xyz");
  }, 1000);
})();
```

Starts the console timer

Prints the console.log message as part of the function operation

Records time at the end

---

console.log will become one of your best friends in web development, as log notes help you find bugs. Get to know your new friend with a little practice and variation.

B.2   Global objects

In Node.js, global objects are accessible throughout any application. You can use these objects at any point in a Node.js application. These objects can contain information about the application or filesystem. The following global objects are used most often in Node.js applications:

- console prints to the console or standard output wherever your application is running.
- __dirname returns the absolute path to the directory location on your machine, as follows:

```
console.log(__dirname);
>> /Users/Jon/Desktop
```

- __filename provides the absolute path to the application directory on your machine, as follows:

```
console.log(__filename);
>> /Users/Jon/Desktop/filename_example.js
```

- process references the process (thread) on which your application is running. This object is the main source of your application's resources and connections to the filesystem.

Some objects appear to be similar to the Node.js global objects but come from other libraries required into your project. These objects are available in most Node.js applications. As you learn to work with the following objects, their use cases will make more sense:

- module references the current module (JavaScript file) in which you're working and allows you to access other variables within that file.
- exports references a key/value pairing object to store a module's functions or objects so they can be shared across other modules. Using this object is mostly the same as using module.exports. In the following example, accessibleFunction is exported for use in other modules:

```
exports.accessibleFunction = () => {
  console.log("hello!");
}
```

- require allows you to import other modules' code into a current module and gives you access to code written outside the current working file. The require keyword is used as follows:

```
const http = require("http");
```

INDEX

MORE TITLES FROM MANNING

Serverless Applications with Node.js
Using AWS Lambda and Claudia.js
by Slobodan Stojanović and Aleksandar Simović

> ISBN: 9781617294723
> 352 pages
> $44.99
> January 2019

Node.js in Motion
by PJ Evans

> Course duration: 6h 14m
> 50 exercises
> $59.99

Single Page Web Applications
JavaScript end-to-end
by Michael S. Mikowski and Josh C. Powell

> ISBN: 9781617290756
> 432 pages
> $44.99
> September 2013

For ordering information go to www.manning.com